Today's Transgender Realities

Vol. 2

Crossdressing in Context

G. G. Bolich, Ph.D.

Psyche's

Press

Psyche's Press
Raleigh, North Carolina
©2007 G. G. Bolich

ISBN 978-0-6151-6577-6

I say to you today, my friends, so even though we face the difficulties of today and tomorrow, I still have a dream. It is a dream deeply rooted in the American dream. I have a dream that one day this nation will rise up and live out the true meaning of its creed, 'We hold these truths to be self-evident, that all men are created equal.'

Martin Luther King, Jr.

Blessed are the peacemakers, for they will be called children of God.

Jesus of Nazareth (Matthew 5:9)

This volume is respectfully and gratefully dedicated to those who make peace, who work for justice for us all, and who see the humanity in every person, no matter how they clothe themselves.

Table of Contents

The Questions

Volume 2: Today's Transgender Realities

Detailed Table of Contents

The Questions

Q. Set 5: How are transgender realities regarded by others? 241

Preface

Can we be honest?

What can you expect?

Let's be candid from the start. The subject matter of this work is controversial. Worse, it is the kind of controversy that often moves beyond mere intellectual disagreement to result in broken relationships and sometimes violence. In preparing this work one particular remark has stayed with me. In a report on violence experienced by transgendered people, the authors wrote, "What is common to most studies of transpeople is their staggering irrelevance to the community at issue."[1]

My intention has been to set forth information that is not irrelevant, either to the transgendered, or to those who find themselves related in some manner to them—which I think is all of us. As the title suggests, this work is about raising questions and offering answers. In the effort to do so, I have drawn both on academic material and on accounts set forth by transgendered people themselves. For example, one question asks how crossdressers describe themselves (Q. 26), while the next offers the results of various formal psychological tests to answer the same question (Q. 27). I have throughout tried to let others speak for themselves. You will find brief quotes from various sources to offer a bit of the flavor of how these other voices sound. In summarizing studies, theories, or personal accounts I have aimed at being concise but fair—and pointed you in directions to follow in order to learn more. Because of the ubiquity of the World Wide Web, whenever possible indication has been made in the endnotes as to where material can be accessed online. At the same time, I have not shied away from offering my own critique of what others have said or my own assessment of the matters about which they speak.

Despite the large number of questions raised, this work barely scratches the surface of transgender realities, including crossdressing. I often refer to 'transgender realities' and I do so quite consciously. I want us to remember that we are examining *realities*—lived experiences that range from very temporary occurrences of minor personal significance to profoundly meaningful matters of personal identity felt and expressed every day. I want us to consider how the *trans* in *trans*gender can mean different things to different people. Nor do I wish us to

1

ever lose sight of how *gender* is basic to trans*gender*. And, because the organizing framework is built around crossdressing, we must also know something about the role clothes play in our lives.

Obviously, I am very ambitious. I hope you are as well. Even something that superficially seems easy enough to describe, like crossdressing, which after all is simply the act of dressing in clothes typically associated with a gender other than the one assigned the wearer, is not really simple when once looked at closely. To understand crossdressing—to begin to truly see transgender realities—takes work. I want to do that work alongside you, serving as a partner in dialog while also offering my modest services as a guide to the vast literature on the subjects considered. Since I am functioning as a guide, you have every right to ask about my qualifications.

Who am I to talk?

One question you may have right away is what my 'position' or 'bias' is on the subject. For example, you might wish to know if I identify myself as a transgendered person. Unfortunately, in my experience, many people screen what they are willing to expose themselves to as they study a controversial topic by using this kind of query. Of course, I know *you* are more fair-minded than that, but the next reader might not be. So, whatever my stance—or identity—may be will have to become a matter of your own judgment (or speculation) as you read the work. I have conscientiously spoken of 'we' and 'us' throughout the book, both when speaking of crossdressers and when referring to noncrossdressers. I wish to convey my conviction that the fundamental humanity that unites us is greater than the differences that we too often let divide, separate, and isolate us. It is a small world we all have to share and a short life we all live.

What I am willing to tell you upfront about myself concerns my qualifications for tackling the subject. I caution you not to infer anything about my being 'for' or 'against' crossdressing from these qualifications.[2] As you know, qualifications do not guarantee people holding reasonable positions or even necessarily knowing what they are talking about! Still, I think you have a right to know relevant portions of my background because they may speak to my level of preparation for talking to you about these things. I don't expect you to take my word on anything from blind trust, but I do hope your confidence in the reliability of my remarks will be strengthened both by my background and by the actual material I set forth.

My background includes more than 30 years working professionally with people, primarily as an educator, but also as a counselor. I hold advanced degrees in the fields of religious studies and psychology, and my teaching and counseling have been in both areas. Because some people view crossdressing as a psychological disorder, my experience in psychology seems relevant. Because

2

some people regard crossdressing as morally or religiously wrong, my experience in religious studies seems relevant, too. In fact, between these two areas, I find most of the questions and concerns about crossdressing that I have encountered from students, clients, and others.

In terms of religious studies, I am seminary trained, holding a M.A. in Theology, and the Master of Divinity—or M.Div.—the degree used to prepare people for professional ministry. My first Ph.D., in Educational Leadership, also focused on religious studies, culminating in a dissertation in the area of New Testament introduction. I am trained in biblical and classical languages (Hebrew, Greek, Latin), and in both traditional and modern methods of translating and interpreting sacred texts. Beginning in 1974, as an instructor at a Bible School, I have taught courses in religious studies at undergraduate and graduate levels in a wide variety of settings, including churches and synagogues, community college, public university, private college, and seminary extension program. These courses have covered matters of ethics, ancient and modern world religions, theology, history, sacred texts, and the relation of religion to psychology. My area of particular interest and specialization has been the religious writings of the period extending from about a century or so before Christ, to the end of the second century after Christ. In addition to scholarly work, I also have been involved in ecumenical work, notably between the Christian and Jewish communities. As a counselor, many people have identified my background in religious studies as an important reason why they chose to come see me.

My second doctorate is in psychology (Ph.D.). Here my interests have been focused on matters of human development and human sexuality. As a counselor I gradually developed a specialization in Trauma Resolution Therapy, principally working with adult survivors of sexual abuse. Today I teach graduate students in counseling about human sexuality. Both as a teacher and as a therapist I have continually encountered curiosity about crossdressing and transgender people. Because of my background in religious studies this curiosity by my students and clients has often extended to specific matters of faith and practice as well as the more specific psychological concerns about whether being a transgender person or engaging in crossdressing is deviant, sick, sinful, or harmful.

Accordingly, this work grows out of many years of interest and experience. I think my background contributes some layers of knowledge that may not be as easily accessible to other professionals whose experience is confined to only one or another of the areas relevant to a full consideration of crossdressing. To these credentials I will add my intention of being fair-minded and honest throughout this work. I intend this work to be educational in nature. At the same time, I am aware that when educating people on controversial subjects it may not be either feasible or even particularly desirable to attempt being completely above the fray and studiously neutral. In truth, I am not neutral on the subject—and I do not know anyone who is. Even scholarly works serve social

3

and political ends, and every work—including mine—must be soberly appraised for fairness. I have every confidence that fair-minded readers who pursue the logic and evidence set down within this work will be able to accurately assess the value of this endeavor.

Introduction

What do you need to know to get started?

Why does any of this matter?

Chances are you aren't looking at this unless you already believe the subject matters. I agree. The fundamental assumption of this work is that transgender realities matter to all of us, whether we are transgendered ourselves or not. They matter because such realities by their very existence pose opportunities for us to explore and expand our sense of sex and gender. In a culture like our own, where sex and gender are so central to the way we define our identities and relationships, such an opportunity must not be missed.

Why this title?

The scope of this work, with all its queries, can be overwhelming—but then sex and gender are precisely that in our culture. You may already feel in over your head just holding this material in your hands. The subject of 'transgender' and 'crossdressing' is perhaps a lot larger than you initially thought—and then 'gender,' 'sex,' and 'dress' are thrown in for good measure! My choice of titles, then, requires a word of explanation.

Crossdressing in Context is meant both to be descriptive and to be implicitly critical of most other works on crossdressing. There are a number of important contexts in which crossdressing must be situated and the separate volume titles indicate these. First and most immediately there is *dress*, especially clothes, without which crossdressing is impossible and by which *gender* is experienced and expressed. Perhaps the greatest failing of studies of crossdressing is the general neglect of the role played by apparel. It is certainly appropriate to focus on gender, but such a focus needs to begin with gender-differentiated clothing. The first volume explores dress and gender, separately and together, in the context of a rich experience and expressive system.

The second volume examines another principal context: *today's transgender realities*, the actual lived experiences of human individuals. This material opens by introducing basic terminology and provides an overview of crossdressing behavior. The next set of questions considers a variety of possible causes of transgender behavior like crossdressing. The volume continues by examining contemporary transgender experience from a variety of perspectives, including how transgender people experience it, examined by a variety of psychological tests, understood legally, and regarded by other people.

The third volume sets crossdressing and transgender realities in *historical and geographical* contexts. The volume begins with a history of transgender realities, revolving around historical depictions of crossdressing, from ancient to modern times. This material includes special attention to the history of theater, as well as modern movies and television. The volume continues with a survey of transgender realities around the world. Collectively, these materials demonstrate that transgender realities have been persistent across times and cultures.

The fourth volume highlights the importance of *religion*. Not only is personal spirituality and religious observance as valued by transgender people as by anyone else, the long history of religions around the world show an involvement with transgender realities that make this area of critical value in properly understanding phenomena like crossdressing. Acknowledging the cultural context in which this work is produced, the first religious sphere considered belongs to Western religions. Thus a careful examination of what the Bible says about crossdressing is followed by how biblical material has been commented upon by Christian and Jewish scholars through the centuries. Following this material a survey is made of the principal religions of the world, both East and West. As in volume 3, the evidence documents an awareness and dialog with transgender realities throughout history and around the globe.

The final volume acknowledges the weight of modern *mental health* in discussions about crossdressing and other transgender realities. Since the medicalization of sex has firmly joined crossdressing behavior to sexuality, this volume begins by examining the theories and evidence allegedly connecting crossdressing and sexual behavior. This is followed by a broader examination of the question whether transgender people, especially those who crossdress, are mentally ill. First this matter is explored by providing a broad historical context—the medicalization of sex—and examining how transgender people often come to mental health professionals' attention. Special terminology like 'gender dysphoria' is explained. The possible connection of transgender behavior to various mental disorders is considered. Then follows a review of contributions on the subject by various scholars since the late 19th century. Given the dominant position the American Psychiatric Association's *Diagnostic and Statistical Manual of Mental Disorders* (popularly referred to as DSM) has attained, a careful look at how crossdressing and other transgender realities have been handled by this model throughout its history also is provided. This, in turn, leads to looking at a variety of treatment approaches that have been tried with transgender clients. The issues involved in such treatment lead to a careful consideration about the wisdom of retaining in the DSM model the categories concerning transgender. Finally, the volume—and the work at large—concludes with a last consideration of whether transgender people need to be changed.

Collectively the five volumes represent one sustained approach to placing crossdressing in context. Although this work broadly is about all transgender realities, the focal point has been the behavior most visibly associated with transgender: *crossdressing*. I treat the subject of crossdressing both as a topic of great interest in its own right and as an entrance into transgender realities. As large as the resulting work is, it could be much larger with a more sustained examination of other transgender realities.

What are the goals of this work?

The structure of this entire five volume work is dialogical in nature. Questions—many, many questions—are raised and considered. The choice of these questions and the way in which they are answered reflects various goals. There are several principal, intentional goals sought by this work, all with the purpose of establishing an understanding in context:

1. to put dress back into crossdressing by situating crossdressing within an experiencing and expressing system built around clothes as the primary vehicle for communicating gender, which is central to our sense of self and relationships;

2. to highlight and explicate the role dress plays both in our affiliations, such as our membership in a gender group, and in our individuality;

3. to explore the basic distinctions between 'sex' and 'gender' in order to better see what transgender is about and how crossdressing is related to each;

4. to use crossdressing—a transgender reality—as entry into other transgender realities, and to see how these realities are similar and dissimilar;

5. to clarify the meaning of terms (e.g., 'transgender,' 'transvestite,' 'transsexual'), while questioning their usefulness;

6. to document transgender realities, especially crossdressing, throughout history and around the world, and to do so with enough depth and breadth to convince even the most skeptical reader of the pervasiveness and significance of these realities;

7. to broaden our understanding of crossdressing by exploring and illustrating the many various motivations behind it and thereby to simultaneously challenge such narrow and erroneous beliefs as that all crossdressing is done because of disturbed gender identity or sexual perversity;

8. to keep in view always that transgender realities are inevitably human experiences, lived by real people, who are worthy of respect and dignity;

9. to set out and place in context the work of others who have written about transgender realities, especially crossdressing, and in doing so engage in dialog with them;

10. to let transgendered people speak for themselves, especially in addressing matters such as what it is like to live as a transgendered person;

11. to examine basic issues of concern to people, such as the morality of crossdressing, the way in which religious traditions have related to transgender realities, the legal issues connected to transgender experience, the relational aspects of being with a transgendered person as a partner, family member, friend, or helper, and the role of sexuality in the life of the transgendered; and,

12. to address the critical matter of the involvement of mental health professionals, including looking closely at the history of study by professionals about transgender (especially crossdressing), detailing the discussion of transgender in today's dominant diagnostic classification system, reviewing the history of treating transgender conditions, considering whether changes need to be made, and examining new models of therapeutic support.

To meet these dozen goals requires some space; hence the size of this work.

Yet, for all this, there are some things underdeveloped. For example, you should know right off that this book is *not* principally about homosexuality. Because that is the transgender reality that receives by far the most attention this work is organized around a different principle: crossdressing. Yes, some homosexuals (but not all) crossdress. And yes, some crossdressers are homosexual. Thus, homosexuals are included within this work. But they are not the focus.

What are 'transgender realities'?

The focus, through the lens of crossdressing, is 'transgender realities.' In choosing the term 'transgender realities' I want to emphasize the multiplicity of expressions that do not fit at the gender poles of masculinity and femininity. A prominent transgender reality—a behavior shared among many transgender people—is crossdressing. I treat all crossdressing as a transgender reality even though not all people whom crossdress identify themselves as transgendered. In other words, just as a self-professed vegetarian may occasionally eat meat, so a non-transgendered person may occasionally enact a transgender reality like crossdressing. In this work I use the broad transgender reality of crossdressing as both entry into other transgender realities and to remind us how pervasive transgender expressions are. But to properly comprehend them they must be retained in their natural contexts.

How is the work structured?

A glance at the questions in the Table of Contents shows an almost bewildering breadth of matters. They are organized into 100 specific questions, each of which entails asking further questions. Those questions cover all kinds of topics, everything from sex and gender to morals and religion. It takes time to cover so much ground and the length of this work reflects my commitment to taking that time. The structure allows you to enter where you like and get answers quickly. By setting everything as answers to questions and encouraging you to dip in wherever you like, an element of repetition is needed to ensure every answer stays embedded in context with enough detail to make full sense to you. So, in reading through the work in a progressive fashion the effect of this repetition will be felt, though hopefully not in too tedious a fashion.

A significant factor adding to the length is my insistence on fleshing out each context with reason and evidence. Too many people disregard arguments because they only see one or two illustrative cases and fail to recognize them as signifying a vast number of others. I wish to create the sense for you of a phenomenon so common and richly varied around the world and throughout history that it cannot be casually dismissed or superficially examined.

I recognize that your interest may not be in all forms of crossdressing, but only a particular kind. You may even only want information on a very specific matter related to that particular kind. As I mentioned above, that is why the organization of this material has been set out as answers to questions, and even then as both shorter and longer answers. I think this is an intuitive and practical approach that will prove useful to you now with the questions you presently have and later with questions still to come. Hopefully, the net effect will be to also prompt other questions and lead you into a larger, ongoing investigation.

On the use and misuse of this work: Who makes the rules?

A final matter about using this work is important to me. Scholarly work is often proof-texted. In other words, readers pick and choose what conveniently supports the position they want to hold. I don't imagine that any of us entirely escape selective recall or purposeful choosing of 'facts' for presentation, but I ask that you play fair with the material included in these pages. When once the whole matter is on the table, or as much of it as can be had, then is the time for making a respectful decision based on evidence and reason.

I know—and so do you—that the matters discussed in this work often engage strong feelings in people. None of my goals include telling you how to feel. However you feel about the matters we discuss I will hope you subject those feelings to scrutiny, evaluate the evidence honestly, and behave with respect toward all. This really matters to me—too many people continue to be harmed.

One of the curious things about freedom is that most of us demand it in very liberal portions for ourselves, but are less charitable toward others. We want to be left alone to do as we see fit, while often insisting that other folk conform to our personal standards as to what is 'right.' Naturally, we generally have at hand one or another rationale for our judgments. Frequently, our logic centers in an opposition to someone else's behavior on religious or moral grounds. After all, it is unseemly to prioritize the fact that the behavior we condemn makes us personally uncomfortable, so we set that truth in second place and justify it by reasoning that we feel uneasy *because* the behavior is inherently—and to us also *obviously*—wrong. Thus we enjoy the best of all solutions: moral and/or religious justification for our felt discomfort. We may even find ourselves justifying unkind remarks, avoidance, harassment, discrimination, or physical violence. Once we convince ourselves something is wrong, it is easy to think whatever is done in opposition must be right. But two wrongs never make a right. Violation of another person's human rights remains evil.

Unfortunately, we may not see that our reasoning is actually just rationalization—a way of thinking that has as its real aim making us less anxious rather than knowing the truth. All we know is that by thinking and judging in certain ways we shield ourselves from uncomfortable feelings. While this may seem useful, when it leads to disruption in our relationships with others and prompts us to words and deeds hurtful to others, then we have become the very makers of evil that we despise.

So let us agree to start in as neutral a position as possible. Instead of assuming that crossdressing is 'right' or 'wrong,' 'healthy' or 'mentally ill,' let us just let it be—and then examine it as best we can. If the subject elicits certain feelings, simply let them be as well. In the privacy of your own reading there is no need to let these feelings be more than they are—one source of information among others. Feelings do not have to motivate you to do anything right now. Simply accept them or set them aside.

You can do this—and you *must* if you are to be fair to yourself and to others. I know that it is very likely you are holding this book either because you crossdress or someone you care about does. Your feelings may be clear, or they may be mixed, but they are not facts that by themselves must determine what you think or do. In fact, by learning more your feelings may change. So be patient with yourself and with others.

Ready? Then let's start asking some questions.

Volume 2:
Today's Transgender Realities

The
Questions

Question Set 2

Who crossdresses—and why?

We all wear clothes, but only some of us crossdress. The very first thing we must do is identify what we mean by 'crossdressing.' Though the word can—and ought—to be debated, here we will use it in a fairly conventional manner. In this work, crossdressing refers to dressing in a manner associated with a gender different from the gender assigned to the person. In this purely descriptive and utilitarian definition all nuances are lost. Regardless of motivation or identity, if someone assigned the gender 'masculine' dresses in a manner associated with the gender 'feminine,' that person is said to be 'crossdressing.' It matters not whether the behavior is partial or complete, sporadic or periodic—for our purposes the person doing so is labeled a 'crossdresser.'[1]

Those of us who do not crossdress are curious as to who does, and why they do it. We may not ask the questions aloud, but when we see someone dressed such that we think they have crossed a gender line we are likely to wonder what it means. Those of us who do crossdress want, like anyone else, to be accepted and understood. In answering the first set of questions, in volume 1, we found that the foundational context for establishing meaning rests in how dress and gender interact in our lives. But those answers may have seemed long on theory and short on personal experience. No matter how interesting or important those questions and answers might be, we likely have more direct and personal queries in mind.

This volume asks those kinds of questions and attempts to answer them using evidence drawn from a wide variety of sources, including surveys and interviews with crossdressers, historical accounts, and observations by professionals in a number of fields, including psychology, anthropology, sociology, literature, and others. The questions asked in this second volume reach across four question sets. They cover issues of motivation, causation, history, culture, personal experience, and social reception. In total, this volume covers about one third of all the questions tackled by the entire five volume series. That makes this a large volume, but perhaps also the one most likely to contain the questions most people have the greatest interest in.

Question set 2—the first in this volume—is organized around exploring the question of *motivation*. But before we can ask why someone might crossdress, we need to explore who does so. We can say, in general terms, that a person of any age and any sex might crossdress. In fact, we can even go so far as to suggest that most of us crossdress at some point in life, with such behavior more common in childhood and decreasing with age. Such an answer may both surprise and frustrate. In itself it also does not answer why we do so.

The *why?* question is the one that most intrigues. Why would any of us want to cross the gender line set and maintained by gender-differentiated dress? We saw in the first volume that gender is very important to our sense of identity and to the roles we occupy in life. We also saw that dress is instrumental in both experiencing and expressing gender. Both points offer a general rationale for crossdressing. We may crossdress to express our gender identity—or to change it. We may crossdress to expand our gender roles—or at least alter them. We may crossdress seeking new gender experiences. Or we may crossdress to construct gender expressions for any number of purposes.

The first question set cannot be put aside in answering the queries in the second set. However, the context of dress will now reside in the background so that the figure of the people who crossdress stands forth. In answering the next set of ten questions we will seek to determine how many people crossdress (Q. 11), and why (Q. 12). The people who crossdress will be looked at in terms of gender (Q. 13-14) and age (Q. 15). We will also look at noncrossdressers, enquiring as to why crossdressing is often seen as entertaining (Q. 16). Then we will focus on major subgroups among crossdressers, starting with homosexual crossdressers (Q. 17). We will also look at three groups affiliated with labels commonly used to identify what is thought a central feature in different groups of crossdressers, such as 'transvestism' (Q. 18), 'transsexualism' (Q. 19), and 'transgender' (Q. 20).

The best way to prepare to enter the context of transgender realities—the overarching theme of this volume—*is to accept this context is part of the world and times we all inhabit.* None of us is completely untouched by these realities, and all of us can profit from better understanding them. Especially if it is true that each of us at some point in our life is likely to have crossed a gender line in dress, we would do well to reflect on when and why we did so. By drawing on our own experience, however limited, we may find some openness to the experience of others. Such openness is essential if we hope to more fully comprehend why crossdressing happens. Even more importantly, such openness is needed if we are to connect to the humanity of others who, like ourselves, desire to be understood and who hope that with understanding will come tolerance, perhaps also acceptance.

Q. 11

How many people crossdress?

The Short Answer. Such a simple question—and so hard to answer! The simple fact is that we don't know how many people crossdress. Certainly more people try it at least once than engage in it regularly. But how common either is remains a matter of guesswork. A number of factors complicate answering the question. First and foremost is the issue of what, exactly, constitutes crossdressing—a matter that we saw earlier (the answer to Q. 10) is less clear than it would seem. If we start with this basic definition—'wearing dress culturally assigned to a gender different from the one assigned the wearer'—we still can draw lines for the behavior widely or narrowly. Very little research pertinent to this broad sense is available. What there is suggests that however common the actual practice might be, the desire to engage in it is even more common; anecdotal evidence suggests more people desire to try crossdressing than actually do. More pertinently, perhaps, crossdressing in a broad sense is so common it has become overlooked as a remarkable activity for the entire feminine gender. Most common presently is the consideration of crossdressing only in a narrow sense, which basically means in the more dramatic sense of the culturally advantaged gender (masculinity) voluntarily appearing in apparel associated with the culturally subordinate gender (femininity). Accordingly, most attention in recent years has been placed on crossdressing males, whether boys or men. This limited focus has not always been the case, but typically so, and in answering this question it will be our focus, too. In this regard, there have been some studies reporting how common the authors believe male crossdressing to be when it is conducted voluntarily and more than once. Estimates range from less than 1% to 10%. About all that can be drawn from that is the conclusion that while the activity is done by a minority of males, no one really knows how many do it.[2]

The Longer Answer. How common is crossdressing? Social psychologist and transgender scholar Richard Ekins remarks, "Although cross-dressing and sex-changing appear to be nowhere, actually they are everywhere."[3] But is this just a media fascination? Movies, literature, music, comic books, theater and television all show crossdressing—and much more often than most of us would reckon we encounter it in real life. Of course, our reckoning presumes we would know it if we see it, which is hardly a warranted assumption.

One value of the media is calling our attention to crossdressing in situations we are likely to find surprising. For example, in the new millennium crossdressing has been used by Muslims both to combat terrorism and to support it.[4] More familiar to us is crossdressing in entertainment media. But even there we might be surprised as we see increasingly frank, sensitive, and often sympathetic portrayals instead of merely playing crossdressing for laughs. Once we start paying attention to the matter we begin to realize how commonly crossdressing images cross our path. But is this apparent ubiquity of crossdressing mostly a matter of a false perception fed by our fascination with what is different and the media images we remember? In other words, are crossdressers really that common, or having been sensitized to the topic do we remember the images we see so well that there seem to be more crossdressing happening than is actually the case?

The answer is elusive. A variety of factors complicate figuring out how common crossdressing is. Even sensitized to the subject there is the possibility that we don't recognize crossdressing when we see it. Some people are adept at 'passing'—being seen as the gender they present rather than the gender they were assigned at birth. Plus, some people only partially crossdress, with the cross-gender items being undergarments that remain unseen. We also must factor in the weight we give to situational crossdressing. We may not count cross-dressing behavior in certain circumstances, such as a man putting on lingerie to play with his wife, or costumed party-goers at Halloween or Mardi Gras, or students dressing for a campus 'opposite sex' day, or attendees at a cult movie showing like the *Rocky Horror Picture Show*, participants at certain rock concerts, or when crossdressing is being done by entertainers. We also may have different estimates as to what qualifies as a cross-gender article of clothing. Are males wearing hosiery crossdressed? Are females wearing a man's sweatshirt cross-dressed? These factors, and perhaps others, all make estimating how common crossdressing is a task that is probably impossible.

So, squarely facing the improbability of offering an answer that will gain any consensus, we are still going to hazard some thoughts on the matter. First, we must examine a bit more closely the key question: what qualifies as crossdressing? We must offer some answer to that before we can decide who qualifies as a crossdresser. Then we can turn to the task of estimating how many people crossdress.

Who qualifies as a crossdresser?

Consider how many women we encounter each week dressed in clothes styles—pants, suits, etc.—traditionally associated with men. Of course, since these have been 'feminized' in various ways, we might want to exclude that kind of crossdressing—but there is no logically compelling reason to do so. Nor does female crossdressing end there. Some research suggests it may be very common for women to sleep with—or in—the clothing of an absent male partner.[5] And throughout history women have used crossdressing intentionally for one or another purpose dependent on being perceived as masculine.

How about children dressed in clothes associated with a different gender? That is more common than one might imagine. Infants are sometimes dressed to reflect what a parent had hoped for in the child's sex rather than what they actually got. Then there is the crossdressing associated with festive events like Halloween. In addition to children being dressed up like members of another gender, many adults do likewise. Ekins' observation seems justified on these grounds alone, let alone the frequent appearance of crossdressing behavior in various media.

Of course, most people want to discount or dismiss all the kinds of crossdressing associated with women using men-like clothes, children being dressed in whatever is handy, people clowning around on a holiday, or entertainers tweaking our noses with their outrageous dress. In short, most people today want to limit crossdressing to men dressing like women. But let's not be too quick to rule out children and adult women crossdressing. In fact, there is a hefty body of literature about crossdressing children. And although comparatively less research exists on the matter of contemporary crossdressing women, the subject has not been completely ignored.

What does research show on how many people crossdress?

In an often-overlooked study, the 1970 research under the auspices of the Kinsey Institute, finally published under the title *Sex and Morality in the U.S.*, 'Gender Characteristics' were examined through a series of questions. One of these questions asked: "How often have you felt you would prefer to wear (opposite sex) clothes?"[6]

Interestingly, women far more often than men affirmed such a preference. About 1-in-7 women (16%) at least occasionally felt such a preference. For men the number was about 1-in-75 (1.5%).[7] This constitutes almost 11 times greater incidence in women than in men. More particularly, given that the range of possible responses was from 'Never' to 'Often,' the percent of women answering 'Often' was more than 30 times that for men (3.3% to 0.1%).[8] Of course, the question asks about 'preference,' not actual behavior, so inferences about what this means must be cautious.

We might rationalize away this finding by claiming that these results from more than three decades ago are outdated. Women today enjoy even greater liberty than before in what they may wear. In fact, many fashions from underwear ('boy shorts') to outerwear ('boy jeans') explicitly bear a name and resemblance to masculine clothing. So perhaps such a question today would find a much smaller response. Yet both the desire then and the reality now for girls and women begs for an examination of *why* those assigned femininity seek masculinity in dress.

For the sake of staying on task that interest must be set aside for now. The question of whether women crossdress will be dealt with, but the existing research literature only supports our trying to estimate the incidence of adult male-only crossdressing. Even that proves difficult for a couple of reasons. First, the behavior is associated with distinct groups who vary in motivation and other important respects. Not all of these groups are always included when estimates of crossdressing are made. Second, most crossdressing appears to be kept secret—hardly surprising given the social costs associated with being a known crossdresser. But this, too, is variable among different groups. No wonder, then, that researcher Richard Schott characterized crossdressers as "notoriously difficult to identify."[9]

Another complicating factor is whether the calculation takes into account occasional as well as regular crossdressing. Many times an estimate is made without specifying if the behavior being estimated is recurrent or sporadic. Obviously, the number ever having crossdressed is higher than the number of those occasionally crossdressing, which is still higher than those frequently crossdressing. Moreover, what exactly constitutes 'occasional' and 'frequent' can vary from study to study. Therefore, comparing estimates across studies is fraught with peril. Nevertheless, some brief review is useful if for no other reason than illustrating the difficulties of fixing on a reliable range for how common crossdressing might be.

Already by the early 1960s, it was acknowledged that the majority of crossdressing by men occurred in private—and secretly. In fact, D. G. Brown, in 1961, flatly declared that 90% of crossdressing was in secrecy.[10] The predominance of secret crossdressing has been well upheld by the research, but only deepens the mystery. But despite the obstacles, some estimates have been offered. The following table illustrates the range of estimates across several studies (and includes data on women when available):

Table 11.1 Estimates of Prevalence of Crossdressing

Study (arranged by year)	Results
J. L. McCary (1978) [11]	Less than 1%
W. B. Arndt (1991) [12]	Less than ½%
S. Janus & C. L. Janus (1993) [13]	3% of women; 6% of men
Vernon Coleman (1996)[14]	10% of men
Lynn Conway (2001-2002)[15]	2%-5% of adult males
N. Langström & K. J. Zucker (2005)[16]	0.4% of women; 2.8% of men

Calculations like those made by Arndt in 1991, or McCary in 1978, that less than 1% of the population engage in transvestic behavior, must be regarded as probably seriously underestimated, if for no other reason than the aforementioned predominance of secrecy, which seem indisputable. An estimate that 3-5% of the adult male population in the United States at least occasionally cross-dress is more plausible,[17] but also may be low. Indeed, a 1982 study of 138 male medical students reports that 11% admit having experienced arousal from crossdressing at some point or another[18]—and that by its nature excludes whatever number might crossdress for other reasons, which would raise the total percentage higher. This conclusion seems buttressed by the work of medical journalist Dr. Vernon Coleman. Based on data collected from over 1000 British men in the mid-1990s, Coleman estimates the incidence of male crossdressing at 10%. But the fact is, we really do not know.

In addition to some of the difficulties mentioned above, there is a substantial issue involved in comparing studies. Each has in mind a particular definition for 'crossdressing' or 'transvestism,' and each has a particular way of measuring its presence. This can be illustrated using two of the studies presented in Table 11.1. The study by Langström and Zucker focuses on 'transvestic fetishism,' which is a subset of the crossdressing population, and their study is restricted to Sweden. Coleman's research, on the other hand, is done in Britain and has a broader view of crossdressing. Further, each study draws on a particular population in its own way, and the representativeness of those sampled must be questioned. Coleman's large group of over 1,000 subjects involves only males and his data is not collected in a rigorous fashion. Langström and Zucker survey the general population of all Sweden, using a random sample of 2,450 adults (ages 18-60), including both men and women. Yet they acknowledge that some parts of the population (e.g. recent immigrants) might be underrepresented and they caution that their definition of 'transvestic fetishism' is based on a single questionnaire item.

For the foreseeable future there seems little reason to suspect these difficulties will be sufficiently overcome to state how common crossdressing is with any confidence. Whether that data matters is largely how important we decide it is in calculating the significance of crossdressing. If we have in mind a threshold number above which the behavior matters and below which it is trivial, then we are likely to want to know how often it happens. In such a case, we are doomed to disappointment. We simply cannot state with confidence how common crossdressing—or any transgender reality—truly is.

Q. 12

Why would anyone crossdress?

The Short Answer: If it is difficult to establish how many people cross-dress, it is at least as difficult coming up with all the reasons crossdressing occurs. In one respect it would not be unfair to say there are as many motivations for crossdressing as there are crossdressers—and these motivations can vary even within an individual. Yet a number of basic, more-or-less common reasons have been discerned for this behavior. A few of these reasons even have led to creating labels to identify certain groups of crossdressers presumed to share the motivation. These reasons typically reflect responses to cultural limitations imposed on gender identity, expression, or roles. The idea of 'gender identity,' in particular, is both important and controversial. Some reasons for crossdressing may motivate both men and women. For example, women have sometimes passed as men to pursue same-sex sexual relationships without public censure. Some men have done the same. While there are some motivations that, historically, males and females have shared for crossdressing, there are also differences between them. These differences also reflect responses to cultural limitations. For instance, women often have posed as men to gain economic opportunities or desired vocations otherwise closed to them. Generally speaking, men have not been motivated by this reason for crossdressing since almost all jobs have been open to them. On occasion, the same stimulus can prompt crossdressing in both men and women for dramatically different reasons. For example, in times of war women may crossdress in order to fight while men may crossdress to escape fighting. The motivations in any given society or time period may be different than those found in other settings. Thus, in sorting out motivations, if various basic themes emerge these should not obscure the underlying individuality of every person who crossdresses.

The Longer Answer: As might be expected, various people offer different reasons for their crossdressing behavior. Nevertheless, across these individual reasons certain basic motivations can be discerned that results in an ability to broadly classify them into distinct categories. Although people always transcend their labels, the identification of groups has been used by researchers to differentiate motivations and other characteristics among those who crossdress. The behavior of crossdressing itself is a hallmark characteristic of the transgendered, despite the fact that not all transgendered people crossdress, and even those who do may only do so sporadically and partially.

In this answer we will explore some of the better-recognized motivations. For convenience, we will begin by setting forth a list of some of the groups into which crossdressers have been categorized. All such classification is meant to do is identify at least one primary, shared motivation for the behavior. Following the identification of these groups we will look at some of the many other reasons documented in history or by testimony of the crossdresser. Finally, we will briefly consider differences in motivation between crossdressers of different gender groups. Because these matters are elaborated upon and illustrated more fully in subsequent answers, our treatment here will be rather cursory.

Can crossdressers be categorized?

While there are more reasons offered by people for why they crossdress than there are groups distinguished by researchers, we may begin with a division into groups based on a primary motivation for so doing:

❑ *Festival crossdressers*—these are people crossdressing only for special festivities, such as a costume party, Mardi Gras, Carnival, or Halloween. (Cf. the answer to Q. 71.)

❑ *Ritual crossdressers*—these are individuals whose crossdressing is associated with ritual, such as puberty rites of passage, or shamanistic or priestly functions. (Cf. the answer to Q. 76.)

❑ *Entertainers*—these include those who only on rare occasions crossdress for a role on stage, in film or for television. (Cf. the answer to Q. 16.)

❑ *Professional imitators*—these entertainers make a living appearing as members of the opposite sex. (Cf. the answer to Q. 16.)

❑ *Drag Queens/Kings*—these are homosexual men or women who dress in a caricature of a different gender (cf. the answer to Q. 17). However, 'dressing in drag' can be done by anyone so long as their use of cross-gender dress is intended to not reflect their gender identity or normal manner of dress.

❑ *Third gender people*—these individuals may crossdress in especially distinctive ways to mark belonging to a gender that is neither masculinity nor femininity.

❑ *Transvestites*—these are people who crossdress either partially or fully, either irregularly or often, either in secret or openly, and for a variety of reasons, but who are almost always heterosexual and who do not desire to change their sex. (Cf. the answer to Q. 18.)

❑ *Transgender* (in the narrow sense)—these are people who crossdress persistently since they live full-time in a gender identity and role different from the one assigned them at birth. They do *not* have the sense of being in a body of the wrong sex and do not seek sex reassignment surgery. (Cf. the answer to Q. 20.)

❑ *Transsexuals*—these folk live with the constant conviction that they indwell a body of the wrong sex and thus dress to gain consonance with their gender identity. (Cf. the answer to Q. 19.)

It should also be noted that these various groups are looked at more closely in answering other questions (see Q. 16-20).

All of the above groups are characterized by a discernible general motive that prompts *voluntary* crossdressing. While it is not our focus here, we should note that some crossdressing is involuntary. Stories abound of so-called 'petticoat punishment,' a practice long employed principally with youth to enforce conformity to social gender expectation in behavior. On occasion, crossdressing also has been incorporated into prisoner abuse and torture. One contemporary example was the scandal of the mistreatment by American soldiers of Iraqi prisoners at Abu Ghraib, where men were forced to wear women's underwear—a tactic evidently adopted from earlier use with detainees at Guantanamo base in Cuba.[19]

Among those who voluntarily crossdress it is easy enough to see how different in nature various groups are from one another. For example, crossdressers labeled transvestites are far more likely to call themselves 'crossdressers' and admit the importance of the behavior to themselves than are those who crossdress for a festive occasion. Not only do motivations differ, but so too do self-perceptions of the behavior and its significance, and the perceptions of others. This last point is especially pertinent when we add the consideration that many other reasons exist for why people may crossdress and how their crossdressing changes the perceptions of observers.

In previous answers we discussed how crossdressing can be used to be, borrow, blend, blur, or bend gender (see the answers to Q. 6-7). These general ideas enter into the service of very concrete intentions. Consider the following partial list of more than two dozen separate motives for crossdressing (which overlaps somewhat with the motivations of the groups identified above):

❑ *criminal activity*—crossdressing provides a disguise making apprehension more difficult;

❑ *employment opportunities*—crossdressing has long provided a way to gain access to opportunities that otherwise would be difficult or impossible to obtain;

❑ *entertainment*—from ancient times to the present, whether at private parties or large public events, crossdressing has been used as one way to entertain others (cf. 'theater,' below);

- *escape*—crossdressing has been used to escape prison, military service, and a variety of other harsh circumstances;
- *exploration*—some crossdressing, especially among children, appears motivated by the desire to explore the experience of a different gender;
- *fashion pleasure*—some people crossdress simply because they like the look and feel of clothing that society has deemed intended for a different gender;
- *festivities*—crossdressing often accompanies celebrations of one kind or another and is a part of recurring festivals like Carnival and Halloween.
- *gender identity experience and expression*—crossdressing offers a way to both experience and express a felt sense of gender for persons whose gender identity is not paired with their sexual body in the way their culture expects;
- *law enforcement*—police officers sometimes use disguises, and crossdressing occasionally facilitates apprehension of a criminal;
- *loneliness*—sometimes people crossdress, donning the apparel of a loved one, as a way of feeling closer while the loved one is absent;
- *love*—much crossdressing across the ages has been motivated by a desire to be with a loved one where otherwise circumstances would frustrate that desire;
- *military strategy*—from ancient times to the present day crossdressing has been used as a way to lay traps, infiltrate enemy lines, and mount surprise attacks in military situations;
- *patriotism*—crossdressing has often been motivated by a desire to serve one's country, especially in times or situations where one sex has been denied the chance to serve in the military;
- *pleasing others*—crossdressing is sometimes motivated by a desire to please a parent, partner, or someone else;
- *political protest and social statement*—as phenomena as different as gay pride marches and feminist dress reform movements show, crossdressing is a way of making powerful symbolic statements about gender and sex;
- *prostitution*—crossdressing is a part of the sex trade;
- *sacred activities and roles*—crossdressing is sometimes employed in religious rites, commonly is associated with shamanism, or is a feature of a sacred office such as priest;
- *safety*—through the ages many people have crossdressed to increase their personal safety, especially when traveling, because their normal sex and gender presentation would have put them at risk;

- *sensual satisfaction*—some people crossdress because they like the look and/or feel of clothing styles and particular apparel associated with a different gender;
- *sexual access*—crossdressing has been used as a way to gain special access to members of a desired sex for sexual activity;
- *sexual arousal*—sometimes crossdressing is pursued for the sexual excitement and relief the act brings;
- *spying*—crossdressing has been used often as a way of spying;
- *stress relief*—often crossdressing is engaged in as a form of relaxation;
- *temporary gender relief and/or exploration*—crossdressing provides a low cost, easily attained and easily reversed way of escaping from one's assigned gender role, with all its expectations;
- *terrorism*—crossdressing is occasionally used by terrorists—both men and women—to add to the confusion and fear of potential victims;
- *theater*—whether drama or comedy, sacred or profane, crossdressing has been a staple of acting and a theme in plays for centuries in places around the world; and,
- *transitions*—because crossdressing involves boundaries it proves an ideal way to signify transitions across lines, such as the passage from childhood into adulthood, or from the mundane to the sacred.

We shall find examples of all of these in answering various questions throughout this work.

What do crossdressers themselves say about why they crossdress?

Having begun with this rough framework, and without exploring further other characteristics of members of these various groups, we will profit from hearing the reasons some crossdressers themselves offer for their crossdressing. As is typically the case, much of the information we have to draw upon comes from adult male crossdressers, most of who would be identified as transvestites, some of who would be labeled transsexuals, and some who might prefer another label (such as transgender). Surveys and interviews are the common avenues for self-report by crossdressers.

In a report published in 1996, based on data from more than 1,000 British men, medical writer Vernon Coleman found strong support for four of the five possible reasons provided to respondents as possible motivations:

- like the feeling of women's clothes (77%);
- want to be like a woman (63%);

❑   provides a sexual kick (59%); and,

❑   helps me relax and deal with stress (48%).[20]

Some of what crossdressers offer as their motivation is known by what they tell mental health professionals. Gianna Israel, a therapist specializing in transgender issues, draws on her experience to affirm that for some people crossdressing occupies an important psychological role—a matter explored more thoroughly in later answers (see especially question set 6). She writes, "Crossdressers are unique among the transgendered because they are satisfied with their natal gender. Yet, a deep fragment of their self must crossdress for mental relief and to experience feelings that cannot be satisfied in their ordinary lives and regular activities. Crossdressing fills these voids."[21]

We might multiply examples from the literature published on crossdressing, but these should suffice to show both that crossdressers indicate a variety of motivations for their behavior and that the significance of the activity for them varies. As can be seen from the above, while crossdressing is generally volitional behavior, it is more compelling for some than for others. Because noncrossdressers often find crossdressing objectionable this felt need is sometimes judged harshly.

What role does 'gender identity' play?

Crossdressing becomes particularly compelling when the motivation is tied to gender identity. We use this phrase 'gender identity' rather often in this work and it requires some special attention. In volume 1 we considered gender at some length, and in another work I have devoted a fair amount of space to the idea of gender identity.[22] Here we will offer only a brief orientation.

Our word *identity* has come to mean a quality of individual self-awareness as a particular person or self who remains relatively constant across time and situations. The English word shows up in the late 16th century, being derived from French, which in turn owed itself to a late Latin form of an earlier Latin root, *idem*, meaning 'same.' This remains the heart of the matter: identity is a persistence of self as known to the self and shown to others. Of course, the matter of persistence is a key idea. While perhaps most people assume their identity is stable and enduring, perhaps it is not as much so as we would like to believe. If we have an identity in reference to gender, then, is it fixed or fluid?

Is Gender Identity Fixed?

The idea of a stable gender identity, while popular and often used, is not without its critics. Three sources of unrest are particularly noteworthy. First, post-modern theorists (e.g., Jean Baudrillard, Jean-Francois Lyotard) critique assumed ways of knowing and unsettle presumed settled notions, such as a strict dichotomy of gender. They invite us to reconsider the idea of gender or identity as fixed realities. Second, post-structuralist theorists (e.g., Jacques Derrida, Jacques Lacan, Michel Foucault) share an aversion to the notion of a fixed and unitary self. They remind us that what we think we 'know' is shaped by our ways of talking about things; we can scarcely conceive of things for which we have no words and our existing words and discourse constrain what we can conceive. Third, queer theorists (e.g., Judith Butler), drawing inspiration in particular from Foucault, challenge heteronormativity—the idea that heterosexual masculinity and femininity should establish what is 'normal'—and view identity as a matter of 'preformativity.' In short, gender is not something we *have* but something we *do*.[23] It should not be hard to see that all three of these approaches are not keen on talk about an 'essential' identity—some immutable quality of being—and so resist ideas of a fixed, natural gender identity.

Nevertheless, though redrawing how identity can be talked about, 'gender identity' remains something that can be discussed. It can, in the traditional manner, be conceived as something fixed and drawn from nature. Or it can be viewed as socially constructed. Or it can be seen as fluid and individually determined. We cannot here go into depth on these or other possible conceptions of gender identity. What we can do is provide some simple clarification as to how it is regarded in this work.

Defining Gender Identity

For our purposes, building on the work in volume 1, we assume that gender is something central to personal identity and social relating in our society. At birth we are assigned a gender (masculine or feminine), based on our apparent sex (male or female), and henceforth are expected to grow as a boy into manhood, or as a girl into womanhood. However, because gender and sex are not the same, and because sex does not determine gender, mismatches between sex and gender can occur. In addition to mismatches involving a simple crossing from one dominant gender to another (e.g., masculine females or feminine males), there are people whose gender does not fit either masculinity or femininity—what we term 'third' gender(s).

In developmental psychology, 'gender identity' is commonly used in a simple and narrow manner to refer to a child's recognition of the self as either a boy or a girl. But this recognition seems more an acknowledgment of gender *assignment* than necessarily of gender *identity*. More often than not, of course, the two are the same. However, there are a fair number of people for whom this is not the case. In either case, we need not assume that gender identity is fixed.

Identity gains its persistent sense not from a sudden, once-for-all decision, but from a gradual accumulation and interpretation of *experience*. As we experience gender for ourselves, both in social interactions and in more private ways, we come to a realization of a particular gendered self. As we talk about gender identity, we need to keep in mind that it is built, sustained, and perhaps modified by experience. To some degree we are always affirming or questioning this persistent sense of our gendered self. Gender identity is much more process than product.

Behind this work's use of the concept lies the idea that gender identity is really *gender self-identifying*, an ongoing process that generally reflects stability, but isn't fixed. In this broader sense of the term, gender identity continues to develop beyond self-identification as labeling and affiliating with a particular gender. Viewed this way, gender identity involves a rich and evolving series of experiences that are then translated in gender expressions. Here, 'gender identity' refers to an ongoing identifying of self in gender terms through both gender experience and gender expression. *Gender experience* refers to the actual, lived gendering done by each of us. Gender experience includes how we feel about our gendered self, how we think of that gendered self, and how we incline ourselves to act based on those thoughts and feelings. This inclination, or will, may or may not always be carried out, but it persists and motivates some behavior consistent with itself. *Gender expression* refers to the behaviors we enact to display gender, whether or not that display is congruent with our gender identity or according to the inclination of our gender experience.[24] It also may or may not be identical at any given moment to our gender role.

Regardless of whether we view the self as fixed or fluid, one or many, at any given moment it achieves a degree of recognition we can call 'identity,' a way of knowing our self in the moment. Gender identity is such self-knowing in terms of gender experience and expression. For our purposes we will consider that *gender identity is an internalized self-construction arising from experience interacting with cultural conceptions and expectations about gender, especially as these relate to the gender assigned the individual.* The value of this formulation is that while it recognizes each of us must wrestle with the weight of culture brought to bear on us through gender assignment and its accompanying socialization pressure, it does not insist that our experience result in a self-construction that must be labeled within the cultural gender scheme. Our experience is what it is. We may find accepted social gender labels more or less fitting. In gender self-identifying we engage in a lifelong process of building, testing, and revising a core aspect of self. The result at any given moment can be called a gender identity, the fruit of experience forged in the context of culture. That forging, or development, must now be our next concern.

Gender Identity As Ongoing Developmental Process[25]

Gender identity can be considered both in a narrow sense along the lines commonly used by child developmentalists and in a broader sense. In the narrow sense it encompasses a process that begins with gender assignment at birth, proceeds through gender socialization to cultivate a gender awareness and culminates in a recognition of how the gendered self is regarded by others. This often also is how the child regards the self, but not necessarily.

A *broad sense of gender identity* posits both that the narrow sense constitutes only one phase of an ongoing process of gender self-identifying, and that even in this first phase there are other elements transpiring that are usually overlooked. The reason these are not typically considered is that they are difficult to establish empirically, especially in the preverbal period, but also in the immature child. So hypothetical constructs set out in this regard must be viewed rather more skeptically. At the same time, they cannot be ignored in light of the observable outcomes in actually witnessed gender identities.

So let us attempt to set out the elements of a broad sense of gender identity, or *the process of gender self-identifying*:

- ❏ Phase I: attaining gender identity (narrow sense).
- ❏ Phase II: gender identity *testing*—confirming or disconfirming through personal experience the product of phase one. It includes:
    - o gender stabilizing—learning that gender persists across time;
    - o attaining gender constancy—learning that gender persists across situations;
    - o reaching gender permanence—applying gender stability and gender constancy to the self and to others; and,
    - o measuring personal experience of gender against the culturally expected label for 'goodness-of-fit.'
- ❏ Phase III: gender identity *stabilizing*—the attainment of a reasonably secure gender identity with some continuing reassessment. The elements of this phase may include:
    - o achieving a goodness-of-fit that persistently stabilizes the gender self-identifying across situations and for a period of time;
    - o cognitive dissonance when elements of gender experience and expression no longer fit as well;
    - o gender identity flux, and perhaps crisis, as competing elements vie to determine the next reasonably stable gender identity; and
    - o recycling of the phase, to a greater or less degree, throughout life.

Phase I, *attaining gender identity (narrow sense)*, we have already discussed. But we must add a comment or two. First, the child at age 3 can label the gendered self as 'boy' or 'girl,' but this really doesn't tell us much about the internal identity experience. After all, what other gender labels are there? The cultural juggernaut of gender socialization admits no other possibilities and lends its full weight to confirming a label consistent with gender assignment. Thus, second, all we can be confident about is that the child has accurately learned the label applied by others.

Phase II, *gender identity testing*, tests the label—the *presumed* gender identity. Typically, gender stability is mastered by age 4. Gender constancy proves a little more elusive. Despite having labeled the self as 'boy' or 'girl,' children between 3-6 view gender as fluid; change one's appearance and the gender changes, too. But by about 6-7 years old most kids have swallowed the cultural lesson that gender is fixed and immutable, both across time and across situations. Shortly thereafter this conclusion is pasted to the gendered self. But the child of 7 still has no other referents for gender identity save 'boy' or 'girl.'

This does not mean children don't search for alternatives. Children are regularly measuring their personal experience of gender against the culturally expected label for 'goodness-of-fit.' How well does the label that has been applied to the gendered self—'boy' or 'girl'—actually fit the self's experience in light of gender expectations and stereotypes? What is a child to do when the label does not wear well?

Consider, for example, the case of elementary school-aged Jodie, who after remarking that all the girls in her class "act all stupid and girlie," declared this judgment did not apply to her "cos I'm not a girl, I'm a tomboy." She succeeded in persuading two male classmates to identify her as a boy—a reasonable judgment because 'tomboy' clearly isn't 'girl' and in a two gender scheme that only leaves 'boy.' The researcher in this study concluded Jodie appeared to be operating at the boundary line between masculinity and femininity—again, a justifiable interpretation where no other gender alternatives are allowed recognition.[26] But we can as easily imagine that Jodie was experiencing a gender identity that neither 'girl' nor 'boy' really labeled; the closest label available that fit her experience was 'tomboy.'

What Jodie may be doing is actively *measuring the 'goodness-of-fit'* between her labeled gender identity and her actual gender experience. She may be acting like a scientist. Psychologist George Kelly's personal construct theory may have some relevance to us in this respect.[27] Kelly views people as rational beings who rely on constructs to construe the environment and anticipate future events. We expect our way of looking at things to make sense and fit internally. So constructs are as valuable as their usefulness for prediction and producing meaning. A child's evolving constructs start few in number and highly dependent on others, especially one's parents. As the child grows, *role-playing* becomes a way to try on and test hypotheses about being a person. Such activity yields for most kids a highly predictable set of outcomes associated with gender conformity as opposed to gender nonconformity. But constructs are highly individual, subjected to continuous testing by experience, and modifiable. They also realize the power of personal choice so that while most children have construct systems that place high priority on *sociality*—predicting the responses and behaviors of others—to guide our behavior, some prioritize another construct. In making an *elaborative choice*, a child selects an alternative aligned with a particular construct because it appears promising to further develop one's construct system. Such choices can consolidate previous gains or seek future ones. Importantly for our consideration, such choices can test, refute, or promote a particular gender identity.

Sooner or later, given the primacy of gender to our culture's conception of self and relationships, a reasonably stable gender identity is achieved. Phase III, *gender identity stabilizing*, begins with and follows from this attainment. It starts with achieving a *goodness-of-fit that persistently secures the gender self-identifying across situations and for a period of time*. The gendered self reaches and maintains, at least for a while, a gender identity that works. It permits a congruence of self-labeling with inner experience and finds outlets, private or public, for expressing that gender. But continuing life experience in an environment where gender expectations change with time and situations may introduce challenges to this security. There may develop *cognitive dissonance* when elements of gender experience and expression no longer fit. What worked before no longer works. The new demands of a different developmental level or interpersonal situation heightens the stakes even as the feasibility of the existing gender identity is called into question. This new instability in the gender self-identifying prompts a degree of *gender identity flux*—a renewed time of testing gender identity in search of a new goodness-of-fit. This flux might persist for a long time if the person is able to tolerate the insecurity of the gender identity, or proves unable to achieve a new stability, or has little incentive to resolve the situation because the price paid for the flux is inconsequential. Perhaps more often, though, flux climaxes in *gender identity crisis*, as competing elements internally vie to determine the next reasonably stable gender identity. Resolution returns the self to a reasonably secure gender identity; there follows recycling of the phase, to a greater or less degree, throughout life.

How significant is crossdressing to crossdressers?

Our somewhat extended discursion on gender identity should help us see why crossdressing can be so significant that crossdressers say they are unwilling or unable to give it up. Because dress marks gender, and because gender is so intrinsic in our culture to the experience and expression of self, crossdressing is highly instrumental in realizing and disclosing a person's gender identity. No wonder, then, it is unlikely to be given up.

Crossdressing by transvestites occasionally has been characterized as a compulsion. Regardless of that characterization, it has proven a behavior very resistant to extinction for most who crossdress (see the answer to Q. 97). That suggests that for these folk the motivations and/or rewards are high—an idea important for understanding why people may crossdress persistently even where social sanctions against it are weighty. So it seems easy to conclude that crossdressing must be very significant to crossdressers.

And it is for many. For some crossdressing meets enduring and deeply felt needs, such as those associated with gender identity. Hence it is likely to occur more frequently. However, mere frequency does not automatically equate with felt significance. Perhaps surprisingly, even among those who crossdress regularly the valuation placed on the behavior varies.

Some crossdress more often than they dress in the manner expected of them by their gender assignment. Yet even in this pattern the perceived significance may vary from one individual to another. Someone who is identified as a transvestite is likely to find the crossdressing itself a highly salient and valued experience. As the label implies, the emphasis is on the clothes. But a transsexual might not regard the behavior as any more significant than anyone else who

31

gives little thought to dressing for the day because there is no sense of crossing a gender line. In truth, in the case of transsexuals it is fair to ask if the dressing behavior is truly crossdressing since the dress is consistent with a stable sense of gender, even if that gender sense is at variance from the birth assigned gender based on body sex.

Complicating matters further is how occasional crossdressing may be assessed. For those who crossdress only for a special occasion (e.g., Carnival, or to entertain others), the occasion itself sets the boundaries. Some who only infrequently crossdress—and then only partially—may find such occasions special and highly significant. Others with a like pattern of behavior may regard it as a casual hobby of no special importance. The significance of the behavior lies embedded in context as much as in the individual. Despite the generalities that can be said about reasons for crossdressing, it inevitably remains a very personal matter with distinct motivational and behavioral patterns whose significance is context-dependent.

Do males and females crossdress for different reasons?

Given the basic individuality of crossdressing, it is fair to ask whether broad differences such as between male and female crossdressers exist. The answer is a qualified 'Yes.' While there is substantial overlap in reasons for crossdressing among members of these gender groups, there also exists a persistent difference in emphasis for the motivation. Historically, we might depict this difference as follows: *whereas males principally seem to be expressing inner qualities in crossdressing, females typically seem to be pursuing external goals.* Thus, while males seem to crossdress to express an internalized gender *identity*, females often crossdress to occupy an external gender *role*. A male often crossdresses to express an inner femininity; a female often crossdresses to seize a masculine prerogative.[28]

Heightened sensitivity to the irrationality of gender-based inequality and sex discrimination have resulted in a modern positive appraisal of women crossdressing to escape their socially prescribed gender role confines. A woman masquerading as a man to improve her economic lot in life has seemed to most of us a perfectly reasonable pretext for an otherwise disapproved behavior. On the other hand, a man crossdressing to express an inner femininity has been widely viewed as an irrational self-emasculation and incomprehensible lowering of social status. In such a context it is little wonder that transvestism as a mental disorder has been seen as the exclusive provenance of males.

Yet we have grounds to question the soundness of the preceding portrayal. First, there are too many exceptions to the above generalizations to make them as useful as they first appear. Second, cultural biases over an extended period of time have colored both what history preserves and how it is interpreted. The historical examples remembered of crossdressing men and women are presumably a fraction of the number who crossdressed and were never known or, if once known, have since been forgotten. Of those remembered, their memory often reflects a selection that carefully confirms preexisting judgments. Thus, it is easier to remember males and females for reasons that support a cultural perception about crossdressing than it is to recall those whose motivations challenge what the majority wants to believe.

In fact, as views about gender and transgender shift, historical examples emerging from obscurity provide support for new ways of understanding. Unfortunately, often enough even these examples have been supplied with an interpretive overlay that first has to be peeled away before a better explanation can be applied. Another obstacle is the willful disregard of evidence that might disconfirm a reigning hypothesis. For example, once a consensus was reached under the medical model of mental health that only males crossdressed for sexual purposes, all effort to investigate that motive in women—or even acknowledge its possibility when it seemed to be present—was discouraged. As a result, the fact that little is known about females who crossdress for sexual arousal has become part of the proof that such very rarely, if ever, occurs.

In answering subsequent questions we must try to remain open to more possibilities and evidence than is generally entertained. If we are serious about understanding why people crossdress, we must be willing to suspend our own culturally preconceived and inherited judgments. Instead, we need to hear what transgendered people say about themselves. We must be willing to admit evidence into consideration that may not fit what we thought was true or wanted to believe. None of these things are easy tasks, but they are rewarding ones when our own humanity is thus expanded and our perception and relationships become enhanced by a nuanced and fuller sensibility.

Q. 13

Do men crossdress?

The Short Answer: Males—both boys and men—crossdress. This phenomenon can be examined in different ways. One path focuses on development in an effort to understand its causes. In childhood crossdressing may happen involuntarily because a parent wishes it. Nevertheless, a sizable percentage of boys crossdress voluntarily. For many of them, the crossdressing is 'experimental' and not pursued with any vigor (what some term 'a phase'). For others, crossdressing becomes a part of their lives and persists into adolescence. Some crossdressing starts in later youth or adulthood—even middle to later adulthood. Crossdressing cuts across sexual orientation, occurring among heterosexuals, homosexuals, and transsexuals. Exactly why it occurs remains a mystery. The evidence suggests a variety of motivations and developmental paths (explored in subsequent answers), and to grasp what crossdressing is all about some sense of this variety is needed. Alongside the range in motivation and development is diversity in historical and cultural expression (also explored in later answers)—which are other profitable ways to try to understand crossdressing. In this respect we find that not only have some males throughout history and around the world crossdressed, they have a wide range of reasons for doing so. What characterizes our situation today is the relatively greater interest in this phenomenon. Perhaps the most remarkable sign of masculine privilege and the patriarchal gender hierarchy comes in our modern preoccupation with male crossdressing. This behavior, whether meant to or not, poses a challenge to the gender hierarchy because it raises the specter of boys and men voluntarily lowering their gender status and privilege to the 'lower' class of girls and women. So a great deal of effort has been expended to explain such behavior as 'abnormal' and 'mentally disordered.'

The Longer Answer: Men crossdress. As best we can tell, some always have (see the answers to Q. 13, 41-47, 49-50). Moreover, this is behavior not confined to the Western world; crossdressing men are found in societies around the world (see the answers to Q. 51-60). Much of this book concerns crossdressing men because they fascinate contemporary society. In past years—and they were not so long ago—it was crossdressing women who drew the most attention (see the answers to Q. 14, 45-48, 68-69). But crossdressing men and boys have always been among us and today they receive more attention than perhaps ever before. While the answers to other questions look more fully at various aspects of this phenomenon, here we will briefly survey the subject.

Why do some men crossdress?

In the answer to the previous question we examined some reasons why people crossdress. We found that differences in reasons permit a degree of generalization into a number of groups. We noted that some groups are characterized by occasional crossdressing in specific circumstances, such as for a festival or party, or for a theatrical role. Others engage in crossdressing more regularly, across a variety of contexts, and because of other motivations. These might include rebellion against stereotyping (as in some drag), or the expression of a gender at variance with the one assigned at birth (as in transvestism or transsexualism). Men can be found among the members of all these groups.

We also noted in answering the previous question that while some differences between why men and women crossdress may exist, we should be wary of exaggerating them. While it may be true that a male often crossdresses to express an inner femininity, and a female often crossdresses to seize a masculine prerogative, there are enough exceptions to prevent forming a steadfast rule. For example, while historically women sometimes crossdressed to hide from enemies, the same has been true for men—including prominent ones. In 1686, during the American colonial period, Sir Edmond Andros, distinguished governor in different colonies for the British crown, ran afoul of the people of Massachusetts and was imprisoned. He attempted escape disguised as a woman, save for his military-style boots, which gave him away.[29] More than 150 years later, the president of the Confederacy during the United States Civil War, Jefferson Davis, suffered a similar misadventure. He was apprehended at war's end while trying to escape wearing his wife's raglan and shawl; his boots also betrayed him.[30]

These figures remind us of another fact of social reality: prominent figures are more likely to be remembered for what they do than the rest of us—and also more likely to escape ruin when caught doing something socially unconventional. Even today there are powerful males who crossdress. In entertainment venues like television or movies few find it remarkable or objectionable for men to portray women (see the answer to Q. 44). In other realms the risk is greater, and so the likelihood that the behavior will be kept secret is higher. For example, some politicians on the national stage crossdress. Psychologist William Stayton, a well-known gender therapist, remarks, "You can't imagine how many politicians can't give a speech in Congress without wearing women's panties."[31] He points specifically to the example of a Senator who wore pantyhose, bra and feminine underwear beneath his masculine blue suit, risking discovery because "it was the only way he could speak calmly before the Senate."[32]

When does male crossdressing start?

Although much is debated about male crossdressing, the matter of when it starts is widely agreed upon. The available evidence (see the answer to Q. 28 for details) indicates crossdressing typically begins in childhood, often very early in childhood (cf. the answer to Q. 14). Sometimes it is voluntary behavior; sometimes not. Why a boy would begin crossdressing is much debated and there are probably numerous reasons. Whatever the 'cause,' the behavior often (but not always) persists.

Some male crossdressers begin this behavior after childhood. Of this group, those who start in adolescence appear to outnumber those who begin in adulthood. Yet there are reports from some adult crossdressers that their behavior began in middle adulthood, or even later. Again reasons vary. Some accidentally discover an erotic quality through an experimental crossdressing. Others say they begin in response to the loss of a loved one. In later onset crossdressing it is unknown how many persist in the behavior. It seems likely that many adult men who experiment with the behavior do not become regular crossdressers.

Why does male crossdressing start and why does it persist?

As already indicated, no one knows for sure why boys or men begin to crossdress. The cause, or causal factors, underlying crossdressing in males remains perhaps the greatest mystery of the subject (cf. answers to Q. 21-25, 29).

Just as intriguing is the question why so many continue the behavior. The negatives surrounding crossdressing seem pretty obvious: widespread social censure, the guilt aroused from violating social norms, the doubt about gender identity often accompanying crossdressing, complications in relationships, and the real possibility of public humiliation, shame, and even violence should the behavior be discovered. That many who crossdress persist despite the risks and, for many, actual experience of many of these negatives attests to the power of the behavior.

Many of us assume that any behavior so persistent in the face of so many possible and actual negatives must itself be negative. In other words, the logic is that only negative behaviors occasion so much social resistance and produce negative consequences. Of course, even a little thought exposes the incorrectness of the logic. Those who opposed racism in the Civil Rights movement in the United States faced both social resistance and many negative outcomes. That did not make the civil disobedience of these folk 'bad behavior.' So whether crossdressing is 'bad' or not cannot be solved by simplistic application of faulty logic. Indeed, the moral and religious questions connected with crossdressing prove surprisingly subtle and complex—and occupy a substantial portion of this work (cf. answers to Q. 3, 61-85).

Most people are at least mildly surprised to discover that the majority of crossdressing men report that crossdressing is a positive experience. In a cost-benefit analysis, apparently the benefits outweigh the costs. Of course, that does not prove that crossdressing is harmless. After all, an alcoholic or drug addict might argue that the benefits outweigh the costs, though others might find that conclusion profoundly wrong. So, analyzing whether crossdressing is harmful—whether to the crossdresser, others, or society at large—is an important matter (addressed in the answer to Q. 32). It is also a matter of concern to mental health experts and their history of involvement with crossdressers is a matter of substantial concern for this work (see answers to Q. 91-100).

How do others respond to male crossdressing?

Differences—especially those that are striking, mysterious, and violate basic assumptions and expectations about how things are, or are supposed to be—may intrigue us, but also often elicit resistance. Some people respond to male crossdressers as though their mere existence brings harm. Historically, various ordinances have been used to discourage crossdressing, at least in public (see the answer to Q. 36). Many regard crossdressing as symptomatic of one or another form of psychological disorder, or of predatory homosexuality, and the phenomenon has been the subject of expert attention for more than a century (see the answers to Q. 95-96).

Of more immediate concern to crossdressers themselves have been the reaction of family and friends. Their reactions fill a wide range, from warm supportiveness to reluctant acceptance to outright rejection. The most examined group of those close to crossdressers has been the spouses and significant others of male crossdressers (see the answer to Q. 38). But another matter of concern has been the reaction of other family members, especially parents and children (see the answer to Q. 39). As with so much else found with this subject, the range of responses from those close to a crossdresser suggest that crossdressing is a complex reality touching on many important aspects of the human experience.

Interestingly, even the reaction of society is more complicated than what we might first assume. We are likely to think that society opposes crossdressing—and for the most part we would not be wrong. But society does not regard all crossdressing alike. Some public crossdressing has a long history of tolerance, even support (see the answers to Q. 60, 71). Many people are not distressed by crossdressing by gay men. Sheila Jeffries notes that, "transvestism in gay men does not seem to promote much disquiet."[33] Indeed, many folk line streets to gaze at gay parades with 'queens' dressed 'in drag.'

The most objectionable form of crossdressing in contemporary Western society is that by male heterosexual adults. Why? The most likely reason concerns our present rigid gender lines and expectations, expressed through heteronormativity. A crossdressing male, especially an ostensibly heterosexual one, challenges received social ideology about the genders and their relations. Under heteronormativity, a crossdressing man both voluntarily lowers his social status—an act for a great many of us that is baffling at best, if not also threatening and upsetting—*and* suggests he has adopted an effeminate homosexuality.

What are male crossdressers like?

Members of any minority population tend to find themselves caricatured by others. The same has been true for male crossdressers. A variety of myths persist, especially that all male crossdressers are homosexual. Another myth is that all male crossdressers want to be women and that given the opportunity most would seek a sex-change operation. Such myths may be reassuring to noncrossdressers afflicted by irrational fears, but they are needless obstacles to comprehending a behavior often blown out of proportion.

The ways in which adult male crossdressers present themselves reveals people much more like others than different from them (see the answer to Q. 26). Of course, in survey and interview situations people may be prone to offer a more positive picture than what is actually the case. Yet psychological testing appears to confirm the general finding that crossdressing men are basically like noncrossdressing men (see the answer to Q. 27). The principal manner in which they differ from other males is in crossdressing.

On the other hand, there may be some usefulness in trying to see ways in which crossdressers differ in life experiences or personality traits, even if these differences ought not to be exaggerated. The dilemma lies in seeking to offer a general portrait that many crossdressers can more or less fit while not creating new stereotypes that distort the more important reality that male crossdressers aren't all that different from noncrossdressers. In examining these matters we shall have to constantly remind ourselves to remain grounded in the data we have and to assess the value of that data.

I hope the remarks in this answer hint at the adventure involved in seeking to comprehend crossdressing. While I have made every effort to consider female crossdressing as well as male, the cultural focus at present is on men. That means that, apart from historical studies, most of the literature on this subject keeps males central. The result for this work is that many answers to questions disproportionately deal with adult heterosexual male crossdressers. Presently they are the group best studied and most discussed.

Q. 14

Do women crossdress?

The Short Answer: Of course they do—far more than men!—if by cross-dressing is meant the wearing of clothes, or fashion styles, typically or tradition-ally associated with the masculine gender. Our best evidence suggests this situa-tion has pertained for as long as gendered distinctions in dress have been made. Prior to the modern era girls and women crossdressed for many reasons, includ-ing a desire to enhance their safety, to gain access to professions and activities otherwise closed to them, and for love—both heterosexual and homosexual. But crossdressing by women has become so ubiquitous in modern Western cul-ture that it is no longer even seen as crossdressing. Instead, today's crossdress-ing woman can advantage herself with clothes originally or predominantly asso-ciated with men (e.g., pants) that have been adapted to become acceptably 'feminine.' When women's clothing looks like that traditionally associated with men (including bearing names suggesting masculinity), it is called 'fashion' in-stead of 'fetishism.' All this aside, evidence unequivocally shows modern women continue to crossdress. Sometimes their reasons are similar to those of their predecessors in bygone times (e.g., safety, love), and sometimes their moti-vation parallels contemporary male crossdressers (e.g., gender identity, transves-tic fetishism). That the reality of crossdressing women remains largely invisible mostly reflects our ongoing preoccupation with what men do. Crossdressing behavior by modern women, particularly in the West, simply does not excite much interest or comment. This situation seriously hampers our overall under-standing of crossdressing because it distorts the reality of the phenomenon. It also limits even more severely than is true for crossdressing men what we can say with confidence about these women. Despite the fact that we know more about crossdressing women of the past than of the present, the totality of what we know is enough for us to conclude that crossdressing has been, and likely remains, an important behavior for some women.

The Longer Answer: Many people are upset at the idea that women crossdress and can be properly termed 'transvestites.' Why is this? The answer is probably obvious, even if not reading through this book in a straightforward fashion. 'Transvestism' is not a term generally used with favor in our culture, and the added reality that it is listed in psychiatric texts as a mental illness adds to distaste for the term. The vast majority of those women who dress in mannish styles regard themselves as unremarkably female, experiencing nothing more than practicality and freedom of expression in their manner of dress. Nevertheless, their behavior is subject to scientific observation and comment.

Harry Brierley, author of a 1979 book on transvestism for mental health professionals, makes the case for female transvestism succinctly:

> Transvestism, literally, is clearly the wearing of the clothes pertaining to the opposite sex. In this sense fashion, particularly the current female fashion for wearing trousers, hacking jacket, waistcoat, shirt, tie and men's cap, or male fashion wearing make-up, are unequivocally transvestite. Because they are 'fashion' does not make them less transvestite nor does regarding them as 'fashion' explain the motivation behind such fashion.[34]

A little more than a decade later, Peggy Rudd, wife of a transgender male, writes with unusual candor about the realization she experienced when she learned the definition of 'transvestite' was 'anyone who crossdresses—who wears the clothes usually associated with the opposite sex.' Rudd remarks: "This definition forced me to consider myself a transvestite when masculine clothing fits the mood or need in my own life."[35]

Perhaps even more to the point, those who contend that women not only do not crossdress, but *cannot*, are ignorant of the consequences girls and women face who actually do crossdress. The eminent recorders of crossdressing, Vern and Bonnie Bullough, pointedly observe that "once women cross over the imaginary line that separates those who toy with men's clothing and those who violate gender norms by impersonating men, the punishments are similar to those meted out to men. These crossdressers are socially stigmatized just as men are."[36]

So why are so many of us reluctant to admit that girls and women may crossdress? The answer lies in our culture's construction of a gender order dependent on power: masculine males have it and if feminine females want it, they can attain some measure of it by masculinizing themselves. Although writing with reference to African discourses on gender, Oyekan Owomoyela makes a telling point about transvestism in Western culture:

> A woman may dress as a man, may wear pants and jackets, even ties, and yet be regarded as perfectly dressed, especially as a modern, "with it" woman. But a man who wears a frock, or skirt and blouse, and a shawl would be a transvestite, somewhat beyond the pale of normality. The inference is that it is alright for a woman to strive to become a man, but not the other way round, since transvestism, according to the general understanding, indicates the gender identity preference of the person who engages in it.[37]

A woman masculinizing herself through dress is reaching up; she is expressing the socially favored gender. However, a man feminizing himself through dress is—in the eyes of the culture at large—voluntarily lowering himself, vacating the social prerogatives socially embedded in cultural patriarchy, and embracing the socially inferior gender identity. While we can readily understand a woman's upward striving, few of us can comprehend or have sympathy for a man giving up his privileged place. It varies so much from cultural values of competition, seeking power, and so forth, that it strikes many of us as a sure sign of mental instability. So, since 'transvestism' has long been culturally coded as mental illness, it cannot be applied to women (since we can understand and empathize with their quest), but we readily stick it to men (since their actions are abnormal and deviant by cultural standards).

Once we set aside our own specific cultural bias toward rewarding masculinity at virtually any expense, the evidence is clear. Despite any disquiet over the notion, women crossdress—and some do so for erotic purposes (the precise aspect used most forcefully to castigate crossdressing males). The connection of female crossdressing and sexuality has been noted occasionally in the psychiatric literature,[38] but mostly before the American Psychiatric Association decided that 'transvestic fetishism' could only be applied to heterosexual males. In the Janus report on sexual behavior, in the early 1990s, 3% of women reported crossdressing.[39] Yet no matter how slight the percentage might be, the Januses offer the observation that, "Women who cross dress have no problem; so called 'tomboys' are fully accepted, but 'sissies' are not."[40]

Why do some women crossdress?

Apparently, women have crossdressed for at least as long as men have. Moreover, people in the past far more often remarked upon crossdressing by women than crossdressing done by men (see the answers to Q. 48, 68-69). The current fascination with crossdressing men is a relatively recent phenomenon. A little reflection may suggest more than one reason why women might want to crossdress. These reasons only partially coincide with reasons offered by male crossdressers.

The pioneering sexologist Havelock Ellis thinks that most crossdressing among women can be accounted for by one or the other of two factors:

❑ for greater facility in making a living; or,

❑ for sexual purposes (i.e., as an expression of their homosexuality).[41]

These explanations remain a common staple for researchers.[42]

When the work worlds of men and women were more sharply divided than they are now, some women turned to male dress as a way of finding entry into realms otherwise closed to them. Of course, in such cases the crossdressing was part of a complete transformation in appearance and manner aimed at helping the woman 'pass' as a man. This behavior sometimes persisted for many years.

In retrospect it is impossible to determine how many of these women would today meet criteria for 'gender dysphoria' (see the answer to Q. 93). That some had yearnings to actually be male is likely, but for others the motivation was economic or vocational.

Ellis' second contention also enjoys ample evidence. Some women have crossdressed as a means of forming same-sex relationships. In some instances, this phenomenon was probably a transsexual female-to-male (FtM) who was pursuing life as a man in every respect, including gender identity. But in other instances, the woman was employing the artifice of appearing as a man so as to enter a relationship with another woman that would be seen by outsiders as heterosexual though it was, in fact, homosexual. Thus, historians John D'Emilio and Estelle Freedman remark that "when working-class women sought to establish same-sex relationships, they often did so by adopting men's clothing and 'passing' as men in order to earn wages and marry other women."[43] (This topic is further explored in the answer to Q. 17.)

Of course, such crossdressing could result in strongly negative consequences. Another pioneering sexologist, Richard von Krafft-Ebing, in his mammoth *Psychopathia Sexualis*, records three instances of crossdressed women living in what he terms 'lesbian love.' The first crossdressing woman, who entered into three marriages with other women, was tried before a court in 1777 and sentenced to six months imprisonment. The second woman's genital sex was discovered after courting another woman. The third lived in marriage with another woman for 30 years before confessing her secret as she lay dying. [44] Other scholars have produced examples of the negative consequences following discovery of same-sex love, and thus reinforcing the motivation to pass as a man in order to avoid discovery and sanctions. In some instances, the deception even extended to the lover!

The reasons set forth by Ellis do not exhaust the possibilities. Literary student Shasta Turner, based on her study of European writings, suggests a fourfold division for female crossdressers:

❑ *crossdressing to avoid unwanted marriages or sexual advances, or to achieve some holy aim*—this type is more common in the Medieval period;

❑ *crossdressing for romantic or sexual purposes*—this includes both those who dress as men to pursue a love for another woman and those who do so in order to remain with a male partner;

❑ *crossdressing in order to obtain positions reserved for men*—such occupations include soldier, sailor, and many more; and,

❑ *crossdressing temporarily for festivals*—Carnival and like occasions find women crossing gender lines, usually in ways deemed inoffensive but which sometimes bring censure (as in appearing in church dressed like a man).[45]

This more nuanced division better reflects the multiple reasons and contexts in which crossdressing occurred.

As social restrictions have eased in various cultures the need for some forms of crossdressing have disappeared. In today's America, while women still are typically paid less for equal work, their open entry into occupations once exclusively the domain of men—such as military life—has eliminated the need for outright disguise. But it does not appear to have eliminated the desirability of some gender mimicry—itself a form of transgender behavior. Evidence supports the impression that women who dress in more masculine clothing do better in the workplace—to a point. There seems to be a delicate, largely invisible gendered dress boundary that invites women to approach for reward, but punishes them if they cross it. In essence, they must project masculine qualities while preserving their femininity. This very goal characterizes the presentation of much women's wear for the workplace. Women must mimic men, but not in too obvious a way.

Similarly, the greater acceptance of lesbian relationships has meant an ability to pursue relationships without recourse to crossdressing to present a heterosexual façade. Yet lesbian couples may utilize gendered distinctions in dress to reflect their relational roles vis-à-vis each other. And lesbians, like gay men, utilize crossdressing for other purposes, such as making very public statements about cultural notions of gender. Moreover, it seems absurd to rule out *a priori* the possibility that some lesbian crossdressing has an erotic quality, and perhaps even a fetishistic one.

Changes over the centuries in religious life have pretty much eliminated the phenomena of the crossdressing female saint. In Euro-American culture women still tend to employ very feminine styles of dress when attending religious services, but rare would be the occasion that a woman would be turned away for wearing more masculine garb, such as pants. The notion of saints is rarer itself, and women in much of the Christian world no longer need masculine disguises to enter into desired forms of spiritual ministry and worship.

In short, the chief historical reasons for women to crossdress have been largely dismissed—and female crossdressing has seemed to largely vanish. But to claim that female crossdressing no longer exists at all is clearly overstating the matter. Jason Cromwell highlights another reason some women have crossdressed: "because they identify as men, whatever that may mean for their particular culture and historical era."[46] Some women apparently still crossdress for this reason, keeping their anatomical sex carefully hidden (e.g., Billy Tipton[47]). Yet, like other historical reasons, this motive for crossdressing appears to have diminished. Today females with a masculine gender identity can identify as transsexual and seek whatever degree of body transformation they desire or can afford.

Does this mean, then, that any suggestion of crossdressing by women today is misplaced? The answer must be no because some females still crossdress for the reasons described above, some crossdress in a manner that in heterosexual men would be labeled 'transvestic fetishism,' and some may crossdress for reasons more associated with our contemporary social reality than for reasons seen in the past. We already discussed the first of these scenarios, using the example of Billy Tipton as a biological female who chose to pass as a man. The second scenario we will examine in a moment. But let us briefly consider the possibility that some female crossdressing may occur for reasons especially associated with today's world.

A story appearing in the news in the spring of 2006 illustrates such a situation. We occasionally hear of cases where after a family break-up the nonresidential parent kidnaps the children and flees. In this story, a mother was arrested in North Carolina some two years after having abducted her two children from her ex-husband, who had been awarded custody. She was accused of having posed during this period as a man. The picture accompanying the story, and the account, depict a heavy-set figure with hair cut short and styled in a masculine fashion, sporting a light mustache, and wearing androgynous clothing. Allegedly she was living with a woman, passing as her husband, and even having her children calling her 'Daddy.' Not surprisingly, at her arrest she claimed she had made no effort to either change her appearance or hide her identity.[48] Yet regardless of the facts of this particular case, it is easy to imagine female crossdressing in such a context—an especially modern phenomenon.[49]

An even more unsettling account of crossdressing comes out of that scourge of modern life, terrorism. In late September, 2005, the Associated Press reported that a woman disguised herself as a man, donning a masculine *dishdasha* (a white robe) and *kaffiyeh* head scarf. She strapped explosives to her body, and went to an Iraqi army recruiting center. There she blew herself up, killing at least six people and wounding more than two dozen others. In the Islamic world the gender dress lines are more strictly drawn than in our own society. That a woman would act in such a radical manner only adds to the confusion and fear sown among potential victims.

Do some women crossdress for sexual arousal?

There also is evidence that some women, like some men, crossdress for auto-arousal. For these female crossdressers the apparent objective is fetishistic—in other words, the crossdressing occurs for sexual pleasure (cf. the answer to Q. 88). Yet one would hardly guess at such a motive from examining the psychiatric or psychological literature. As therapist Arlene Istar Lev observes, "The possibility of erotic transvestism in females is ignored, as is the existence of all fetishistic behaviors in females."[50] Indeed, female crossdressing for sexual arousal is excluded by the criteria for 'transvestic fetishism' in the *Diagnostic and Statistical Manual of Mental Disorders, 4th edition* (DSM-IV).[51] As far as the DSM model is concerned, the condition only occurs among heterosexual males, or at least is only 'disordered' when done by such men.

Yet investigation reveals that there is evidence of female crossdressing as a transvestic 'clinical condition.' For example, in the early 1920s psychoanalyst

Emil Gutheil reported the case of a woman who not only experienced pleasure she spoke about in terms that recall the sexual response cycle (excitement-orgasm-relief), but who expressed "lustful satisfaction" just dreaming of cross-dressing.[52] Psychoanalyst Lawrence Kubie, in 1974, recalled his 1932 report of the case of a 15-year-old transvestite girl.[53] Robert Stoller—one of the best known and most often referenced authorities on transvestites and transsexuals—in the early 1980s presented three case studies of fetishistic crossdressing in women. In one, the woman reported that she felt "very excited immediately" when putting on men's Levi jeans and that the resulting sexual tension became uncomfortable if not relieved. Stoller was struck in each case by a strong masculinity that apparently had been present in these women since childhood. He thought that the fetish represented an unconscious meaning to the patient, which once brought to consciousness would deprive the fetish of its power to arouse.[54] Still, Stoller himself resisted applying the term 'transvestite' to women. Nevertheless, unsought and even denied, such experiences continue to emerge. In the mid-1990s, Lorraine Gamman and Merja Makinen, in their study of female fetishism, remarked, "our research has found that in a few cases at least something like sexual fetishism was involved in a woman dressing as a man, lesbian, heterosexual, or bisexual."[55]

That such cases remain relatively rare in the literature does not necessarily mean more instances do not exist in the world of lived experience. In fact, they most likely point to two other facts: first, that female fetishistic transvestism truly does exist, and that however much it exists, it is pretty much ignored. The latter likelihood says much about how values connected to crossdressing have changed over the years while adding little to our actually understanding the modern female experience of this phenomenon. For the present, the dimensions of this phenomenon remain largely unexplored.

What about Female-to-Male (FtM) transsexuals?

Strangely, little attention also seems granted to the crossdressing associated with female-to-male (FtM) transsexualism. But then, perhaps psychiatrist Ira Pauly's observations in 1974 remain apt. His study of 80 cases of female transsexuals found in the scientific literature from 1922-1970 reveals that interest in female cases lags behind study of male cases by about a decade. He offers two possible explanations: the greater prevalence of transsexualism among biological males or what he calls 'gender centricity'—"a phenomenon in which male students of gender identity attend predominantly to the explanation of masculine gender identity and disorders thereof."[56]

When genetic females who are psychologically male dress in the clothes associated with men, is it crossdressing? With regard to their biological sex and assigned gender, the answer is "Yes." With respect to their gender identity and pursued role, the answer is "No." And, after sex reassignment surgery the answer must be emphatically "No!"[57] Still, at least with regard to childhood behav-

47

ior, dressing in the clothes of the opposite sex will be regarded as crossdressing—and it does occur in girls.[58]

Pauly, in his review of 80 cases, finds that 90% of the subjects crossdressed in childhood. Overall, one-fifth (20%) did so only occasionally. However 16% did so consistently and more than half (54%) did so 'as often as possible.'[59] Yet there remains a persistent inclination to view this behavior differently in females than in males, both in childhood and later. For example, French psychoanalyst Colette Chiland overgeneralizes the situation by remarking of the young transsexual female, "When she dresses as a boy, there is no sign of the erotic component found in boys who cross-dress."[60] Though this remains a common enough belief, it merely repeats stereotypes about both young male and female transsexuals—stereotypes challenged by actual facts.

Pauly, for instance, reports facts about young female crossdressers parallel to what we find with young male crossdressers. These children typically try, at least at first, to comply with their gender assignment and socialization. During school they dress and act as girls. Outside of more formal contexts, as on the weekends, they relax into their inner preference for more masculine expression. In sum, says Pauly, they are forced to live a dual existence—one harder to maintain as they grow older.[61]

At least there may be some slight advantage compared to male-to-female transsexuals. Even though a normal part of pre-operative therapy for all sex reassignment candidates is living full-time in the identity and role of the opposite sex—including dressing as a member of the opposite sex—this aspect often is better socially tolerated for FtM transsexuals than for MtF transsexuals. Probably the factors that produce this situation include both that our culture has much greater tolerance for women appearing at least somewhat like men, and that women seeking to be men are moving socially upward, while men seeking to be women are moving socially downward.

In sum, crossdressing females constitute a phenomenon interesting in its own right and significantly different in many respects from male crossdressing. That this crossdressing is less studied reflects current social values. Yet there is much that may be learned both from studying female crossdressing of the past and in the present. There also is value in comparing and contrasting female crossdressing with male crossdressing. Hopefully, the future will witness more attention to contemporary female crossdressing.

Q. 15
Do children crossdress?

The Short Answer: In some respects the question of crossdressing children is more complex than asking about crossdressing adults. On one hand, the situation is like this: children appear in clothes associated with a different gender, sometimes by personal choice and sometimes not. So, while it is true that children crossdress (or are crossdressed), the situation is not precisely the same as for adults, where any crossdressing is likely to be a voluntary act. On the other hand, transgender behavior typically begins early in life and crossdressing is frequently reported as having begun early in childhood. The age at which crossdressing occurs may be an important factor, with crossdressing more likely widespread at younger rather than at older ages. If it persists as a child becomes older, despite censure from peers and others, then the behavior marks intentionality consistent with more than transient transgender exploration. Some mental health practitioners think special attention to crossdressing in children is important because if caught early it can be 'corrected' so that gender and sexual development may proceed along the path most others follow. Other professionals believe this goal is unnecessary and perhaps immoral since it relies on a particular cultural view of what constitutes 'normal' and 'healthy' gender and sexuality. In any event, what is clearly apparent is that boys who demonstrate gender-variant behavior are far more likely than girls to be censored and brought for psychiatric intervention. This situation clearly reflects the gender hierarchy of our culture; boys conformity to gender expectations is culturally more valued than that by girls.

The Longer Answer: There are both similarities and differences in cross-gender behavior in adults and children. For one thing, children by virtue of their dependence on parents face different issues than do adults. The acceptance or rejection of their stated wishes and behavior by one or both parents greatly influences many aspects of their experience and the developmental path they embark upon. Most parents reinforce cultural expectations of assigned gender role. In fact, research indicates adults in general are exceedingly reluctant to attribute feminine characteristics to boys.[62] Thus 'transgressions' like crossdressing are typically met with disapproval and discouragement. Such pressures to conform to expected gender behavior are reinforced by people outside the family, too. As children grow older peer pressures to conform to gender expectations increase.

Figures like doctors, clergy, and schoolteachers serve as guardians of culture, lending their authority to reinforce conformity. That such responses from parents and others so often do not extinguish either the wish or the behavior is testimony to the power of transgender realities. In any event, crossdressing by children is not unusual.

Do children in our culture crossdress?

We err if we think children in our culture are indifferent to what they wear. Modern kids, from a very young age, are keenly conscious of dress and concerned about their own and that by others. We already have seen (in volume 1) how this begins at an early age in terms of gender consciousness and dress, and how gender expectations exert pressure on both boys and girls. As children develop, the expectations they receive from society are strongly internalized. Those expectations, by and large, privilege masculinity such that both boys and girls soon learn what constitutes masculinity; femininity is first and foremost non-masculinity. In a gender hierarchy where masculinity rules, even girls have incentive to master what characteristics exclude them.[63]

But judgments about gender-differentiated apparel do not appear full-blown at an early age. Research shows instead that children gradually learn to sanction conformity and disapprove nonconformity. In the mid-1980s, a study conducted with children of various ages (from kindergarten through sixth grade, found that attitudes about cross-gender behavior by peers changed from more to less tolerant over time. Curiously, children across all ages were relatively accepting of the idea of cross-gender behavior, but in terms of their own behavior they showed an unwillingness to actually play with such peers.[64]

In the mid-1990s another study furthered investigation into this matter. The researchers were particularly interested in how flexibility with regard to gender roles operates across development. First, they distinguished two kinds of flexibility: traditional flexibility, wherein a recognition exists that either males or females have the ability to engage in similar behaviors even though all won't, and evaluative flexibility, wherein a judgment is made as to whether males and females should engage in the same behaviors. They designed a way to study flexibility in both aspects toward gender transgressions as demonstrated at three developmental points: among four year olds (N = 24), eight year olds (N = 40), and young adults (N = 46). They found that while traditional flexibility increased over time, "evaluative judgments of masculine transgressions actually became more negative with age." They suggest this may be one reason stereotypes—which are characterized by inflexibility—may be so difficult to overcome.[65]

In adolescence these are reflected not only in dress choices, but also in body satisfaction. Some research suggests that as adolescence progresses, satisfaction with both body and clothing diminishes. Moreover, gender differences in the measures of satisfaction point back to the strong influence of societal gender expectations for both boys and girls. [66] It hardly requires a stretch of the imagination to think similar processes are at work among those of us who struggle with rigid gender identity and role expectations.

Issues of gender, dress, and social behavior proceed right from birth. All children at times engage in behaviors more typical of the opposite gender.[67] This includes dressing in clothing adults regard as more appropriate to the opposite gender. So, simply put, kids crossdress. We know this both from retrospective reports by adults and from observational reports of children by their parents. Sometimes, especially with very young children, the crossdressing is initiated and sustained by a parent or other guardian. As children learn to dress themselves some choose voluntarily to wear the garments of the opposite sex. Among such children this crossdressing may be merely experimental or it may be more constant. Some of these children continue to crossdress through adolescence and adulthood.

How many children crossdress and who are they?

We can say with virtual certainty that the actual occurrence of crossdressing among children is more frequent than what we know about. This conclusion follows from knowing that crossdressing early becomes a secret activity for most who do it. Thus observation by parents becomes less likely and probably in some instances the behavior, when it is observed, is explained by the parents to themselves in such a way that they are able to avoid a label like 'crossdressing.' In such cases they will not report such behavior when asked about crossdressing. As well, adults looking back may be reluctant to admit having practiced crossdressing in childhood. Conversely, it is relatively unlikely anyone would fabricate a report of having engaged in crossdressing in childhood. Thus, all estimates are probably best viewed as on the low side of actual practice.

Crossdressing in children as an interest of researchers has been less than that for adults. Once again this reflects cultural values; what children do in dress behavior is generally seen as less meaningful and important than what is done by adolescents and adults. Also, especially in very young children, the behavior is prone to a variety of explanations to avoid the stigma associated with crossdressing. Despite such forces at work, crossdressing in children has been a feature of reports for a long time. The early psychoanalysts remarked on it in case studies. In 1960, a brief report on the matter was published in the *Journal of Pediatrics*. [68] But with the rise of the modern DSM model (cf. the answer to Q. 96) to prominence, more attention and study has been given to this subject.

Not surprisingly, most empirical research has focused on boys. This is because crossdressing by girls is unremarkable in our present society and because many view crossdressing by boys as worrisome. Accordingly, as is so often the case in answering questions with regard to crossdressing, we are left to rely principally on data collected for males. Most of that material is garnered from adults through retrospective studies. However, there is some information utilizing actual observation of boys, and that is where we shall begin.

In the mid-1970s a report on an ongoing longitudinal study of boys, already seven years in the making, released some results. The boys, all under age 11 at the study's onset, were part of research on "atypical and typical psychosexual development."[69] Some 60 boys represented 'atypical' development in having demonstrated variant gender-role behavior. These boys were matched with a sample of 50 others who showed typical gender-role behavior. The former group were identified as 'feminine boys' while the later were identified as 'masculine boys.' Both groups exhibited some incidence of crossdressing behavior. Among feminine boys it was a defining characteristic: 98% had crossdressed. However, nearly one-fifth (19%) of the masculine boys also had crossdressed. [70]

What are characteristics of crossdressing children?

Much more can be said about the childhood of crossdressers than will appear in this answer because the matter is considered in another place (see the answer to Q. 29). However, it seems appropriate here to at least briefly explore the observed characteristics of crossdressing children. Once more, most of what we know has come from study of the behavior in males. Among boys, the majority of crossdressers come from one or another of what are three distinct groups in adulthood: heterosexual transvestites, homosexuals, and male-to-female transsexuals. To which group a boy might someday belong is not certain based on childhood characteristics, nor are these three groups the only possibilities for a child. We err if we believe an individual's destiny determined by any behavior in childhood, but we do not err if we discern patterns in childhood that often extend to particular paths in later life.

Perhaps the best known researcher in exploring matters related to this topic has been Richard Green. In introducing one study comparing 'feminine' and 'masculine' boys, Green remarks:

> The rationale behind the study rests on the retrospectively recalled childhood behaviors of adult males with an atypical sexual identity. The majority of transsexuals, transvestites, and homosexually-oriented adult males recall their childhood as characterized by a preference for the clothes, toys, games, and companionship of girls and, in the case of transsexuals, the wish to be a girl . . . . [71]

Green's longitudinal research tested the accuracy of such recollections by looking at children and discovering what their parents observed. Those children identified as 'feminine' boys in Green's study had certain characteristics distinguishing them from another group of 'masculine' boys, and mirroring the reports of adult males with atypical sexual identities. These characteristics included:

- *Play differences*:
  - less participation in rough-and-tumble play;
  - greater interest in play-acting, more likely to play house, and more likely to play a feminine role, especially the mother.
- *Peer relations*:
  - a greater likelihood of choosing to be a 'loner';
  - more often being rejected by same-sex peers;
  - relating best to girls of the same age, or older.
- *Parental relations*:
  - a greater preference for the mother, including as a role model;
  - more often being separated from the biological father prior to age 5.
- Other characteristics:
  - a strong likelihood (83%) of expressing a wish to have been born a girl;
  - a greater likelihood of having been hospitalized at least once, and earlier in life; and,
  - almost universal crossdressing (98%), which begins before age 6, and is usually frequent.[72]

In Green's study, so-called 'feminine' boys were far more likely to crossdress than 'masculine' boys.

But we must be careful not to make the adjectives 'feminine' and 'masculine' into value-laden judgments. 'Feminine' applied to boys will be pejorative to many folk, just as 'masculine' applied to girls will be viewed negatively by many. Yet such judgments are neither natural nor necessary, especially if gender is as fluid and socially constructed as many current theorists argue. What matters here is that the evidence found by Green suggests that crossdressing is just one aspect of cross-gender behavior and one part of a larger pattern that has bearing on personality and relationships as well.

What about crossdressing children outside modern Western culture?

Crossdressing not infrequently has been associated with initiatory rites into adulthood. Remember, 'adolescence' as such is a modern invention; traditionally, children use some culturally recognized rite of passage to enter adult life and responsibilities. Puberty is a natural marker for such transitions. Both in ancient and modern times crossdressing behavior has featured in such rites.

Academically referred to as 'ritual transvestism,' crossdressing associated with the passage into adulthood is viewed by some scholars as constituting a transitional rite characterized by a regard of the youth as neither child nor adult, and so standing outside society's normal statuses. [73] This 'in-between' or 'outside' position permits a temporary flexibility in gender behavior that helps mark the transition taking place. Thus behaviors like crossdressing not only escape censure but can be viewed positively as signs of desired developmental change.

Although such practices today are commonly thought to stand outside Western culture, we have only to look to Europe's past to find such rites. Among the ancient people of Crete, for example, the Festival of Ekdusia at Phaistos appears to have been such an initiation. As reconstructed by some scholars, the rite was inspired by the legend of Leucippus (cf. the answer to Q. 43). Male youth, garbed in feminine dress, put off these clothes and donned adult male dress in the context of ceremony highlighted by the taking of an oath of citizenship.[74]

The exact symbolic meaning of crossdressing in such a context is often unknown. In some instances it may constitute an act of appropriation whereby some perceived quality of another gender is taken into oneself. In others it may stand for a social status; a crossdressed male, for example, stands in a status similar to that of females. Boys are often seen as part of a gender cluster also including girls and women—all members marked by lower social status. The conspicuously crossdressed boy who publicly and deliberately casts off feminine garb to don the masculine apparel expected of men thus declares his passage into a sphere of gender privilege and power.

Or the behavior may represent a developmental transition out from the orbit of the feminine (under the power of women like the child's mother) and into the realm of social life dominated by the masculine. Until only a few decades ago, boys in our culture wore clothes not much different from that of girls, including dresses. As they grew older and more independent, they would move from such clothing to costumes designed to show their increasing status even though not yet men. Breeching ceremonies exemplify this.

Perhaps more than one element is in play, or other meanings attach to rituals where crossdressing behavior is employed to help mark developmental progress. Whatever the specific case may be, we must realize the crossdressing is neither incidental nor frivolous. It is purposeful and meaningful.

Q. 16

What do people find entertaining about crossdressing?

The Short Answer. Crossdressing has been used for entertainment for centuries. Curiously, though, few have asked why so many of us find it entertaining. Thus, solid data is lacking to answer this question, which matters because of what it says about our attitudes and values. We are left to speculate on why, though not on the readily observable fact. That people do find some crossdressing entertaining is obvious, as witnessed by its popularly as an activity associated with various festivities, the attendance at clubs where crossdressing entertainers are featured, and the recurrence of the behavior in theater and movie presentations. Two plausible reasons for the popularity of crossdressing entertainment converge on the relation of dress to gender. First, there seems to be social and psychological safety in merely observing a behavior that in other public contexts would likely be viewed as transgressive. This safety defuses anxiety that might otherwise be present and in this relaxed state it is possible to be amused or otherwise pleased by what we see. Second, as a consequence of this safety, we are free to vicariously utilize the performer's crossdressing to explore gender. Typically, we do so in ways designed to keep anxiety associated with such exploration at bay by making the process one filled with parody and laughter. In social environments like our own, where gender issues have become more visible and public tolerance appears to have increased, some serious explorations through entertainment also become more likely. Crossdressing is no longer just played for laughs. More and more it is portrayed in serious entertainment as behavior warranting sober reflection about another way to be human.

The Longer Answer. What exactly is it about crossdressing that draws our attention? Why do so many of us find it entertaining? Are those who crossdress for our entertainment themselves really crossdressers?

The latter two of these queries are seldom asked. Perhaps the answers seem obvious. Or perhaps the questions seem trivial. Yet asking such questions may shed some light on an aspect that is probably as ancient a practice as crossdressing itself. In so doing it may even provide a glimpse into ourselves.

Are crossdressing entertainers really crossdressers?

Are professional entertainers who dress in the garb of members of the opposite sex to be considered crossdressers? How we answer such a query certainly says much about how we regard crossdressing. In the broadest sense of the term, anyone is a crossdresser who dresses in clothes associated with the opposite sex. But since over the course of a lifetime that includes the majority of us, many of us prefer a more restricted sense. Perhaps most of us think of crossdressers as those who rather regularly dress in clothing associated with the opposite sex. Some of us may be even more restrictive and think of crossdressers as only those who do so exclusively for reasons associated with sexual pleasure (as in transvestic fetishism), or gender issues (as in transvestism and transsexualism), or social commentary (as with drag queens), or entertainment (as with professional female imitators).

So we return to our question: Are professional entertainers who dress in the garb of members of a different gender to be considered crossdressers? Most of us would hedge our answer by wanting to know if the entertainer crossdresses professionally either principally or exclusively for a living. Thus, for most of us, actors like Robin Williams (*Mrs. Doubtfire*), Dustin Hoffmann (*Tootsie*), the Wayans brothers (*White Chicks*), Hillary Swank (*Boys Don't Cry*), or Felicity Huffman (*Transamerica*) are not crossdressers because their crossdressing only occurred in a specific context, for a specific role, for a limited duration. But what about, for example, professional female impersonators (aka 'gender illusionists')?

Claudine Griggs writes, "For a professional female impersonator, crossdressing is a defining behavioral characteristic that makes him transvestic."[75] In other words, many of these performers not only appear as women in their work, but present the same gender in their private lives. Their crossdressing is not casual, nor is it merely for professional gain. Their vocation is also an avocation. In such cases, the entertainer certainly qualifies as a crossdresser in the eyes of most observers.

Obviously, the determinant lies not only in how crossdressing is defined, but also in separating the behavior from a 'condition' (the crossdresser); the behavior can occur without the latter's existence. Set the boundaries liberally enough and anyone who ever dresses in a single article of apparel (from shoes through underwear and outerwear to earrings and hats) associated with a different gender is a crossdresser. That likely would make all of us at least occasional crossdressers. Set the lines restrictively enough and only a small group of people fit—which is what some of us seem to want to do by making crossdressing always and only about heterosexual males who dress up as women for their sexual jollies. But then where do entertainers fit in?

Of course, each of us will draw our lines where we will. For myself, cross-dressing happens when a person is in the garb of a gender different than the one they were assigned at birth. It doesn't matter whether it is a baby girl dressed by her mother as a boy, or an adult man voluntarily putting on a dress. Nor does it matter whether it is done for laughs, or for sex, or for some other reason. For the term to have much face value it must describe the behavior, not the motivation or context or meaning. So, when Dustin Hoffmann dressed as Tootsie, he was crossdressed. Female impersonators are crossdressed.

Whether the behavior means one must be further labeled as a 'crossdresser' seems to me an illogical move. Some people try to do this with crossdressing, just as some try to do it with sexual orientation (i.e., one same-sex sexual encounter makes one homosexual). The problem with the logic becomes apparent when applied to other things. A person overeating one time is not thereby a glutton; a person who hits a home run is not thereby a 'sultan of swat.' We readily see with most behaviors that an occasional incidence does not equate with a habitual pattern and that labeling such incidental acts as though they reflect some sort of permanent condition is absurd.

So, in the interest of rationality, we shall refrain from such a connection. A 'crossdresser' is someone who engages in the behavior often enough, and with enough significance, as to warrant a descriptive label that says this behavior matters to the individual. That may or may not be true for a crossdressed entertainer. Fortunately for us, we are under no obligation to determine if this is the case, nor does it seem a particularly desirable or meaningful thing to try.

The more significant question is: Why do we, the observers, find cross-dressing entertaining? To answer that query let us start with an indirect approach.

Who is entertained by crossdressing?

It may seem curious to ask who is entertained by crossdressing. Obviously, both men and women are. Yet the question affords a way to approach the issue of why it is found entertaining. Consider the matter this way: what appeal could there possibly be for men in watching other men masquerade as women? Especially in a culture steeped in homophobia as an aspect of defining masculinity, this is a serious question.

Theater scholar Kate Davy pointedly remarks, "Female impersonation, while it certainly says something about women, is primarily about men, addressed to men, and for men."[76] But if it is an 'address' of sorts, what does it say? There are multiple possibilities and any number of them might be at work. For instance, female impersonation can either exaggerate male-female body differences and masculine-feminine gender differences—or minimize them. Either kind of performance makes a statement, and either one can be unsettling or reassuring. If laughter is provoked, it may be of a kind meant to discharge anxiety, or the kind prompted by an unexpected but welcome revelation.

57

Entertainment, of course, includes more than laughter. We may feel we have been entertained when we are challenged to think in new ways, shown possibilities we dimly imagined, if at all, or find our feelings engaged by rapport with the performer or character being portrayed. Men may find female impersonators entertaining because of the sheer escapist value of watching a spectacle far removed from their ordinary life. Others may like the sexual eroticism of the atmosphere or find it pleasant to be attracted to the performer or character. Some may find temporary identification with the performer—male to male—a way to escape the burdens of the masculine gender role. Others may be entertained by the wish to in some manner be like the entertainer, whether as a person less inhibited, more in touch with a feminine side, or attractive (albeit as a 'woman' rather than as a 'man'). Some may be entranced by the imaginative possibilities of a transgendered reality.

The possibilities are numerous—precisely why such a broad range of males, including the most masculine to the most effeminate, find such entertainment appealing. Similarly, women may find numerous reasons to be entertained. They may find comfort in a spectacle that proves a man can't be a woman. Or, conversely, they may be impressed at the characterization and find hope that at least some men can be 'more like a woman.' No less than men, women may be entertained in any number of ways, through laughter, reflection, wonder, or empathy.

Men impersonating women typically is probed more for meaning—and meaning is more often found—than in women impersonating men. Florence King, writing in the National Review, humorously suggests, "Why there is no lesbian equivalent of the female impersonator: Because there's nothing to do. If you want to impersonate a man, all you have to do is sit still, stick to the subject, and say things once instead of three times. This lacks entertainment value."[77] More seriously, college student Helen Bode observes that female 'kinging'— drag by women—reveals through imitation how men's posturing is an act, and that coupled with jokes about small penises, male stupidity, and vulnerability, elicits laughter at a flawed masculinity.[78]

What is entertaining about witnessing crossdressing?

Even a quick survey of the plays and movies where crossdressing has been featured (see the answer to Q. 44) would show that most often they are comedies. Crossdressing is played for laughs—and gets them. This trait is not merely a recent one, either. Crossdressing on stage has been garnering laughs for centuries. Why is that?

Some of us might argue that the sight of a man in a dress is inherently laughable. But that rather misses the point because some reason exists for us to think it silly. The most plausible explanation is that most of us find crossing the gender divide to be an act of folly—and foolish things can be laughed at. By laughing at the crossdressed entertainer we keep crossdressing itself relegated to the realm of the foolish. Today the laughter is aimed at men in female garb, whereas in other times women drew the laughs. But is that all there is to it?

Philosopher Ivan Illich proposes that 'travesty'—the transvestism of festivals such as Carnival—permits serious business to be done under the pretence of pretence. A publicly crossdressed woman at festival time, for example, constitutes a lampooning of men without actually threatening a social order where males dominate. In Illich's view, examining travesty in public festivals provides an excellent look at how ritual mockery actually preserves traditional gender lines.[79] Perhaps, then, we are entertained because we can both vent our frustrations at gender restrictions by applauding crossdressed entertainers and still feel secure because the gender lines are reaffirmed.

Maybe we can vicariously crossdress through witnessing someone who is. Through them we test the waters, imagine what we would look like, speculate on why we might do so, and glimpse the probable outcome. The laughter the entertainer fetches is the laughter we can imagine aimed at ourselves. Thus our laughing becomes, in part, sheer relief. We have experimented secretly and safely because we have done so vicariously.

Most likely, a variety and a mix of reasons explain why we find crossdressing entertaining. But I think Illich right in at least one respect—something serious accompanies the mask of laughter. As with all abiding humor, the laughing defends us against anxiety, whether it is individual or cultural in origin. Matters of sex, gender, identity, and appearance all matter dearly to us. When they converge in the way they do in crossdressing, some anxiety is aroused. The exploitation of that in entertainment is also a form of exploration.[80]

Q. 17
Why do some homosexuals crossdress?

The Short Answer: One of the most common myths about crossdressing is that only homosexual males do it. This means many people erroneously assume that all crossdressers are homosexual. The facts are rather different. First, some crossdressers are homosexual and some homosexuals crossdress. Or, to put the matter another way, while some homosexuals crossdress many do not and of those who do, it is generally occasional rather than habitual. This is true for both gay men and lesbian women. Second, as with heterosexuals, the reasons motivating crossdressing are diverse and include both issues of identity and sexuality. Indeed, the appropriateness of the term 'transgender' for homosexuals can be questioned on the grounds that many, perhaps most homosexual adults embrace and manifest gender in accord with their birth gender assignment. In fact, increasingly various studies are finding a significant portion of homosexuals who more strongly endorse and embrace the stereotype of their assigned gender than is true for many heterosexuals. But because our culture has for some time associated male same-sex sexual desire with effeminacy, a well-established link between homosexuality and transgender experience exists. Certainly, some homosexual men have exploited this link to critique it and to challenge the wider society to reexamine its artificially constructed notions of gender. Perhaps the most famous of all forms of crossdressing—drag—is a calculated manipulation of crossdressing to send a message. However, the original shock value of drag, which once prompted reflection by many, now has receded, as drag has become passé for the majority of observers. So while drag may still intend to send a message, it has also developed into serving other functions.

The Longer Answer: The most visible population of the various groups often linked together as sexual minorities or as transgender people, homosexuals are also the most watched, researched, and commented upon. Yet, for all that they remain widely misperceived by the heterosexual community. Those most vitriolic in voicing their homophobia are unlikely to know—or even want to know—that some of the people in their own lives are gay or lesbian. But it would be a rare person inhabiting a narrow world indeed who does not come into contact with homosexuals. As the U.S. 2000 census data shows, homosexuals are found in both metropolitan and rural areas and in every region of the nation.[81] Their largely invisible presence attests to a number of realities including, of course, that many remain largely or entirely in the closet to avoid homophobia. But they are also largely invisible because most live lives indistinguishable from their heterosexual counterparts. They may differ in the object of erotic attraction, but little else.

Homophobia, though, can only survive by stressing the otherness of homosexuals and doing so such that being different is equated with being bad. Thus it is popular among heterosexuals to speak about a homosexual 'lifestyle'—though they never seem to talk about a heterosexual lifestyle![82] Clearly the word 'lifestyle' is being used pejoratively and an implicit 'deviant' is attached unspoken in front of it. Similarly, speaking of 'preference' instead of 'orientation' encourages seeing homosexual sexual attraction as a matter purely of choice (meaning deviant choice), unlike the presumed naturalness of heterosexuality. Since the existence of choice is necessary to establish moral culpability, this terminology is used by homophobic individuals to justify their moral judgment about homosexuality—even if it is kept purposely implicit.[83] Ordinary language is employed to maintain a quiet homophobia based on accentuating and rejecting the perceived otherness of homosexual people.[84]

Another way to 'prove' the deviant otherness of homosexuals is to claim they all engage in behaviors placing them outside the norms for gender and/or sexuality. Because of our culture's gender hierarchy, and the stake it has in protecting masculine privilege, gay men are subject to much more scrutiny and criticism than lesbian women. Indeed, we should go further and recognize that all men are subject to a strangling set of gender expectations such that the merest hint of femininity—whether in appearance or action—carries the risk of being labeled gay and accordingly ostracized. For instance, the American Studies and Comparative Literature scholar Ben Sifuentes-Jauregui observes how "for women, 'effeminacy' is a quality that is not only acceptable but encouraged; however, that same quality for men labels them as 'homosexual.' This immediate labeling of an effeminate man as a homosexual happens because the spectrum of gender and sexual signs is so severe, so dichotomized—and even so arbitrary."[85] What isn't arbitrary is protecting masculine privilege at any cost; too much social power is at risk for those whose hold on it proves increasingly tenuous.

By connecting homosexuals to crossdressing, and proclaiming that crossdressing is all about deceiving others to gain sexual contact, homophobia evokes the anxiety most people have over sexuality and specifically liberates fear in some of them. What most of us fail to see is how conveniently homophobia plays into the hands of those wanting to hold onto power. Homophobia is a blunt instrument in gender politics and if it does nothing else it certainly protects masculine privilege. Unfortunately, it also does much more than that. Associating all homosexuals with all crossdressers not only distorts the facts, it does so in a way that harms all crossdressers and also all homosexuals through false, negative stereotypes that fuel intolerance and violence. A certain kind of masculine man profits from the victimization of other men—both those who are effeminate and those whose masculinity is not of the dominant kind in society.

Not surprisingly, then, both heterosexual crossdressers and homosexuals fight the myth that all crossdressers are gay. Heterosexual crossdressers point out that most male crossdressers are not homosexual; the best estimate is that the percentage of crossdressers who are homosexual is about the same as the percentage of homosexuals in the general population.[86] Homosexuals point out that while some gays and lesbians crossdress, most do not, at least not regularly.[87] Since our concern is with crossdressers, we shall focus in answering this question on those men and women who identify themselves as homosexual and who also at least occasionally crossdress.[88]

The question whether homosexual crossdressers differ in significant ways from heterosexual crossdressers has received surprisingly little study. In general, they seem to share some characteristics and differ in others. Among the traits they share are a variety of reasons motivating the crossdressing and a range of frequency and completeness to the crossdressing. In a limited study of 16 adult gay men and 9 gay adolescents, Ethel Person and Lionel Ovesey conclude that homosexual crossdressers (HCDs) differ from their heterosexual counterparts in interests and mannerisms, as well as object choice (i.e., a desire for same-sex partners rather than opposite sex). Person and Oversey also find that HCDs differ in other ways, such as in their gender identity, developmental history, and the circumstances in which the behavior occurs.[89]

No less than is true for heterosexual crossdressers, homosexuals may engage in crossdressing for a variety of reasons. Among these are:

❑ dressing in drag to celebrate gay pride;
❑ dressing in drag for theatrical or entertainment purposes;
❑ seeking sexual arousal; and
❑ because they are supposed to.[90]

We shall examine these reasons, but divide our discussion into an examination first of gay men and then of lesbians.

Why do some gay men crossdress?

Dressing in Drag

We must give one phenomenon priority because it is the kind of crossdressing most associated with the homosexual community: dressing in drag. The term, as used in this work, refers to crossdressing meant to be seen as such, and intended to be provocative. Drag is performance crossdressing and may be meant as entertainment (e.g., Drag 'Queens' and 'Kings'), or public declaration of identity (e.g., 'I'm gay and proud of it'), or challenge of cultural conventions (e.g., 'I don't fit your gender categories—deal with it!'). Drag can be performed by either males or females, homosexuals or heterosexuals, but it is always a conscious public act rather than a private personal one.

Because the term 'drag'[91] can be applied to any person it may be argued that too much has been made of the connection to the homosexual community. Writing for the *Chicago-Kent Law Review* Kelly Kleiman argues, "the connection between drag and gay men is at best vestigial, like the appendix, and thus can be removed."[92] On the other hand, anthropologist Esther Newman observes: "Not all gay people want to wear drag, but drag symbolizes gayness. The drag queen symbolizes an open declaration, even celebration, of homosexuality."[93] Certainly the strong association of drag with gay men is largely the result of very public celebratory parades featuring crossdressed men.

Both inside and outside the gay community dressing in drag is variously appraised. Gay advocate writer Mark Thompson offers the hope that drag might someday lead "to the realization that within each one of us lies the potential for a more balanced—and androgynous—human spirit."[94] But others see crossdressing as reinforcing the stereotype of gay men as effeminate. And feminist scholar Amanda Swarr argues that the term "indicates a rupture between gendered appearance and sex that essentializes anatomy."[95] In short, drag itself both challenges our existing gender order and, paradoxically, reaffirms it.

So why would gay men choose drag as a way to express gay pride? For some the presentation as a 'drag queen' is meant to ridicule social stereotypes. Roselle Pineda argues that the "politics of drag" differentiate it from transvestism because the latter imitates traditional gender roles while drag subverts them through parody.[96] Research confirms that homosexuals are much like heterosexuals in every respect, with sexual orientation the great exception. Yet social stereotypes present homosexuals as very different from heterosexuals, especially in being 'sissies'—effeminate men who crossdress. Through crossdressing in public parades the gay man can both challenge and mock what he perceives as social nonsense.

While celebrating gay pride may be a chief reason for dressing in drag, it is not the only one. Some gay men do so for theatrical or other entertainment purposes. For them, crossdressing is an integral part of the performance presentation. In fact, in this context, sociologist Steven Schacht has identified what he calls "four emergent renditions of doing female drag":

❑ *High brow female impersonators*—the crossdressing by gay men as part of the Imperial Court System (ICS), where clothing is worn consistent with the gender of any title held by the individual (i.e., a 'princess' wears female attire), is done for utilitarian purposes—to garner and reflect power and authority within that setting, rather than to express femininity. These men do not crossdress outside this setting.

- *Female illusionists*—the crossdressing is for performance purposes and the men use hormonal treatments, but not sex-reassignment surgery; many also live as women outside their performance venues.
- *Professional glamour queens*—the most popular form of doing drag, the crossdressing is done by gay men and, as the name suggests, for money.
- *Professional camp queens*—the crossdressing is done by gay men to present intentionally exaggerated images of women for entertainment.[97]

As with so many other matters about crossdressing, 'doing drag' is far more multi-faceted than most imagine.

Crossdressing for Erotic Arousal

Some homosexuals—like some heterosexuals—crossdress for erotic purposes. These may be divided into two distinct and very different kinds:

- crossdressing to elicit arousal in others; or,
- crossdressing for self-arousal.

Some gay men crossdress to excite sexual attention from others. This is most evident among crossdressing gay prostitutes. But, we would be wrong to assume that all gay crossdressers are prostitutes, or promiscuous. Like their heterosexual counterparts, they may crossdress only in the context of an exclusive, intimate relationship. As British writer Adrian Gillan noted, "wearing bras, panties, and other feminine garments [may] serve to enhance the thrill of a more traditional sexual encounter between two gay men."[98]

Some gay men crossdress to accomplish sexual arousal in themselves. Why? Lorraine Gamman and Merja Makinen offer the most sensible answer: "Explanations vary and there is no consensus about the motivation of either homosexual or heterosexual transvestites who achieve erotic pleasure from wearing the clothes of the opposite sex."[99] That said, the evidence suggests that some of these men would meet the criteria for transvestic fetishism in the DSM-model (cf. the answer to Q. 96), if that model did not restrict the diagnosis to heterosexual men.

Why do some lesbians crossdress?

Some people reserve the use of the term 'drag' to men. When women crossdress, they suggest the term 'drab'—'dressed as a boy.'[100] Others have no objection to applying the term 'drag' to lesbian crossdressing, but speak about 'drag Kings'[101] rather than 'drag Queens.' In any event, by whatever name, some lesbians do crossdress.

'Kinging' is a form of drab/drag done for entertainment in which women imitate men. This imitation extends beyond dress to incorporate posture and mannerisms. Well-known male figures like Elvis Presley are popular objects of imitation. However, 'kinging' also often draws attention to masculinities other than that of our culture's normative White masculinity. For example, through a technique called 'layering,' the Drag King can selectively show to an audience glimpses of minority masculinities such as those found among ethnic males or the 'dyke' or 'butch' presentation by some females. Such performances are thus both entertaining and provocative as they highlight the constructed, performative nature of gender itself.[102]

Authors Gamman and Makinen suggest that some contemporary lesbians crossdress as part of one or another lesbian dress code. A certain 'boyish' look—whether patterned on famous lesbian figures of the past or not—is used to signal other lesbians. But sometimes the look sought is intended not only to signal other lesbians but to defiantly tweak homophobic noses.[103] This use of crossdressing explicitly highlights the use of dress at the center of an elaborate and complex expressive system that can be used effectively in communication.

Like gay men, lesbians can also use crossdressing to openly declare being homosexual by capitalizing on the myth that all crossdressers are homosexual. At the same time, as indicated above, they are both protesting the myth and intentionally confronting those homophobic people who are scandalized by such public dress. Yet, as Gamman and Makinen point out, the crossdressing can also celebrate female strength.[104] As others have discovered, crossdressing is capable of saying more than one thing at the same time.

Despite the reluctance of the mental health community to acknowledge it, some female crossdressing is associated with sexual purposes.[105] These essentially amount to these reasons: crossdressing to gain access to other women, or crossdressing for sexual arousal independent of another person.

Some lesbians crossdress to pursue relationships with other women. This has been true historically,[106] but even in today's more tolerant society this sometimes occurs.[107] Many lesbians stay 'in the closet'—refraining from any public disclosure of their sexual orientation. Masquerading as a male can be a means of keeping their sexual orientation hidden while still seeking at least some degree of sexual fulfillment. (And in societies where women are more severely limited in their opportunities, such guise carries the additional hope of expanded avenues to pursue success financially and in terms of social status.)

Some lesbians may find crossdressing arousing in the fetishistic way described in clinical literature for transvestic fetishism (cf. the answer to Q. 96). Unfortunately, the literature relevant to this matter is sparse and not particularly illuminating.[108] In cases where female fetishistic crossdressing is described the focus is not on the subjects' sexual orientation. However, such reports are typically found in the writings of psychoanalysts, who typically view male crossdressers as at least latent homosexuals. Gamman and Makinen remark, "Our research has found that in a few cases at least something like sexual fetishism was involved in a woman dressing as a man, lesbian, heterosexual, or bisexual."[109] At any rate, this matter merits more attention than it has received.

Q. 18

What is 'transvestism'?

The Short Answer: The term 'transvestism' is derived from two Latin words and means 'crossdressed.' The mental health community adopted this particular word after it was coined in the early 20th century (as a part of the so-called 'medicalization of sex') to provide a scientific name for crossdressing behavior. In the first half of the 20th century transvestites were commonly assumed to be homosexual, either openly or latently. This popular conception ran counter to the research showing that most crossdressers identify as heterosexual and typically are or have been married. Gradual recognition and acceptance of the differences found among those who crossdress led to a restricting of the term transvestism to only some kinds of crossdressing. Thus, all transvestites crossdress, but not all crossdressers are transvestites. In time the term 'transvestism' was especially attached to the adjective 'fetishistic' and used to refer to those who crossdress for sexual arousal and satisfaction. Eventually, in the last quarter of the 20th century, the compound label of 'transvestic fetishism' was established as a psychological disorder that by definition could only be applied to heterosexual adult males. Despite these historical developments, the term itself merely refers to crossdressing. Thus, various people have used it in either broader or narrower senses. Along these lines there have been various efforts to differentiate among transvestites. The result has been more labels such as 'nuclear' transvestite or 'marginal' transvestite. However, there remains no universally accepted system for classifying transvestites and not everyone agrees such efforts are warranted or desirable. The persistent inconsistency in usage of the term has caused some difficulties for people seeking to understand crossdressing and how it is generally regarded.

The Longer Answer: The term 'transvestism' reflects a desire to provide a scientific label to classify a certain kind of behavior—crossdressing. Over time, the exact meaning of the term has changed to reflect an ever more narrow application to one particular group of people. We shall briefly examine the history behind the term, as well as specify its definition. But first we should recognize a basic axiom: all transvestites are crossdressers, but not all crossdressers are transvestites.

'Transvestism' is a simple word that has managed to become a term enthusiastically adopted by some, despised by others, and bewildering to a great many. Whatever we may think of it, the word seems to carry power because it names behavior that carries significance, whether valued positively or negatively. As American Studies scholar Ben Sifuentes-Jauregui graphically comments, "Transvestism is an act that penetrates and tampers with those who witness it . . . . Transvestism is about the raw touching, gentle tampering, and, literally, fucking up of any fixed notions of gender."[110] How can one rather odd and cumbersome word be freighted with so much emotional weight?

What does the word mean?

The word itself is a simple compound. The Latin word for 'clothes' or 'dress' (*vestitus*) is joined to the preposition meaning 'across' (*trans*) to form transvestism: 'cross-dress.' Thus, 'transvestism' merely means being clothed in dress associated with someone of a gender different from the wearer's. This is the sense in which the word is almost always meant. The 'transvestite'—the person practicing transvestism—is crossing an established and recognized gender line in clothing to wear apparel designed for a gender that is not the wearer's own assigned gender (which may or may not be the gender the individual desires or identifies with).

However, complicating matters, the Latin *trans* can also mean 'beyond.' A few contemporary people who might be said to be engaged in transvestism argue they are not crossdressing because though the clothes they wear may be associated in some broad way with a particular gender group (e.g., pants with men), the apparel they are wearing has been specifically designed either for the wearer's own gender (e.g., a woman wearing feminine pants), or is somehow 'beyond' gender. In this sense of 'beyond gender,' transvestism is a label that could be applied to women who wear suits designed for women, men who wear skirts designed for men, or anyone who wears androgynous clothing. However, when the term is used in this manner and applied to people wearing clothes such as just described, a strong negative reaction is elicited. This is partly because 'transvestism' is generally understood to mean purposeful transgression of gender lines, and not dressing 'beyond' gender lines. More pertinently, the negative reaction comes from the recognition that the term 'transvestite' is not a good thing to be called.

In fact, many crossdressers—and here we mean folk who make no bones about the fact they are intentionally wearing clothes designed for a different gender—also get upset when the term transvestism is applied to them. They recognize not only that those who use it typically aren't offering praise, but that the word is often used in a more restrictive sense to refer to people who crossdress for autoerotic arousal. In other words, some people use the word 'transvestite' to refer to all crossdressers, but assume that all crossdressers engage in the behavior as a prompt to masturbation. It is easy to see why many crossdressers find the term offensive when they sense that is what the user means by it.

It is unfortunate that the term has come to mean so many different things. As is evident throughout this volume, the terms 'crossdressing' and 'crossdresser' are preferred to 'transvestism' and 'transvestite.' In part this is to avoid the pre-assigned meanings the latter terms have come to mean to many, especially since those pre-assigned meanings vary as widely as they do, along with a range of predetermined value judgments connected to the varying meanings. Still, we should recognize the term 'transvestism' isn't going away any time soon. To understand better how we have come to be where we are, we need to look at a little history.

What is the origin and history of the term?

In 1910, the pioneering sexologist Magnus Hirschfeld introduced the word 'transvestism' to name crossdressing behavior in his book *Die Transvestiten* (*Transvestites*).[111] Hirschfeld was following a time-honored tradition in the scientific community by looking to a classical language—in this case Latin—to classify an observed phenomenon. Hirschfeld's own sense of crossdressers was that they are people occupying a position between masculine and feminine genders. His term was soon adopted widely, though not always with the same understanding.

While many latched on to the term 'transvestism,' they did so without sharing Hirschfeld's sense of it. The label 'transvestite' was applied rather indiscriminately to any and all, male or female, who crossdressed, save for those who did so purely for entertainment or at sanctioned occasions such as Carnival. Later, it became more narrowly applied in order to distinguish a subset who practice this behavior ('transvestites') from others who also crossdress. This subset of crossdressers was still viewed as including both males and females, but could be distinguished from other crossdressing groups such as homosexuals in drag or transsexuals. Still later a further narrowing of the term excluded females.

How could such a distortion of Hirschfeld's research conclusions come about? First, not everyone concurred with Hirschfeld's conclusions about transvestism and the people to whom that term was attached. Second, competing ideological agendas were at work, and those who supported the rival viewpoint had considerably more influence in the psychiatric community. Where Hirschfeld had identified most transvestites as heterosexual, early psychoanalysts believed they were either explicitly homosexual or latently so—and their view largely carried the day.[112]

To be sure, there were those who defended Hirschfeld's research and who agreed the evidence showed most transvestites were heterosexuals. On the other hand, their support was modified somewhat by their own ideas and applications of the research. For example, Havelock Ellis, a pioneering British sexologist, found much that he agreed with in Hirschfeld, but he personally preferred the term 'Eonism' to that of transvestism. His quarrel with the label of transvestism was that it is misleading. By placing the focus on crossdressing he felt that other, more important psychological elements were overlooked.[113]

Ellis ultimately lost that particular argument. The term transvestism prevailed, though exactly what it covers and to whom it is appropriately applied have continued to be matters of debate. The principal argument in recent decades has been whether transvestism should be used in a broad or general sense to merely stand as a synonym for crossdressing. This was the way the term was used by many psychiatrists and it remains a popular use for many in the general public. Psychoanalyst Robert Stoller did not concur with this usage, arguing that the term transvestism ought to be reserved for only instances of crossdressing motivated by fetishistic sexual arousal.[114] Stoller's view mostly prevails, at least within mental health circles, though there persist many individual practitioners who continue to use the terms 'transvestism' and 'crossdressing' synonymously.

Finally, one problem that plagues use of this term—and most of the gender vocabulary we use—is that it keeps us firmly within a questionable two gender scheme that derives most of its power historically from an essentialist perspective. In such a view, gender is fixed and immutable, a property of being, determined by biological sex. Consequently, words like 'transgender' and 'transvestism' are locked into an understanding in terms of two fixed genders. Social anthropologist Andrea Cornwall captures the problem nicely: "To call someone a 'transvestite' involves making a series of prior assumptions about them. These cluster around the notion that there is some original 'sex' or 'gender' to which they 'really' belong: transvestites *cross*-dress, they do not just dress."[115]

As a result of the tendency for so long to see all crossdressers as the same—transgressors of a fixed dichotomy between masculinity and femininity—and to attach to them erroneous ideas, today the term 'transvestite' is widely shunned by crossdressers. Nevertheless, within psychiatric nomenclature the label remains. We need next to see how it is used in mental health diagnosis.

What is 'fetishistic transvestism'?

For reasons sketched in other places, the term 'transvestism' has come to be used by mental health professionals principally in a narrow sense and increasingly with reference to the following set of ideas:

- ❑ Transvestites are males who dress partially or wholly in clothes associated with females.
- ❑ Transvestites are heterosexual.
- ❑ Transvestites use their crossdressing largely or entirely for sexual arousal and relief.

These ideas are the heart of the mental health diagnosis of 'transvestic fetishism' (see the answer to Q. 96).

This is the kind of crossdressing that seems to most fascinate many of us—and is the form most likely to be found objectionable. The term 'fetish,' elaborated elsewhere (see the answer to Q. 88), has a decidedly negative connotation for most of us. This is only natural given how the term is almost always attached to comments that ridicule or denigrate the behavior being described. So when connected to crossdressing, 'transvestic fetishism' immediately sounds bad to us, even if we don't quite know what it means.

But 'fetish,' like 'transvestism,' is a neutral word that was originally chosen in the interest of trying to be scientific. It appeared to observers that those who crossdressed for sexual arousal and relief were using the clothes as ancient people might a fetish—that is, as possessing magical power. Certainly, the effects were strong: not only did sexual potency increase, but the wearer could feel transformed. What worried some observers, though, was that this effect might become so pronounced that the wearer would give up pursuing normal sexual relationships in favor of the satisfaction obtained through crossdressing. If this were to happen the consequences for relationships would be serious.

Whether the term 'fetish' is an unfortunate one or not is debated. The biggest problem is that the word today is more often than not divorced from its original sense and context. Because it largely has taken on an association with sexual deviancy or perversion it no longer functions as a neutral descriptor. It is a pejorative adjective attached to a pejorative noun—almost universally people will reckon 'transvestic fetishism' as a highly undesirable label, and see it not as a scientific label for particular behavior but as a sensationalistic proclamation of harsh judgment. To the extent this latter sense exercises influence even on mental health practitioners this designation is an unfortunate obstacle to care.

Another problem with the designation 'transvestic fetishism' lies in it incorrectly being generalized—including by some mental health professionals—to include all crossdressing practiced by non-homosexual males. In other words, the label often functions as a group tag for all male heterosexual crossdressers. Worse, it defines the common link among them as crossdressing for sexual reasons, especially self-gratification through masturbation. But researchers working with crossdressing boys and men know the reality is far more complex. Not all transvestites—in fact, probably not even most—meet the criteria for inclusion in a group characterized by 'transvestic fetishism.' Therefore, it is important we look at what kinds of important distinctions exist among transvestites.

Are there different transvestite types?

Let's begin broadly. There have been a number of attempts to differentiate kinds of crossdressers. Some aim merely to separate out groups with large and clear distinctions (e.g., professional entertainers from drag queens). Others focus on a particular group—especially adult male crossdressers—and try to differentiate subgroups. In recent years it has been common to focus on three groups of crossdressers (mostly male), typically along axes of sexual orientation and gender identification. The groups thus constructed range from those with the strongest heterosexual orientation and weakest feminine gender identification (transvestites), to those with a complete feminine gender identification, regardless of sexual orientation (transsexuals), to those with a complete homosexual orientation regardless of strength of feminine gender identification (homosexual crossdressers).

Devor's Proposal

Such broad divisions have some obvious utility. Nevertheless, it should be noted that some researchers reach for a much wider manner of differentiating groups and subgroups. Sexologist Holly Devor, for example, has articulated a comprehensive scheme to capture a taxonomy for what she terms 'gendered sexuality.' Her basic classification method proposes to factor in genetic sex (male/female) and sexual orientation (heterosexual or homosexual), together with social gender (man/woman) and sexual orientation (straight or gay/lesbian), plus the summation of these two as 'gendered sexuality.'

The notion of 'gendered sexuality' is important because individuals in sexual relationship with one another—even if only in fantasy—interact such that they express something that involves both sex and gender, but which can vary. In a 'non-normative' situation, for example, by using these various factors the same person might be classified in more than one way depending on the particular relationship. For example, a crossdressing female with a heterosexual orientation may express masculine gender (as a straight man) in relation to a crossdressing male (who is expressing feminine gender). However, the same individual in a different relationship, while still female with a heterosexual orientation, may express herself as a lesbian woman in relation to another woman. [116]

There is much to like and admire in Devor's effort to sketch a rudimentary taxonomy. But to date it has not caught on. We seem, instead, to remain mired in older, static, rigid and unrealistic classification systems. In this reality, when something does not fit smoothly, rather than recognize the dynamic continuum that actually exists, we generally resort to ever finer splitting of hairs by creating yet more categories and subcategories—or by ignoring any reality that doesn't fit the scheme. With that unfortunate state of affairs in mind, we must turn now to some other classification notions.

What are some designations for male transvestites?

Over the years a number of different designations have been proposed to distinguish among the different presentations of crossdressing. This began with Hirschfeld's identification of ten patterns that covered all crossdressers.[117] Havelock Ellis favored a simple division into categories that today would be identified as transvestites and transsexuals.[118] In his review of the literature at mid-20th century, Narcyz Lukianowicz identified four types of transvestites, differentiated by sexual aim: *a*-sexual; *auto-mono*-sexual; *hetero*-sexual; and, *homo*-sexual.[119] By the end of the century researchers were clear that different types of crossdressers existed, but attention had narrowed to one group with respect to this behavior.

Today's reductionistic tendency to view crossdressing as almost exclusively male, and transvestism as a phenomenon of heterosexual males, has narrowed classification schemes. The following table summarizes some of the proposals for subgroups among transvestites:

Table 18.1 Proposed Transvestite Groups

Study	# Subjects	Proposed Groups
Harry Benjamin[120]	NA	Three of his six types of crossdressers are transvestites (pseudo, fetishistic, and true).
Neil Buhrich & Neil McConaghy (1977)[121]	34	Femmiphilic transvestism used, though a distinction is noted among subjects concerning degree of feminization desired.
Neil Buhrich & Neil McConaghy (1979)[122]	22	Building on previous work, distinguished 3 subtypes for fetishistic transvestism: nuclear, marginal, and fetishistic transsexualism.
Neil Buhrich & Trina Beaumont (1981)[123]	222	[1] Nuclear transvestites: subjects content with their crossdressing. [2] Marginal transvestites: subjects desiring feminization, either by taking hormones or through surgery.
Richard Docter (1988)[124]	110	Of his 9 crossdressing patterns, 5 include heterosexual crossdressers, but only 2 are named as forms of transvestism (fetishistic and marginal).
Richard Ekins (1997)[125]	NA	Avoiding labels of people, he identifies 3 forms of behavior representative of 'male-femaling': [1] body femaling (changes in secondary sex characteristics); [2] erotic femaling (goal is sexual arousal); and [3] gender femaling (expression of feminine gender).

Conclusion
As may be obvious by now, a great many things about crossdressing prompt debate. When even basic terms prove controversial, communication and com-

prehension are greatly complicated. This situation helps explain why this work is as long as it is—and it is really only an introduction to the subject. As for the term 'transvestism,' in this work both the broader and narrower sense of it can be found. Overall, we shall prefer the term 'crossdressing' to 'transvestism' and 'crossdresser' to 'transvestite' to avoid confining our treatment to any one sub-group among those who dress in clothes usually associated with a gender other than the one they were assigned at birth.

Q. 19

What is 'transsexualism'?

The Short Answer. During the course of the 20th century a new name was given to a transgender reality that has existed for millennia: 'transsexualism.' Though the name caught on and remains popular, it can be misleading because it suggests one's sex might be changed as casually as one's clothes. But while a transsexual may change the body's sex presentation, the person does not regard this as changing sex. Instead, the body is being altered to reflect the true sex experienced psychologically. This position privileges the mind/brain as the most prominent sex organ rather than the genitals. The term 'transsexualism' references an experience of a profound disagreement between one's sexual designation (and genital presentation), and one's gender identity, or as some prefer, 'brain sex.' This may mean a person assigned at birth to the female sex experiences the identity of a boy/man trapped in a girl/woman's body (female-to-male transsexual, or FtM), or a person assigned to the male sex experiences the identity of a girl/woman trapped in a boy/man's body (male-to-female transsexual, or MtF). This internal dissonance is resolved in favor of the mind/brain by changing the genitals, (which is less resistant to change than the psyche). Thus, transsexual people are commonly distinguished from other transgender people by their seeking body modifications, including sexual reassignment surgery, to produce a match between mind/brain and body. Over the course of the 20th century, through both law and medicine, transsexual people gained greater control over their lives. Transsexualism remains a popular term despite having been passed over in the standard psychiatric classification system in favor of the prejudicial label 'Gender Identity Disorder' (GID), and by many others in favor of the broader term 'transgender.' Despite the stigma still attached by official classification as a mental disorder, a pronounced trend has been evident in some societies of dropping GID as a psychiatric diagnosis. The depathologizing of transsexualism is a change welcomed by the transgender community.

The Longer Answer. I think it important to start by acknowledging the preference today expressed by many people who could be called 'transsexual' for the term 'transgender' instead. The preference for the latter term rightly calls attention to the fact that 'gender' rather than 'sex' is at the heart of the matter.

However, the term 'transgender' also is appropriated by others and put to different uses (see the answer to Q. 20). I am afraid that to adopt the term 'transgender' here may cause confusion elsewhere. As inadequate as the term 'transsexual' is, the term is more readily recognizable as referring to a discrete group of people who are the object of contemplation here. So, with apologies and the desire not to offend anyone, I have retained the term transsexual both in this answer and elsewhere in the book as a simple means of keeping various groups distinct.

Transsexualism is important in the study of crossdressing both because many transsexuals crossdress long before they seek sex reassignment surgery and because dressing in the clothes of the gender they will be living in after such surgery is a standard part of pre-operative preparation. Although the general public shows greater awareness and understanding of transsexualism today than previously, there remains much ignorance about it. This answer attempts to cover areas basic to comprehending transsexualism, especially with regard to crossdressing.

As a preliminary note, we should be aware that much of the moralizing done about transgender people becomes especially negative when transsexualism is discussed. An essentialist position that maintains we have a given, 'essential' nature—specifically, one that predicates gender on a foundation of biological sex—is prone to argue that transsexuals act against Nature (or God) in seeking sex reassignment surgery. The argument presumes that being made male requires being masculine; being made female requires being feminine. But the naivety of the position becomes clear when it is seen that 'maleness' and 'femaleness' are based entirely on the apparent sex anatomy of the individual—the appearance of the genitals. That the brain is the principal sex organ in the body is irrelevant to people who care more about what is found between the legs than what resides between the ears.

If we wish to debate the moral rightness of sex reassignment surgery, perhaps we should ask first whether it is a greater good to force change upon the brain and psyche than upon the gonads. Decades of modern medical practice were devoted to trying to change the transsexual psyche, with so little success and so much misery that even the most committed to seeing transsexualism as a mental disorder were finally compelled to conclude that health is more attainable by altering superficial sex appearance than by trying to alter deeply rooted identity. This was not a concession to moral depravity, but a recognition that psychology is not independent of the brain—the mind is rooted in the body, but some parts of the body are far easier to change than others.

So if we wish to apply such facts to our moral reasoning, perhaps we may discover that the picture changes if we regard an 'essential' nature to be one rooted between the ears rather than the legs. If Nature (or God) has crafted an individual with a brain of one sex and gonads of another, should it not be the brain that receives priority? The transsexual's gender sense can still be regarded as founded upon sex (if one so chooses), as long as sex is better understood.[126]

What does the word 'transsexualism' mean?

The term 'transsexualism,' which literally means 'cross-sexed,' refers to the experience of a conflict between one's anatomical sex and one's culturally assigned gender identity. Hence, transsexuals commonly explain the experience as feeling they were born in a body of the wrong sex. This means a person born with the anatomical features of one sex experiences the gender identity associated with the opposite sex to such a complete extent that the discord between this identity and the body which houses it drives the individual to do lifelong behaviors designed to bridge the gap. Ultimately this may mean seeking sex reassignment surgery (SRS). It feels right to such individuals to change the body to match the psychological reality.

Note that above we distinguished between anatomical sex (Nature) and culturally assigned gender (Nurture). In our culture gender is strictly assigned based on superficial anatomical presentation at birth. Transsexualism in our culture reflects a disjunction between the socially normal and expected pairing of anatomical sex and assigned gender—either 'masculine male' or 'feminine female.' Perhaps Judith Shapiro best catches the essence of transsexualism in our cultural context when she remarks that it is the "suspension of the usual anatomical recruitment rule to gender category membership."[127] In the transsexual individual gender identity is not congruent to the cultural rule that it be paired simply, clearly, and only with the biological sex assigned partnership to it.

What is the origin and history of the term?

The reality of transsexualism is much older than the word. Descriptions that today would garner this label can be found throughout history, even into the ancient world (see the answers to Q. 41, 43). Medical descriptions date back to at least the early to mid-19th century.[128] However, the word itself entered the terminology of mental health less than a century ago. Pioneering sexologist Magnus Hirschfeld coined it in the early 1920s to differentiate between those who crossdressed ("transvestites") and others for whom crossdressing was not sufficient by itself ("transsexuals").[129] The term gained modest support when David Caulfield used it in a publication at mid-century.[130] But it was principally Harry Benjamin, an endocrinologist by training, who helped popularize the term with his publications in the 1950s-1960s.[131] Benjamin, who knew Hirschfeld in the late 1920s and was a staunch supporter, adopted Hirschfeld's terminology and carried the field with it.[132]

A marker event occurred in 1980 with the appearance of the *Diagnostic and Statistical Manual of Mental Disorders, 3rd edition*, (DSM-III). For the first time, transsexualism was included in this classification and diagnostic system, albeit under the label 'Gender Identity Disorder' ('GID'; see the answer to Q. 96). Its hallmark quality was called 'gender dysphoria' (see the answer to Q. 93). In subsequent revisions and new editions, GID would undergo significant changes (e.g., the cessation of the use of the term 'transsexualism'), reflecting a lingering unease over how best to characterize the situation. As the 20th century concluded, the text revision to the 4th edition of the DSM revealed the significant influence of investigators such as Susan Bradley, Richard Green, and especially Ray Blanchard (see the answer to Q. 95).

How prevalent is transsexualism?

The exact number of people who qualify as transsexuals is unknown and a matter of some debate. DSM-IV, frequently regarded as an authoritative guide, offers figures of roughly 1 per 30,000 adult males and 1 per 100,000 females.[133] Richard Carroll writes that "these numbers are likely to be a significant underestimation" because the negative judgments attached to labels like 'transsexual' or 'Gender Identity Disorder,' encourage transgendered people to stay relatively hidden.[134] Ray Blanchard, a very influential voice on the committee that revised DSM-IV (DSM-IV-TR, the text revision published in 2000), estimates prevalence at 1-in-40,000 to 1-in-50,000 adults, with males being from 2-4 times more likely to have the condition.[135]

Lynn Conway, active in educating people about transsexualism, argues that a more accurate estimate for male-to-female (MtF) transsexuals may be as high as 1 per 500 adult males. Conway arrives at this figure as follows:

> We first estimate the number of postop women in the U.S by accumulating the estimated numbers of sex reassignment surgeries (SRS) performed on U.S. citizens and residents decade by decade. We then divide that number by the number of adult males in the country. The result is a rough lower bound on postop prevalence, which we find to be about 1:2500. In other words, at least one or more in every 2500 adult males in the U.S. has had SRS and become a postop woman. The prevalence of untreated intense MtF transsexualism must be many times that number, and is perhaps on the order of 1:500.[136]

Conway notes that the number of sex reassignment surgeries for U.S. residents has grown dramatically since the 1960s. Then, the number was about 1,000 for the entire decade; today some 800-1,000 are done each year. She estimates that between 1990-2002 some 14,000-20,000 sex reassignment surgeries were done on U.S. citizens, either in the country or abroad. After adjusting for deaths among the post-operative population of MtF transsexuals since 1960, Conway arrives at an estimate of 32,000 living post-op females in the U.S. Since the estimated adult male population for ages 18-60 is 80 million, the resultant ratio is 1 per 2,500. This, Conway contends, is the low end estimate for prevalence since it only addresses those who have actually had surgery. She argues that the number of those experiencing intense transsexualism is at least three to five times higher, or some 100,000-200,000 untreated transsexuals. Adopting an estimation figure of 160,000 (pre-op plus post-op), Conway reaches her final figure of 1 per 500.[137]

Conway offers other ways to come at the same problem and each time demonstrates that the prevalence is markedly different from that calculated in the DSM model. The different figures offered can be seen in the samples in the following Table:

Table 19.1 Prevalence Estimates for Transsexualism in Select Societies

Country (Year of Study)	Prevalence
Australia (1996)[138]	2.38 per 100,000
Denmark (1980)[139]	2.1 per 100,000
England & Wales (1974)[140]	1.9 per 100,000
Germany (1996)[141]	2.25 per 100,000
Netherlands (1986)[142] (1996)[143]	1-in-18,000 (M); 1-in-54,000 (F) 4.72 per 100,000
Scotland (1999)[144]	8.18 per 100,000
Singapore (1988)[145]	1.58 per 100,000 1-in-2,840 (M); 1-in-8,333 (F)
Sweden (1967)[146] (2003)[147]	1 per 103,000 1.9 per 100,000
United States (1974)[148]	1 per 100,000 (M); 1 per 130,000 (F)

It must be noted that in their overview of transsexualism, Aude Michel, Christian Mormont and J. J. Legros, when summarizing 9 studies from 1968 to 1996, conclude that prevalence rates vary both by era and by country, with a wide range reported among studies.[149] Comparisons between studies are complicated by differences in collecting and calculating prevalence. As a group, however, the studies show that reported figures are growing larger when compared to earlier research. While the actual situation remains somewhat unclear, it seems quite plausible that the DSM estimates are low.

One area where there is widespread agreement is that there are more MtF transsexuals than FtM. In 1966, Harry Benjamin found a proportion among his clients of 8:1 male-to-female, but noted that other investigators have found a 4:1 or 3:1 ratio.[150] Jan Wilander, in Sweden, found a lower ratio: 2.5:1 male-to-female, about the same time as Benjamin's work.[151] A 4:1 male-to-female ratio was reported in the 2000 Scotland study. A 1971 report of the relative proportion of this population that was born male or female found a ratio of 2.7:1, male-to-female, among the 599 self-designated transsexuals involved in the study. They compared this ratio with earlier estimates of 2.8:1 found in 1967, 3.3:1 found in 1953, and 4:1 found in 1968.[152] All nine studies reported in Michel, Mormont, and Legros found a greater prevalence among males.[153] On the other hand, data reported from Hong Kong's only sex clinic treating transsexuals found slightly more FtM clients than MtF presenting over the period 1991-2001.[154] What to make of these differences remains unclear.

What are the characteristics of transsexualism?

The hallmark characteristic of transsexualism is the strongly felt experience of being in a body of the wrong sex. An epidemiological and demographic study found that transsexuals typically report having experienced strong feelings of being in the wrong sex body from childhood on, though they generally seek their first consultation about this sometime in early to mid-adulthood (age 20-45).[155] Similarly, a study of 200 male and 100 female transsexuals in Singapore found that transsexual feelings begin in childhood.[156]

Prince and Bentler, in their 1972 survey of 504 male crossdressers, note six characteristics simultaneously occurring among transsexuals:

- ❑ low heterosexual interest;
- ❑ preference for feminine self;
- ❑ taking female hormones;
- ❑ desire to live feminine role;
- ❑ feeling trapped in the wrong body; and,
- ❑ desiring sex reassignment surgery.[157]

At the end of the 20th century, the DSM-IV-TR diagnostic criteria listed four salient characteristics:

- ❑ a strong and persistent cross-gender identification—one not expressing merely a desire for any perceived cultural advantages of being an other sex;
- ❑ persistent discomfort with one's own sex, or sense that one's assigned gender role is inappropriate;
- ❑ the absence of a physical intersex condition; and,
- ❑ clinically significant distress or impairment in an important area of functioning, such as the social or occupational arena.

There are, accompanying the first two of these, qualifying distinctions between children as one group, and adolescents and adults as another.[158]

Ray Blanchard, Head of Clinical Sexology Services at the Clarke Institute of Psychiatry in Toronto, California, proposes a twofold division for transsexualism. In 'homosexual transsexualism,' transsexuals erroneously believe themselves to be heterosexual because of the mental disturbance that prompts them to see themselves as members of a biological sex other than their anatomical presentation. Both males and females are represented in homosexual transsexualism. In 'nonhomosexual transsexualism,' Blanchard proposes, the persons are almost always males. They may be bisexual, heterosexual, or asexual (not erotically attracted to either sex).[159] For a variety of reasons Blanchard's ideas have proven especially controversial within the transsexual community.[160]

What causes transsexualism?

What causes transsexualism remains unknown. Both environmental and biological factors have been proposed, with the latter receiving increasing attention in recent years. There have been various ways the range of alternative explanations have been presented; the following offer two rather different examples.

Paul Federoff of the Centre for Addiction and Mental Health in Toronto, Canada, proposes that five major ways of understanding transsexualism exist. These explanations variously propose that transsexualism is:

❑ *a delusional disorder*—from the standpoint of apparent sex, the statement 'I am trapped in the body of the wrong sex' is factually wrong, so such belief constitutes a delusion and adhering to it fixedly makes it a disorder;

❑ *an overvalued idea*—the transsexual has fixated on an idea others may share, but in such an insistent and inflexible manner that an emotional commitment to it comes to enchain the person's behavior;

❑ *a variant of normal*—transsexualism is a variant, albeit an extreme one, of gender identity and thus not pathological;

❑ *a lifestyle choice*—the transsexual may be voluntarily committed to adopting a sex/gender identity and sex/gender roles that they have idealized; or,

❑ *a physical disease*—transsexualism originates in biological causes, such as abnormalities in the brain, and thus produces symptoms such as gender dysphoria.[161]

In their overview of transsexualism, researchers Michel, Mormont, and Legros list five principal areas of investigation, three of which are biological. These five are:

❑ *perinatal hormonal abnormalities*—an atypical hormonal environment before and around the time of birth has been thought by some to be a contributing factor, though most who experience such an environment do not develop transsexualism;

❑ *alteration of gonadotrophin secretion*—during the sexual differentiation of the brain into 'male' and 'female,' a deficit of androgen (male hormone) can lead to reversed sexual behavior in rats, but whether something similar occurs in humans has been disputed;

- *sexual morphological differentiation in the brain*—a portion of the hypothalamus (a region in the brain important to sexual behavior), known as the central subdivision of the bed nucleus of the stria terminalis (BSTc), is different in volume between males and females, with this region in transsexuals similar to that found in members of the opposite sex;
- *the non-conflictual hypothesis*—the psychological development of the MtF transsexual is typified by a long and pleasant symbiotic relationship between mother and son such that the son identifies with her gender; and,
- *conflictual hypotheses*—transsexualism is conceived as a psychological compromise to internal conflict, whether that conflict arises because of a defense against homosexuality, or as a result of disturbances in the separation-individuation phase of development, or as a manifestation of a personality disorder, or some other hypothesized conflict.[162]

Although it seems reasonable to suppose that a biological foundation exists, the way transsexualism plays out behaviorally is undoubtedly influenced by the culture the individual resides within, as well as by individual factors. It may be that some seek sex reassignment surgery because of the cultural pressure on people to present a congruence between body sex and gender presentation. Thus, some individuals who might otherwise be content to remain in the body sex of their birth may be led to change their genital presentation to conform to an insistent cultural pressure. Ironically, then, our culture's refusal to admit a 'third gender' in our cultural gender scheme may be a factor in prompting body modifications, including sex reassignment surgery.

What is the relation between crossdressing and transsexualism?

Noelle Howey, daughter of a MtF transsexual, very succinctly summarizes the relation between dress and transsexualism: "Being a transsexual isn't just about clothes, any more than being a woman is. However, that doesn't mean clothes are meaningless either. Clothes are a representative of identity—for men, women, everyone in between."[163] Indeed, based on interviews with transsexuals, sociologist Sally Hines concludes that gendered appearance, and especially the role of clothing, is placed in an important position in differentiating transsexual and transvestite identities.[164]

Transsexuals experience and express dress differently than do others who clothe themselves in fashions associated with the gender opposite the one they were assigned at birth. For transsexuals, dress is used in a manner like most other people—to express a primary gender identity and gender role that remains relatively constant. For them, their manner of dress is consistent with their gender, and this identity is relatively more persistent than that found among those labeled transvestites, whose gender expression may change from masculine to feminine or perhaps some point between. Thus, transsexuals do not see their manner of dress as crossdressing. And they are right—at least in terms of agreement between experienced gender and dress representation of gender. But from the perspective of a wider public, which pairs genitalia with gender, anyone who dresses in gender-associated clothing different from that associated with a specific sex is crossdressing.

But crossdressing is about gender, not genitalia. Thus, someone crossdresses when there occurs a mismatch between the gendered clothes being worn and the gender status assigned the wearer. Those who assign to a MtF transsexual the gender status of a man will inevitably view feminine dress as a mismatch and call what they are seeing crossdressing. Those who successfully 'pass' as a legitimate member of the gender they are dressed as will not be viewed as crossdressing, unless the observer knows that the assigned gender varies from the gender presentation. In short, crossdressing is a matter of perception and judgment.

Whether we like it or not, or agree or not, many folk are still going to see transsexuals as crossdressers because their genetic sex remains the same whether they receive hormone treatments and surgery or not. So, in that regard transsexuals—whether preoperative or postoperative—belong as part of the larger picture of crossdressing. On the other hand, considering transsexualism is even more justified by its undeniable place as a prominent transgender reality. So how might we put these various matters together?

Preoperatively, many transsexuals might be said to crossdress, especially in light of the latter half of our definition. A preoperative transsexual commonly presents a public gender identity and fills a gender role inconsistent with what is actually felt privately. So, technically, we could argue that such a person is crossdressing either because what is being worn is inconsistent with the public gender identity and role, or with the private gender experience. Either way, at some points in time crossdressing is happening. However, postoperatively, it seems highly impolite to suggest a transsexual is crossdressing merely because her or his clothes are associated with a genetic sex different from the constructed one. Once congruence and constancy are achieved, then crossdressing by its very name is excluded, though the argument may still be made that the person represents a transgender reality because of the manner in which the match between gender and anatomical sex has been attained.

In broad strokes, some crossdressers are transsexuals, but not all transsexuals are always or necessarily crossdressers. The research tends to regard crossdressing and transsexualism along the lines of the general public's perception: crossdressing is wearing clothes associated with the gender paired with the sex opposite the one the person is genetically. In this context, a study released in 1971 of 599 self-designated transsexuals reports that a little more than half of its subjects (52%) crossdress a significant portion of the time, while nearly a quarter (23%) claim never to crossdress. This study also finds a difference between MtF and FtM transsexuals. Males more frequently experiment with crossdressing (15% to 5%), but females, if they crossdress at all, are more likely to do so frequently.[165] On the other hand, a small sample of 28 transsexuals (15 FtM; 13 MtF) at a Hong Kong sex clinic reports nearly 93% crossdress at least once a month—and that includes all the MtF clients.[166] Also a 1979 study, with another small group (15 FtM transsexuals), finds that 80% of them crossdressed in childhood.[167] Tsoi's study of 200 male and 100 female transsexuals in Singapore concluds that crossdressing in childhood is an early sign of transsexualism and occurs earlier in females than in males.[168]

What has been legal reasoning about transsexualism?

Transsexualism has been the subject of a number of important legal cases, one of which is summarized in a later answer. In this answer, however, we are less interested in the particulars of individual cases and more in the general conclusions, which reflect basic reasoning about transsexualism. Not surprisingly, given the complexity, cultural values, changing social mores, and subject content, there has not been uniformity in reasoning or conclusions. On the whole, however, it can be argued that slowly the legal prospects for transsexuals winning recognition and gaining essential human protections have improved. A basic review of these matters is found in the answer to Q. 36.

Legal scholar Andrew Sharpe, in a variety of publications, documents the issues and history of English law with reference to the transgendered. He notes that the legal reasoning with reference to transsexuals has undergone changes. Previously courts largely followed the logic set forth in the landmark case of *Corbett v. Corbett* (1970), which gave priority to the notion that a person's sex is determined at birth. Despite the fact that April Ashley was a post-operative MtF transsexual, the court ruled that 'she' remained a 'he.'[169]

An alternative logic in a 1968 New York case (*Re Anonymous*) determined a person's sex based on 'psychological and anatomical harmony' between the individual's psychological convictions and post-operative sexual anatomy. This latter logic relied also on a post surgical body's capacity for sexual desire and performance, as a 1976 New Jersey case made plain in ruling that the mere creation through surgery of operational sexual anatomy is not enough; there must be an accompanying 'psychological and emotional orientation to engage in sexual intercourse.' This logic stresses *functionality*—the real sex of the person is a function of their ability, psychologically and physically, to perform sexually. Sharpe argues that, "It is through an analysis around functionality that law comprehends and makes sense of the desire for and the fact of sex reassignment surgery. In this regard law conflates gender identity and sexual desire in thinking about transgender persons."[170]

More recently, Sharpe detects a shift from functionality to aesthetics. In examining a 1995 New Zealand case (*Attorney-General v. Otahuhu Family Court*), Sharpe notes that the reasoning applied departs from the 'psychological and anatomical harmony' logic. Instead of insisting on the transsexual person's sexual capacity to perform, this case merely required for a valid marriage that both persons present with the apparent genitals of different sexes—one male and one female. Instead of heterosexual capacity, a bodily aesthetic predominates. While Sharpe recognizes this change can be viewed as an advance for transsexual people, he also sees it as problematic in that it still retains a judicial anxiety over the pre-operative transsexual body and the specter of homosexuality.[171]

In the broadly shared cultural framework of Australia, New Zealand, Great Britain and the United States, this analysis resonates. The persistent obsession over the sexual orientation of transsexuals, with an accompanying designation of homosexual based on chromosomal sex rather than gender identity or post-operative sexuality reflects the general culture's connecting of transsexuality (and transgender at large) with a particular—and largely disfavored—sexual orientation. However, given the generally conservative nature of judiciaries, the slow trend documented by Sharpe may be seen as another demonstration of the cultural shift in perception of transgender. How deep this shift is in substance remains to be seen.

Who are some notable modern transsexuals?

The best historical evidence, though scanty, suggests transsexual individuals have been around a long time (see the answers to Q. 41-42, 48-49). But only fairly recently have they had recourse to effective surgical means of changing their visible sexual anatomy.[172] We would be remiss in any consideration of the brave pioneers who sought and underwent sex reassignment surgery (SRS) if we did not also recognize the courageous physicians who sought to alleviate their patients' suffering. Harry Benjamin, in his classic work *The Transsexual Phenomenon*, observes that surgeons conducting SRS often faced punishment for breaking the law. In Europe, for example, a law commonly referred to as the 'mayhem statute'—which dated to the reign of Henry VIII—could be applied to doctors who undertook to 'convert' a person from one sex presentation to another. Even as Benjamin was writing in 1966, he was aware that such operations remained illegal in much of the modern world—a situation that persists.[173] Yet compassionate physicians then and now often risk their own well-being to promote the well-being of transgender individuals.

The earliest recorded effort at SRS took place in Berlin in 1912. Magnus Hirschfeld, who later coined the term 'transsexualism,' referred a female patient to a surgeon for what was an incomplete operation.[174] Early attempts at male-to-female (MtF) changes took place in Berlin in 1920, though the first complete operation did not occur until 1931, when two of Hirschfeld's colleagues referred a man named "Rudolph R." (later "Dorchen") to surgeons.[175] A number of individuals are known to have undertaken a complete transformation during the 1930s.[176] Today, SRS is available in a number of countries, though it remains illegal in many. The following persons (whose stories are told in the historical present tense) represent a host of transsexual pioneers.

Einer Wegener/Lili Elbe

Among the most famous of early cases is that of Einer Wegener (1886-1931), a Dane who after his MtF operation in 1930 has an autobiography appear under the name Lili Elbe.[177] Wegener begins the process of transitioning more than a decade before a series of experimental operations. The first of these, which happens in Berlin (and after examination by Hirschfeld), removes his genitals. Later operations transplant ovaries into him, and construct a rudimentary vagina. These surgeries contribute to Wegener—who is issued a new Danish birth certificate under the name Lili Elbe—dying not long after. Elbe, reflecting both the ignorance and exaggerated dreams of the times, had hoped and believed that the surgeries would make it possible for her to not only be married, but even to have children.[178]

Arnold-Lèon/Arlette-Irène Leber

Another notable early case is that of Arnold-Lèon (b. 1912), who becomes Arlette-Irène Leber after surgeries completed in 1942 and an important court case that concludes in 1945. (For more on Leber's story and case, see the answer to Q. 36.)

Laura Maud Dillon/Laurence Michael Dillon

The individuals mentioned thus far all began life as biological males. Historically, more males have sought sex reassignment surgery than have females. However, from a very early time there have been some FtM transsexuals who have undergone SRS. Author Pagan Kennedy makes the case that the first 'man-made man' was Michael Dillon.[179]

Dillon is born Laura Dillon into a wealthy London family on May 1st, 1915. But life is immediately complicated by the death of her mother just a few days later, followed by her father's giving her and a brother over to the care of aunts to be raised. Her father dies while Laura is still a child.

Nevertheless, her family's wealth and status ensure Laura access to a fine education. After attending an exclusive girls' school, she enrolls at St. Anne's College, part of Oxford University. Her tomboyish childhood had yielded to increasing discomfort as puberty produced unwelcome changes. She responds by efforts such as tying down her breasts with a belt. Mannish in appearance, with her cut short and a deep voice for a woman, she favors masculine dress. Laura proves an excellent athlete at Oxford. But she struggles to fit in, trying without satisfaction to establish an identity as a lesbian. She graduates in 1938.

Experiencing the self as a man rather than as a woman, Laura follows a course similar to the one others in a similar circumstance have taken. She lives a life largely separate and isolated from others. For employment, work as a garage hand is undertaken. The ongoing disjunction between psychological identity as a man and a female body spurs Laura to seek out ways of changing the latter.

As the 1930s end, her life begins to change dramatically through the ministrations of modern medicine. In 1939, she finds a physician willing to administer male hormones and becomes the first female documented to receive testosterone treatment. The hormone soon has a visible effect, as a beard readily grows. In 1942 she undergoes a mastectomy. As the operations move forward, other changes accompany them. Over the course of the next few years, pioneering plastic surgeon Sir Harold Gillies will perform a series of body-altering operations, culminating with the construction of a phallus.

In 1944, Laura succeeds in changing her birth certificate to indicate birth as a son named Laurence Michael Dillon. Her older brother, Sir Robert Dillon, reacts by refusing further relationship. Now going by 'Michael,' Dillon enters medical school in 1945 at Trinity College in Dublin. During the years 1945-1949, living as a man, the medical work to complete the transition continues under Gillies and his colleague Ralph Millard. In all, there are more than a dozen surgeries required.

As his medical education nears its completion, Michael meets another individual on a path transecting his own life course. The person is Roberta Cowell, a pre-operative MtF transsexual, who in 1951 becomes the first male to complete sex reassignment surgery in the United Kingdom. Michael and Roberta forge a friendship that develops into something more. A year after first meeting, he proposes marriage. It is not to be. Roberta, who had been a captain in the Royal air force during the war, as well as a racecar driver, has goals of her own—including publishing, in 1954, the story of her life. The disappointed, and worried, Michael keeps to the high seas, fearful of his secret becoming known. He will remain single the remainder of his life.

Upon graduation from medical school, in 1951, Michael Dillon becomes a ship's doctor and travels to many parts of the world. But an action he had undertaken earlier proves instrumental in leading to disclosure of his sex change and to unwanted publicity. Michael had presented his changed birth certificate to *Debrett's Peerage*—a long-established guide to British titled aristocracy. They had agreed to amend their listing, a change that would establish Michael's claim to the title held by his estranged (and childless) brother upon his brother's death. However, *Burke's Peerage* had not similarly changed their listing. In 1958, the paper *Sunday Express* investigates and publishes news of the sex change.

Michael has no desire to be known in this manner. He seeks refuge in a Theravada Buddhist monastery in Bengal. But their rules prevent his becoming a monk. Instead, in the last years of his short life, he finds a new home in a Tibetan monastery in the Himalayan mountains. Study there leads to another name change, as he becomes Lobzang Jivaha, a Tibetan monk. The learning he acquires there, and his own experiences, lead him to write two books. One is a biography of an 11ᵗʰ century yogi, the other (*Imji Getsui*) is his account of life in a Buddhist monastery. He dies at age 47 in 1962.

James Morris/Jan Morris

One of those who has helped present to a wider public the experience of being transsexual is noted travel writer Jan Morris. Fellow writer, the novelist Jennifer Finney Boylan (herself a MtF transsexual) declares Morris' book *Conundrum* "the one book on transsexuality that has been most frequently read by persons who otherwise would prefer live burial to 'gender studies.'"[180]

Morris (b. 1926) is born James Humphrey Morris in Somerset, England. Early attracted to writing, James works as a journalist for the *Western Daily News* of Bristol before becoming an officer cadet at Sandhurst Military College. Service in World War II (1943-1945) includes postings as an intelligence officer in what is then called Palestine, as well as in Italy. Following his exit from military life, Morris attends Oxford University. There his interest in writing is continued by editing *Cherwell*, a student magazine.

In 1949, the same year as entering Oxford, James marries Elizabeth Tuckness, who is aware of his conviction of being a woman trapped in a male body. The couple have five children and remain together when, after more than 20 years of marriage, James undergoes sex reassignment surgery to complete his transition into full-time life as a woman.

Morris is successful in his chosen career as a writer. As a staff reporter at *The Times* (1951-1956), in 1953, he is witness to the British conquest of Mount Everest. Later he moves to *The Guardian* (1957-1962) where he is a foreign correspondent, based mostly in the Middle East. Leaving journalism, James moves to writing as an independent author. Among Morris' works is the trilogy *Pax Britannica* (1968-1978), a history of the British Empire begun while still a man but completed after becoming a woman.

Morris begins hormone treatment in the 1960s. James has become Jan. Sex reassignment surgery is completed in 1972 when Jan is in her mid-forties. The tale of this experience is recounted in *Conundrum* (1974; reissued 2006), a book that generates much attention and not a little controversy. In this autobiography Jan recounts the long journey that commenced with an awareness already by age 3-4 of being in the wrong body, a journey that leads eventually to hormone treatments and surgery. Like others who have told of the changes they experience in both body and mind through the transitioning, Morris offers testimony to both:

> It is not merely the loss of androgens that has made me more retiring, more ready to be led, more passive: the removal of the organs themselves has contributed, for there was to the presence of the penis something positive and stimulating. My body then was made to push and initiate, it is made now to yield and accept, and the outside change has had its inner consequences.[181]

Among the more than 30 books Morris has published are both works about places (e.g., *Coast to Coast: A Journey Across 1950s America*), people (e.g., *Lincoln: A Foreigner's Quest*), and novels (e.g. *Our First Leader, Trieste and the Meaning of Nowhere*). In 1999, Morris is honored as a Commander of the British Empire.[182]

George Jorgensen, Jr./Christine Jorgensen

By far the most famous case in the United States of a MtF transsexual is that of Christine Jorgensen (1927-1989). Probably more than other case, this one brought transsexualism into public awareness. Born genetically male, and named George Jorgensen, Jr., the boy grows up in the Bronx, New York. Later, Jorgensen will describe that child as frail and introverted, who avoided rough and tumble play, and dreamed of 'a pretty doll with long golden hair' for Christmas.[183]

Graduating from High School in 1945, Jorgensen is drafted into the Army not long after the conclusion of the Second World War. After his time of service, Jorgensen returns to New York. Deeply dissatisfied with the experience of living as a man while identifying as a woman, Jorgensen learns of the sex-change operations available in Europe. At the age of 26, after three operations, 'he' becomes 'she' and takes the name Christine Jorgensen. Though Jorgensen has not intended or desired publicity, the 1952-1953 operations in Copenhagen, Denmark, generate news on both sides of the Atlantic. *The New York Daily News* runs the story under the headline, "Ex-GI Becomes Blonde Beauty: Operations Transform Bronx Youth."[184]

Although Jorgensen contracts to tell her life story exclusively to *American Weekly* magazine for $20,000, there is a flurry of competing stories published about the sex change. Christine becomes the object of fascination and intense attention. The stories reflect the controversy surrounding what Jorgensen has done, with some being sharply critical and others warmly supportive. The publicity, both good and bad, help her financially. As she remarks in a 1979 interview with *Newsday*, "It's enabled me to make a lot of money."[185]

The publicity also enables many to speak openly about an issue that is part of the sexual revolution then beginning to emerge. The timing of the event— and the attractiveness of Christine—help draw and hold attention. Jorgensen makes an ideal 'poster child' for transsexualism. Her story is dramatic (an ex-GI!), and the change likewise (blonde bombshell!). But more, she is able to communicate both verbally and through her autobiography the transsexual experience in a way that helps others understand how a person might engage in a course of action so radical that matters we think central to life—the body's sexual identity, a personal name, and a conventional gender role—should all be changed. In changing the self, Jorgensen helps change society.

Richard Raskin/Renee Richards

Richard Raskin (b. 1934) is thrust into the national spotlight in the mid-1970s when the former male player enters the world of women's professional tennis as Renee Richards. Perhaps no area of public endeavor has tried harder to keep men and women separate than that of sports. The higher the level of competition, the more pronounced the gender divide. Thus the case of a trans-gendered tennis player creates a firestorm of controversy. While many Americans are still accustoming themselves to the reality of transgendered people, the notion that someone might change sex and cross the gender divide to compete in athletics is a controversial idea—one especially opposed within sport itself.

The desire to be more successful as a woman's tennis player than Raskins had been as a male performer is not his motivation to change sex. That desire has been there for a very long time. As an adult looking back on childhood, Raskin/Richards points to certain environmental factors as instrumental, regardless of whatever biochemical forces may also have been at work. An older sister, herself pronouncedly tomboyish, introduces her brother to crossdressing and the creation of a feminine persona, 'Renee.' Throughout childhood, adolescence, and well into adulthood two personas vie for dominance.[186]

In many respects, Raskin's masculine life is of the sort others envy: a Yale graduate, a veteran of the armed services, and a successful medical professional. Inwardly, though, the struggle continues. In the late 1960s, Raskins begins taking hormones in preparation for sex reassignment surgery abroad. But when the moment actually arrives, he backs away. Instead of surgery to become a female, Raskins returns to the States and actually begins steps to alter his body back to fully male. He marries, has a child, and divorces. Finally, in 1975, at age 40, he undertakes SRS.

A successful ophthalmologist, Raskins is also a successful amateur tennis player, nationally ranked in the men's 35-and-older division. In 1976, now under the name Renee Clarke, the 41-year-old enters a tennis tournament in La Jolla, California. A reporter, astounded that this tall (6'2") newcomer has dethroned the defending ladies champion, investigates and learns 'Clarke's' true identity. Accusations are made that this is a man masquerading as a woman. The resulting publicity becomes magnified when Renee enters a tournament warm-up to the U.S. Open, the country's premier tennis event. Both the U.S. Tennis Association and Women's Tennis Association respond by revoking their recognition of the tournament, and 25 of the 32 women entered withdraw. This does not end the matter. Renee declares she will enter the U.S. Open and the governing tennis bodies react by requiring all women participants undergo a genetic test of their sex. Richards' refusal to submit to this test prevents her participation in the Open, but does not resolve the larger conflict. Taking the matter to the state Supreme Court in New York, Renee wins. The Court rules she is female and that the requirement of the sex test had been discriminatory. The way is thus paved for her to play professionally as a woman, which she does until retiring in 1981 at age 47.[187]

After retiring as an active player, Renee serves briefly as tennis coach for one of the world's most prominent players, Martina Navratilova. Then she returns to practice as an ophthalmologist. In 1983 her autobiography, *Second Serve*, is published. This account is rendered into a made-for-television movie by the same name broadcast in 1986 and starring Vanessa Redgrave in the lead role. Richards continues to practice medicine, eventually taking a high position at the Manhattan Eye, Ear and Throat Hospital. In 1999, in an interview for *Tennis* magazine, Renee expresses her belief that many of her difficulties stemmed from having undergone her transition from man to woman so late in life. She discourages others from seeing her as a role model for late transitioning, but also acknowledges her role in helping challenge the public stereotype of trans-gendered people as sexual perverts.[188]

Vernoy Wayne Martin / Jayne Wayne County [189]

In the modern world transgender individuals are commonly shunted to the margins of society. If they present publicly as transgendered they face many employment barriers. One realm, however, where being transgendered has been more accepted is entertainment. Some of today's best-known transgendered people are entertainers, especially in music. Internationally, there are figures like Dana International in the Middle East (see the answer to Q. 53), and Harisu in the Far East (see the answer to Q. 52). In the West, too, there are transgender entertainers, though typically they not as well-known or as well-received as elsewhere.

Vernoy Wayne Martin (b. 1946) is a trash/glam/punk rock performer bet-ter known under the name Jayne Wayne County (adopted for the stage). Born and raised in a small Georgia town in the American south, County says in her autobiography that she grew up a 'sissy boy.' She attributes her transgender identity to both biological (estrogen injections received by her pregnant mother) and environmental forces (pervasive feminine presence and emotionally distant father). As a young boy County felt comfortable garbed in feminine clothes and playing with dolls. Typical of transsexual children, County recalls expressing the wish to be a girl and a strong identification with female role models.

Rock & roll music proves an important early influence and even as a child County puts on performances while dressed as a girl. Crafting a series of short plays, County begins performing locally. Her first significant public perform-ance is at Atlanta's Looking Glass Club. But County has loftier ambitions and so strikes out for New York City, joining in the avant-garde theater there. Still identified as a man, performing under the name Wayne County, it is an off-off Broadway role as a lesbian kleptomaniac in the play *Femme Fatale* that leads to a series of other roles, including that of Viva in Andy Warhol's *Pork*. Success on stage leads to other opportunities, most notably in the music industry.

County becomes a DJ at Max's Kansas City club, and in 1972 begins per-forming there dressed as a woman. County develops a style of rock music in-spired by the New York Dolls and gains notoriety for an outrageous act, backed by the band Backstreet Boys. But County grows frustrated and disillusioned with an inability to gain recording contracts in the U.S. Greener pastures across the Atlantic beckon and so County relocates to London in the late 1970s, arriving as that city's punk movement blossoms. Now backed by The Electric Chairs, County enjoys commercial success, releasing a series of albums between 1977-1979.

At the end of the decade, County goes to Berlin, only to reemerge a new person. Now known as Jayne County, the performer returns to the United States in 1980. Since then, County has continued to perform and to release albums. She is perhaps the best known transsexual performer in this country. In 1995, her autobiography appears under the title *Man Enough to Be a Woman*.

Conclusion

Just how far society has come remains to be seen. Advances in some countries, such as the United States, have been made on the legal front (see answer to Q. 36). Unfortunately, violence remains all too common (see answer to Q. 37). Moreover, in the view of most mental health professionals, transsexualism—as 'Gender Identity Disorder'—remains a 'mental disorder' (see answers to Q. 96, 99). On the other hand, at the end of 2002, the British Lord Chancellor's Office published a policy report declaring unambiguously that transsexualism is not a mental illness.[190] Whether this conclusion will become widespread is not yet known.

Q. 20

What does 'transgender' mean?

The Short Answer. 'Transgender' is a key term, one used increasingly often, but also one without a fixed meaning. Literally, 'transgender' means 'cross gender' (just as 'transvestism' literally means 'cross-clothed,' or 'crossdressed'). Though the term is widely used, it often is left undefined so that what is meant by it must be inferred from context. Various people mean different things by 'transgender.' Some use it as an embracing term encompassing various subgroups; others use it in a narrower sense to reflect one group with distinguishing characteristics—most often transsexuals. A narrow sense is actually the original one, but not as a synonym for 'transsexual.' Rather, the narrow meaning refers to those who live full-time in the identity of a gender different from the one they were assigned at birth, but without seeking sex reassignment surgery. Such individuals are sometimes called 'transgenderists.' In this volume the use of the term almost always refers to its broader, more general meaning. In other words, 'transgender' is employed as an umbrella term under which a variety of people are put who share the characteristic of not easily fitting society's sense of gender conformity.

The Longer Answer. Since most of us think we know what is meant by 'gender,' the key to the term 'transgender' is the meaning of the prefixed 'trans.' In its simplest and most direct sense it means 'to cross,' so that 'cross-gender' and 'transgender' both mean to move from one gender presentation to another. Since in our culture gender is so closely paired with anatomical sex, crossing gender is typically understood to mean presenting in a gender not paired by our culture with the person's anatomical sex. Thus, a female who presents as masculine is displaying transgender.

But 'trans' is affixed to a variety of other words that lend depth and coloration to the term 'transgender.' For example, consider the word 'transgression.' Some people view transgender as a transgression of gender rules and boundaries; the word 'transgender,' for them, is decidedly negative. On the other hand, consider the word 'transcend.' Some people view transgender as a transcending of too-narrow gender rules and boundaries; the term 'transgender,' for them, is definitely positive. Other instances of how 'trans' might be construed—any of which can influence how one views the term—include 'translate' (transgender as rendering the gender associated with a different sex into a gender paired with one's own sex, as in biological males who represent a certain language of femininity through their crossdressing), 'transform' (transgender as reshaping gender in distinctive ways), or 'transition' (transgender as moving from one gender to another while dragging one's sex along behind, as in transsexuals who live as a gender before undergoing surgery to become anatomically the sex typically paired with that gender).

If we try to structure such multiple uses of the prefix 'trans' and elucidate its various meanings we arrive at the following list, which is not exclusive of other possibilities: the trans in transgender can mean

- ❏ to cross from one gender to another, leaving each gender intact;
- ❏ to violate gender boundaries;
- ❏ to move beyond artificial gender confines;
- ❏ to reinterpret gender and sex pairings;
- ❏ to create gender, as in 'third gender' realities; or
- ❏ to change gender.

These meanings can exist alone or in combination.

Clearly, what first may seem a simple matter presents unexpected complexity. This impression is reinforced when we turn to other matters, such as history, to help us. We find both that the term is fairly recent, but that even in its short existence it has come to have a variety of uses.

Terms antecedent to 'transgender,' such as 'transgenderal' or 'transgenderist,' have been around since at least the 1970s. Coined by transgender pioneer activist and organizer Virginia Prince, the term originally intended a narrow meaning (see below). However, by the mid-1990s it had gained wide circulation and popularity as an umbrella term. Today it can claim being the most widely used term to refer to a number of groups of people whose gendered reality does not strictly conform to the simplistic dualism of masculine/feminine.[191] This history, though, means the word has carried—and still does—more than one meaning. This persists in causing confusion and necessitates we examine both the broader and narrower applications of the term.

Defining the word 'transgender' is difficult; applying it to various individuals is even harder because the use of the term is controversial. There are both wider and two narrower senses for the term 'transgender.' The word itself permits a range of applications since it simply means 'cross' (or 'across') gender. Both broad and narrow uses of the term merit some exploration. But initially it should be noted that the term was first used in a narrower sense and only later became used in a wider one. Currently, both uses of the word are relatively common and exact meaning must often be inferred from the context.

It is common in much literature, particularly legal literature, to find 'transgender' used either as a synonym for 'transsexual' or as a term embracing two subgroups, 'transsexuals' and 'transgenderists.' This is because much legal literature is with reference to laws concerning either sex reassignment surgery for transsexuals, or identity paper changes, which affect both transsexuals and transgenderists. In any event, a reliance on careful scrutiny of context will help avoid misunderstandings. Remember that we live in a creative period where the lively conversation on gender is still working to establish a clearer vocabulary.

In its wider sense, what does 'transgenderism' include?

The more common use of the term is in its broad sense. For example, Walter Bockting, among the best known experts on transgender conditions, remarks that "transgender people are a diverse group of individuals who cross or transcend culturally defined categories of gender."[192] Similarly, sex therapist Richard Carroll observes that, "the term 'transgendered experience' is currently used to refer to the many different ways individuals may experience a gender identity outside the simple categories of male or female."[193]

'Transgender,' in short, can be an umbrella term, whether applied to members of various identifiable groups or used to describe different gender experiences regardless of group affiliation. Personally, I like the phrasing of the Gender Public Advocacy Coalition (GenderPAC). In a 1997 report GenderPAC offered a description of transgendered people that fits well a broad sense of the term: "Transgendered people are people who manifest gender characteristics, behavior, or self-identification typical of or commonly associated with persons of another gender."[194]

As useful as these descriptions are, they do not actually list any groups already existing under other labels. One description of the term, offered by Thom and More, rectifies this situation by proposing that 'transgender' names "the community of all self identified cross gender people whether intersex, transsexual men and women, cross dressers, drag kings and drag queens, transgenderists, androgynous, bi-gendered, third gendered or as yet unnamed gender gifted people."[195]

With this list in mind, the term 'transgender' in its wider sense may be used to embrace members of the following groups (each listed with a defining characteristic), who also are commonly referred to as 'sexual minorities':

- ❑ *bigendered*—those who perceive themselves as both masculine and feminine;
- ❑ *gender impersonators*—professional impersonators of a gender different than the one assigned them at birth (typically male impersonators of females);
- ❑ *homosexuals*—those whose fixed erotic attraction pattern is toward members of their own sex (and thus contrary to the majority gender pattern);
- ❑ *intersexed*—those born with ambiguous genitalia or sexual characteristics that make simple identification as male or female impossible;

- ❑ *third gender people*—those who perceive themselves as belonging to neither gender pole but instead possessing a separate sense of gender;
- ❑ *transsexuals*—those who have a persistent sense of inhabiting the body of the wrong sex, and who typically pursue body-altering strategies including hormonal and surgical treatment; and,
- ❑ *transvestites*—those who dress in the clothes associated with the opposite gender, including those who do so occasionally or regularly, and others who choose to live as members of the opposite sex without sex reassignment surgery (the latter often being referred to as 'transgenderists').[196]

The appropriateness of one or another group being placed under this large umbrella is often debated. What they often have in common is what sociologists Patricia Gagne and Richard Tewksbury call "quests to find room to be themselves within a system that made no space for them."[197]

Interestingly, the term can be applied even more widely than as used above. Dallas Denny, founder of the American Educational Gender Information Service, Inc. (AEGIS), suggests that the term can be interpreted as "transgressively gendered" and applied to anyone who either dislikes or is uncomfortable with gender stereotypes. She points out that in this respect, only the John Wayne stereotypical masculine man and the Marilyn Monroe stereotypically feminine female are not transgendered! Further, she argues that even American society as a whole can be called transgendered because over the course of its history there has been a progressive relaxing of strict male/female gender norms.[198] But while Denny's observations are not devoid of merit, especially in calling us to think more broadly than we are accustomed to do, they do not reflect the general manner in which the term 'transgender' is employed.

A chief motivation for this wider sense of the term has been to increase the influence of the members of the separate groups by bringing them together. This has met a mixed reception. Some accept it with the reasoning that what affects one group typically affects them all and that certain characteristics are shared enough to warrant a broad inclusion. Others object to being affiliated with different groups from the fear of being confused for actually being members in these other groups. For example, heterosexual transvestites may object to being viewed too closely with transsexuals or homosexuals because these two groups may have more social stigma attached to them, perhaps even in the view of the transvestite. Some homosexuals object to the term because they do not crossdress and see themselves as already members of a distinct group whose identity might be compromised by association with transvestites and transsexuals.

Homosexuals, in particular, might raise a valid objection. A great many adult homosexuals embrace and experience gender consistent with their birth assignment. In short, homosexual men may as fully identify as masculine men as do heterosexual men, and homosexual women may as fully identify as feminine women as do heterosexual women. For these individuals the designation as transgender seems incorrect at best and offensive at worst. It does not help that the historic association of homosexuality with transgender was forged on the notion that gender and sex are inseparable, and that same-sex desire (especially among men) is inconsistent with gender and sex norm expectations.

Therefore, some justification beyond just history is needed for the inclusion of homosexuality among transgender realities. While the perception of heterosexuals about homosexuals is significant in its own right, we ought fully to reckon with the self-experience and self-identification of gay men and lesbian women. One reason to include homosexuality as a transgendered reality may exist in the developmental backgrounds of homosexuals. Gay men, for example, commonly exhibit gender nonconformity as children and are often labeled 'sissies.' Further, numerous studies of adult gay men suggest that, compared to heterosexual males they do, on average, exhibit greater gender nonconformity. That fewer adults than children show such behavior may be explained by a variety of factors, such as learning to bow to peer pressures to enforce gender conformity.[199] In sum, the significant overlap in gender nonconforming behaviors among homosexuals and others called transgender seems to warrant their inclusion under this broad umbrella, though for any given individual the term may be more or less accurate.

In a similar manner, members of the intersexed community may object to their inclusion. Many, perhaps most intersex individuals grow up with a sense of congruence between their assigned sex and assigned gender. Of course, there have been notable cases where such congruency has not developed; these individuals are indisputably transgendered. The inclusion of the whole group has stemmed less from such individuals than from the general public's willingness to cluster together any and all who do not readily and neatly meet the expected standards for both sex and gender. In other words, if an individual has some anomalous sex situation, that alone is deemed enough to assume a problematic gender situation. Because so many societies strongly pair sex and gender, with the latter dependent on the former, intersexed individuals have long been studied in terms of how societies handle realities along the borders of sex and gender. There seems so much profit to be gained from continuing this practice that for academic purposes the inclusion of intersex as a transgender reality, while often misleading, seems warranted—as long as we understand the context in which it is occurring.

In the wider sense described above, those who crossdress belong to the transgender community because their manner of dress expresses a crossing over from their assigned gender to a different gender. But since, as we have seen, those who crossdress include a wide range of people with sometimes vastly different reasons for doing so, this label has never fit completely comfortably. As we shall see presently, not even crossdressers agree on which label is most descriptively appropriate.

In its narrower sense, who are the 'transgendered'?

Some prefer restricting the scope of the term 'transgender.' In this more limited sense, transgender is applied to a specific group whose distinguishing characteristics separate its members from other groups. In this manner is the word used as to describe a particular subset of sexual minorities in the abbreviation GLBT: Gays, Lesbians, Bisexuals, and Transgendered.

This was the term's original intention. Virginia Prince claims to have coined the terms 'transgenderism' and 'transgenderist' to refer to people who live full-time as members of the opposite sex but without intending sexual reassignment.[200] Prominent theorist Richard Docter prefers to confine the term to refer to those who live for periods of time fully in the identity and role of a member of the opposite sex.[201] Sexologists Bonnie and Vern Bullough follow this usage in their 1997 report of research with 372 adult male crossdressers, of whom they find 11% meet this description.[202]

But today many transsexuals prefer the designation transgendered. They correctly see it as more accurate for their situation. This preference is thought by some to have gained widespread agreement among those who others might call transsexual. Among the advantages of this use is that the term can encompass both pre-operative and post-operative individuals who live in a consistent gender identity and role different from the one they were assigned at birth. Thus the term can include those meant by Virginia Prince as well as those often called transsexual. The disadvantages include failing to distinguish what some see as important differences between the two subgroups thus joined under one term. Others believe that restricting the term transgender in this way unfairly and inaccurately excludes others who have as legitimate a claim. Accordingly, a narrow use may fragment and weaken the collective power possible when various subgroups unite under a term they all can justly embrace.

What about third gender people?

Distinctly 'third gender' people are known at least throughout southern Asia, Africa, and the Americas.[203] But modern Western societies have been particularly resistant to the designation 'third gender.' One consequence of the medicalization of sex, with its tidy bipolar sex-paired-with-gender scheme, is that the very label seems to legitimize something not an option within this cultural framework. Other terms, such as homosexual, intersexed, transvestite, transsexual, and transgender, all can be fit within the cultural bipolar system— we need simply see them as deviations from the norm. Of course, for those thus included, the unfortunate consequences include marginalization, and being seen as abnormal, unnatural, and/or disordered. Further, with the success of

Western societies has come the exporting of their cultural values to other societies, whose members are often all too eager to embrace Western perceptions and biases in the hope of gaining entry into greater prosperity. Accordingly, Western resistance to the idea of third gender people has led in many places to a reframing of perceptions so that such people have been recast under modern Western labels—and increasingly treated according to Western prejudices.

Such decisions carry consequences. What if the Western gender scheme is empirically unjustified? What do we lose by refusing to acknowledge other genders? Anthropologist Will Roscoe remarks, "Third and fourth genders . . . help us to perceive all that is left over when the world has been divided into male and female—the feelings, perceptions, and talents that may be neither."[204] Denying diversity does not make it disappear; it merely removes it from easy reach to enrich ourselves.

Despite socially unfriendly forces, both in non-Western societies and in the West there persist people who experience themselves as not existing at the gender poles. Even in the United States there are people who self-identify as 'third gender.' Little study has been done on such folk, though in a cultural framework that implicitly denies the very idea this must almost certainly be the case. What modest research there is merits special attention and given the controversy over the notion needs to be broached here in our consideration of fundamental terms.

Clinician Ingrid Sell is one professional who has taken self-identified people at their word and sought to understand their life experience. In a study published in 2004, she reports on 30 male and female individuals, ages 29-77. Among her findings concerning their developmental experience are:

❑ Awareness of being differently gendered occurred very early for most (90%) of them, typically by age 5.

❑ Female third gender people experienced less pressure to conform to their assigned gender during childhood.

❑ In adulthood, social pressures to gender conform varied according to gender presentation—those who could more easily 'pass' as a member of their assigned gender experienced less pressure.

❑ Coping with gender pressures and ostracism was met in different ways: self-imposed isolation, taking on leadership roles, projecting a 'don't mess with me' appearance, engaging in creative arts, excelling in school, and using substances.[205]

Sell wisely regards her data in a context larger than just Western culture. She notes how American third gender people have life experiences and characteristics parallel to third gender folk elsewhere in the world. In many places such individuals, precisely because they are situated between the gender poles, are seen as a valuable resource for their insights and abilities to mediate. Such mediation often extends not only to working with the dominant gender groups (i.e., bridging men and women), but also other groups and often between this ordinary world and a sacred world beyond. In this latter regard, third gender people often gain legitimacy in their sacred roles by exhibiting a greater sensitivity to spiritual matters. Sell found among her subjects both that they were very likely to have been called upon to mediate between men and women (77%), and that they were especially likely to have experienced a transcendent spiritual event and/or exhibit paranormal-type abilities (93%). Further consistent with such people's experiences elsewhere in the world, these American third gender people were likely to be healers (43% work in health and helping professions), and to be highly creative and artistic (47% were writers, musicians, or performers; an additional 10% were in other very creative fields). She remarks, "Perhaps, as non-Western cultures recognize, there is indeed an element of spirit or 'calling' involved in our being men, women, or mediators between."[206]

As is true for many persons labeled 'transgender,' the participants in Sell's study showed some ambivalence toward the designation. From our discussion above, we can readily see why—'transgender' is a term with wide possibilities of meaning and application, which means it also carries easy potential for misunderstanding. There is no easy solution to the dilemma posed by our current muddled situation. Time will tell what position on the word will prevail. For the present, for this work, the wider and more general sense of the term will be used. My reason is principally for the sake of clarity: the various subgroups are typically distinguished in the literature and since the material in this book relies on that literature those distinctions are preserved.

Do crossdressers regard themselves as 'transgendered'?

While most folk don't like being labeled—including those who crossdress—they also recognize a need, even desirability, for an accurate descriptor to name the groups they belong to, whether 'Protestant' or 'Catholic' among Christians, 'Democrat' or 'Republican' among politicians, or 'heterosexual,' 'homosexual,' or 'bisexual' when sexual orientation is being discussed. The best labels express an affiliation someone voluntary selects. But lacking that, many still cling to them because they offer some sense of belonging—or at least of not being alone—and carry some promise of explanatory power.

Thus many crossdressers confess to a sense of relief in first encountering the term 'transvestite.' The word, they say, tells them there are others like themselves—and that reduces somewhat the sense of alienation and anxiety experienced in doing what the culture says is deviant. Some labels—like 'transvestite' or, for that matter, 'crossdresser')—carry negative connotations for some people, but they are hard to escape. In a 1999 online survey, over 1,000 male crossdressers addressed this problem of what name they preferred for this group. The largest number preferred the simple descriptor 'crossdresser' (43%). Less than one-fifth (19%) preferred 'transgendered,' and even fewer preferred 'transvestite' (11%).[207]

While some crossdressers identify with the term 'transgendered' (or 'transgendered person'), others prefer 'trans person' or 'gender-variant person.' Alternative terms have proliferated. Today some individuals under the transgender umbrella use one or more of the following: 'gender-bender,' 'gender outlaw,' 'gender trash,' or 'gender queer,' among many others.[208] To attempt using a wide number of variants in this work would invite more confusion than understanding, so we shall use transgender, transvestite, and transsexual—in each instance seeking to make the meaning clear in context.

The answer to the question, 'What's in a name?' is—much power. Though terms like 'crossdresser,' 'transvestite,' and 'transgendered' all are descriptive in nature, it is their connotations rather than their denotations that figure in how we regard those of us who adopt—or are labeled—with such terms. Only time will tell whether the current connotations persist or are gradually replaced by others. At present, those connotations are as diverse as the groups that use them, ranging from expressions of derision to ones of pride.

Finally, there is another dimension to such naming that must be considered. Is transgender a gendered reality independent of masculine and feminine? Though the debate is by no means settled, not all participants in it consider that terms like 'transgender' or 'third gender' are appropriate as descriptors of a separate gendered reality. For example, Ana Mariella Bacigalupo, an anthropologist who has focused on the Mapuche people indigenous to Southern Chile, contends that such words and the very notion of 'third gender' draw upon Western gender binarism and reinforce that culture's idea that sex and gender are naturally paired so that gender, like sex, becomes an attribute regarded as fixed. In Bacigalupo's eyes, this denies the culturally variable and context specific nature of the realities Westerners term 'transgender.'[209]

While culture is certainly a powerful force, shaping gender expressions as well as the social vehicles they inhabit, there are good reasons not to ignore transcultural features. Gender, as we have seen, is not completely independent of sexed bodies. Even in cultures where gender is constructed in terms of social roles, those social roles themselves depend in part on the differences in male and female bodies. In every culture there is recognition of male and female bodies—and bodies not clearly either. In every culture there is also recognition, however grudging, of gender presentations not clearly masculine or feminine. Some global descriptor parallel in utility to masculine and feminine seems desirable, even if separate transgendered realities within specific societies are referred to by particular names—a practice we shall also pursue. At present, for all its limitations, 'transgender' is such a term. In one sense, then, it will be used throughout this work as a global descriptor for gender presentations separate from masculinity and femininity, though each of these may be used for convenience to describe particular features in ways understandable to those of us who live in a two-and-only-two gender system.

Question Set 3:

What causes crossdressing and trans-gender realities?

In the late 1980s, Richard Docter introduced his own theory about cross-dressers by stating, " I agree with other gender researchers . . . who have con-cluded that the causes of transvestism and transsexualism remain largely un-known."[210] As of this writing the situation remains the same. But that does not mean there is any lack of hypotheses about the cause of these and other kinds of crossdressing. Inevitably, virtually all scholars will conclude that completely separating Nature from Nurture is impossible and that some complex interac-tion occurs between them to provide the causal framework for crossdressing. In all likelihood, the proportion of influence will prove to vary from one situation to another, or at least from one kind of crossdressing to another.

With the caveat that no final answer is yet possible, some of the variety of hypotheses about the cause of crossdressing can be examined. In the answers to the next few questions a variety of supposed causal factors are investigated. While it is artificial to do so, my treatment looks at Nature and Nurture sepa-rately. I begin our tour with biological explanations, which appear to have gained ascendancy in the current discussion.

Question Set 3:

What causes cross-dressing and trans-gender realities?

Q. 21

Is a transgender reality like crossdressing 'natural'?

The Short Answer. If one embraces the notion that *Natura non facit salut* ('Nature makes no leaps'), then gradations between male and female are expectable and acceptable, as are those between masculine and feminine. Such a notion presupposes a biological foundation generating diversity across a range of natural realities. Certainly, the sheer persistence of transgender realities through history and their appearance across cultures suggests a biological component, perhaps even origin. Otherwise we should expect a more significant variation in incidence and display across cultures and across time than we actually encounter, as well as a sizable number of cultures where transgender realities are absent. Such does not appear to be true. So, even if a behavior like crossdressing is learned, it seems probable that some predisposing biological factors (e.g., genetic influences or physiological processes) are at work. Virtually from the beginning of the modern scientific effort to understand it, biology has been considered as a force to be reckoned with in grappling with the origin of transgender realities, including crossdressing.[211] In order to answer the question of how Nature is involved a number of lines of potential evidence must be examined. These include discovering whether transgender realities (including crossdressing) occur in other species and whether that has any bearing on human behavior. It also requires looking at possible evolutionary and genetic factors. Finally, it means investigating human biology. All these sources suggest the possibility that transgender realities like crossdressing are, in some sense, 'natural.'

The Longer Answer. One of the enduring debates about transgender realities is whether ultimately they derive from biological origins (Nature) or environmental ones (Nurture). Among transgender people there is a common sense that their experiential reality, which they typically become aware of at an early age, is natural and rooted in biology. In this vein, anthropologist Jason Cromwell writes, "However much they may pass, transpeople, whether they identify as trans or not, are always aware of their transness—an awareness situated in their bodies."[212] In this answer we shall explore possible lines of reasoning and evidence suggestive of biological origin for transgender realities.

One broad possibility is that transgender realities are an aspect of something inherent to being human. Psychoanalyst Lawrence Kubie, in 1974 recalling remarks he made in 1932, observes that his comments then concerning transvestism in a 15 year old girl have only garnered more evidence over the years for a basic thesis: crossdressing reflects a human drive to become both sexes. Kubie suggests that "latent and unconscious transvestite tendencies might well be more widespread than is generally realized, and this may be a manifestation of impulses which might be 'more or less universal' . . . ."[213] Of course, ideas about the 'bisexual' nature of human beings can be found in Freud, and in Jung, and indeed in various forms before them. But Kubie's specific suggestion about crossdressing adds a new dimension.

Is crossdressing 'natural'—something part of the essence of humanity?

Since at least the time of the formation of the Hippocratic Corpus,[214] people have speculated about a biological origin—or at least contribution—to gender and to transgender realities among people. In modern times evolutionary psychologists have insisted that "an evolutionary account of gender roles does not deny socialization or cognitive influences on human behavior, but it does assume that human thought and human learning unfold within a wider biological context."[215] Contemporary speculations have looked both to the psychophysiology of transgendered people and to the wider world of Nature. We shall examine each path, beginning with the latter.

One way to investigate any proposed naturalness to transgender realities is to investigate whether similar things occur in nonhuman animal species. Some transgender realities, such as intersex conditions and homosexuality, have been observed and documented in a variety of nonhuman species. Matters of gender presentation have received less attention as they pose different difficulties. For example, how can we talk about crossdressing in animals? To do this requires considering human use of clothing as a kind of behavior for which at least rough parallels occur in nature. But just such parallels may exist. To get started we need to return once more to sorting out the issues of sex and gender.

Do other animals crossdress?

Transgender Realities in Nature

Some transgender realities, such as homosexuality, are well-known in Nature.[216] As yet, unfortunately, they remain relatively unacknowledged by human beings, including many scientists. However, evidence continues to mount for greater sexual and gender diversity in Nature than typically recognized. At the forefront of presenting this evidence is well-respected Stanford biologist Joan Roughgarden. In her *Evolution's Rainbow*, Roughgarden uses the metaphor of the rainbow to discuss natural variability. So profoundly robust is variation in Nature that, as she puts it, "biological rainbows" frustrate our scientific efforts to catalogue living beings; "nature abhors a category."[217]

Yet Roughgarden knows that in the midst of diversity occur likenesses that invite grouping; so we have identified species. What, though, do we do about the diversity *within* species? Are some variations flaws? This question is the critical one—and evolutionary biologists are divided on it. Some regard intraspecies variability as merely reflecting a norm and imperfect deviations ('mistakes') ranged around it. Others believe such variability a natural good in its own right. The judgment made on this matter has many ramifications, including how apparent sexual and gender diversity will be interpreted and evaluated.

Roughgarden herself has a rich appreciation for the rainbow and documents copiously the natural variability in sex and gender. With respect to the former, she points out that in Nature most bodies make both eggs and sperm, either at the same time or at different times during their lives, and thus are not neatly classifiable as 'male' or 'female.'[218] In fact, even in species where individuals always and only make eggs (unambiguously female) or sperm (unambiguously male), multiple forms of males and females are possible.[219] With regard to gender a similar situation exists. There are species with multiple genders. Even within species where there are only two types of sexed bodies there can be more than two genders.[220] Further, something roughly analogous to transgender is found among nonhuman species where 'masculine females' and 'feminine males' can be found, and where individuals are known to change gender as they age.[221]

Animal Transvestism

Still, even granting all that, the idea of crossdressing animals probably seems absurd on the face of it. Unless clothed by human beings, animals do not wear clothes. But if crossdressing in humans involves one sex taking on the appearance of the other, then 'crossdressing' does occur in nature. *Sexual mimicry* in other species is well documented and occasionally referred to as 'crossdressing' or 'transvestism.' Biologist Bruce Bagemihl contends, "Transvestism is widespread in the animal kingdom and takes a variety of forms."[222] Bagemihl divides such transvestism into two kinds: *physical* (or morphological) and *behavioral*. Similarly, other scientists, writing in the prestigious journal *Nature* remark, "One well-documented alternative male reproductive pattern is 'female mimicry,' whereby males assume a female-like morphology or mimic female behavior patterns. In some species males mimic both female morphology and behavior."[223]

Do not be misled by this comment to think that such animal transvestism is confined to males. Examples of mimicry are found in a variety of species, and among both males and females. In morphological, or physical, transvestism the sexual mimicry ('crossdressing'), says Bagemihl, can entail "almost total physical resemblance between males and females, or mimicry of only certain primary or secondary sexual characteristics." When it comes to behavioral transvestism, continues Bagemihl, "an animal of one sex acts in a way that is characteristic of members of the opposite sex of that species—often fooling members of their own species."[224]

Among 'crossdressing' insects are sweat bees,[225] butterflies,[226] beetles,[227] and fruit flies.[228] The phenomenon has been observed in fish,[229] birds,[230] reptiles,[231] and mammals.[232] Mimicry of the opposite sex fulfils important purposes, advantaging the individual who practices it.[233] For example, Bagemihl cites the case of male terns who mimic female food-begging patterns to steal food from other males—a behavioral transvestism which confers a clear survival advantage.[234] A closer examination of some other instances of how mimicry functions in various species may make the notion that sexual mimicry among humans is 'natural' more plausible.

One of the best-studied examples of animal 'crossdressing' behavior—where an individual of one sex masquerades as the opposite sex—is the red-sided garter snake (*Thamnophis sirtalis parietalis*). In this species some males actually emit a pheromone that deceives other males into perceiving them as females. Such male snakes have been dubbed 'she-males' (a term also sometimes used for some human male crossdressers). The behavior is not homosexual as these 'she-males' mate with females. In fact, compared to 'normal' males, the 'she-males' are far more successful in mating. Thus, this 'crossdressing' behavior apparently demonstrates sexual selection at work, conferring a reproductive advantage to such males.[235]

More recently, an alternative explanation for this behavior has been advanced. Researchers Bob Mason and Rick Shine studied red-sided garter snakes as they emerged from winter hibernation and began seeking mating opportunities. Mason and Shine find that, rather than increased sexual success, the behavior maximizes survival. By attracting other males, who swarm around them, the 'she-male' garter snakes acquire both warmth and protection from predators. Thus, the behavior reflects natural selection for survival rather than sexual selection for reproductive advantage.[236]

Of course, some may object that such an example is far removed from humanity. A more valued instance might be obtained from among mammals. In Africa's Serengeti, the spotted hyena may afford such an example. In this female-dominated society, female hyenas possess sexual organs remarkably resembling those of males. The clitoris looks like a penis. A swollen clitoris functions as a ritualized greeting signaling submission and is thus an important mechanism for reducing aggression by other, dominant females. This social function thus utilizes a sexual signal that has been converted for non-sexual communication.[237]

Once more objection may be raised that such a species is too far removed from the human species to be very instructive. So let us turn to primates. More than 30 years ago, zoologist John Hurrell Crook noted that just as male mimicry of female genitalia can be found among Old World monkeys (*Cercopithecoidea*), so female mimicry of male genitalia can be found among some New World monkeys (*Ceboids*).[238] Primatologist Andreas Paul lists female mimicry as an alternative mating tactic in mate competition.[239] And ethologist Wolfgang Wickler observes that among primates both sexes may utilize sexual signals 'emancipated' from their original context and now used for social greeting.[240]

Clearly, then, animal mimicry presents something that can be argued to be analogous to human crossdressing. Yet drawing parallels between animal and human behavior is always fraught with difficulty and controversy. So what are we to make of these examples? To help us answer that we need to turn to evolutionary psychology.

What are some evolutionary factors perhaps involved in crossdressing?

Sexual Mimicry and Human Behavior

Evolutionary psychology seeks explanations for human behavior in the mechanisms of evolution. To reason out cause we examine consequence, or as an evolutionary psychologist might put it, "from an evolutionary perspective, the first questions one asks about a physical or behavioral feature is: What is its function?"[241] The functions favored by evolution include basic natural processes such as natural selection and sexual selection—mechanisms seen above to be at work in 'crossdressing' animal species. Before trying to view human crossdressing as rooted in evolutionary processes, let us briefly review. Sexual mimicry in nature often is used to confer reproductive advantage to an individual and is thus an aspect of sexual selection. But as seen in our examples, at least in some instances, mimicry of the opposite sex apparently occurs for nonsexual purposes. The advantage may be survival, as in the case of the garter snake, or reduction of same-sex aggression, as in the case of the hyena. In other instances, mimicry functions to reduce aggression from competing males.[242]

If sexual mimicry among other species is so common, then perhaps such behavior among human beings is less surprising. If such mimicry among other species can fulfill different purposes, then perhaps it is not so far fetched to think something similar is happening among human beings. If animal 'crossdressing' is sometimes used for social signaling rather than reproductive advantage, perhaps at least some crossdressing men and women also pursue the behavior for nonsexual reasons. There is no compelling reason not to imagine such possibilities. But the question remains: if human crossdressing can be understood in an evolutionary context, what advantage does it procure for the individual practicing it?

There may be a range of possible advantages, some of which pertain to some crossdressers and different advantages to other crossdressers. For example, there may be a reproductive advantage for some crossdressing males who thereby gain access to women's company in social environments where the sexes are sharply segregated. Or, there may be a reproductive advantage gained in cultures like our own where men hide their crossdressing from prospective mates, yet demonstrate transgender behavior that diminishes their aggression and enhances their sensitivity such that some women are more drawn to them than to aggressive males. Or, the gain may come from lowering the aggression of other male competitors, who do not see the 'feminine' male as a threat.[243]

There may be advantages only indirectly related to reproductive advantage, if at all. For example, crossdressing females may find the behavior allows them to escape the aggression of males if they can successfully 'pass' as male. Or crossdressing by either sex may serve as one of nature's ways to keep the sexes from too great a distance from each other; nature prefers to move incrementally and hedge her bets for survival through diversity. In this case, the advantage to the individual lies in finding a particular environment where there is a good fit between self-expression and social acceptance. Some cultures reserve a place of tolerance, even esteem, for the transgendered, such as in work niches (e.g. entertainment, religious roles, or the sex trade), or in geographical places (e.g., large cities). In sum, a number of possible advantages can be conceived for sex/gender mimicry among humans, of which crossdressing occupies an instrumental but not exclusive place.

Crossdressing as Attachment Substitute

Another evolved biological system important to human beings is attachment. Some crossdressing may be explained by attachment theory. This theory, first formulated by John Bowlby, who drew both upon ethology and object relations theory, posits attachment as a biologically rooted evolutionary system.[244] In attachment we seek to attain and then maintain proximity to those we perceive (often unconsciously) as better able to cope than we are. Attachment theory has proven successful at explaining many aspects of human relational behavior. It is applicable to some crossdressing.

There are instances where crossdressing apparently has developed in response to the loss or absence of a loved one. Much like psychiatrist Donald Winnicott's 'transitional object' functions for children,[245] the donning of the loved one's clothes seems to function for some adults as a symbolic substitute for a significant other. There have been anecdotal reports of elderly men crossdressing in the spouse's clothes after her death.[246] Literature also reports instances where women have donned the absent lover's clothing as a way of feeling close.[247] Shakespeare may have had something like this in mind in *Twelfth Night* when Viola, believing her twin brother Sebastian to be dead, crossdresses.[248] Indeed, this notion has even been presented in various television commercials.[249] Perhaps in some way crossdressing engages the attachment biology and reduces the distress caused by absence or loss.

Crossdressing as Biologically Predisposed Environmental Response

There may be other ways in which crossdressing is at least partly rooted in evolutionary biology. Adaptation—'fitting' one's environment—is a matter of a complex reciprocal interaction between body and environment. Basic to this interaction is our ability to receive sensory input, sort and interpret it, and respond adaptively. Our sense of touch, for example, is intrinsic to our physical survival and to our psychological well-being. Touch facilitates human bonding and, as we have seen with attachment biology, transitional objects—tactile substitutes for absent human figures—are important in development. Many of us remember fondly a favorite stuffed animal or soft blanket which brought to us feelings of safety, warmth, and a sense of the comforting presence of a parent.

However, we vary temperamentally in our degree of sensitivity to stimuli. Hypersensitive tactile responsiveness may produce negative feelings and reactions in some of us when we are exposed to certain touch sensations that others manage without a second thought.[250] Perhaps a contributing factor in some male children preferring feminine articles of clothing is a biological predisposition toward their softer textures coupled with an aversion to the harsher touch of masculine apparel. Sidney Chu, a specialist on so-called 'tactile defensiveness' in children notes specifically that some children may avoid rough textures in clothing and at the same time express an unusual preference for softer styles and textures.[251] Perhaps some children initially gravitate toward crossdressing because of a biologically-rooted preference for the softer tactile stimulation of feminine apparel. This material may also add warm, comforting feelings associated with the maternal presence they represent.

While I know of no research explicitly investigating this possibility, there is indirect evidence along two lines. First, some scientific research has noted instances consistent with the reasoning just outlined. Patricia Gail Williams, Anna Mary Allard and Lonnie Sears observe that it is not uncommon in the literature on autism for reference to be made concerning gender crossing behavior. They present a case study of two young boys diagnosed with autism who exhibited preoccupation with feminine gender-stereotyped activities and objects.[252] Subsequent to this report other research has investigated the coincidence of these kinds of developmental disorders with transgender realities.

The second line of evidence resides in psychological testing done with self-identified crossdressers (see the answer to Q. 27). That research finds a tendency toward behavioral patterns that may be rooted at least in part by a temperamentally driven avoidance of over stimulation from the environment. A highly reactive central nervous system and/or hypersensitive tactile responsiveness may contribute to the pattern of choices that produce crossdressing behavior in some individuals. (This conclusion also fits well within the matters we found in answering Q. 2.)

Crossdressing as Biological 'Play'

Although looking at nature invites some consideration of whether cross-dressing might be an evolved characteristic, it doesn't automatically suggest what its function might be. Can evolutionary psychology offer any other clues as to why this kind of behavior may have been adopted and still persists? Psychologist Richard Smith suggests that both homosexual and transvestite behaviors can be regarded as biological 'play' rather than as pathology. In the same way that activities like painting have no apparent survival value, yet are valued all the same, crossdressing does not have to be seen as indicating a psychological illness.[253] It may be pursued simply for its pleasurable qualities.

But I doubt this explanation will prove satisfactory to many people, especially crossdressers who find something more serious and substantial than 'play' transpiring in their lives because of crossdressing. Though I would argue that few things are more serious than play, I do think more consideration might be given to whether a human parallel exists to any of the functions sexual mimicry is seen to play in other species. Could it be, as speculated above, that crossdressing is behavior designed to gain access to sexual partners—an instance of sexual selection? Or could its function sometimes be an attempt to reduce aggression by others? Can human crossdressing be understood as an evolved communication system? Or is the notion that human crossdressing constitutes a form of sexual mimicry at all like what is found among other species too fantastic to imagine?

Crossdressing and Imprinting

One effort to find a human parallel to behavior in other species is the attempt by British ethologist Glenn Wilson to see in the development of fetishistic behavior an example of an imprinting-like process in humans. Imprinting is biologically programmed learning that occurs during critical periods of development. Perhaps the origin of crossdressing lies in such a process. According to this hypothesis, male infants are biologically predisposed to associate particular sights with genital arousal. What an infant experiences helps build associations that will persist lifelong. If a male infant sees unclothed female parts such as the breasts, he is likely to associate such sights with pleasurable arousal and establish a pattern that will regulate later sexual associations, such as arousal to the buttocks and genitals of females. If, on the other hand, at a critical time in development the infant is instead exposed to objects related to his mother's body, such as articles of clothing, but not her body itself, a different arousal pattern may be established. In this instance, articles of female clothing stand in (i.e., are 'fetishes') for her body. Once established, these learned associations prove very resistant to extinction.[254]

Are there genetic indicators?

Alongside evolution, genetics is an essential potential contributor requiring examination when considering any 'natural' basis for transgender realities, including crossdressing. Genetic contributions to sexual behavior seem a logical deduction given the crucial role played generally by genes. But more than a half century ago, psychiatrist George Wiedeman warned that no specific genotype can be assumed to produce a behavior such as crossdressing.[255] The caution is as applicable today, despite the attractiveness of searching for genetic factors.

Demonstrating the nature of a hypothesized contribution, especially in human beings, can be difficult. Nevertheless, some research has established specific genetic contributions to sexual characteristics and behaviors in mammalian species such as rats or mice. For example, in a study hailed as a landmark, researchers reported in 2003 evidence for 54 genes involved in differential sex expression, with at least 7 murine (mice) genes displaying differential expression before any hormonal gonadal influence, which typically has been regarded as the most decisive factor on the developing brain.[256] Other research has substantiated that sex chromosome genes do, in fact, contribute directly to the formation of sex differences in the brain.[257] These differences have been investigated in matters such as intersexed conditions, homosexuality and transsexualism. To a far more limited extent, they also have been explored with reference to heterosexual crossdressing.

Intersex and Genetic Evidence

Intersexed conditions, broadly speaking, result from genetic variability from a karyotype (complete chromosomal picture) other than 46, XX (generic female) or 46, XY (generic male), occurring in perhaps 1-of-500 individuals, or from a variant genetic condition in a 46, XX or 46, XY karyotype. An instance of the former situation is found in Klinefelter Syndrome, where the karyotype is 47, XXY. The additional X chromosome may yield any number of effects, most mild, with the most common being undersized testes. An example of the later situation is found in androgen insensitivity syndrome (AIS), where the karyotype 46, XY—typically associated with normal male sexual development—yields a generally female genitalia presentation. AIS is not a deviation from the expected 'normal' karyotype, but it is an abnormal presentation. AIS results from a genetic variation in the X chromosome and is heritable. These examples, alongside others, result in anatomical variations of a greater or lesser degree—and that is where cultural values in a sex and gender dichotomous society enter in.

Regardless of sex chromosomes, the human embryo develops along the same path until the seventh week of gestation. From this common template external genitalia are differentiated such that there is a range of possible mixed presentations alongside those that look fully male or completely female. All of these possibilities are prompted and mediated by genetic factors. For example, the external genitalia may look essentially female, but with a large clitoris. On the other hand, the genitalia may look basically male, although the penis is unusually small. In some instances there is a mixed presentation of male and female characteristics, giving rise to the labels 'pseudo-hermaphrodite' and, when the sex characteristics seem equally balanced between male and female, 'true hermaphrodite.' These varying presentations, all keyed by genetic triggers and triggered by endocrine releases, result in a wide range of intersexed conditions. Typically, when external manifestations do not meet culturally accepted standards for 'maleness' or 'femaleness' medical interventions are made to bring the presentation into conformity, and gender assignment is made to match the sex presentation, irrespective of the possible long-term psychological consequences (cf. the answer to Q. 5).[258]

Our culture strongly favors a pairing of masculine gender identity with male genetic sex and feminine gender identity with female genetic sex—despite the fact genetic testing is seldom done; instead, reliance is made on visual inspection of genitalia to determine it. Put another way, there is a cultural expectation that gender differentiation will follow predictably from sexual differentiation: masculinity will follow maleness and femininity will follow femaleness. Of course, this occurs often enough to reinforce the cultural bias and, for many, lend it the weight of being 'natural.' But as John Bancroft, director of the Kinsey Institute, points out, sexual differentiation can lead to intersex conditions and gender differentiation in this population can be instructive. "The fact that some intersex individuals can be brought up successfully in the gender which best matches their degree of gender differentiation rather than their sex chromosome constitution indicates that there is a degree of plasticity in this process."[259] Genetic sex is *not* gender destiny.

Homosexuality and Genetic Evidence

Homosexuality also has been researched with regard to genetic roots. Probably the best known and most widely remarked upon has been the study led by Dean Hamer, based on data from the families of more than a hundred homosexual males. That study implicates a particular stretch along the X chromosome (inherited from the mother) designated the Xq28 region.[260] Since then a number of studies have yielded inconsistent results. A notable study led by Brian Mustanski, published in 2005, was a sweeping investigation involving 456 individuals from 146 families with two or more gay brothers. It directed attention for further research to three new areas of genetic interest outside the X chromosome: 7q36, 8p12, and 10q26. This study furnished further evidence of the difficulty in establishing the contribution of individual genes to a characteristic undoubtedly involving multiple regions of DNA for its development and expression.[261] Presently, a growing number of lines of evidence suggest a genetic component.[262]

Transsexualism and Genetic Evidence

There also exists relevant research with reference to transsexualism. Some speculation exists of possible ties between intersexed conditions and some instances of transgender, especially transsexualism.[263] For example, congenital adrenal hyperplasia (CAH), the most common cause of intersexed conditions among those bearing XX chromosomes, results in the adrenal glands producing an androgen precursor rather than cortisone. This then leads to virilization anatomically (e.g., a large clitoris and/or labia that resemble scrotum), and behaviorally (e.g., tomboy behavior). CAH has in some instances been linked to female-to-male (FtM) transsexualism.[264]

Richard Green points out that, accepting the usually cited prevalence rates for transsexualism (1-in-10,000 males; 1-in-30,000 females), the odds for, say, two male siblings both being transsexual—assuming random selection—are 1-in-100,000,000; the chance co-occurrence in both parent and child is also highly improbable. Yet, in research reported in 2000, he found 10 such pairs from a patient pool of about 1500 individuals.[265] This kind of finding certainly invites reasoning that some genetic component is involved, especially when environmental hypotheses such as role-modeling have been ruled out, as was the case among Green's parent-child pairs.

Familial incidence is used in testing ideas about whether a genetic component exists of a behavior. Most usually, data comes from case studies. Researcher Neil Buhrich, for example, presents a case study where the familial situation suggests a 'constitutional' factor at play. The case involves a father and son, both heterosexual, and each engaged in crossdressing. But the son is unaware of his father's crossdressing. Moreover, in neither situation can Buhrich find environmental factors to explain the adoption of this behavior.[266] Another case study examines the family history of a 13-year-old boy diagnosed with Gender Identity Disorder (GID), who has two crossdressing uncles on his mother's side.[267] Another study, reported in 1985, offers the first documented case of transsexualism in sisters. The sisters are independently diagnosed. No likely environmental explanation for their transsexualism is found for either sister, raising the suspicion that other factors are at play.[268] Though sorting out the shared environmental influence of their family-of-origin from any presumed genetic/biological factors is probably impossible, the case affords an intriguing possibility.

Richard Green's above-mentioned report offers 10 sets of siblings or parent-child pairs where there is co-occurrence of 'gender dysphoria,' either as transsexualism (GID), or as GID with transvestism. The ten cases cover a range of relationships (e.g., twins and non-twins, same sex sibling pairs and opposite sex sibling pairs, father and son, father and daughter), and combinations (e.g., transvestic parent and transsexual child, sibling sets of GID). Such familial patterns, given the unlikely possibility of chance occurrence, suggest a genetic component may be involved.[269]

But not all investigators concur. Croughan and associates, utilizing interviews with 70 adult male crossdressers, conclude based on family histories that the data does not support seeing crossdressing as a familial disorder. They find just 4% of their subjects reporting a first-degree family member who is also known to have crossdressed.[270] Like so many other things, this matter remains unresolved.

Is there evidence in human brain anatomy studies?

Various explanations also have been proposed for crossdressing from evidence of anatomical and/or physiological differences in the brain. Here we examine anatomical differences.

Are the brains of crossdressers anatomically different from those of noncrossdressers? The question is intriguing, but not easy to investigate. To do the kind of close inspection desirable requires post mortem examination. In the mid-1990s, a team of Dutch researchers reported such a study in the pages of the prestigious journal *Nature*. Their groundbreaking work looks closely at an area in the brain—the central subdivision of the bed nucleus of the stria terminalis (BSTc) in the hypothalamus—known to be essential for sexual behavior. The volume of this area is larger in men than in women; in male-to-female (MtF) transsexuals this area is female-sized. The authors write, "Our study is the first to show a female brain structure in genetically male transsexuals and supports the hypothesis that gender identity develops as a result of an interaction between the developing brain and sex hormones."[271]

The researchers were able to collect their data from six MtF transsexuals over a span of 11 years. They sought a portion of the brain that meets two important characteristics: it is sexually dimorphic (meaning it varies between males and females), and it is not influenced by sexual orientation. Comparative studies with other mammals (i.e., rats) suggested the BSTc was a good place to look. Sure enough, it met both criteria they needed: the BSTc volume in heterosexual males turns out to be on average 44% larger than in heterosexual females; the volume in homosexual men is comparable to that in heterosexual men, but significantly larger than in heterosexual females. There is no correlation between BSTc size and sexual orientation among the MtF transsexuals.

In MtF transsexuals, the volume of the BSTc is not statistically significantly different from that of heterosexual females. This anatomical difference is significant because of the implications for physiological functioning. The BST presumably holds an important place in behaviors related to masculinity. In investigating possible explanations for what they observe, the researchers conclude that the small size of the BSTc in MtF transsexuals cannot be explained by differences in adult sex hormone levels. Rather, it appears this area's volume is established by the effect of sex hormones during prenatal development.[272]

At the beginning of the 21st century, another team reported findings concerning neural organization in the brain of transsexuals.[273] Neurons are brain nerve cells that communicate messages by means of chemical messengers. The kind of neurons investigated in this study are called somatostatin neurons because they release somatostatin (SOM), an important hormone used to regulate other hormones by inhibiting their release. The SOM neurons examined in this research are found in the same region of the hypothalamus as studied in the earlier research reported above—the BSTc.

The researchers studied the somatostatin-expressing neurons of the BSTc in 42 brains of deceased patients; 26 of these also had been used in the earlier study discussed above. The subjects include roughly equal numbers of presumed heterosexual males and females, and homosexual males, as well as six MtF transsexuals and one FtM transsexual. After carefully ruling out a number of possible confounding factors, the team finds a number of statistically significant results. First, the number of SOM neurons in the BSTc of heterosexual males is 71% higher than in heterosexual females. Second, the number of SOM neurons in heterosexual and homosexual men is comparable. Third, and most significant for our understanding, the number of SOM neurons in MtF transsexuals is similar to that of heterosexual females while being 40% less than in heterosexual males; the one FtM subject has SOM neuron numbers "clearly in the male range."[274]

The researchers note that these observed differences exist independent of sexual orientation. Their analysis argues against the idea raised by some that the difference in neuron numbers results from changes in sex hormone levels during adulthood. Rather, this work argues for the establishment of these neuronal differences earlier in development. Pointing to other studies, they suggest the influence of perinatal exposure to androgens (male sex hormones) as instrumental in the organizing of the development of the BSTc and its SOM neurons. They also remark that "a direct action of genetic factors" should not be ruled out.[275]

Both studies above lead us to more specific attention to the role of hormones.

Is there evidence in human physiology studies?

Hormonal Factors

The highly influential sexologist John Money once admitted, "There is a possibility that, heterosexualism, bisexualism, and homosexualism—maybe transsexualism and transvestism also—are to some degree determined in a rather direct way by the amount of androgenic influence on the brain in prenatal life."[276]

This was not a new idea even then. Endocrinologist Harry Benjamin was contemplating the biological contributions to transsexualism in the 1950s and speculates on genetic and hormonal influences in his 1966 landmark study *The Transsexual Phenomenon*.[277] In 1971, the French researcher Philbert, building on studies from the late 1960s, observes that depriving the developing male of androgen makes possible an expression of female-type behavior during adulthood. Philbert notes, however, that the presence of female hormones neonatally does not appear to be needed for this later feminine expression. Moreover, he points out that transsexual males do not respond to high doses of male hormone administered during adulthood. Putting these matters together produces his conclusion: "Female psychosexual differentiation in transsexualism could be a passive spontaneous phenomenon due to the early relative lack of the masculizing principle—testosterone."[278]

In Money's own theoretical framework, as set forth later in his *Gay, Straight, and In-Between: The Sexology of Erotic Attraction,* he proposes that sexual orientation and gender identity/role are formed out of an interaction of Nature/Nurture. A biological foundation provides predispositions activated by environmental factors during periods of critical sensitivity in development. Or, as he summarized it, the interaction is among "nature/critical period/nurture."[279]

In the decades since Money's admission growing evidence suggests that he was correct about an important role for hormones in prenatal development related to sex and gender development. We already noted that until the seventh week of development, the male and female embryo are visibly undifferentiated sexually. Genetic coding then prompts the development of either testes or ovaries. This gonadal sex then translates into a phenotypic sex as 'male' or 'female.' Masculinization-producing male external genitalia requires the operation of three hormones: testosterone, its metabolite dihydrotestosterone, and antimullerian hormone. Both the seventh and fourteenth weeks are periods of critical sensitivity; males exposed to too much or too little of a hormone may experience a larger or smaller effect, with some subtle consequences perhaps not emerging until much later. Irregularities in any of the processes described above can prompt unusual sexual development, which may display itself in one or more ways, from a chromosomal level (e.g., intersexed conditions, discussed above), to a gonadal level, to the phenotypic level.

A variety of brain chemicals are known to be involved in sexual behavior, such as the neuropeptides corticotropin-releasing hormone (CRH), and thyroid-releasing hormone (TRH), and especially gonadotropin-releasing hormone (GRH).[280] One contemporary researcher, psychologist Geert De Vries, notes that hormones produced by the gonads (i.e., testes and ovaries) are important throughout life. In our early development they help establish whether we will exhibit behaviors more typical of a male or of a female; later in life they help regulate our sexual behavior. Gonadal hormones can exert strong control over hormones that are sexually dimorphic (meaning they differ significantly in male and female brains). Vasopressin, for instance, is a sexually dimorphic hormone implicated in aggressive behavior: males have twice the number of neurons producing it as do females. This hormone is regulated by gonadal hormones.[281]

In a review of nineteen studies on the behavioral effects of prenatal exposure to hormones, a team led by June Reinisch (former director of the Kinsey Institute) reports that such exposure can play a profound role. Concentrating on individuals whose prenatal hormonal environments were atypical, it becomes clear that various hormones have specific effects. For example, prenatal exposure to an androgen-based synthetic hormone exerts a masculinizing and/or defeminizing influence on behavioral development. On the other hand, prenatal exposure to progesterone (a naturally occurring female hormone), or progestin (a synthetic female hormone) has a feminizing and/or demasculinizing influence, especially on females.[282]

In addition to more general reviews, some studies have examined specific hormones and/or conditions. For example, a 1992 study speculates that a physiological chain rooted in a brain anatomical difference may be important in understanding a female-type pattern of hormone secretion observed in MtF transsexuals. This chain begins with an area of the anterior hypothalamic nuclei that have been linked to male sexual orientation. The neuronal density in this area is greater in heterosexual males. This region may alter gonadotropin releasing hormone (GnRH) function, leading to a pattern of gonadotropin hormone secretion more like that found in females.[283]

One hormone of particular interest has been luteinizing hormone (LH). A 1982 report looks at the possible relation between LH and transsexualism. The research compares ten different aspects of hypothalamic and pituitary function in 13 MtF transsexuals and 7 heterosexual males. The data collected finds a high-frequency, high-amplitude pulsatile secretion of pituitary LH in MtF transsexuals. The researchers suggest that transsexualism perhaps is related to a difference in the way LH is secreted.[284] The following year, a team of researchers reports that MtF transsexuals with a homosexual orientation, after estrogen stimulation, show a rise in LH—just as do genetic females.[285] In 1995 another examination of LH, this time in 9 MtF transsexuals, finds that a decrease in LH pulse frequency may be a marker for transsexualism. At the same time, the researchers note that the subjects also show normal testosterone levels, an indication that the subjects might be maintaining normal qualitative LH secretion.[286]

Some speculation has focused on the possible role of aromatase, an enzyme that converts the 'male' hormone testosterone into estradiol, a potent estrogen. Aromatase inhibition is part of the hormonal treatment of female transsexual patients.[287] When aromatase is inhibited in male rats, their sexual behavior is feminized. In human males aromatase dysregulation may also be implicated in transgender realities. Aromatase excess in human males slows pubertal maturation and prompts the development of larger than normal breasts (gynecomastia). Physician Robert Jasiniski suggests that boys born with gynecomastia may prove more likely to have gynecomastia at adolescence and transgenderism.[288]

Alongside research investigations like those just described have been efforts at theoretical construction. John Money's work, for example, articulates what he terms 'gender transpositions'—or variations from what he posits as the most favorable evolutionary position: exclusive heterosexuality.[289] Responding to some of Money's ideas, Richard Pillard and James Weinrich propose a "periodic table model" for gender transpositions. Their sociobiological model gives prominence to the role played by both prenatal and perinatal hormonal fluctuations.[290]

As others have, they note the importance of critical periods during development when such hormonal fluctuations may play a dramatic role in altering brain formation from the normative evolutionary pattern. Together with genetic and environmental contributions the resulting variations constitute degrees of masculinization and/or defeminization of the brain. The consequence is a range of sex and gender differences among human beings. However, these differences fall into one or another of four broad groups depending on the masculizing or defeminizing that occurs. Thus, the quadrants of their model contain those who are "masculinized and defeminized" (e.g., typical heterosexual males), those who are "unmasculinized and undefeminized" (e.g., typical heterosexual females), those who are "unmasculinized and defeminized" (e.g., male-to-female transsexuals), and those who are "masculinized and defeminized" (e.g., most homosexuals).[291] Not surprisingly, such theories remain controversial.

Jean Wilson, while concluding that it appears "inescapable" that androgen action is "important for male gender role behavior and probably for male gender identity as well," points out a basic logical dilemma with gonadal hormone studies. The same data can be evaluated in diametrically opposed ways. Those favoring an environmental explanation for transgender behavior relegate the role of hormones to, at best, a secondary position. Those who advocate that gonadal hormonal influences are important determinants of gender identity point to evidence such as discussed above, but are confronted by an intractable problem. As Wilson puts it, while gonadal hormones may be important determinants of gender identity/behavior, they also control development of the external genitalia. This anatomical presentation is then used by others for sex and gender assignment. Accordingly, gender identity and anatomical sex are almost invariably the same.[292] In short, the ability to sort out biological effects from environmental ones is complicated and difficult. This same observation remains pertinent when we turn our attention elsewhere.

As the brief review above suggests, most of the attention has been devoted to gonadal hormones. The influence of hormones on the developing brain remains a critically important area of investigation, but not the only one. The role played by hormonal changes at puberty has also been implicated in the development of transgender behaviors like crossdressing. The suggestion has been that these changes enhance a specifically erotic component to acts like crossdressing in many young males and thus leads to fetishistic transvestism, which may persist well into adulthood.

Researchers Gilbert Herdt and Martha McClintock posit another possible hormonal influence on the development of crossdressing behavior: the maturation of the adrenal glands (adrenarche) that occurs in the years preceding puberty (typically ages 6-10). As the adrenal cortex matures it releases the hormone dehydroepiandrosterone (DHEA), which when metabolized yields estradiol and testosterone. They point out that early sexual attraction emerges coincident with this maturation and before gonadarche.[293] Herdt and McClintock view adrenarche as paving the way for the later developments associated with gonadarche. This "adrenal puberty" permits experience and expression of sexual awareness and attraction, which becomes markedly noticeable and stable around age 10. The result, these scholars contend, are important in the rise of "sexual subjectivity" including the rise of sexual attraction.[294] The possible role played by these events on the development of transgender identity, crossdressing behavior, and related matters has been almost completely ignored.

Finally, some cases of transgender development in the United States, Canada, and Europe may stem, at least in part, from the involvement of chemicals introduced into the mother's body when the person was *in utero*. Educator Scott Kerlin, in a paper presented in 2004, points to a possible link between prenatal exposure by males to diethylstilbestrol (DES)—a drug used to prevent miscarriage—and the development of a transgender identity. DES exposure in pregnant women was most likely in the period from 1941 until the 1970s, and perhaps 1-3 million U.S. males had such *in utero* exposure. Kerlin notes that previous research investigated such possible psychosexual impacts as feminization and demasculization in such males. Other research established a number of effects, such as abnormalities of the reproductive system. The study Kerlin reports involved more than 100 members of the DES Sons International Network and employed the principles of grounded theory in qualitative analysis. Kerlin found that when members were asked to choose one term regarding gender, sexual identity, or sexual orientation most descriptive of their self-definition among close friends, of those responding, two-thirds (66%) chose a term fitting within the broad umbrella of 'transgender' (see the answer to Q. 20): 'transsexual' (36.5%), 'transgendered' (15%), 'intersex' (3.1%), 'androgynous' (9%), or 'eunuch' (1.5%). Although these figures represent a disproportionately high occurrence compared to the general population, and are certainly suggestive, Kerlin notes his research is both preliminary and ongoing.[295]

Neurotransmitter Factors

Neurotransmitters—the chemical messengers so important in the brain— also have been implicated. One hypothesis is that the so-called 'paraphilic disorders' (which include those associated with the behavior of crossdressing) are associated with unusual neurotransmitter functioning. The specific idea is that the neurotransmitters belonging to the monoamine family (which includes serotonin, dopamine, and norepinephrine) are somehow involved. Though both dopamine (DA) and serotonin (5-HT) are implicated in sexual behavior, attention has focused on serotonin with regard to the paraphilias.[296] It must be noted, though, that the research on the biological bases of the paraphilias has focused on such serious problems as the treatment of pedophiles, not on conditions associated with crossdressing.

Might crossdressing be rooted in the experience of dress?

All of the above lines of inquiry might profit from a turn toward the foundational context described earlier in this work (volume 1). If we begin with the independent reality of clothing, material of substance that when brought into the realm of the senses elicits physiological responses, then we may make better progress than we have thus far. Our bodies vary; our genetic predispositions vary; the environments in which our bodies are placed and to which they must adapt, vary too. All of these variations, though, intersect and interact in the concrete reality of each individual life. At the center where these things meet is that other physical and symbolic reality called dress.

Dress contributes significantly to our personal and social boundary system.[297] One aspect of this is that dress offers each of us a physical shield between ourselves and our environments, including our social environments with all their pressures and demands. Through that shield we can express something either true to our experience of the self or at variance with it. This particular aspect is widely recognized and remarked upon, both in general and with reference to crossdressing. Less recognized is the role dress plays in personal experience and shaping the contents of the self. Dress, as a kind of 'second skin,' becomes incorporated, literally; it becomes part of the embodied self. As a boundary, then, dress possesses both independent substance and yet becomes part of our body substance.

The influence of the physiological changes elicited by clothing, prompting changes in psychological affect and cognition seem obviously pertinent to understanding crossdressing, yet there appears to have been no careful study of this.[298] Consider an important fact: an aspect of how dress is gender differentiated is not merely its look but also its feel on the skin. More than merely an expression of beliefs about the genders, differences in the look and feel of clothing may be presumed to elicit varying physiological and psychological changes in the wearer. Because different kinds of clothing are culturally associated with one or another gender, so also will be the effects produced experientially by wearing them. In other words, wearing dress associated with a different gender teaches the wearer to experience that gender.

Logically, if a boy—for whatever reason, constitutionally or environmentally—is exposed to feminine apparel and finds the resulting experience richly satisfying, because the feel and look of the clothes prompts changes physiological and psychological associated with pleasure, then the boy will seek to repeat such experience. The initial experience may be largely independent of either consciousness of gender differentiation in dress or concern about gender differentiation. In short, the initial experience may have little or nothing to do with gender per se. The child may not be seeking to express anything; the experience is satisfying in and of itself because the clothes in their independent reality offer a venue for pleasurable sensation. This child's body interacts with the physicality of these clothes such as to produce a pleasing experience. The experience is not one of crossdressing so much as simply an experience of dressing.

Because, however, the clothing is gender differentiated the experience must become more fully realized as crossdressing. For some children this is translated into a pleasurable feeling associated with sexuality and over time may develop into what mental health professionals term 'transvestic fetishism.' For other children whatever sexual component is present becomes secondary to the relief and generalized pleasure associated with temporary affiliation with another gender through periodic practice of crossdressing. These individuals may be identified as transvestites or transgendered (in the narrow sense of that word) individuals. For yet other children the experience is deeply tied to a developing sense of gender at variance with birth assignment; the experience of gender differentiated clothes resonates with a sense of gender identity to such an extent the body itself feels wrong and the child becomes someone identified as transsexual.

The result is this: comprehending the influence of dress on physiology and psychology offers a plausible hypothesis for a common ground underlying the multiple developmental pathways of transgender connected to crossdressing. For at least some crossdressers, early experience of clothing associated with each gender may have produced significantly varying results. A preference for the experience accompanying dress assigned to the other gender presents then a psychological challenge to the individual. The different ways in which the individual solves this challenge leads to one or another transgender identification. As long as dress remains gender differentiated any continuing experience of dress associated with a gender other than the one assigned at birth will necessitate some personal reckoning of gender that makes some transgender identity likely, if not inevitable.

Conclusion

In the early 1980s evolutionary psychologists Martin Daly and Margo Wilson offered an observation: "It is not at all easy to tease apart the contribution that different developmental factors make to the sexual differentiation of brain and behavior."[299] Since that time significant advances have been made in the study of such matters. Nevertheless, the situation remains substantially the same in many important regards. We still don't have a clear understanding of how biology figures into the etiology of transgender conditions or crossdressing behavior. We remain ignorant of how a larger picture may best fit the bits and pieces that specific studies are identifying.

Still, the notion that biology is involved has been persistent from the beginning. Indeed, even among indigenous peoples this idea can be glimpsed. In various settings manipulations of the body through diet or other physical means have sought to align body presentation with a perceived 'natural' condition at variance with anatomy. For example, the Waria of Indonesia (see the answers to Q. 57, 78), in the days before access to hormonal treatments and surgery, used to take *jamu*, a traditional medicinal drink.[300]

Whatever else may be said on the matter, this much is clear: biological factors, no matter the extant of their role in crossdressing behavior, are subtle, complex, and interactive. They not only are intermixed with one another, they are inescapably interactive with environmental factors. The more we learn, the more likely it becomes that biological factors are more important than previously recognized. But that recognition has not made the specifics so much clearer that anyone can state with confidence that this or another factor is solely or principally responsible for causing crossdressing. More certain is that new revelations will continue to emerge from biopsychological research and offer new light on crossdressing.

If such research directs its attention to the role dress plays in human physiology and psychology, then perhaps especially relevant results may emerge. However, that role, as we have seen, necessitates also serious reckoning of the environment. Culture informs how we regard dress, craft clothes, and change fashions. Our use of dress, including crossdressing, cannot escape its cultural context. Because culture relies on learning, environmental influences through parents, family, and social institutions all are candidates for helping explain crossdressing. It is to these matters we must next turn.

Q. 22

Is a transgender reality like crossdressing learned behavior?

The Short Answer. Environmental explanations for crossdressing have a long history, dating back to the early days of study during the medicalization of sex. By far the most popular has been the psychoanalytic hypothesis that cross-dressing stems from a family dynamic where the crossdressing son affiliates closely with a dominant mother while the father is physically or emotionally distant (or absent). This hypothesis relies mostly on interpretation from case studies of individuals in counseling. But there have been numerous other models as well, many of them variations on a theme, but some offering different emphasis on various other environmental factors. What these models have in common is the conviction that the observed behavior is not innate, or biologically founded and derived, but rather learned, and that this learning develops over time.

The Longer Answer. Whether or not a biological component—even foundation—is ever determined for some or all crossdressing behavior, the importance of environmental factors will remain. Our concern here is in exploring whether such factors constitute a better explanation for crossdressing than do biological factors. Much earlier, in answering Q. 7, we considered one such environmental explanation—the pressure exerted on both males and females, but especially the former, to conform to social gender identity and role expectations. Perhaps crossdressing provides a measure of relief from such pressures. But this hypothesis, which receives additional consideration here, is just one among a number of alternative explanations.

Some crossdressers believe their behavior stems from the family environment they experienced during childhood.[301] Over the years a number of social scientists and mental health professionals have joined them in this belief. For decades, much speculation about the cause(s) for male transvestism has centered on 'pregenital psychopathology'—psychological disorder originating before puberty.[302] Since this is the developmental time when parental influence is strongest, perhaps *parenting* plays a role in the adoption of crossdressing. Of course, at one time it was especially popular to attribute virtually any unusual or pathological behavior to deficient parenting. This explanation was used for conditions ranging from autism to xenophobia. The realm of human sexuality was no exception; homosexuality was commonly explained as caused by family dysfunction. So, too, crossdressing.

Those who view crossdressing as learned behavior look for factors in the environment associated with developing the behavior; they are largely developmental models. Although some of these models, particularly earlier ones, either minimize or disdain biological factors, others recognize the possibility of biological factors playing a role. However, in each of these models the decisive element is thought to be one or more factors in the environment, and the primary environment examined is the child's family. That is not to suggest that cultural factors may not play a role, nor that yet other matters may influence the hypothesized learning of transgender behavior. But the role of parents is typically emphasized.

Since crossdressing generally begins before puberty, and since parents are (arguably) the principal influence in a child's life, suspicion that some kind of parental role is involved comes naturally to theoreticians. The dominant model used in this respect stresses a particular pattern in the family with regard to the parents—a strong maternal presence and a distant, or absent paternal one. However, a different model suggests that it is a rejecting maternal presence that may prompt crossdressing in some boys. Another model emphasizes the role that desire by one or both parents for a child of the opposite sex may have in facilitating the development of crossdressing. Yet other models suggest the importance of the father as a role model in stimulating crossdressing in a child, or speculate about the involvement of other kin.[303] Another model hypothesizes a series of steps that must be realized for crossdressing to become so firmly established that one can speak legitimately of a 'transvestite.' A few models de-emphasize developmental elements in favor of conditioned learning along the lines of behaviorist thinking. Finally, some models seek to incorporate a number of factors, which may or may not include ideas already listed.

Psychoanalytic models, in particular, have focused on disturbed parent-child relations. Typically, the mother-son relationship is viewed as most decisive in the formation of crossdressing. The father's role is generally regarded as secondary in contributing to the situation wherein crossdressing begins and is nourished. This situation is usually described as arising early in childhood (before age five). Among various psychoanalytic interpretations—based on case studies—crossdressing has been viewed variously as:

- ❑ a failure in early separation of the boy from his mother, wherein by imitating her, he becomes her;[304]
- ❑ serving the function of 'restitution' for an early separation from the mother;[305] or,

❑   as a 'transitional object' to compensate for a sense of abandonment.[306]

Regardless of the specific nature of the symbolic function crossdressing is envi-
sioned to perform, these interpretations, and others like them, favor theory
dominated by the rule of nurture over nature.

As is obvious from the above introductory remarks, no consensus exists on
what environmental factors may prove decisive in producing transgender identity or behaviors like crossdressing. In the remainder of this answer we shall
examine a number of alternatives, some more popular and influential than others, but all enjoying at one time or another advocates. We shall begin with an
idea already introduced, that crossdressing—at least among males—is prompted
by a desire for escape (or at least relief) from the masculine gender role.

What is the 'Escape from Gender Role' model?

The anthropologist and psychologist team of Robert and Ruth Munroe remark that anthropologists traditionally have explained male crossdressing as a
vehicle of escape from gender role expectations.[307] In this model, males who
cannot face the demands of the masculine gender as set forth in their society
seek relief or escape from such demands by affiliating with femininity. In many
societies this move is a sanctioned one with the transgender male coming to
occupy a new gender role with its own set of expectations. In societies like our
own, where the move is not sanctioned and no third gender role exists, the
feminine male faces punitive sanctions. Accordingly, most do not find a full
escape from masculinity but in private are able to accomplish some measure of
temporary relief.

Unlike most of the models described in this answer, which rely on case
studies, anecdotal reports, or the theorist's intuition, this model has received
some empirical testing. The Munroes specified the model in terms of the demands placed on the energy and time of males to contribute to the basic subsistence economy of their society. Their hypothesis was that in societies where the
demand was higher in males than females the potential escape value of crossdressing should be maximized and accordingly there should be a higher incidence of its occurrence than among males in societies where they contribute
less to subsistence activities. They examined 73 societies for which ratings existed both with respect to male transvestism and the sexual division of labor in
subsistence activities. The results confirmed their hypothesis: in every society
where male transvestism was documented, males had the greater role in subsistence activities. What matters, apparently, is the quantitative contribution of
males, not differences in the tasks undertaken by each sex. Males unable to cope
with the social gender expectation are provided a sanctioned escape through
their transvestism.[308]

Crossdressing by males is not sanctioned within our culture and masculine
gender expectations are expected to be met, not escaped. Still, perhaps the gen-

der role hypothesis, albeit somewhat recast, offers an explanation for at least some of the male crossdressing seen in Western culture. Our society, in particular, is characterized by greater rigidity in expectations about gender identity than occurs in many other places. Despite more relaxed gender role expectations in many aspects in recent years, the linking of gender identity to gender roles, and making both dependent on body sex, carries consequences, especially in gender development. Our society's gender role socialization exerts enormous pressure to conform and carries penalties for those who do not. But whatever benefits conformity allegedly accrues for us, there are attendant costs as well. Not all of us fit comfortably within our assigned gender identity and role. The gender socialization process can produce conflict, both within the individual and between the individual and others.

Gender role socialization is enforced in myriad ways. Social tolerance is a powerful force in motivating individuals and their families to conform to social norms. As sociologist Jason Schnittker shows, other people receive gender norm conformity as 'normal,' while atypical gender behavior prompts labels and negative appraisals.[309] This was demonstrated, for example, in 1990 research with 80 college undergraduates. They were given questionnaires probing their attitudes toward 'tomboys' and 'sissies'—both labels applied to relatively nonconforming children. The instrument also asked them to speculate concerning the future, adult behavior of tomboys and sissies compared to typical girls and boys. Not only are sissies regarded more negatively than tomboys, they are also projected to be more likely in adulthood to continue their cross-gender behavior. The students view sissies as likely to be less well-adjusted than others. They also expect them to be more likely than other boys to grow up to be homosexuals.[310] Since homophobia is an important force in the construction of masculinity in our culture, the implied threat of being or becoming one is used even by children to coerce gender conformity. Given such attitudes and expectations, it is easy enough to envision the pressures all children experience, and none more so than those who find conformity challenging or impossible.

Those who do conform can pose a risk to those who do not. As Lisa Hinkelman and Darcy Haag Granello find in their research, those who most conform—the 'hypergendered'—are also those most likely to hold negative attitudes toward persons labeled as mentally ill.[311] They caution:

> To the extent that this finding generalizes to the population at large, mental health counselors may want to work to limit the interactions of their clients with persons who hold rigid hypergender beliefs or at least give their clients some skills to counter possible negative interactions with the hypergender people in their lives.[312]

This warning would certainly seem applicable to the transgendered, so commonly labeled as 'psychologically disordered,' or 'mentally ill,' who are in hypergendered people's lives.

Manuel Zamarripa and his associates note that restrictive gender role socialization can place stress on both boys and girls, but the negative effects seem particularly obvious with boys because they are the objects of the most rigid and restrictive patterns of socialization. As Zamarripa and colleagues write, "many traditionally masculine values that are so prized in our society also lead to various aspects of psychological distress."[313] In particular, masculine values devalue in men the expression of so-called 'feminine' traits such as emotional expressiveness. Socialized to place success above emotionality, the restrictive nature of the masculine gender role can lead to depression. Further, in relationships with other men this restrictive gender socialization can lead to avoidance of affection toward them for fear of being 'feminine' or 'homosexual.' Thus restriction of affection toward other males also produces anxiety.[314]

Many males respond to anxiety and depression by self-medication through the use of alcohol or recreational drugs. Others may adapt by crossdressing. The behavior at least temporarily sets aside masculine gender role oppression. Some males escape the pressure by permanently abandoning the masculine identity and role. Thus, this model can be used to explain the differences between, for example, transvestites and transgenderists. The former leave the masculine role for a time; the latter abandon it entirely.

In light of considerations like the above, is it implausible to speculate that at least some crossdressing is a response to gender role pressures? Perhaps the higher incidence of crossdressing observed in males in our culture makes sense in light of the greater pressure—and attendant conflict—they face in gender role socialization and nonconformity. Maybe crossdressing, especially that labeled 'heterosexual transvestism,' constitutes an escape from the excessive, rigid, unrealistic pressure of the modern male role. Certainly, many students of crossdressing have hypothesized that an aspect of its pleasure is the relief it provides from the masculine gender role.[315]

However, casting crossdressing in the light of the larger society, while appealing to anthropologists, is not the favored explanation of other social scientists, such as psychologists. The latter group, more accustomed to working with smaller social units or individuals, have focused on the possible role played by family dynamics. This does not, of course, preclude the possibility that both larger and smaller social systems produce dynamic influences on individual development, choices, and behavior.

What is the 'Dominant Mother/Distant Father' model?

Environmental explanations have a long history, and none more so than those that place the parents at the heart of what transpires—with one particular constellation of factors most often traced. In a report published in 1960, for example, a psychiatrist explained two cases of transvestism in males as a confluence of the following factors:

❏ Early difficulties in male identification either because of an absent father or because of parental rejection.
❏ Feminine identification enhanced by:
   o close visual contact of a little sister;
   o over-protectiveness by the mother; or,
   o being dressed in girls clothes.[316]

Is there evidence to substantiate such an explanation?

Most of the support has come from psychoanalytic interpretations in case study research.[317] But there are larger studies that may be relevant. One such study, reported in 1971, involves 599 self-identified transsexuals (73% male). When asked to name the family person they felt closest to, most name either their father or mother, with each sex expressing a preference for the parent of the opposite sex.[318] However, no explanation is given as to why, so whatever use is made of this finding must be limited. Another 1971 report examines 18 adolescent crossdressing boys and their families. A dozen of these boys, diagnosed as transvestites, share similar family patterns. The father is distant and passive, while the mother encourages feminine behaviors like crossdressing either openly or subtly. In these families there is also a sister who is felt to be the mother's favored child. The crossdressing boys are observed as engaging in their crossdressing less for sexual arousal than as part of their desire to appear feminine.[319] Robert Stoller, in 1979, also notes in 9 cases the outcomes for boys with fathers who do not properly fulfill a normal role in their sons' lives. Stoller identifies this parental failure as an important factor in the boys developing significant feminine behavior.[320]

A much larger study, conducted in the mid-1980s, uses the Parent Characteristics Questionnaire (PCQ) to explore whether "non-normative parent sex-role qualities" are instrumental in the development of homosexuality and/or transvestism. The PCQ measures five personality traits (intellectuality, dependence, affiliation, endurance, and aggressive-dominance) in terms of their relative distribution between mother and father. Accordingly, three groups were administered the PCQ: 228 heterosexuals (106 male; 122 female), 97 homosexuals (34 male; 63 female), and 77 transvestites (all male). The subjects' perceptions of their parents afford the data. The results find that non-normative parent sex-role traits are significantly different for both lesbians and transvestites from heterosexuals and male homosexuals.[321] These results lend some support to the notion that parent characteristics may indeed play a part in the development of gender different behavior like crossdressing.

For the most part, this psychoanalytic model has portrayed the mother-son relationship as symbiotic—an entanglement that prevents the boy from adopting a masculine gender identity. The warm closeness of the relationship smothers the kind of separation-individuation the child needs, and the father is not available to help. But psychiatrist Susan Bradley advances a different hypothesis. She still affirms the strength of the mother's influence, but in a different manner. Bradley hypothesizes that boys who adopt crossdressing may do in response to an overtly rejecting mother. For example, an adolescent boy may feel intense anger at the mother for her rejection. But such strong feelings may prompt anxiety, which crossdressing—together with sexual arousal and relief through masturbation—lessens. As Bradley puts it, "The use of maternal garments may act as a fantasized protector against fear of loss of the mother at these times."[322] A similar theme was advanced by Kenneth Zucker and Ray Blanchard in 1995. They also thought that in adolescence crossdressing by males may be a facet of mother-son conflict.[323]

In 1995, psychologist Zucker and psychiatrist Bradley collaborated in writing *Gender Identity Disorder and Psychosexual Problems in Children and Adolescents*. In it they contend that for both boys and girls cross-gender behavior (including crossdressing) arises within a dysfunctional family setting, one where familial stress and frustration are high. Especially when this happens in early childhood at the time the child is learning gender, vulnerability to poor parent-child interactions can lead to adopting cross-gender behavior. This response is defensive and though it provides relief for a time it is problematic.[324]

Zucker and Bradley, in part citing earlier research, note that those most at risk seem to possess a sensitive nature, which experiences high arousal in stressful situations. In boys, this may contribute to feeling inadequate as males, avoiding both rough and tumble play and same-sex peer relationships. If their mothers experience instances of male aggression in an especially strong and negative fashion, they may actively encourage their sons to be different, discouraging normal boyish aggressive play and rewarding more feminine behaviors. The boy may experience his mother's intense feelings as directed at him. Zucker and Bradley write:

> The boy, who is highly sensitive to maternal signals, perceives the mother's feelings of depression and anger. Because of his own insecurity, he is all the more threatened by his mother's anger or hostility, which he perceives as directed at him. His worry about the loss of his mother intensifies his conflict over his own anger, resulting in high levels of arousal or anxiety.[325]

Fathers in such settings may disapprove of what is happening but keep themselves at a distance from it. The result can be growing discord in the family. The boy's anxiety at last finds some relief in cross-gender behavior, such as crossdressing with masturbation.[326]

Perhaps paralleling the situation with crossdressing boys is that encountered by crossdressing girls. Psychiatrist Ira Pauly investigated 80 cases of female transsexuals in the literature between 1922-1970. He reports that in those cases where the mother-daughter relationship was considered, more than a third (36%; N=28) experienced their mothers as cold and rejecting. However, this must be balanced against another finding: when the matter of the mother's relationship to the father is considered, 83% (N=18) of the subjects claim their mothers were in some need of protection by them from the father—hardly the picture of a 'dominant' mother.[327]

What, then, of the opposite side of the equation—the absent father? Overall, the psychoanalytic hypothesis of the influence posed by a father's absence has not been strongly supported. More systematic research has failed to confirm it. For example, a comparative study involving over 200 men (65 transvestites, 33 male-to-female (MtF) transsexuals, 57 homosexuals, and 61 men whose sexual orientation remained unidentified), finds no support for this idea. Specifically, the hypothesis was tested that transvestites and transsexuals will be more likely to have grown up in a family headed by a female (an idea also often held to be true for homosexuals). This hypothesis is refuted by the data collected. Indeed, for all three groups—transvestites, transsexuals, and homosexuals—absent fathers are no more common than in the general population.[328] On the other hand, one study finds evidence of a parent sex-role reversal in transvestites' parents, with the fathers appearing to their sons as more dependent and affiliative in behavior compared to the perceptions of non-crossdressing males.[329] Overall, today this model enjoys less favor than it once did.

What is the 'Parental Wish for an Opposite Sex Child' model?

Psychoanalysts have often speculated that a parent's wish—especially the mother's—for a child of the sex opposite of the actual one of a child is a factor in the development of crossdressing.[330] That the mother would play a critical role if she held such a wish seems obvious—she typically provides the primary care, including the selection of clothes and dressing of the child.[331] Sociologist Gregory Stone offers trenchant insight into how her role affects males, and may lead to crossdressing: "Their first reflected glimpse of themselves was provided by the eyes of a woman—a woman who, in fact, saw many of those men as girls. Some were dressed as little girls."[332]

What kind of evidence might there be for the role of such a wish? As indicated earlier, appeal is often made to the case history of individual patients in treatment. But are there broader lines of evidence?

Some 1970 research under the auspices of the Kinsey Institute, finally published with the title *Sex and Morality in the U.S.*, examines 'Gender Characteristics' in a series of questions. Two questions addressing actual behavior possibly related to crossdressing drew different response frequencies. Questions were asked concerning any sign while growing up that either parent would have preferred the respondent to have been born the opposite sex. When it came to the behavior of fathers, four times as many females (1.5%) as males (0.4%) affirm that such a sign included his preference in how he wanted his child to dress.[333] Yet when it came to the behavior of mothers, more than twice as many males

(1.6%) as females (0.7%) affirm that such a sign included her preference in how she wanted her child to dress.[334] For those answering affirmatively in either scenario, significant percentages of both males and females report that this continued at least into adolescence.[335]

So we are returned to our question: Might a parent's wish to have had a child of the opposite sex play a crucial role in the development of crossdressing? We do have data that indicates a fair number of male crossdressers remember wishing as children that they had been born female. For example, Neil Buhrich and Trina Beaumont find in studying 222 American and Australian adult male crossdressers that nearly one-third (30%) remembered having such a wish at least once a week during ages 6-12.[336] Perhaps such wishes at least sometimes reflect at some level, conscious or not, a perception of a parent's wish for an opposite-sex child. More pertinently, in his review of 80 cases of female-to-male transsexuals reported between 1922-1970, Ira Pauly finds nearly two-thirds (62%; N-16) of the subjects in cases where the question came up remember their mothers as having preferred a boy instead of a girl.[337]

Researchers Neil Buhrich and Neil McConaghy studied the relationships with parents during childhood of men in three distinct groups: homosexuals, transvestites, and transsexuals. In examining the relationships with parents of the 34 male transvestites and 29 male transsexuals, Buhrich and McConaghy find that in both groups there were significantly more mothers who had hoped for a girl than was true for mothers of homosexuals. Yet, there was no evidence of a pathological relationship with the mothers. Also, in all three groups, the father was likely to either have been absent or to have shown little interest in them.[338] Despite these general findings, no specific factor in the childrearing environment could be identified to explain the child's homosexuality, transvestism, or transsexualism.

What is the 'Influence of Cultural Beliefs' model?

An interesting possible variant on the above model is presented by a case study published in 2001. A genetic male child in Thailand displays transgender behavior reflecting his parents' belief that he is the reincarnation of his maternal grandmother—an idea echoed in the boy's own claims as he grows older. A birthmark on the child prompted this belief. The researchers who published this case speculate on the role parental expectations may play in the formation of transgender behavior, as well as the part played by cultural beliefs.[339]

Another indication of the possible influence of cultural beliefs—with reincarnation again at the center—comes from the case of girl who claims to recall a previous life as a male. Her observed gender dysphoria is interpreted within the cultural context (southeast Asia) as the impress of this former life. Because belief in reincarnation is common among Hindus and Buddhists in this part of the world, the observed behavior is afforded a nonpathological context and thus does not arouse the concern such behavior generally creates among Western families.[340] The belief that *karma* accrued in one life produces effects in the next is not infrequently appealed to by transgender individuals in Eastern societies as an explanation for why they are as they are (cf. volume 3 of this work).

What is the 'Father as Role Model' hypothesis?

While most research has focused on a possible role by the mother, some has examined the possible role of the father. What if the father is a crossdresser and this behavior becomes known to his sons? David Krueger presents the situation of a crossdressing father and three crossdressing sons. All three sons began their crossdressing in early adolescence. Krueger thinks that the father's role modeling played a significant part in the behavior exhibited by the sons.[341] However, while social learning theory has established the power of observation and imitation of models in learning, including gender learning, this hypothesis has not received much support. Abundant examples exist of families in which the same-sex offspring are aware of the parent's crossdressing but show no inclination to imitate it.

What is the 'Transvestic Career Path' model?

Some theorists have attempted to explain crossdressing as a process that takes advantage of miscues in development. In the broad sense of 'development,' this can be said of probably all of the models investigated in this answer. Each, in its own way, suggests something went wrong in childhood. As we have seen, proposing a failure in parent-child relationships has been one manner of explaining how crossdressing begins and is established. But there are other ways of seeing the matter, some of which are explained in the rest of this answer.

For example, in 1970, sociologist H. Taylor Buckner, based on interviews with seven adult male transvestites, hypothesized a series of steps that must be taken before one becomes a crossdresser. His steps are:

- ❑ First, usually sometime between ages 5-14 the boy associates some feminine item of clothing with sexual pleasure, usually through masturbation.[342]
- ❑ The youth next perceives some heterosexual difficulties, whose origins may be varied, but which generate a fear of inadequacy.
- ❑ In the third step, he blocks any possible homosexual outlet, whether from a learned aversion or because of a lack of opportunity. With steps 2 and 3 in place, he reverts to feminine dress for sexual satisfaction.
- ❑ Fourth, his masturbation fantasies are elaborated into the development of a feminine self. As with other steps, a variety of factors may enter into a person taking this step.

❑ In this, the fifth step, usually accomplished by age 18-20, cross-dressing becomes a permanent part of the personality. Only now can the individual be termed a 'true' transvestite. The gratification pattern involving crossdressing has become a fixed part of the identity, including (for many) a feminine alter-ego, so that as both male and female he can carry out various cultural patterns of heterosexuality.[343]

Obviously, a sample size of just seven subjects should give us pause. However, in various forms the internal logic of this model is not uncommon. Buckner conceives of crossdressing as learning that is responsive and progressive in nature. The idea is that an individual in encountering a life difficulty may draw upon something previously learned, apply it, extend it, and in time make it a basic part of the personality. Such logic has been used by various theorists in connection to any number of matters.

What is the 'Behavioral Conditioning' model?

The conviction that crossdressing is learned elicits a number of notions as to exactly how the learning proceeds. We have already examined a couple of these. A few theorists have stressed learning in the sense of behavioral conditioning. These researchers downplay the predominant role of developmental processes, arguing that such conditioning may occur at any time in life, even if it proves more common in childhood. Though various elements may be involved in the learning process they all converge in conditioning a person's response through a specific behavior. This may be conceived as either classical conditioning (as in Buckner's first step, described above), or operant conditioning, or both.

Along these lines, the eminent American sexologist Alfred Kinsey tries to explain crossdressing in his 1953 volume *Sexual Behavior in the Human Female*. Noting that crossdressing occurs in both males and females, but is far more common among males, he argues the explanation lies in a sex-based difference in learning: "Transvestism provides one of the striking illustrations of the fact that males are more liable to be conditioned by psychologic stimuli."[344] Because human beings rely on conditioning throughout life for learning—always subject to modification through experience as they interact with their environment—conditioning leading to crossdressing behavior might happen at any time.[345]

Without departing far from the importance of developmental considerations, sexologist John Money also proposes learning factors as critical. In Money's estimation the formation of a 'paraphilia' (a condition in which normal objects of erotic attraction are displaced by unusual ones), such as crossdressing, is rooted in childhood conditioning. Money proposes explaining individual patterns of sexual interest in terms of 'lovemaps' (explained further in the answer to Q. 95) formed during childhood. The paraphilic lovemap is constructed before puberty from a variety of experiences, all with some sexual component, that together represent a deviance from normal lovemap development. Thus crossdressing has its origin in "the neglect of healthy sexual learning in childhood." But, coupled with this neglect, Money points to the role played by "abusive discipline and assaultive punishment" attending discovery of child sexual play.[346] Further, in puberty, hormonal changes enter in and also play a role, thus suggesting a biopsychosocial model of multiple factors. While Money confesses that all of the facts that are needed to fully explain the rise of crossdressing remain unavailable he is confident that those that are available support his general conclusion.

The behaviorist explanation for learning has been applied to transgender people by some mental health professionals. Behavioral therapists think that anything that is learned can be unlearned; unwanted behavior can be modified or extinguished. Thus, behavioral therapy of crossdressing has sought to eliminate the behavior through aversive conditioning. However, despite a wave of early enthusiasm for this process, longitudinal studies have indicated this approach is not particularly effective (see the answer to Q. 97).

What are 'Multi-Factor' models?

As just seen, various models (probably the majority of them) propose more than one factor involved in the etiology of transgender conditions and behaviors like crossdressing. Many psychoanalytic models posit multiple factors involved in the development of crossdressing. For example, in 1964 Anna Freud presented a sample study plan for the treatment of transvestism that recognized three developmental stages, with a variety of possible causal factors.[347] The stages identified are:

- ❏ Stage A—the common children's game of 'dressing up.' At this stage, crossdressing serves "a variety of role-plays and fantasies in which the sex differences play no part or are transcended easily."[348]
- ❏ Stage B—in boys in the early school years crossdressing, whether open or secret, may flow from one or another of a number of causes:
  - ○ the mother's original wish for a girl;
  - ○ gender envy; or,
  - ○ an attempt to recapture a lost female object through identification.
- ❏ Stage C—the adult crossdresser.

Freud notes that "unexpectedly," the second stage is not found to be characterized by sexual arousal through crossdressing.[349] In a contemporaneous work, Freud also cautions that determining the exact meaning of the child's crossdressing "is difficult to assess, even in the cases under analysis."[350]

Perhaps the most complex attempt related to understanding crossdressing is represented by Peter Bentler's effort to specify 32 factors involved in the development of a feminine sex role in males. By this he hopes to differentiate between homosexuality, transsexualism, and transvestism. Of these 32 factors, a dozen are common to all three conditions; two prove unique to homosexuality, two others are unique to transsexualism, and six are unique to transvestism. Prenatal feminization of the brain—a biological factor—is named for homosexuality and transsexualism, but not for transvestism. Since the latter is most associated with crossdressing, Bentler probably sees this behavior as principally due to environment. This seems confirmed when looking at the list of behaviors Bentler sees as associated with transvestism and transsexualism, which includes nonoptimal stimulation during infancy, and training in impulse control, harm avoidance, and behavioral inhibition. Unique to the development of transvestism is an emphasis on intellectual success. These and other environmental factors Bentler names are present in the years when crossdressing starts. For transvestites there is also the anxiety reduction associated with orgasm while crossdressing—a powerfully self-reinforcing behavior.[351]

Conclusion

We have sketched in this answer, and the previous one, a number of hypotheses about the origin of crossdressing in individuals' lives. None have captured the support of a majority of professionals and the quest to come up with a satisfactory explanation continues. For most scholars today the answer seems to reside in recognizing two facts: no one explanation suffices for all (or perhaps even the majority) of individuals, and no one factor is likely to emerge as especially determinative. We have not exhausted the subject. The next three answers continue our examination of causality. They have been set apart because each, in its own way, merits special attention.

Q. 23

Is a transgender reality like cross-dressing developmental (i.e., "just a phase")?

The Short Answer. We have seen that the idea that development occupies an important role is common to both biological and environmental explanations of crossdressing. The idea that crossdressing does not spring forth fully realized but develops gradually and is rooted in developmental processes probably stems from several noncausally related factors, including its prevalence in childhood, its episodic nature, and its nonpersistence in some individuals. Because development is commonly conceived of as proceeding through distinct stages, it can be appealing to regard transgender behavior as just one phase a child may pass through. This way of thinking is sometimes clung to by parents who hope what they are seeing in a child will not persist or develop further. The idea that they are only seeing a passing phase thus offers them comfort and hope. But there is no support for the notion that crossdressing is 'just a phase' that many individuals pass through on their way to attaining gender identity. One consequence of the dashing of this false hope is the conclusion some parents reach that their child's persistence in this 'phase' means they have become developmentally stuck—they have, in effect, experienced a 'developmental failure.' The idea that crossdressing represents a developmental failure is a complex matter, depending on exactly what is meant by the terms 'developmental' and 'failure.' However, this hypothesis is also not widely supported.

The Longer Answer. In the previous answer we explored various ways in which crossdressing has been explained as an outcome related to one or more facets of childhood development. But we hardly exhausted the idea and one or two more particular matters merit further investigation. Foremost, we should consider the notion that experimenting with crossdressing is a normal phase of childhood experience. Secondarily, we should then ask if crossdressing that persists represents a failure in this experimental phase ending. Perhaps persistent crossdressing reflects a kind of developmental arrest, where one gets stuck in immature behavior. To address this we must first examine the idea that cross-dressing constitutes an experimental and transitory situation—a 'phase.'

Is crossdressing a normal phase of childhood?

Might crossdressing be 'just a phase' that many children pass through? The idea seems common enough. The *Diagnostic and Statistical Manual for Mental Disorders, 4th Edition, Text Revision* (DSM-IV-TR) notes that it is typical for children to be referred about the time they are ready to start school because what the parents had viewed as a phase that would pass was still continuing.[352] Behavior that parents find easier to overlook at ages 2-4 becomes a concern at ages 5-7. So are transgender behaviors like crossdressing signs of a phase kids often pass into and then out of?

While it is true that many small children may experience some degree of crossdressing, for it to be 'a phase' would require it to be something rather widespread and dependable in its course. No evidence suggests that to be the case. In fact, as Richard Schott's work suggests, crossdressing in childhood is highly variable even among those who regularly crossdress in adulthood. Schott discovers among his 85 sample male subjects that early experiences with cross-dressing ranges widely in time of origin and frequency. Some are so dressed in infancy, others start later; some are fully dressed as girls, others only partly so; some crossdress regularly, others only occasionally.[353] And these findings seem supported by other research.

The situation with children who display transsexual characteristics is also unclear. One of the hallmark signs of early onset transsexualism (known in the DSM model as 'Gender Identity Disorder'—see the answer to Q. 96) is the ex-pressed desire to be a member of the opposite sex. Curiously, such expressions sharply decrease after age 6 or 7. This might suggest that the earlier vocalization was a passing wish—a phase now past. But, as Kenneth Zucker and Susan Bradley point out, the children may stop expressing the wish not because it has gone but because they have learned such a wish is unacceptable to others.[354] Whether the change in what is voiced represents a genuine internal change is thus a matter that cannot be resolved on this point alone. On the other hand, some children who voice such a desire do not develop other transsexual charac-teristics later; perhaps, for them, it was just a passing experience.

Is crossdressing a developmental failure?

Another, related explanation has been that crossdressing represents a de-velopmental failure. Often implicit in this thinking is that some crossdressing in early childhood is innocent and natural—'a phase'—but when it persists some-thing has gone awry. Specifically, the presumed 'failure' is double: on the one hand, the child has failed to identify properly with the same sex and, on the other hand, has failed by over-identifying with the opposite sex. Crossdressing

140

manifests from this presumed double failure, though the latter element is decisive. This idea has been around more than half a century; Janet Thompson, in 1951, proposed that crossdressing can principally be explained by "faulty, incomplete or distorted sex identification."[355]

More recent research calls into question the prominence of childhood in the development of crossdressing. The authors of one comparative study suggest their findings indicate that psychoanalytic theories of crossdressing have overemphasized childhood, at least with regard to relations with parents.[356] In other words, merely because it often appears first in childhood does not necessarily mean it results from something unique to childhood. Crossdressing is unlikely to be adequately explained as either 'a phase' of development, or 'a failure' in development.

Q. 24

Is a transgender reality like crossdressing caused by sexual abuse?

The Short Answer. Where crossdressing is viewed as aberrant, even pathological behavior, it is tempting to look for an aberrant or pathological cause. This might be brain 'dysfunction,' or a 'disturbed' family—or sexual abuse. The thinking seems to be that the violation occurring in sexual abuse results in a variety of disturbances, with crossdressing being one. Why this might be so is not generally articulated. However, the possible correlation between childhood sexual abuse and crossdressing has been examined, albeit not greatly. To date, evidence does not support the notion that sexual abuse causes crossdressing. Nevertheless, in *some* instances for *some* individuals there may be a significant connection between childhood abuse, particularly sexual abuse, and the development of crossdressing. This seems more often the case in females than in males.

The Longer Answer. Sexual abuse is a frightful reality in Western culture. In the United States a common estimate for how many females are affected is 1-in-3 (33%) by age eighteen. For males a common estimate is 1-in-5 (20%) to 1-in-4 (25%), but is harder to come by because of less reporting. By any standard, these numbers are horrific. Occasionally speculation is raised regarding any role abuse may play in the adoption of crossdressing behavior, especially transsexualism.[357] This matter has received limited attention. One study published in 2003 reports having compared a group of 41 transsexuals with 115 psychiatric inpatients. The research used three instruments: the Interview for Dissociative Disorders, the Dissociative Experiences Scale, and the Childhood Trauma Questionnaire. The findings indicate no particular risk for dissociative disorders, but the transsexual subjects when compared to the general public show a greater incidence of having experienced emotional maltreatment. The results offer modest support for the idea that childhood trauma might affect the development of sexual identity in transsexuals.[358] That, however, is a far cry from any claim that abuse *causes* transsexualism.

Still, the idea of abuse as a cause of transgender identity or of behaviors like crossdressing appeals to many people as an explanation for what otherwise seems to them incomprehensible. Even popular literature plays with the supposed association.[359] However, anecdotal evidence from crossdressers themselves strongly suggests that a majority of them did not experience abuse in childhood, thus limiting any causal role of abuse in explaining crossdressing.

What is the evidence with regard to female crossdressers?

Most research with reference to crossdressing females concerns female-to-male (FtM) transsexuals. For them, dressing as a male in the postoperative stage can hardly be called 'cross'-dressing. Whether the term is appropriate before sex reassignment surgery is debatable, but for our purposes here we shall include FtM transsexuals in trying to answer this question.

Sexologist Holly Devor reported in 1994 a study investigating child abuse and transsexualism. Devor, noting that both childhood physical and sexual abuse are commonly reported in the histories of FtM transsexuals, interviewed 45 subjects. She finds that more than a third (38%) of her subjects report "significant" child abuse. Of these, nearly two-thirds (63%) experienced physical abuse (generally early, often, and by the father); over half (52%) were sexually abused (about two-thirds (64%) by older males; 92% involved genital contact); and more than a quarter (29%) report emotional abuse. Adding to the problem, those abused are likely to have experienced more than one form of abuse.[360]

While these figures are sobering in themselves, they require comparison to norms for the population. While these change to some degree from year to year, and from decade to decade, at least some reference point is needed. The 2002 Child Maltreatment figures for the United States may offer a rough baseline. Those figures show that of child abuse victims, 20% experienced physical abuse and 10% sexual abuse.[361] Clearly, the figures for Devor's subjects are much higher. So, does such abuse and the dissociation abuse typically generates account in a causal fashion for transsexualism in these women? Devor specifically refrains from drawing that conclusion. We simply do not know.

If it is a causal factor for some, then the reason why remains elusive. The psychoanalytic notion of the ego's defense against anxiety by identification with the aggressor could be one possible hypothesis. Equally plausible is the idea that transgender behavior is pursued as an escape from the gendered condition that made victimization possible. By becoming a different gender, or sex, the aggressor may find the person undesirable. But these are simply speculations. There has not been enough research as yet to offer us better ideas.

What is the evidence with regard to male crossdressers?

As with most matters, when it comes to crossdressers most of what we know in reference to this question comes from males. So, if we use a baseline of

20% experience of sexual abuse for the general male population, we can start by trying to see what percent of crossdressing males have this experience in their background. For those that do, it can be asked what, if any, role the sexual abuse has had in their adopting of crossdressing.

A population-based study conducted in Sweden and reported in 2005 finds that 19.4% of those identified with transvestic fetishism experienced sexual abuse at some point. The authors, noting that only 12.4% of other respondents acknowledged such an experience point to experience of sexual abuse as one variable significantly related to transvestic fetishism. However, the percentage of those saying they have ever been sexually abused before age 18 is only 8.8%, and the actual number of respondents identified with transvestic fetishism is only 36. The authors themselves admit conflicting statistical analyses of the data.[362] Caution in applying the results is thus warranted.

A 1999 online survey with male crossdressing respondents offers a reporting of abuse at less than 1-in-6 (15%), a rate likely lower than for the general male population. The average of the initiation of the abuse proves just under 9 years old, and for somewhat more than half (55%) the abuse preceded the advent of crossdressing. Yet most (58%) of those who have been abused do not believe it was a factor for them in starting to crossdress, though some (10%) do think it was a factor and almost a quarter (24%), while unsure, think it might have played a role.[363]

Therapist Lin Fraser says that when she encounters the coincidence of crossdressing and a history of child sexual abuse the development of the cross-gender identity can be a result. However, she also notes that in such cases the therapist is also seeing dissociative states and multiple personalities.[364] Neither condition is common with crossdressers. In such cases the motivation for crossdressing is likely to be significantly different than what is found among other crossdressers.

In sum, abuse may play a role in the formation of crossdressing for some crossdressers. That role may be most prominent in FtM transsexuals. It does not seem to be a significant factor for most other crossdressing groups, but may play a role in the specific life experiences of certain individuals. Like so many other areas, this is one that would profit from further research.

Q. 25

Is a transgender reality like crossdressing a choice?

The Short Answer. A question many of us want to know concerns whether crossdressing is a matter of choice. The interest in asking such a question lies in the implied consequence: if it is not a choice, then the matter is settled and one must simply learn to live with the reality. If it is a choice, then it can be undone by choosing differently. Moreover, the existence of choice is fundamental to moral will. Where people have choices, those choices can be morally evaluated. Thus, those who condemn transgender behaviors appeal to choice as providing grounds for passing moral judgments. Clearly, the answer to this question informs much of the personal response to crossdressing we are likely to make.

The Longer Answer. Oftentimes the ideas of 'free will' and 'choice' become synonymous. Yet those who espouse one form or another of determinism are quick to point out that choices remain important. The difference between free will positions and those of determinism are not really about the presence or absence of choices, but about the degree to which those choices are constrained by factors other than an individual's will. Science depends on cause-and-effect chains and those are comprised of identifiable factors that impinge upon, influence, and constrain human will and behavior. Therefore, it seems wise to think in terms of how free our choices are in light of the number and power of forces acting on us.

In that light, the available evidence suggests that crossdressing often is a choice strongly constrained by powerful forces. Whatever its cause, crossdressing appears to be a behavior that is very hard to stop. Certainly, if it was a matter of simply willing to stop, many crossdressers would—but not because they find the behavior unpleasant or wrong. Because of the negative social and relational consequences associated with being caught crossdressing, most crossdressers have at one time or another tried to stop the behavior. Croughan and associates, in a 1981 report of adult male crossdressers observe that 97% have tried to stop. However, a majority try only once, and less than a third try three

147

times or more.[365] Furthermore, these efforts fail; temporary 'abstinence' seems the most likely outcome, with shorter rather than long duration the norm for such abstinence.[366] As Harry Benjamin observed back in 1966, the notion that transvestites can simply use willpower to cease their crossdressing is "nonsense." [367]

Most habitual crossdressers come to accept crossdressing and even to embrace it as a positive force in their lives. In so doing, choices are being made. But once more the issue is whether those choices are purely or primarily a matter of individual will, or constrained by a variety of factors. We can choose, too, to regard others' behavior either strictly in terms of individual willing, or with reference to many causal factors. That choice also carries consequences.

What is the moral dimension of choosing crossdressing?

Are crossdressers weak-willed or willfully sinful? Those are certainly possible explanations, and we may favor one or the other if we insist on seeing all matters in terms of morality and will. We may believe that a crossdresser chose to start the behavior and can choose to stop. We may believe that failed efforts to stop reflect a weak will. We may believe that those who actively persist in crossdressing and enjoy it suffer from a seared conscience. But if we conclude that crossdressing is immoral behavior that results from individual choice, and that it can be stopped by the same act of will once transformed by moral change, then we are likely to brush aside all talk about other possible causal factors, whether biological or environmental.

While the simplicity and clarity of such thinking may seem irresistibly desirable to some of us, I cannot endorse it. The end of such logic is to reduce scientific investigations to irrelevancy and leave all of us prey to the moral values and judgments of those few who hold real power to enforce their will. That path historically leads to oppression rather than liberty, divides rather than unites, and harms rather than helps. We all know areas in our personal experience where we certainly feel less control, less power, and more constrained by factors beyond our will. If nothing else, such experiences can move us to feel compassion for those we may feel are trapped in behaviors we may believe are wrong or ill-advised.

There are choices involved in crossdressing. How we estimate the power of those choices will influence how we view crossdressers. How we value the role of individual will and how we judge the morality of crossdressing will also influence our view. To acknowledge that choices are made by crossdressers says surprisingly little in itself. It is our other choices—about religion, morality, social values, and so forth—that really shape our judgments. The attractiveness of science is that it offers common ground where we can all speak the language of reason and evidence in an effort to understand behavior. We don't have to set aside moral or religious convictions, but we suspend our certainty that we know enough to pass life-altering judgments on matters where reason and evidence provide pause. In short, we need not choose between science and religion when there are so many advantages to employing both in being human.

What is the psychological dimension of choosing cross-dressing?

If we decide to rely on science to help us understand why some among us choose to crossdress, we may find a number of more-or-less plausible explanations for why crossdressing starts and then is sustained (see, for example, the answers to Q. 21-22). But since our focus here is on the issue of *choice*, it seems appropriate to consider in particular the one psychological dimension most often put forth in this regard: obsessive and compulsive behavior. In other words, some people speculate that crossdressing is a behavior similar in its dynamics to that found in obsessive-compulsive disorder.

Forensic psychiatrist John Bradford points to four similarities between obsessions and compulsions, on the one hand, and sexual disorders on the other. Since these may be relevant to understanding crossdressing, we need to review them:

❑ Obsessions are similar to sexual fantasies.
❑ Compulsions, in general, are similar to sexual compulsions.
❑ Obsessive-compulsive disorder (OCD) and sexual disorders are often comorbid, and often co-occur with anxiety or mood disorders.
❑ Physiologically, as seen in pharmacological treatments, there is significant overlap between OCD and sexual disorders. [368]

Bradford notes that such similarities have led to the suggestion that a number of disorders, including the paraphilias (among which is transvestic fetishism), might be profitably grouped under the heading "obsessive-compulsive spectrum disorders."[369] However, Benjamin Saddock and Virginia Saddock summarize the research situation as this: "The data support the hypothesis that paraphilias and related disorders are on the *impulsive* rather than the *compulsive* end of the obsessive-compulsive spectrum" [italics added].[370] Yet this, too, may not apply to crossdressing, as we shall see in a moment.

One persistently specific hypothesized link is between transvestic crossdressing and obsessive-compulsive disorder (OCD). Research into this matter has depended largely upon case study reports. For example, Carmita Abdo and colleagues reported in 2001 two cases of men diagnosed both with transvestic fetishism and OCD. They note four possible explanations for this co-existence: the two conditions may be independent and associated in these men by chance; crossdressing may be a symptom of the OCD; OCD may be a symptom of the transvestism; or, they may represent different points along a spectrum of like disorders—a position they favor with reference to these individuals.[371]

On the other hand, some personality research conducted with crossdressers not uncommonly finds a modestly more pronounced tendency toward control of their impulses.[372] This might suggest that most crossdressers are *less* impulsive than the general population, but that for those who are crossdressing it may serve as an outlet to control their anxiety. This would agree with other research that suggests stress relief and coping with anxiety as important motivations in crossdressing for many persons. In short, a connection between crossdressing and efforts to control anxiety may be a better link than that between crossdressing and either impulsivity or compulsiveness.

What should we conclude about the cause of crossdressing?

As with proposed biological factors, proposed environmental factors appear to be subtle, complex, and interactive. No one hypothesis has prevailed and different ideas have come and gone in favor. In the last few decades, biological explanations have become more in vogue, just as they have in many other areas of psychology. In no small measure this trend has resulted from more sophisticated instruments to study the human body, especially the brain. Whether this trend will persist for a long period is less certain than that it shows no sign of abating for the foreseeable future.

Despite the increased attention given to biological factors, presently the dominant path used in explaining transgender realities like crossdressing is that environment and biology are involved together in some as yet poorly understood interaction. Further, there seem to be different factors involved in differing crossdressing behaviors. The mechanisms involved in transsexualism, for instance, seem somewhat different from those involved in transvestism. But we remain a long way from a satisfactory explanation for crossdressing. Perhaps the best word on causality for now remains that offered by Alfred Kinsey in a 1953 letter to Harry Benjamin in which he offers various explanations for different cases of crossdressing and concludes, "There seem to be as many factors as there are individual cases."[373]

The similar conclusion drawn more than a half century ago by Janet Thompson seems well substantiated today: there is no common denominator.[374] People crossdress for all kinds of reasons and the origin of the behavior in any particular individual may be unknown. That most of us want to find universal answers and wish the security of assured moral judgments must be subordinated to a greater desire to hold for others what we want held for ourselves. That means openness in the face of uncertainty, accompanied by the generosity of spirit that all moral codes and religious traditions endorse as part of what makes us truly human.

Our uncertainty over causality beckons us to be flexible and creative. Perhaps we would be better served recasting causality as the possibility that crossdressing is both 'natural' (as something that appears regularly in Nature), and 'environmental' (as something occurring in a man-made setting), regardless of individual factors. The multiplicity of causal possibilities, together with the high individuality of human cases, should give us pause about too facile judgments on how transgender realities like crossdressing arise. As well, if gender is viewed as a social construction, then gender variations may be different but they don't have to be deviant. Intersexed individuals do not have to be attached to 'male' or 'female' labels to be okay. Transgendered people do not have to be seen as abandoning their 'true gender,' but can be viewed as expressing their own gender. In this view, crossdressing behavior may be seen as social expression, and the crossdresser as a gender performer—like everyone else—regardless of 'cause.'[375]

What are the consequences of our views?

Each of the alternative explanations considered in this and the previous four answers represent possible, more-or-less plausible explanations for why crossdressing happens. Yet there is an additional, very real and quite consequential matter to consider. The conclusions we draw about origin elicit other trains of thought, including a valuation of the behavior in light of what we presume causes it. Therefore it is important we pause to ask what consequences follow from the explanations we adopt.

Part of our reasoning in this endeavor must also include a new perspective on dress (see volume 1). Crossdressing depends on dress primarily with regard to gender, but not entirely separate from sex. The importance both of gendered distinctions in particular clothing and the power of the dress silhouette mean many possible combinations of crossdressing behavior with gender and sex. No one explanation is likely to fit all crossdressers—or even necessarily the same crossdresser at different times. What we can be confident of is that crossdressing cannot happen without dress, which in turn is inseparable from gender and sex, physical reality and symbol, experience and expression. We can also be confident that the better we understand these things the less likely we will be to make facile judgments, typically hasty and general in character.

Inevitably, what we comprehend guides our expectations about how others should appear and behave, as well as think and feel. With changed expectations come altered judgments. Ideally, the more we know the more accurate our judgments will become. Unfortunately, we all tend to be self-serving in both our expectations and our judgments. We want to be both 'normal' and 'exceptional.' If we can find ways to clearly appraise ourselves as normal, then we cling to them as standards by which to judge others. For some of us, being exceptional means the most conformity to gender stereotypes—a 'man's man' or a 'lady's lady.' That can be done without danger to society's separation of the genders. When being exceptional means blurring conventional gender lines, though, our sense of normality is threatened.

For many of us, where biological sex and gender identity agree and gender roles feel comfortable, exceptions to this chain of agreement (sex—gender identity—gender role) seem more than merely unusual. They cause implicit doubt on the solidity of our own normality. Most of us like things clear-cut; gradations in appearance (too tall, too thin, too short, too fat, too whatever) disturb us and invite negative judgments if for little more reason than to reassure us about ourselves. Somehow the scientific desire to classify becomes a social tool by which to separate one person from another, with some categorized as 'not okay' based on a value judgment (e.g., 'It is good to be like me, and not good to be too different from me'), rather than unambiguous evidence of personal distress or impairment in function. In short, we must beware creating judgments of someone else's sin or sickness merely for our own convenience.

So how ought crossdressing be regarded in light of hypothesized causes of it? Obviously, each of us will make a decision for ourselves. My concern is that most of us are short-sighted when it comes to history. We don't know where our views have come from and so we placidly regard them as timeless. We shy away from realizing that much of what we think we know may not be as true as we want it to be. It is easier to turn a blind eye to matters we do not see as directly involving us, or passing conventional judgments in lieu of finding out the facts for ourselves. We forget that the goal in changing what we see is to see better.

We ought to do our best to see as clearly as we can what causes behavior, both because we value such knowledge in its own right and for the benefits we may thereby confer on others. As a general precept, we do well to adhere to the wisdom of Hippocrates in seeking first to do no harm. Beyond that we might aspire to the Golden Rule—the wish to regard and treat others as we would like them to do toward us. Thus, if we can, we want to see others as okay just as they are. We need evidence to decide otherwise. If we can legitimately view matters about sex, gender and dress along the lines that allow us to find difference rather than dysfunction, then let us do so. If the multitude of possible causal factors urges us to not draw general conclusions, especially ones prone to be used to justify unnecessary interventions, then we may be happy to keep studying the matter, trying to stay open to new evidence, and remaining resolute that whatever causes crossdressing, the crossdresser is a person worthy of respect and good will.

At this point in time, my personal conclusion is that the evidence of causality broadly distills to a perspective on 'transgender' variations as *sui generis*.[376] Ongoing evidence suggests increasing support for biological factors interacting with environmental ones. Among the latter, cultural pressures seem the most salient. Certainly they exert their force not only through broad social values and expectations, but instrumentally through social institutions like the family. Nevertheless, regardless of the cause or causes, I remain persuaded the effect of our conclusions on the issue matter more than our theories. This volume concerns the lived experience of real people—our friends, our family members, the people we work for and beside. We need to resolve to keep their humanity, and our own, in the highest position.

Question Set 4:

What is it like to be a transgendered crossdresser?

If it is nothing else, human experience is diverse. While there is a certain usefulness to generalizing apparently common elements of behavior into categories that bear labels to facilitate some kinds of communication, we would be amiss to ever think any particular person is just the sum of a category of characteristics. Lived experience is dynamic, vital, variable, and holistic. We are all unique.

So trying to answer what it is like to be transgendered ultimately cannot yield more than partial answers. 'Transgendered' is just a label, and often a misleading one at that, in a realm where a sufficient vocabulary is still being developed. As we have seen (in the answer to Q. 20), the term is applied to a variety of people. They can be further sorted by other characteristics into subgroups. Yet all the labeling, sorting and describing in the world fails to capture the real lived experience of any individual. If we forget to see genuine individuals in all their particularity all our supposed knowledge remains nonsense.

In this question set we will seek to keep individual experience in sight even while we resort to the conventions of academic analysis and discourse. For each question in this set material will appear from one real person, who graciously consented to consider each question in turn and answer it from individual experience. 'Lee' (a pseudonym) is a White, middle-aged professional, biologically male, assigned to masculinity at birth, and self-identifying as transgendered. Lee read draft material provided for each question, thus having those answers in view when forming personal responses. The drafted remarks were edited, but he approved each final result before it was incorporated. To make Lee's answers easy to see, they have been set apart from the rest of the text in boxes.

Alongside Lee's responses is information drawn from other sources. These materials abstract experience, creating lists of characteristics and forming categories. Of particular importance in creating answers to these questions has been the use of surveys and interviews with transgendered people. Over the last few decades a number of these have appeared. Most of those utilized here appeared in the academic literature, but I have not been opposed to some cautious use of material from other sources. The guiding principle throughout was to give, as much as possible, a voice to transgendered people to speak for themselves in describing what transgendered reality is like.

In that interest, as has been the case throughout this volume, reports of research are written in present tense. This can produce confusion if the limited results from a particular study done years ago is thought to be representing all present day crossdressers. But I have tried to be careful in reminding that no one study, or even set of studies, should be made more than what it is: a partial contribution to our effort to construct a larger picture. Even that larger picture must remain incomplete; there remains much to learn.

As a personal aside, I strongly recommend supplementing this material with as much exposure as possible to firsthand, autobiographical accounts. None of us can speak for all of us, whether transgendered or not, but in these individual stories is writ the story of humanity, in all its flaws and strengths. Increasingly, as witnessed in the answer to Q. 44, transgender realities are being sensitively and sympathetically portrayed in mediums such as television and film. These, too, offer avenues to learn more about transgender people.

Q. 26

How do crossdressers describe themselves?

The Short Answer. Transgendered people have been researched in a number of different ways. Research has utilized surveys, interviews, and other instruments with people who practice crossdressing in such a manner that they themselves, or others, identify them as 'crossdressers.' Unfortunately, most of what we know comes only from male crossdressers. That information shows that most male crossdressers are heterosexual, generally well-educated and affluent, have been or are married and have children. They start crossdressing in childhood, the behavior persists, and often they find crossdressing a vital means of expressing aspects of themselves otherwise not accessible. The majority do not find the behavior constitutes a mental disorder and so do not seek treatment for it. Commonly when counseling occurs in connection with crossdressing it is because a significant other has insisted upon it.

The Longer Answer. A basic difficulty long hampered discussion of male crossdressers: the ones who were talking were not crossdressers but noncrossdressers, typically psychiatrists and other health professionals. The subjects they were discussing, often in case studies of one or a few individuals, were in treatment and usually in distress. In short, much of the scientific literature, especially the older literature, paints a picture of crossdressers distorted by the population it is drawn from. Much of what we knew in the 20th century prior to the 1970s came from a group sharing three characteristics:

❑ male;
❑ heterosexual (though often seen as at least latently homosexual); and
❑ receiving psychological treatment.

A real question posed itself: do these individuals represent most crossdressers?

If the first difficulty is whether a clinical population of male crossdressers adequately represents the larger group of male crossdressers, a second difficulty is whether limiting study of crossdressers to males is appropriate. Anyone familiar with the history of crossdressing is struck by the preponderance of attention given to female crossdressers prior to our contemporary scene. Yet today the attention is almost exclusively fixed upon male crossdressers. Moreover, in a third complicating difficulty, though it is known that some homosexuals also crossdress, the research focus has been on heterosexual males. In large part this has been because of the desire to highlight a single behavior—crossdressing— that distinguishes a group of heterosexual men from other heterosexual men.[377] Yet this focus on heterosexual males represents a bias in data collection that inevitably distorts the overall picture.

Of these difficulties, perhaps the most problematic, historically, has been an over-reliance on data collected from those crossdressers most distressed by their condition, or whose crossdressing became attached to some other circumstance (e.g., relational problems) that resulted in seeking professional help. Because so much of the data historically has been obtained from a 'clinical population'— people in treatment for some condition, whether crossdressing or not—the resulting portrayal has tended toward an extreme, especially given the interpretations put to the behavior by professionals predisposed by their own unexamined cultural bias to regard it negatively. In short, this subset of the much larger crossdressing population, most of whom never seek counseling with reference to crossdressing, may not be a representative sample and certainly often has not been studied dispassionately. Therefore, as time progressed and new perspectives on gender helped open up the research perspective on transgender, the conclusions drawn only from such research were increasingly seen as needing to be balanced against data drawn from a wider group of crossdressers and without the lens of preconceived pathology. In essence, the new task became to let crossdressers speak for themselves, in settings outside mental health facilities, and to listen without preconceptions of pathology.

How do we let crossdressers speak for themselves?

That is where surveys, interviews, and various tests voluntarily undertaken by nonclinical groups of crossdressers enter in. Since the early 1970s these have played an increasingly important part in learning about adult male crossdressing. Through these various instruments crossdressers have a chance to describe themselves, both directly (as in interviews or through surveys), and indirectly (as through various tests). The results can then be compared and contrasted with those found with a clinical population.[378] Unfortunately, by their very nature such studies cannot claim to include representative samples. If anything, together they are only broadly representative of those crossdressers more open to disclose their crossdressing and willing to assist in research. Yet, the results across studies is both illuminating and often compellingly consistent.

In this answer the focus is on what such instruments reveal about male crossdressers. I have sought to emphasize the information gained from research into the lives of crossdressers who are not part of a clinical population. At the same time, where relevant, I have included information from clinical studies, too. In every instance I have sought to make the nature of the research and the population from whom it was obtained clear. In addition, one transgendered person ('Lee') has provided personal material relevant to each subsection's question. Lee's story is uniquely individual, and should not be read as a template all male crossdressers adhere to. It has value both because it is a concrete example of a lived reality and because it reminds us that all our efforts to draft broad descriptions and shape specific categories pales against the richness of life, which persists in a diversity defying tight specification. The best way to understand any human behavior remains to know individuals.

What is childhood like?

A number of research studies have investigated what childhood is like for male crossdressers. Much of this research is retrospective: adults remembering back. The material in this section can be profitably set alongside that in the answers to Q. 28-29. Here only a brief overview is offered, drawn from what crossdressers themselves report.

Birth Order

Some research indicates a greater likelihood of male crossdressers being a firstborn child. The following table illustrates the findings:

Table 26.1 Percent of Crossdressers Who Are Firstborn

Study	# Subjects	Firstborn
Prince & Bentler (1972)[379]	504	50%
Schott (1995)[380]	85	40%
'Yvonne' (1999)[381]	1,316	41%

These percentages are substantially higher than national norms for families where the firstborn is male.

What do such figures mean? Various explanations are possible. Psychological theorists, for example, speak of the 'dethronement' of the firstborn when a new child enters the family. Perhaps efforts to renew and reinforce affiliative ties with the mother lead some sons to adopt crossdressing as a means of identification. Adlerian theorists point to the characteristics typical of firstborns, who tend to take rules and role responsibilities very seriously, perhaps leaving them more vulnerable to gender role pressures. Other theorists note that all males in our culture are placed under heavy gender role expectations. Perhaps, then, crossdressing is adopted by some males as a way of easing away from such burdens or expressing rebellion against the artificial confines in which they find themselves. These are all speculations, of course, and no one knows what significance—if any—birth order has for crossdressing.

Relation to Parents

The family background of crossdressers—particularly crossdressing males—receives attention in many studies (cf. answer to Q. 22). This research is important because of efforts to explain the origin of crossdressing in some kind of family dysfunction. If so, it apparently is not the result of a broken family. A study of 110 crossdressing males, reported by Richard Docter in 1988, shows that four-fifths (80%) of them come from intact families.[382] But that in itself says nothing about the nature of the child's relationship to his parents.

A common idea has been that transvestism in males results from a dominant mother and an absent father (see the answer to Q. 22). Yet self-reports from most crossdressing males do not seem to support this hypothesis. Prince and Bentler's 1972 survey reports that about half (51%) of their subjects identify their father as the dominant parent. Moreover, nearly three-quarters (72%) affirm that their father provided a good masculine image for them.[383] A survey study conducted by Docter and Prince a generation later, patterned on the 1972 survey, finds similar numbers: a little more than three-quarters (76%) reared by both parents through age 18 and a like number (76%) reporting their father provided a good masculine image.[384]

The comparative studies published in 1978 by Buhrich and McConaghy,[385] and the report in 1995 by Schott,[386] also find no support for the hypothesis of a disturbed relationship with the mother. However, at least one study does find evidence of a parent sex-role reversal in transvestites' parents, with the fathers appearing to their sons as more dependent and affiliative in behavior compared to the perceptions of noncrossdressing males.[387] And Schott's 1995 report suggests that relationships with fathers may be viewed less positively than those with mothers; more than two-thirds (68%) of his subjects put the father-son relationship on the lower end of a continuum, with judgments ranging from 'neutral' (31%) through 'fairly negative' (20%) to 'very negative' (17%).[388]

Happiness

One might suppose that crossdressing contributes to being less happy in childhood, if for no other reason than fear and the consequences of being caught.[389] Plenty of research suggests that transgender children, especially those who crossdress, are at risk for displeasure, even rejection, from other family members (see the answer to Q. 29). In light of the possibly disastrous consequences of the behavior we might expect a learned association between crossdressing and punishment that would help extinguish the behavior, or at least render it so fraught with anxiety as to become unpleasurable. Yet Schott's study reports that more than half (55%) of the 85 male crossdressers he surveyed recall positive emotions of enjoyment and happiness from crossdressing. Transsexuals, on the other hand, are emotionally neutral about their crossdressing since, for them, it is 'normal.'[390] Perhaps all this says is that pleasure exists in the act for those who succeed in not being caught, or who live in supportive family environments. Or perhaps it reflects the power of crossdressing to produce congruent and positive feelings that outweigh the risks or even the punishments. In either instance, this fact alone does not speak completely to the larger question of whether childhood overall is remembered fondly as a generally happy time.

While relatively few studies probe crossdressers' assessment of their childhoods as happy or unhappy, the results of those that do seem to be fairly consistent, as the following table shows:

Table 26.2 Recollected Happiness in Childhood

Study	# Subjects	Happy	Mixed	Unhappy
Bullough, Bullough, & Smith (1983)[391]	65	38%	39%	23%
Bullough & Bullough (1997)[392]	372	42%	46%	12%

The overall picture, as the Bulloughs conclude in their 1997 study, is one of a "more or less normal childhood."[393]

Education

Academic performance also has been investigated. Those crossdressers who participate in surveys and interviews are generally well-educated, as the following table shows:

Table 26.3 Educational Attainment

Study	# Subjects	B.A. +
Prince & Bentler (1972)[394]	504	37%
Croughan, et al. (1981)[395]	70	36%
Docter (1988)[396]	110	53%
Docter & Prince (1997)[397]	1,032	65%
'Yvonne' (1999)[398]	1,141	43%
Docter & Fleming (2001)[399]	516	73%

In understanding the above figures, it is important to also bear in mind the norms of the time. For instance, in the 1960s far fewer people attended or completed college than was the case in the 1990s.

161

However, academic attainment and academic experience are different matters. Despite their attainment, many crossdressers may feel inadequate as students. The earlier reported comparative study with 65 male transvestites and 33 male transsexuals finds that both these groups describe their performance as somewhat poorer than do other groups. Still, more than a third (35%) of transvestites report having been "excellent" students, and only 11% say they were "poor" students. The numbers for transsexuals are a bit worse: 30% "excellent," but 21% "poor."[400] Such figures should be placed in the context of overall school experience, which is often problematic (see the answer to Q. 37).

Crossdressing in Childhood (cf. answer to Q. 28)

We saw a moment ago that many crossdressers remember childhood crossdressing as a happy experience. The vast majority of crossdressers start this behavior in childhood, typically before puberty. However, no uniform practice can be discerned after it starts. Some do it more often than others. Some do it more completely than others. Croughan and associates find that even initial efforts vary widely: about half use only undergarments, most of the rest use some combination of under- and outer-garments, while just 10% start fully crossdressed. By adolescence, more than half are crossdressing partially or fully at least once a week, and the percentage of those so doing rises after age 30.[401] Schott's 1995 survey finds that while nearly half (45%) only crossdress infrequently in childhood, a sizeable minority (13%) do so regularly. But, as Schott also finds, one factor does unite most childhood experiences—they are kept secret. More than three-quarters (78%) keep their crossdressing secret, with the highest percentages among nuclear transvestites (83%) and the lowest among transsexuals (69%). Of the 22% who are more public, it is because another family member encourages and supports the behavior, at least up to school age.[402]

Lee's Remarks

Hi. Call me Lee. I agreed to answer these questions because it feels like a safe way to say some things that matter to me. So let me get started, but let me begin by stressing I am only speaking for myself. I don't pretend to speak for anyone else. I may share some things in common with their experiences, but I imagine a lot of things are different, too.

I am the firstborn in my family. During my growing up years my parents had the best marriage of anyone I knew and, frankly, that remains true. My father is the head of the family, though my mother rules the household; the overall effect is a pretty egalitarian relationship. My father was—and is—a man's man: independent, strong, well-versed in all the matters American males are supposed to be capable in. He made his living doing a man's work come rain or shine, with never a complaint. I would have to affirm emphatically that he provided a masculine role model—one I have never come close to approximating. I admire him immensely and we have a strong relationship—but I am not a man like him.

Growing up, I was closer to my mother, who was always available and often needed as I was a small, frail, often sickly child. Childhood was difficult for me in many respects and I was eager to grow up. I was not a particularly happy child, nor an especially unhappy one. I poured myself into academic pursuits, the one arena where I excelled. I have completed schooling through the attainment of an advanced degree. Crossdressing was part of my childhood from an early age, certainly by age 5.

What are some demographics of adult crossdressers?

Occupational Social Status

Male crossdressers are represented in a range of occupations, some lower and others higher in social status. Prince and Bentler's 1972 report shows that among its subjects one out of six (17%) are either president of a company or business owners.[403] But, as found with other matters, there are differences between crossdressing subgroups. Male transvestites fare better than male transsexuals in matters of occupational social status. The 1983 comparative study referenced elsewhere in this answer finds that nearly two-thirds (64%) of transvestites rank above the national median in occupational prestige. This compares to less than a third (31%) of transsexuals and homosexuals (30%) ranking above the national median. Transvestites are also well above the undifferentiated group they are compared to (64% to 48% above). The authors comment:

> [T]he transvestite sample was heavily represented in the mainstream white collar world, including engineering, accounting, teaching, sales, and clerical work. These men clearly are high prestige workers, and, except for the two hairdressers and the performing artists, were not represented in stereotypically feminine jobs.[404]

Similar findings pertain in later studies reported in 1988 and 1997, though in the latter with relatively more representation in technical and professional groups and relatively less in unskilled positions.[405]

Transsexuals may not fare as well as transvestites. A study published about the same time as Bentler and Prince's work, of 599 transsexual respondents to a survey, reports, "Most respondents clustered in the lower middle-upper lower and lower socioeconomic classes. Since male respondents were drawn to employment usually considered feminine, the overall effect was to lower the socioeconomic level of that group." However, the authors of the study note mitigating factors that might be influencing the findings, such as reluctance by transsexuals in higher economic classes to respond to the survey.[406]

Perhaps pertinent to this area is the research done by clinician Ingrid Sell about Americans who identify as 'third gender' people. Her study of 30 such folk, including biological males and females, with ages ranging from 29-77, finds that compared to the general population a disproportionate number (43%) work in health and helping professions. They also are more likely than the general population to be engaged in highly creative and artistic endeavors; nearly half (47%) are writers, musicians, or other performers—and 17% earn a substantial portion of their income from their art. As Sell perceptively notes, these characteristics parallel cross-cultural evidence about the activities of third gender people elsewhere around the world (cf. the answers to Q. 51-59).[407]

Marriage and Family

A substantial number of crossdressers are married—or have been. Among crossdressing men who identify themselves as heterosexual, the majority are, or have been, married and have children. This finding has been consistent across various studies, as the following table shows:

Table 26.4 Marital Status & Children

Study	# Subjects	Married	Children
Meyer, Knorr, Blumer (1971)[408]	599	19%	4%
Prince & Bentler (1972)[409]	504	78%	74%
Croughan, et al. (1981)[410]	70	77%	--
Docter (1988)[411]	110	82%	59%
Docter & Prince (1997)[412]	1,032	83%	69%
'Yvonne' (1999)[413]	1,205	75%	74%
Docter & Fleming (2001)[414]	516	82%	71%

The first of the studies in this Table differs from the others in some important respects. First, its subject pool is entirely comprised of self-identified transsexuals. Second, it includes both males and females (73% males). This study differentiates between marriage and cohabitation, and the percentages increase to about 47% if cohabitation is included.[415] Nevertheless, this study, though reflecting a more difficult historical period for transsexuals, may indicate that they are less likely to marry than other crossdressers.

But does crossdressing make marriage a rocky road? Prince and Bentler's study reports that more than a third of their subjects who divorced cite their crossdressing as one cause.[416] Yet Docter's analysis of his research subjects suggests they do not appear to be extraordinarily at risk for divorce.[417] Overall, the rejection of such behavior by a spouse certainly can't be seen as lending itself to marital health and stability, but it also does not seem to predict an inevitability of distress and divorce (cf. the answer to Q. 38).

Religious Affiliation

Surveys and interviews consistently reveal a broad pattern of religious affiliations. As might be expected, since the research has largely been done in the United States or in societies sharing a similar religious heritage, most crossdressers identify themselves as Christians. The data can be displayed as follows:

Table 26.5 Religious Affiliation

Study	Roman Catholic	Protestant	Jewish	Other
Meyer, Knorr, & Blumer (1971)[418]	10%	15%	.3%	4%
Prince & Bentler (1972)[419]	23%	57%	4%	16%
Croughan, et al. (1981)[420]	20%	66%	7%	7%
Docter & Prince (1997)[421]	24%	38%	3%	35%
'Yvonne' (1999)[422]	28%	29%	2%	41%

Religious affiliation does not appear to be associated with an increased likelihood of crossdressing. (On such matters, see volume 3 of this work.)

Intriguingly, Sell's research finds a related feature that may be significant. In her study, the vast majority of people identifying as 'third gender' experience two facets associated in other parts of the world with shamans: mediation and transcendent spiritual events. More than three-quarters (77%) recount being asked to mediate between men and women because they are viewed as having a perspective wide enough to see both sides. Many also mediate with other groups (e.g., racial, cultural, sub-cultural, age-differentiated). More strikingly yet, 93% report one or more transcendent spiritual events and/or what others would term 'paranormal' abilities. Sell notes that these numbers far exceed what other research finds for members of the general population. "Perhaps," she concludes, "as non-Western cultures recognize, there is indeed an element of spirit or 'calling' involved in our being men, women, or mediators between."[423]

Lee's Remarks

I grew up in a home where my mother was very active in the church, which meant that we kids were as well. Ours was a Protestant church, and I suppose I'd say it was a Protestant upbringing I received, with an emphasis on the value of work, self-control, and morality. My parents, well-read themselves, always strongly supported my schooling and eventually I ended up a teacher, though looking back it seems more like I drifted into the profession as a compromise between my various ambitions, tempered with a fair dose of uncertainty about how I fit into the world.

Most of my career has been spent teaching college undergraduates in state-sponsored schools. After embarking on this career I followed a conventional path, marrying and becoming a father. My marriage ended in divorce, though I don't attribute that to being transgendered since my wife had no inkling of my crossdressing nor did I ever discuss matters of sex or gender with her. She expected a husband who would fulfill a masculine role in a socially conventional manner; I only partially succeeded. I suppose in that sense being transgendered played a role in our marriage ending, because I was unable to be the man she wanted—a fact she constantly reminded me of. After some years single, I re-married.

My present wife has known since before we married that I crossdress. She does not fully understand why I crossdress, and has made only occasional, sporadic efforts to understand. She barely tolerates it, and then only when I keep it as hidden as possible. I am disappointed she closes herself off from me in this way, but given how so many people in our society are, I am not surprised, nor do I condemn her. But it does elicit a sense of loneliness for me in the one relationship where I least desire being alone.

To her credit, my wife struggles with the issue, and seems to sometimes at least glimpse it as a matter of my gender and identity rather than some weird quirk of my personality or some kinky sexual thing. While she feels it unfortunate I have not the same freedom as she does to be herself openly, she also is emphatic that I refrain from such freedom around anyone, including herself. In her mind, if I am transgendered whether crossdressed or not, why should I ever be crossdressed? It's a fair question, but my answer seems to elude her.

I am not magically changed by crossdressing, but I do experience a greater sense of completeness and satisfaction when dressing in a manner that fits me. I am transgendered whether crossdressed or not, but when I am crossdressed my gender appearance balances my body appearance, and that permits a sense of completeness, relaxation and satisfaction I do not otherwise have. Perhaps part of the difficulty for my wife (and maybe others) is understanding how clothes can play such a strong role for me when they hold a significantly less vital role in her own life.

What are some psychological characteristics?

Crossdressing for Personality Expression

A common refrain among crossdressers categorized as 'transvestites' is that crossdressing facilitates a full expression of personality that otherwise does not occur. While crossdressed there is an experience of greater access to feelings coupled with an enhanced pleasure in living.[424] Docter and Prince's survey of over 1000 male crossdressers finds four-fifths (80%) feel crossdressing allows them to express a different part of themselves.[425] Similarly, a 1999 online survey finds that 74% respond affirmatively to the query, "In your opinion, do you exhibit a different personality *en femme* than when you present as a man?"[426]

Neil Buhrich, in interviews with 33 crossdressing males in a transvestites' club, finds that these men commonly report feeling more at ease when crossdressed. There is also less experience of the burden of traditional masculine demands. Similar reports are found by Buhrich in a comparison group of 24 transsexual males. However, Buhrich finds that transvestite males show more compulsive and narcissistic behaviors than their transsexual counterparts,[427] though this finding is relative to a specific population and should not be unduly exaggerated or over-generalized.

Crossdressers and Counseling

There is perhaps a certain irony that much of what even mental health professionals think they know about crossdressers often comes from a very narrow segment of the crossdressing population. Most crossdressers never seek counseling, either for their crossdressing or anything else. In this respect, apparently, they are like the population at large. The 1972 survey of 504 subscribers to *Transvestia* magazine find that more than three-quarters of the respondents never sought a professional's opinion about their behavior.[428] The 1981 research by Croughan and associates of 70 subjects uses broad parameters in order to designate about half (49%) as a 'treated group'; they are placed in this group if they have ever been seen by a professional in connection to their crossdressing. Within this group, half of the men self-referred for treatment—a number less than one-quarter (24%) of the total pool, and also similar to earlier findings.[429] When counseling is sought, it often is for relational issues. This proves true for 1-in-7 (16%) of Croughan and associates' group of subjects.[430] The online survey of 1999 finds that almost 15% of respondents who had been married, are married, or are in a relationship have tried marriage counseling, and almost three-quarters (72%) feel their counselor was accepting of crossdressing, yet most (62%) do not feel the counseling proved helpful.[431]

Lee's Remarks

I can emphatically affirm that I crossdress to realize and express myself. Put bluntly, I only feel fully who I am when crossdressed. Here's the deal: I know I am not a female. But I have never identified as a masculine male either. I get that one can be a heterosexual male and still not have the sense of being a man—that fits my experience. I don't pretend to understand why or how, but crossdressing always lets me feel like myself. Maybe I should just be content with seeing myself as a feminine male and leave it at that, though my fuzzy sense about all this is that I need another gender alternative to fit myself in. For now I sometimes live with the term 'transgender,' though for me that means 'bigender' or, better, 'third gender.' Believe me, I have tried to make sense of my crossdressing, and much of what I have read about it resonates with me, but at day's end all I am certain about is that I feel most myself when crossdressed.

As for having a different personality, I don't know. I guess I see it more as my full personality is present when I'm crossdressed—or at least is more fully experienced. When I'm not crossdressed, I have to fake a masculinity that isn't true to my sense of self and which never fits comfortably (though it reassures my wife, who desires me to be a masculine male, despite having actually come to love me as a transgendered one!). I suppose it's true I feel relief from the demands of the masculine gender role because I am not pretending to be masculine when dressed in feminine clothes. That feels both good and right.

As for counseling, I have never sought help for crossdressing because it has never been a problem for me. In fact, quite the opposite is true. I feel crossdressing may do more to keep me sane than just about anything else! I wish the world I live in was more accepting of people in general, and certainly I wish they were more accepting of people like me. Personally, I think intolerant, violent people are a lot more in need of therapy than those of us who dress in unconventional ways!

What is the sexual orientation of crossdressers?

Research consistently finds that most crossdressers—regardless of sex—are *heterosexual*. Yet the notion that crossdressing means the person is homosexual has been a persistent myth. In all likelihood, for many who hold this erroneous view the idea was planted and then reinforced by images of drag queens in a visible homosexual community. But data obtained from crossdressers paints a far different picture. The vast majority—at least four-fifths (80%)—are heterosexual. (For more complete information, see the answer to Q 55.)

Lee's Remarks

My sexual desires have always been directed toward women. This was never an ambiguous matter for me. In my adolescence I never experimented with sex with any male peers. I started dating at age 15, had several girlfriends before my wife, and was conventionally sexually active with them. I guess all this makes me a pretty ordinary heterosexual.

What is the preferred gender identity of crossdressers?

Gender identity is clearly of strong interest to crossdressers. In the 1972 Prince and Bentler survey, subjects are asked which statement from a list applies to them. The choices are:

☐ "I feel myself to be a woman trapped in a male body";
☐ "I feel myself to be a man who just has a feminine side seeking expression"; or,

❏ "I feel myself to be a man with just a sexual fetish for feminine attire."

The first and last alternatives are not strongly endorsed (12% for each); the middle choice is strongly endorsed (69%).[432]

In a study of 222 male crossdressers in America (N=126) and Australia (N=86), published in 1981, Neil Buhrich and Trina Beaumont report that when crossdressed more than three-quarters of these men claim they feel like a woman. Interestingly, almost a fifth (18%) also report feeling this way when dressed in masculine clothing.[433] A generation after the Prince and Bentler study, the Docter and Prince survey of 1032 male crossdressers, reported in 1997, finds nearly three-quarters (74%) of these men identify themselves as a man with a feminine side, and more than half (60%) prefer the masculine and feminine gender identities equally.[434]

Gender identity issues may differentiate crossdressers from noncrossdressers, but they likewise can differentiate some crossdressers from other crossdressers. Buhrich and Beaumont's 1981 study separates results for 'nuclear' (satisfied with crossdressing, less intense feminine identification, and stronger heterosexual interest) and 'marginal' (desire for at least partial feminization by hormones or surgery) transvestites. Marginal transvestites are more likely to report feeling like a woman when crossdressed than are nuclear transvestites (90% to 69%). A similarly large margin is found in percentages for this feeling even when dressed as a man (26% to 9%).[435]

The 1983 comparative study cited earlier, involving male transvestites, transsexuals, homosexuals and others, also demonstrates this differentiation among crossdressers, though using broader groups. While transvestites are most likely to identify themselves as males with a feminine side (46%), more than a third (37%) prefer characterizing themselves as a "person who enjoys opposite sex clothing," and 11% favor the description "woman trapped in a male body," though they are not categorized as transsexuals. Still, this last choice is dwarfed among transvestites when compared to its selection by transsexuals (64%). More than a quarter (27%) of transsexuals prefer the even stronger descriptor, "woman."[436]

Lee's Remarks

Should I worry if I don't find myself fitting snugly into any of the boxes? Perhaps I am self-deceived, but as best I can tell, I don't particularly feel either masculine or feminine—but how are those supposed to feel anyway? I either feel like myself, or I don't; when I am crossdressed is when I feel most like myself. If that means I'm feminine, okay. But where does that put me? I don't feel like a woman trapped in a man's body, but how can I know what it feels like to be a woman so that I might feel like one trapped in a man's body?!? On the other hand, I often do feel trapped in a man's body that has never felt exactly right. I am not comfortable in my own skin and don't ever remember being so.

I will confess that given what I know, witness, and experience, that if I had to choose to be at one or the other end of the gender spectrum, I'd prefer the feminine end. But why do I have to choose? Put me in the middle, or outside your little gender box scheme and let me be. I just want to be who I am!

What is crossdressing behavior in general?

(Also see the answers to Q. 29-34, and 90.)

Transsexuals and transgenderists (those living full time in a gender different than the one assigned them at birth) might be expected to crossdress most or all of the time. But that is not necessarily so, at least for transsexuals. Although we must reckon with how times have changed, in the 1971 research reported earlier, of the 599 self-identified transsexual participants, fully 23% deny ever crossdressing at all—though whether that reflects regarding their behavior as noncrossdressing where others would judge it as crossdressing is unknown. More than half (52%) report some crossdressing, and the authors note a distinct difference between male and female transsexuals. Though the latter are less likely overall to try crossdressing, those that do seem more committed to the practice.[437]

With a different population in view (heterosexual transvestites), Prince and Bentler find that their subjects generally embrace crossdressing. Most (72%) express the hope of expanding their crossdressing activities and the vast majority (85%) prefer full costume (including wig and makeup) to partial crossdressing. Among individual items, there is a preference for lingerie (32% indicate most interest in these kinds of items), but more than one-fifth (21%) simply state they like all feminine items. Most have never tried to "pass" in public as a woman. A mere 1% of their sample express a hope of restricting their behavior in an effort to stop it. Still, more than two-thirds (69%) have experienced a "purge" (doing away with their feminine items) at one time or another.[438] A generation later, almost all (93%) the crossdressers surveyed by Docter and Prince also express a preference for complete crossdressing, but remain reticent about appearing in public while crossdressed. Struggles over crossdressing are still evident, too; three-quarters (75%) have at one time or another purged.[439]

If no other reason than cultural norms, crossdressing creates at least some degree of internal conflict for most crossdressers. While negative feelings may lead to purging, it neither stops the behavior nor accurately predicts how crossdressers will continue to feel. In fact, Prince and Bentler discover a wide range of feelings about crossdressing among the men who practice it. Less than a quarter (22%) report feelings of shame or guilt, and those feelings are dissipating. More than three-quarters (78%) express positive perceptions of their crossdressing. About a third (32%) feel free of guilt, and more than one-fifth (21%) believe crossdressing has made a valuable contribution to their life.[440]

Lee's Remarks

My relationship to clothes is this: I endure wearing masculine clothing; I love wearing women's clothing. I like soft colors and fine fabrics. I find soothing the sensation of camisoles against my skin, and the thick comfort of long cotton socks. But skirts are my favorite article of dress. I enjoy how a long skirt feels, looks, and even sounds. When I am completely crossdressed, I feel alive, secure, at peace. Because I cannot wear feminine clothing as I'd like, I select as androgynous clothing as I can find, while wearing feminine underwear, except for when I go out in public.

I have never tried to pass as a woman in public. I have no desire to do so. That does not mean I have no desire to be crossdressed in the company of others. I would love the freedom to be who I am anytime and anywhere I want to be—and dress accordingly. I am very careful how I dress and I have been fully crossdressed in the presence of others while wearing women's clothes easily perceived as androgynous because I am not presenting as a woman. People in such cases see what they want to see. No one has challenged me, questioned me, or exhibited any unease. Still, I wish I had the kind of home where I could relax and wear what I want when I want, regardless of how feminine it is perceived to be.

But let's get real—other people are not about to let me do that. I hate that I am forced to pretend to be masculine; that doesn't mean I'm interested in pretending to be a feminine female. As long as we are all stuck having to be one or the other, I am stuck, too. So I keep my crossdressing private. Only a couple of people know of it.

I prefer to be fully crossdressed, but I generally compromise with social logistics and end up being partially crossdressed. I don't use jewelry or makeup, nor do I use a wig. Far from trying to be someone I am not, I crossdress to be who I am. I like the look and the feel of feminine clothing. I more often wear feminine underwear than outerwear, but that's because of visibility issues. I feel neither guilt nor shame over being who I am or dressing accordingly.

So why do I keep my crossdressing secret? What world do *you* live in? If I tried to pass as a woman I'd be living as much a falsehood as I do having to pretend I'm a man. If I dressed as a woman without trying to pass as one all I'd do is risk violence from intolerant bigots. So keeping my crossdressing secret is a rational choice and not one born of shame.

Q. 27

What is the profile of a 'typical' cross-dresser?

The Short Answer. There is an abundance of information about crossdressers. This material encompasses personal anecdotes, historical accounts, anthropological and sociological observations and analyses, and psychological research. Though this volume touches on all of these sources, in this answer the focus is on empirical research with regard to demographic and personality characteristics. The research offers a somewhat mixed bag of findings but generally supports the conclusion that crossdressers are folk pretty much like everybody else. Whether speaking of personality, mental health, or sexuality, crossdressers are not as different from noncrossdressers as many of the latter fear. Especially with regard to overall mental health, major reviews conclude that crossdressers are no more liable to mental disorders than are noncrossdressers. Perhaps surprising to noncrossdressers, some research suggests that when crossdressers are crossdressed they actually do better psychologically than when not crossdressed. (Also see the answers to Q. 26, 94 and 98.)

The Longer Answer. The material here is meant to stand alongside that found in answering Q. 26 so that those who wish to do so may compare and contrast the results found through surveys and interviews (last question) with other instruments (e.g., case studies and tests). Let us begin with a capsule overview. Transgender therapist and columnist Gianna Israel offers a succinct reminder:

> Transgender individuals can come from any racial, economic, or religious background. They work in many types of fields; there are transgender physicians, teachers, insurance underwriters and auto mechanics. Finally, most transgender persons have families, and a large proportion have children. This knowledge should be passed on to other family members and relatives who are misinformed or who are afraid of catching 'transgender germs.'[441]

Crossdressers are, first and foremost, *persons*.

What are some general characteristics?

Writing in 1970, sociologist H. Taylor Buckner offers the following generalizations for what he learned from surveys completed by 262 adult transvestites:

- ☐ The ordinary transvestite is male.
- ☐ He is most likely married.
- ☐ If married, he probably has children.
- ☐ Almost all claim to be exclusively heterosexual.
- ☐ The crossdressing is generally done in private.
- ☐ There is rarely trouble with the law.
- ☐ Any difficulties associated with crossdressing tend to be between he and his wife.[442]

This profile of the adult male transvestite in the United States apparently has remained constant over the last few decades. To the above list can be added this often observed characteristic:

- ☐ Sexual arousal associated with the crossdressing tends to abate with age.[443]

Also worth noting is that these characteristics may hold true for individuals in different societies that share the same general culture.[444]

Lee's Remarks

The characteristics listed by Buckner all fit me: I'm biologically male, married with children, heterosexual, and very private about crossdressing so that I can avoid transphobic responses. I have never been in trouble with the law for anything—and aim to keep it so.

I do wish to comment on the 'additional' characteristic. Sexy clothes are arousing whether they are on me or on my partner. But then, they are supposed to be! On the other hand, I don't need to wear any clothes to be aroused. Nor does simply being crossdressed arouse me. Put all this together and I have a hard time agreeing that any sexual arousal I feel connected to crossdressing is either more or less than when I was younger. When it is a part of sexual activity it is pleasing, because it simply is a part of who I am, and I'm a sexual being. But I don't require being crossdressed to be excited, and generally have not been crossdressed during sex. Finally, I have always found it irritating and demeaning that so many people fixate on the connection between crossdressing and sexual arousal—that just misses the boat as far as I'm concerned.

What are some personality characteristics?

In the mid-1970s, researcher and theoretician Peter Bentler sought to articulate a rough and preliminary list of 32 factors involved in the development of a feminine sex role in males. His interest yields a typology useful with three groups: homosexuals, transsexuals, and transvestites. Some of his factors indicate developed personality traits. All three conditions, he feels, show an emphasis on independence, with an absence of same-sex affiliative behavior. Transsexualism and transvestism he associates with training in impulse control, harm avoidance, and behavioral inhibition. For transvestism alone he also finds an emphasis on intellectual success.[445]

Bentler is noted for being a careful scholar. But do his observations correspond with other studies? What does research through actual personality testing reveal? Fortunately, there are a number of such studies employing a variety of personality tests. The overall picture looks like this:

❏ Personality tests show that crossdressers are more like members of the general population than they are unlike them.

❏ In the ways that crossdressers as a group are different from general population norms, the differences are generally not statistically significant (i.e., the findings are judged to not be the products of chance), and even less likely to be clinically significant (i.e., the findings do not suggest psychopathology).

❏ In addition to personality features, crossdressers are also more like than unlike the general population in sexual functioning. In fact, one team of researchers characterizes the situation as being that crossdressers are virtually indistinguishable from noncrossdressers in both personality and sexual functioning.[446]

❏ One area where crossdressers display a consistent difference from others is in greater feminine gender affiliation. Yet, not all crossdressers show the same level of difference; transvestite and transsexual groups can be distinguished from homosexuals and from one another.

❏ As with other groups, there are some differences between those crossdressers who are "distressed" and seek treatment, and those who do not seek treatment. Thus, the subjects of any study should be noted when interpreting the results.

These broad conclusions can be illustrated by consideration of a number of specific studies, to which we shall now turn. (These are generally presented in chronological order within each section.)

Projective Tests

A number of different personality tests have been used to compare crossdressers to others. Among these some have been projective tests. This kind of test assumes that an individual's personality will be projected outward as they interact with ambiguous stimuli, such as inkblots or pictures. Some of the best known projective tests are the Rorschach and the Holtzman Ink Blot tests, and the Thematic Apperception Test (TAT).

One early study, conducted by Peter Bentler, Richard Sherman and Charles 'Virginia' Prince, dates from 1970. In it, 25 male crossdressers not in therapy are administered the Holtzman Ink Blot Test. This projective test consists of a set of 45 inkblots presented the individual sequentially, with only one response per card permitted. The results obtained are then compared to norms for the general population. Crossdressers, this research finds, tend to respond more to the form of the inkblots than to their color or shading, a response style associated with relative rigidity of personality. Although crossdressers exhibit some greater preoccupation with the body, and elevated levels of anxiety and hostility, overall they do not differ significantly from the general population. The researchers conclude that "the scores for transvestites seem to indicate generally organized and intellectually adequate thought processes."[447]

Transsexuals also have been administered projective measures. A 1980 report examines test results for an individual obtained over a 9 year span. The first testing occurs 6 years before sex reassignment surgery (SRS). At this time, the tests used include several projective instruments as well as the Wechsler Adult Intelligence Scale (WAIS) and a neuropsychological test (the Bender-Gestalt). Specifically, the projective tests are the Holtzman Ink Blot Technique, the Draw-a-Person (DAP) test, and the Thematic Apperception Test (TAT). The Holtzman already has been described. The DAP provides the test subject with a 9½"-by-12" blank sheet of paper, plus a pencil, with instructions to draw a picture of a person. After completing it, the subject is asked to then draw a picture of a person of the opposite sex from that of the first drawing. The TAT presents a series of pictures and asks the respondent to tell a story concerning each. Initial results for the person disclose significant distress, including suicidal tendencies. This situation leads to psychotherapy. After SRS, re-testing reveals depression accompanied by guilt and identity conflicts. Psychotherapy continues. A final evaluation reveals significant changes. Mood has greatly improved, anxiety has decreased, and intellectual functioning is good.[448]

Different projective testing with a group of transsexuals is reported in 1982. In this study, the Rorschach inkblot test is employed. This test is the most widely used projective instrument. A series of 10 bilaterally symmetrical ink blots, on 5"-by-9" cards, are presented in order. The subject is asked to describe fully what is seen in each. In this study, 20 transsexuals (10 male-to-female (MtF) and 10 female-to-male (FtM)) are administered the Rorschach both before and after sex reassignment surgery. The results of these tests are then compared to norms drawn from subjects in the general population. There proves to be "a lack of obvious difference from norms for the general population."[449]

As will be seen below, other projective tests also have been employed in various studies. These have included the DAP, the Franck Drawing Completion

Test, and the Animal and Opposite-Animal Drawing Technique (AOADT). Among these, the DAP appears to be the most widely used. Since these tests have been principally used in gender identification assessments, they are considered under that section.

Mixed, Multivariate & Multiple Instrument Assessments

In 1965, a report is published that contains the results of tests performed on 19 adult male transvestites. On one instrument, the Maudsley Personality Inventory's Extraversion Scale, these men average one standard deviation below the norm (-1 SD), meaning they are significantly less extraverted (hence, more introverted). On the other hand, a +1 SD average is found on the Neuroticism Scale, indicating greater than average anxiety—a finding affirmed by scores on the Willoughby Anxiety Scale. Finally, gender testing reveals average scores indicating greater feminine identity than found in most males. [450]

Peter Bentler and Virginia Prince did a comparative study reported in 1969, which involves 181 adult male crossdressers, 1,029 norm subjects, and 62 control subjects. The crossdressers are not clients in clinical treatment. The research examines variables on the Personality Research Form (PRF), Form BB, an instrument used to measure normal personality traits. A total of 22 traits are assessed through the 440 items of the test. The results show crossdressers are "clearly more controlled in their impulses" as reflected in these traits:

❑ a tendency to avoid risks of bodily harm alongside a dislike of exciting, but potentially dangerous activities;

❑ a concern to maintain neat and organized personal surroundings;

❑ a preference for routine over new and different experiences;

❑ a tendency toward deliberate rather than spontaneous acts; and,

❑ a reluctance to express feelings and wishes.[451]

Another set of differences between these men and those they are compared to concerns "the degree and nature of interpersonal orientation," as exhibited in the following traits:

❑ being relatively withdrawn socially;

❑ tendencies toward introversion;

❑ a preference not to be the center of attention;

❑ less nurturing (e.g., in doing favors or offering sympathy);

❑ less concern for approval from others;

❑ less likelihood of seeking roles of dominance—or enjoying them;

❑ a dislike of arguments and conflict, and,

❑ being relatively more self-reliant and autonomous.[452]

A study subsequently published by Bentler and Prince in 1970 involves a similar number of male transvestites. They recive a standard psychopathology inventory test along the lines of the Minnesota Multiphasic Personality Inventory (MMPI). The research discovers no gross psychiatric symptomatology in its subjects. It does note, though, that on average these men are slightly more constrained in their impulses.[453]

The MMPI also has been used with transsexual subjects. In 1979, 27 MtF transsexual candidates for SRS are administered the test. The data obtained is then compared to that gained from 50 male medical patients (24 kidney transplant candidates and 26 possibly having a psychophysiological disorder). The results confirm an absence of psychopathology in the transsexual subjects.[454]

Also reported in 1979 is research involving 17 FtM transsexual candidates for SRS, in a comparative study with 40 lesbians and 59 female heterosexuals, focused on self-esteem and psychological well-being. The researchers use the Tennessee Self-Concept Scale (TSCS), an instrument comprised of 100 self-descriptive items. The TSCS measures more than just self-esteem. It examines a variety of aspects of a person's self-concept, including both external (e.g., social) and internal (e.g., identity) factors. While the FtM transsexuals individually vary in measures both of self-concept and adjustment, as a group they are not appreciably different from the other groups.[455]

Transsexuals awaiting SRS are subjects in a 1981 study. The 22 persons are administered both a standard mental ability test and a comprehensive personality test. For the former, the Wechsler Adult Intelligence Scale (WAIS)—the most widely used measure of adult intelligence—is employed. It has both vocabulary and performance tests. For the latter, the Minnesota Multiphasic Personality Inventory (MMPI) is used. It consists of more than 500 statements to which the respondent must answer 'true,' 'false,' or 'cannot say.' A total of 10 clinical scales are reported, which provide a measure of any psychopathology. Results on the WAIS prove mixed: subjects score congruent to their genetic sex except on a measure of conceptual styles, where scores are congruent instead with their gender identity. The MMPI finds no major psychopathology processes involved in the subjects.[456]

A team in 1991 reports a study of 24 men diagnosed with transvestic fetishism and receiving treatment. They are interviewed in addition to being administered two psychological tests. Personality traits are measured by Costa and McRae's NEO Personality Inventory (NEO-PI). This instrument is a 181 item questionnaire based on the five-factor model (OCEAN) of personality. Sexual functioning is assessed using the Derogatis Sexual Functioning Inventory (DSFI). It employs 255 items to measure 10 dimensions.[457]

The data obtained from these instruments is then compared to data from 26 men diagnosed with other sexual paraphilias. The researchers' analysis of the comparison leads them to conclude the two groups are more alike than dissimilar on most dimensions of the NEO-PI and the DSFI. Both groups are higher than general population norms in N ("Neuroticism"), and lower in A ("Agreeableness"). Among key findings concerning the male transvestites in treatment in comparison to the general male population are these:

- ❏ Relatively high levels of neuroticism (a personality trait associated with tendencies toward anxiety, depression, self-consciousness and vulnerability to stress) are common.
- ❏ Relatively high levels of hostility also are found.
- ❏ Relatively high levels of role identity with femininity prevail.
- ❏ Relatively low levels of agreeableness are seen.
- ❏ Relatively low levels of emotional intimacy (whether because of need or capacity) also are observed.[458]

It should be remembered that these crossdressing subjects are all in treatment and have received a specific diagnosis of transvestic fetishism—a particular kind of crossdressing discussed more fully in volume 4. The personality traits of this group may not be generalizable to the wider crossdressing population.

In fact, another limited study involving 13 crossdressing men, reported by Chris Gosselin and Sybil B. Eysenck, finds rather different results. Researchers administer the Eysenck Personality Inventory (EPI) to these men both while crossdressed and when not crossdressed. Results show that the men, while crossdressed, score significantly lower on the Neuroticism scale. They also score lower on Psychoticism but higher on Extraversion.[459] In sum, these men demonstrate less anxiety and are more at ease and outgoing when crossdressed. This study also provides an interesting counterpoint to other research by Gosselin and Glen Wilson using the Eysenck Personality Questionnaire (EPQ), among other instruments. In 1980, based on data obtained from 269 adult male crossdressers who are not in treatment, the researchers report that crossdressers rank higher in introversion and neuroticism compared to norms from other adult males.[460] Perhaps, as crossdressers themselves claim and their partners often endorse, the crossdressed condition produces notable changes in psychological functioning.

Mary Hogan-Finlay, in her 1995 Ph.D. dissertation in psychology, compares a sample of 101 "non-clinical cross-gendered men" with an equal number of heterosexual controls. The comparison examines demographics, childhood experiences, psychological functioning and gender issues. The transgendered men are sorted into three distinguishable groups: transsexuals (27%) and two groups of transvestites (83%) differentiated by degree of "physiological fantasies" of being a woman. Hogan-Finlay finds that transsexuals display more "gender disturbance" than transvestites or controls and show the highest levels of "psychological distress." But she does not find support for transvestism as a mental disorder.[461]

George Brown and associates report another sizeable study in 1996. This research involves 188 subjects classified in one or another of three conditions: 83 transvestites (44% of the subjects); 44 transsexuals (23%); and, 61 transgendered (33%; a group equivalent to what other researchers term the 'marginal transvestites'). They are further differentiated by whether they have received treatment or not into four groups: 'no treatment' (81 subjects; 43%); 'treated for psychological problems' (49 subjects; 26%); 'treated for transvestism' (41 subjects; 22%); and, 'treated for gender change' (17 subjects; 9%). The study examines these subjects both with reference to personality characteristics and for sexual functioning. Personality traits are measured by the NEO-PI; sexual functioning is assessed using the DSFI.[462]

With regard to personality characteristics, the researchers conclude: "Overall, the personality profile of this sample of 188 male cross-dressers did not deviate substantially from the NEO-PI normative sample of community-dwelling men."[463] Specifically, crossdressers score in the normal range on all personality dimensions of the NEO-PI except one. For the 'O' ('Openness') dimension, crossdressers are in the high range for Fantasy, Feelings, and Values scales.[464] Such scores are not intrinsically negative.

The researchers reach a similar conclusion about sexual functioning. The DSFI results reveal that crossdressers do not deviate dramatically from so-called 'normal' male heterosexual subjects. A modest difference is found in one respect. As a group, crossdressers' scores are lower in the area of the DSFI that indicates they are more likely to endorse a poorer body image.[465] (However, a 1977 study of 67 transsexuals finds that progression from a no treatment stage, through hormonal treatment, to SRS leads to increased body satisfaction, as measured by the Body Image Scale (BI-I), which considers 30 body features evaluated along a 5 point scale.[466])

Brown and colleagues, then, find that at least some male crossdressers demonstrate personality and sexual functioning much like norms obtained from the general male population. They also suggest their data raises questions with regard to the adequacy of the DSM model (see the answers to Q. 94, 98-99).[467]

In sum, while some differences can be found between crossdressers and the general population, these generally seem not to rise to a level of either statistical or clinical significance. When clinically significant differences are found, not surprisingly they are with crossdressing subjects in treatment. The personality differences observed between crossdressers and noncrossdressers may be accentuated when the crossdresser is tested while in the crossdressed condition. Indeed, an interesting issue raised by personality research concerns differences between the crossdressed and non-crossdressed condition. As seen above, some differences have been observed. The same is true for issues of gender identity and role, a matter to which we must now turn.

Lee's Remarks

Probably anyone who has gone through an undergraduate and graduate experience has had to take some psychological tests in one or another class. At least, I remember taking a few, both intelligence tests and personality tests. I no longer recall the names of either of the intelligence tests. As for the personality tests, I remember doing the MMPI, the Kersey Temperament Sorter, the BSRI, and one or two others that I no longer remember well. Evidently none of them raised any concerns because no one ever took me aside and suggested counseling. I recall testing high in introversion, which fits. I also could have told the examiner I tend toward anxiety and low mood, both of which tests also indicated. Those are chiefly the results I remember, save for the BSRI.

What does testing show about gender affiliation?

Let us begin where we just left off: differences found in crossdressers when crossdressed as compared to when they are not crossdressed. Kurt Freund and colleagues, in 1982, propose that crossdressers—transvestites (and not just transsexuals)—experience cross-gender identity.[468] But perhaps an important differentiation between transsexuals and transvestites is not only the degree of cross-gender identity, but also its *constancy*. In other words, transsexuals experience greater cross-gender identity and do so more constantly than transvestites, who may experience this cross-gender identity only when crossdressed. Thus historian Peter Ackroyd, alongside many other observers, notes that feminine gender characteristics do not predominate when the crossdresser is not crossdressed but is occupying his male gender role.[469]

What has research revealed?

Personality testing also reveals that crossdressing males express a stronger feminine gender identity than do other males. Researchers Neil Buhrich and Neil McConaghy, in the late 1970s, work with a group of 64 male crossdressers (transvestites and transsexuals). These subjects are divided into two groups based on their degree of feminine gender identity. Both groups are compared to two other groups (homosexual and heterosexual men). Four tests are administered to measure gender feelings and behavior. These tests are: the California Personality Femininity Scale (CPF-Fe), the Draw-a-Person (DAP), the Franck Drawing Completion Test, and two subtests (Information & Vocabulary) of the Wechsler Adult Intelligence Scales (WAIS).

The DAP has been described above. The CPF-Fe Scale is comprised of 38 True/False items. The Franck test provides 36 simple, but incomplete line drawings to be finished by the subject. Results from the scores obtained indicate that two of tests (CPF-Fe & DAP) support the crossdressing males' expressed degree of feminine gender identity. On the DAP, whether the subject expresses a moderate or a high feminine gender identity, they are significantly more likely than most men to draw a female figure first. (This result parallels that found in a 1972 report by Richard Green and colleagues about "feminine boys."[470]) Both the CPF-Fe and DAP apparently measure some aspects of gender feelings and behavior in various men. But the authors speculate that they measure different aspects. The CPI-Fe, for example, differentiates transvestites and transsexuals from homosexuals, but the DAP does not.[471]

The DAP has also been employed in helping to predict successful candidates for sex reassignment surgery (SRS). A 1982 study reports that the DAP, used in conjunction with the Animal and Opposite-Animal Drawing Technique (AOADT), yields results indicative of which prospective candidates for SRS are most likely to undergo the surgery. The study's subjects are 9 genetic males and 10 genetic females. All are administered both the DAP and the AOADT. Results show that MtF candidates who draw a member of the opposite sex first on the DAP are most likely to complete SRS. The AOADT provides another differentiation. Those who complete SRS draw second animals who are congruent with their biological sex significantly more often than do MtF or FtM transsexuals who have not had SRS.[472]

Peter Fagan and associates employ a different instrument in assessing 21 male "distressed transvestites" in comparison with 45 married heterosexual males. Using the Derogatis Sexual Functioning Inventory (DSFI), the team finds that the crossdressing males endorse a more feminine self-representation. In self-description they prefer adjectives generally associated with gender role stereotypes for women.[473] A pronounced feminine gender role definition is also found using the DSFI with 31 MtF transsexuals in a 1978 study.[474]

A 1981 study reports the results of a battery of tests given to 24 adult men (ages 21-35), who are placed in three matched groups: transsexual, homosexual and heterosexual. The tests include the Bem Sex Role Inventory (BSRI) and the Rosenberg Self-Esteem Scale (RSES). The BSRI uses 60 characteristics, 20 each that are designated 'masculine' or 'feminine' and 20 that are considered 'neutral.' Scores on the BSRI indicate whether someone endorses a stereotypical gender role or a more androgynous one. Androgyny has been linked with more positive psychological and social outcomes than found for those who embrace gender stereotyped roles. The RSES is perhaps the most widely used instrument for assessing self-esteem. It has 10 items commonly scored along a four point Likert scale, with response options ranging from "strongly agree" to "strongly disagree." The three groups differentiate as follows:

❑ transsexuals show most identification with the feminine role and score lowest in self-esteem;

❑ homosexuals report the most identification with the masculine role and score the highest in self-esteem; and,

❑ heterosexuals score as masculine to androgynous and display moderately high levels of self-esteem.[475]

The correlation of identification with the feminine role and lower self-esteem perhaps reflects the somber social reality for males who express as females in a culture where masculine males dominate.

In 1982, sociologist John Talamini reports on a study using the BSRI. In the research, matched groups of heterosexual males who don't crossdress and those who do score differently. The crossdressing males score significantly higher in androgyny.[476] Perhaps the endorsing of a more feminine gender identity and/or role leads to greater androgyny among these men. Talamini feels that "crossdressing is somehow bound up with the universal personal drive toward androgyny."[477]

In 2001, Richard Docter and James Fleming explore transgender identity through 26 items of their 70 item questionnaire administered to 516 adult males (ages 19-78), 88% of whom are identified as transvestites who periodically crossdress fully as women and 12% who are identified as transsexual. The 26 items have content such as "I wish I had been born a woman," "I do not enjoy functioning as a man," and "My true gender is feminine." All 26 items receive some endorsement with factor loads ranging from .48 ("I daydream of being a woman at least 10 times per day") to .92 ("I would choose to live as a woman"). There is overlap between the two groups on this scale, with the mean score for transsexuals (20.9) somewhat higher than for transvestites (12.2).[478]

Although androgyny has been correlated with positive outcomes, the results of the above studies cannot be made to prove that the self-representations of crossdressing males are healthier than that of noncrossdressing males. Indeed, it is to the question of whether crossdressers suffer more psychopathology that we must now turn.

Lee's Remarks

I must confess having had some anxiety at the prospect of taking the BSRI. However, it was done in such a manner that all the results were carefully kept confidential. I was as honest as I could be and mightily relieved when the results indicated androgyny. That was a term I was just then becoming acquainted with and it attracted me because it offered an alternative to masculinity and femininity. Although my ease with the word has lessened over time, I still prefer describing myself as androgynous to either being masculine or feminine, though my term of choice to myself is 'other-gendered.' I wish, though, someone would come up with a word that better fits me.

Do crossdressers suffer more psychopathology?

(Also see the answers to Q. 94, 98.)

The entry for transvestism in the *Encyclopedia of Psychology* (2nd ed.) summarizes the situation succinctly:

> Concerning their psychological makeup, transvestites as a group are no more neurotic or psychotic than matched control groups, although they do tend to be more controlled in impulse expression, more inhibited in interpersonal relationships, more dependent, and less involved with other people . . . . Interestingly, over three-fourths of transvestites consider themselves to be a different personality when crossdressed, perhaps experiencing in female clothing a significant facet of their psychological makeup that cannot otherwise be expressed . . . .[479]

Even among those who experience adverse consequences from crossdressing such that they seek professional help, there does not appear to be a significantly higher occurrence of psychological disorders. Inasmuch as a later question (Q. 94) addresses this matter more fully, all we need note here is that the personality and gender characteristics associated with crossdressing in men cannot be said to predict more psychopathology than what is found in other men. Indeed, many of the characteristics can be viewed as defensive reactions formed in environments that deny as much freedom of self-expression as other males enjoy. Whatever conclusions are drawn, caution must be used. Individuals always transcend the generalizations made about whatever groups they may belong to.

Q. 28

When does crossdressing usually start?

The Short Answer. Crossdressing, at least among males (for whom data is easier to acquire), begins early. Most crossdressing boys begin this behavior prior to puberty. Many report having started in early childhood.

The Longer Answer. One of the more often studied matters associated with crossdressing is 'age at onset.' Interest in knowing this is tied to a desire to understand what causes crossdressing. However, the question as to when crossdressing usually starts is complicated by two important factors. First, crossdressing in very young children is more likely done by someone else's choice. The age at which it may be voluntarily undertaken may be in doubt in some cases. Still, there is no reason to doubt that in the majority of cases as the child grows older he or she initiates the behavior, either by expressing a preference to a parent or by dressing him- or herself. Second, data is more abundant for boys than for girls because of our contemporary fixation on male crossdressing and bland disregard for female crossdressing. Accordingly, the findings reported below must be qualified by the influence of these two factors.

At what age does crossdressing start?

Research finds that crossdressing in males typically begins in childhood and is well established by the end of adolescence. Here are the findings of some studies:

Table 28.1 Age at Onset

Year	Researchers	# Subjects	Findings
1951	Janet Thompson[480]	50+	Proposed that crossdressing begins prior to age 5.
1962	H. Taylor Buckner[481]	262	Before 4.9 yrs. old (14%); between 5-9.9 yrs. old (39%); between 10-17.9 yrs. old (39%); after age 18

			(8%).
1972	V. Prince & P. M. Bentler[482]	504	More than half (54%) before age 10.
1976	Peter Bentler[483]	42	Two-thirds (67%) of the heterosexuals before age 11; half (50%) of homosexuals before age 11. About 1/3 (33% and 36%) of all before age 5.
1976	Richard Green[484]	60	Three-quarters (75%) before age 4; only 3% after age 6.
1977	Neil Buhrich & Neil McConaghy[485]	34	Usually in childhood; almost always before age 15.
1981	J. L. Croughan, M. Saghir, R. Cohen & E. Robins[486]	70	94% before age 14; average age at onset 8-11 years old.
1981	Neil Buhrich & Trina Beaumont[487]	222	Almost half (45%) before age 11 and almost half (49%) between 11-19.
1983	Bullough, Bullough, & Smith[488]	65	Almost three-quarters (73%) before age 10.
1987	Richard Green[489]	66	Most commonly by age 2-3.
1988	P. J. Fagan, T. N. Wise, L. R. Derogatis, & C. W. Schmidt[490]	21	Behaviorally bisexual, average age at onset was 8 years old; heterosexuals, 11 years old.
1988	Richard Docter[491]	110	4% before age 10; 79% between 10-15; 18% between 15-20.
1990	A. M. Verschoor[492]	292	Before age 12 for 61% of transvestites (N=69); 87.5% of transsexuals (N=133).
1994	C. D. Doorn, J. Poortinga, & A. M. Verschoor[493]	191	Early onset transsexuals and transvestites typically begin before age 12.
1995	Richard Schott[494]	85	Half by age 7; 97% before age 13 (puberty).
1996	Vernon Coleman[495]	1,014	Average age 13 (range 4-70)

1997	Bonnie Bullough & Vern Bullough[496]	372	Median age of 8.5 years old. 34% by age 6; 91% by age 14.
1997	R. Docter & V. Prince[497]	1,032	Two-thirds (66%) before age 10; 29% between 10-20 years old.
1999	'Yvonne'[498]	1,203	More than four-fifths (83%) before age 12; only 2% after age 21.
2001	Yik Koon Teh[499]	507	Most between ages 11-20.

It should be noted that such studies typically are retrospective, using adult males who identify themselves as heterosexual. One study—that reported by Richard Green in 1976—focuses on this behavior as observed in children by their parents. Two studies—by Peter Bentler in 1976 and by Yik Koon Teh in 2001—focus on transsexuals, the latter with the *Mak Nyahs* of Malaysia, thus reminding us of the cross-cultural nature of crossdressing.[500] All are from the scientific literature except the 1999 survey reported by male crossdresser 'Yvonne,' which is available online. Together, this collected body of research clearly indicates an early origin to the behavior, a finding already known to psychiatrist Narcyz Lukianowicz in his review of the literature in 1959, where he notes a "general agreement" then existing that crossdressing typically begins in early childhood.[501] This finding is perhaps the most constant one known about crossdressing.

Alongside it might be placed the data from clinician Ingrid Sell's study of 30 Americans who self-identify as 'third gender' people. Among them, 90% reported an awareness of being gender-different from their peers, typically by age 5.[502]

Lee's Remarks

My earliest memory of crossdressing comes from the years before I started school, so I must have been 4 or 5 years old. Of course, that was very partial crossdressing; it was easy to have access to feminine clothes with a mother and sisters about the house. I'm actually less sure when I first started full crossdressing. It was in youth, but it was much more infrequent than it would become.

Why might crossdressing start later in life?

Not all crossdressers start crossdressing in childhood—or even in adolescence. Why might someone start crossdressing in adulthood? Some anecdotal evidence, as well as some literary evidence, suggests that some adults begin crossdressing in response to the loss of a loved one of a different gender. But while this is the most attested reason it is unlikely it explains all instances. It may be that a transgender identity emerges more fully in the greater security of adulthood and thus provides a liberty to begin behavior that was earlier desired but not acted upon.

Q. 29

What is a crossdresser's childhood and adolescence like?

The Short Answer. Crossdressing typically begins in childhood, often before school age. It tends to progress from irregular and partial efforts to more regular and complete crossdressing. While sexual arousal may not be prominent at first, it often becomes so later. This may be both because the early sensual pleasure of the feel of certain clothes becomes specifically associated with erotic pleasure, and because the culture reinforces the idea that cross gender use of clothes must have an erotic component. While crossdressing complicates childhood in some respects, in some cases it is not the occasion of traumatic events at home, while in other cases it is. Both in our society and in other lands transchildren often encounter significant obstacles. Because transgender realities are ranged along a spectrum, different developmental outcomes may occur. Still, transchildren in Western societies commonly share experiences of ridicule and rejection in childhood that lead to social marginalization and an increased sense of isolation. However, most not only survive childhood to become as well-adjusted as other folk, but many also recall childhood in generally positive terms (cf. the answer to Q. 26).

The Longer Answer. The danger in framing a question about childhood and adolescence in terms of a single behavior is that it might erroneously suggest to others that the behavior in view so defines childhood and adolescence that other matters are irrelevant. We must not err in thinking that crossdressing or transgender experience and identity so completely define growing up that we conclude nothing else matters. While transgendered realities shape an individual they do not entirely define the person. Though surviving in society may require accepting a label by which others try to hold a transgendered person, being a person will always transcend being transgendered.

At the same time, however, we can hypothesize that gender may typically occupy a larger role in shaping the self-identity precisely because gender non-conformity and the responses it elicits from others heightens awareness of the process for transgender children. This process is further complicated by the lack of social support that often occurs. Parents commonly respond to crossdressing with efforts to promote gender conformity in their child, including punishment for nonconforming behaviors, and then growing concern when resistance occurs, or the sheer persistence of transgender behavior continues. Even where parents may wish to be supportive, any efforts to do so are likely to meet with resistance from others, including extended family, teachers and health professionals. Social workers Gerald Mallon and Theresa DeCrescenzo remark:

> Virtually no social supports are in any of our child welfare or educational institutions for children or youth who are gender variant. Parents who attempt to negotiate a fair accommodation for the gender variant child will undoubtedly meet misunderstanding, incredulity, and resistance, even hostility, from almost everyone they encounter.[503]

With this perspective in place, we can inquire about how crossdressing shapes growing up. In doing so we can explore common features of childhood and adolescence related to transgender behavior. At the same time, we can both acknowledge individual uniqueness in personal experience and broadly suggest various patterns often found among those who crossdress. In short, we can employ a label like 'crossdresser' as a means to signal certain differences of experience and behavior from others without sacrificing an underlying appreciation for the singular person in all of her or his individuality.

What are some common features of a crossdresser's childhood?

In answering other questions we have considered when crossdressing first starts (Q. 28) and the retrospective reports of adult male crossdressers about their childhoods (Q. 26). That material we can summarize in the following points:

- ❑ *early onset*—typically, crossdressing begins before adolescence, often well before it;
- ❑ *two parent families*—most crossdressers come from families where both father and mother resided in the home;
- ❑ *not unhappy*—most crossdressers do not characterize their childhoods as especially unhappy;
- ❑ *pleasure in crossdressing*—most crossdressers recall childhood crossdressing as a pleasurable activity;
- ❑ *anxiety over discovery*—commonly crossdressers also recall anxiety over being discovered, and thus trying to keep the behavior secret;
- ❑ *progress in degree and regularity*—generally, crossdressing begins as partial crossdressing done irregularly, but with time it often becomes more frequent and complete; and,

❏ *growing eroticism*—the pleasant sensations associated with crossdressing often become connected to erotic arousal as childhood progresses into adolescence.

This developmental pattern, discerned in the United States, may hold true in different societies as well.[504]

The above points suggest a more-or-less regular pattern of development. Some research supports this idea, but not all. Though many young people may share some broadly common experiential themes, these developmental features hardly hint at the intensely personal experiential reality. Richard Schott's 1995 survey of 85 crossdressing men references anecdotal details offering a picture of great variety in the developmental course of crossdressing. Often childhood is complicated by this behavior that makes the child different from peers. They might feel isolated, confused, conflicted by self-doubt and guilt. Yet Schott observes:

> Other members of the sample, more frequently those who identify as nuclear transvestites, were originally bothered and confused by their compulsion to cross-dress, but seem to have taken their cross-dressing more in stride and have integrated it (with varying degrees of success) into their adult lives. For them, the extent of disclosure to family members and the degree of acceptance by the spouse seem to be the major remaining issues. Some of this group have gone beyond integrating their feminine persona and have taken initiative in forming self-help and outreach groups or become involved in public awareness programs.[505]

Lee's Remarks

I agree with Schott's assessment, at least as far as it relates to my own experience. As I said earlier, I started crossdressing around age 4 or 5 years old. It's funny, but I don't remember my mother being all freaked out when she discovered me doing it. Still, somehow or another I got the message this was an unapproved activity and one that I best do in secret. That always bothered me to some degree, but I guess having learned it at so early an age I digested the lesson so thoroughly that I never have really questioned or challenged the need to keep it private. At any rate, I soon developed some anxiety over being caught, but the experience was so pleasurable I never stopped. With several females in the family there was never a lack of available items to use. I would have preferred to have my own, and indeed began purchasing articles of my own as soon as I grew old enough (and brave enough). Also as I grew older I clued in more to the need to keep crossdressing secret if I wasn't going to make my life even harder than it was.

In truth, my childhood was complicated by matters far more significant to me than my occasional crossdressing. I was a small child, frail and often ill. Al-

191

though I was not conscious of doing anything out of the ordinary for a boy, I do remember often being bullied and I recall being teased as a 'sissy' on more than one occasion. I preferred the company of girls, but I think it would be erroneous to say my activities were largely feminine. I believe part of my preference for feminine company was a greater sense of acceptance, as well as relief from bullies, and to some degree because my personality and interests fit better with the girls I was around than with the boys I knew.

I confess to having had much ambivalence about my body even as a child. But given the many physical difficulties I experienced that seems understandable apart from any crisis of gender or sexual identity. I do remember, though, as a small child pulling my penis back between my legs so that it and my testicles would disappear. I can remember an occasional wish to not have such encumbrances, but I do not recall them as either strong or persistent. Likewise, I remember occasionally envying girls, but I also recalling wishing I could be more like other boys. I was, so to speak, stuck between genders, though as a child I had neither the words nor the thoughts to articulate my feelings.

What are difficulties and outcomes transgender children may face?

Over time almost all crossdressers adjust to a life made different by their crossdressing. But individual experiences and their outcomes vary widely. Mallon and DeCrescenzo remind us of the consequences often produced by a hostile environment: anger, anxiety, depression, fear, low self-esteem, self-mutilation, and suicidal ideation. What is worse, they point out, is that such symptoms of distress are often interpreted as further proof the problem resides in the child rather than in the environment.[506]

Socialization Pressures

All of us experience socialization into gender roles and, as our parents typically hope, into gender identities in line with the gender assignment made at birth. But this picture only simplifies a complex reality. Sociologist Emily Kane points out that many parents stray from—and thus expand—normative conceptions of gender. However, as she also observes, this happens to a far greater extent with girls than with boys. In interviews with 42 parents (24 mothers; 18 fathers) of preschool age children, she finds both mothers and fathers often celebrate gender nonconformity in their daughters. On the other hand, while some support of gender nonconformity is offered sons, it is tempered by negative responses as well. Kane reports that, "In stark contrast to the lack of negative response for daughters, 23 of 31 parents of sons expressed at least some negative responses, and 6 of these offered only negative responses regarding what they perceived as gender nonconformity." What parents prove especially likely to object to is a son wearing dress typed feminine (e.g., pink or frilly clothing, skirts, dresses, or tights). And fathers play an especially large role in seeking gender conformity by their sons.[507]

Children actively assist and cooperate with gender expectations. Gender variant children generally do so as well. The difference between them and gender conforming children is their relative lack of success. Although some people interpret nonconforming gender behavior as rebellion, transgender children are no more likely to be rebels than any other kids or youth. But because conformity to a gender sense that remains alien to their own experience is difficult, they fail more often at it. Put in another way, they most often succeed at being who they are than in pretending to be who they aren't.

Unfortunately, attaining a stable gender identity is complicated by life in a gender system admitting only two valid alternatives. Even the growing acknowledgement of 'transgender' defines it in terms of crossing from one gender to the other, thus retaining the gender dichotomy. So those who find they can't fit at one pole are only offered the option of trying the other. For those who find this option also doesn't work well carving out an identity can be especially challenging. The absence of a third gender alternative doesn't keep third gender people from existing, but it poses a serious obstacle to healthy gender self-identifying. It is remarkable, then, that some carve a path to such an identity, a path today aided by greater awareness of gender flexibility outside our own culture.

Some transgender children quit trying to comply with gender socialization. They remain steadfast in expressing what they experience, even though this fetches harsher penalties. The stress thus placed on them can be enormous. Both those who try to comply, and those who stop trying, are at risk. The former suffer the pains associated with trying to be who they are not; the latter suffer the wounds inflicted by those who will not support who they show themselves to be. Efforts to prevent a child from exploring and developing their individual gender identity can lead to a gender-conflicted adult.[508] Mallon and DeCrescenzo warn that prolonged and pervasive social stigmatization can lead from the low self-esteem of youth to internalized self-hatred as adults.[509]

Variable Outcomes

As Schott's retrospective study of adults indicates, some fare in adulthood better than others, though most do all right. When male transvestites, for example, are differentiated into distinct groups by their level of satisfaction with crossdressing alone ('nuclear transvestites'), or by a desire for further feminization, such as through taking hormones ('marginal transvestites'), some differences emerge that suggest the latter group may have more problems than the former.

A study from 1981 by Neil Buhrich and Trina Beaumont provides some illuminating data. They examine 222 adult male crossdressers in America (N=126) and Australia (N=86). They find that nearly one-quarter (24%) overall are called "sissy" during childhood. But marginal transvestites are more likely to be labeled in this manner (29% to 17%).[510] Given the pejorative associations with the term, we might expect this labeling to correlate to some degree with peer difficulties such as ostracism or being bullied.

Another study, by Neil Buhrich and Neil McConaghy, compares 34 adult male crossdressers with 20 non-crossdressing 'control' subjects. The crossdressers are differentiated into two groups along the aforementioned lines. While both groups report significantly more feminine behaviors in childhood than do the control subjects, there also proves to be a significant difference between the two crossdressing groups. The 'marginal transvestites' report more feminine behavior in childhood than do the 'nuclear transvestites.'[511] Since childhood peers are known to rigorously enforce social expectations related to gender role, presumably this higher incidence of more feminine behavior also becomes associated with a greater degree of conflict with peers about gender performance.

Violence

Indeed, such conflict can lead to varying degrees of violence. Shannon Wyss, in recounting the stories of transgender youth, remarks that because of their peers' hatred—one mirroring adult prejudices—teens publicly expressing their transgender identity often find themselves in unsafe situations. Many lose their friends, face ongoing harassment, and discover that teachers and school staff refuse to intervene, sometimes even suggesting the ill treatment transgender youth experience has been brought on by themselves. In such environments survival rather than learning becomes the priority. As a consequence, Wyss notes, transgender youth are at special risk for self-destructive behaviors.[512]

Often the blame for such behaviors is placed on the transgender identity itself. This attribution conveniently sidesteps the environmental pressures mounted on the individual. We dare not excuse the violence practiced against transgender youth. Blaming the victim is morally indefensible. The actual incidence of aggression against transgender youth is staggering (see the answer to Q. 37). For those youth who ponder coming out, the knowledge of possible consequences offers serious incentive to stay in the closet. The courage of those who do otherwise should not be underestimated or dismissed.

Variable Outcomes Reprised

If we return to the distinctions made by Buhrich and McConaghy, in general 'marginal transvestites' do not fare as well as 'nuclear transvestites.' Whether measured in terms of demographic factors (e.g., occupational status), or psychological ones (e.g., gender dysphoria), the 'marginal transvestites' typically have a rougher go in life. It is hardly a stretch of the imagination to think they may have, on average, less happy childhoods. Inasmuch as this seems to be the case with transsexuals, as a group, it seems that the further a genetic male is along the continuum of feminine identification, the more he is at risk, in childhood and adulthood both.

But we must also temper our remarks with an awareness that in many studies the crossdressers surveyed or interviewed are those most willing, even eager, to share their life experiences and perspectives. Those whose childhoods encounter the most difficulties may never have the same opportunities to be heard. Their voices may be stilled by violence or they may have survived by learning to stay in the shadows. Jody Norton reminds us of a sobering reality: "While transchildren turn up in all classes and races, the poorer, less educated, and darker skinned you are, the more likely you will find it necessary to resort to prostitution, with all the risks of violence (by others on the street, by tricks, by police), arrest, drug involvement, and disease that accompany street life." As Norton observes, many transchildren when they reach adolescence leave home, sometimes cast out, sometimes escaping, sometimes wishing to spare family any further public shame.[513]

What are some common features of a crossdresser's adolescence?

Evidence suggests most crossdressing males keep their crossdressing secret. However, the secret may be exposed. This event, say Mallon and DeCrescenzo, is likely to precipitate an emotional crisis not merely for the youth, but for the entire family. Because most keep their gender issues hidden as long as possible, when they come out the revelations generally produce surprise, even shock—not a scenario conducive to positive outcomes. Those transgender youth who 'out' themselves may not fare any better; though a range of family responses are possible, rejection is one strong possibility.[514]

A principal concern of other family members is what this behavior means for the youth's sexuality, especially the individual's sexual orientation. The mere occurrence of crossdressing in childhood cannot be used to predict a future outcome either in sexual orientation or gender identification. Some so-called 'effeminate' boys grow up to be married heterosexual crossdressers, some eventually are revealed as male-to-female (MtF) transsexuals, and some know themselves as gay men.[515] Efforts to confidently predict a certain outcome are absurd. That doesn't mean they don't happen. Family members can panic, filled with a dread for the future that is fueled by homophobia and transphobia.

These family reactions further complicate the developmental tasks of adolescence. Ego psychologist Erik Erikson famously frames the challenge of adolescence as a basic sense of 'identity versus role confusion.' Among other things, for Erikson this means youth are concerned with "what they appear to be in the eyes of others as compared with what they feel they are . . . ."[516] The normal tasks of identity formation are complicated for most transgendered youth by the additional and pressing issue of their gender identity, plus any exposure that occurs. In the eyes of others there is reflected the gender role expectations that lie at variance with what they feel they are. This conflict, whether hidden from others or not, can lead to role confusion. Erikson believes that for most youth the struggle for identity involves a danger of role confusion in which the risk can be an inability to settle on an occupational identity. But where role confusion is based on "strong previous doubt as to one's sexual identity," the risk is more pronounced. Even so, Erikson expresses confidence that, "if diagnosed and treated properly," a positive outcome can occur.[517]

Treatment, of course, is a major issue—one we shall have to largely leave until volume 5. What exposed transgender youth face, with or without treatment, are very practical concerns. What will this mean for opportunities in gaining employment? In finding housing? In attaining health care? What will this mean for personal safety? For future relationships? While all youth face such questions, the societal response to transgender makes these questions even keener—and more problematic—for transgender youth. The bleakness the future may seem to bode, coupled with the present stresses they experience, can lead transgender youth to attempt suicide. Some succeed.

Any yet . . . most believe the future is not writ for them. They struggle and they survive. Perhaps surprisingly, the self-confirmation and affirmation of their gender identity proves crucially instrumental in that process. As Mallon and DeCrescenzo point out, a development of a sense of 'realness'—both internalized and as perceived by others—is very important for most transyouth.[518] They are also right that the future *is* open—for them and for us. The vast majority of transgender youth become as reasonably well-adjusted as the rest of us. If social tolerance continues to grow and someday develop into acceptance, then the future will look even brighter for us all.

Lee's Remarks

I do not recall fantasizing myself as a female or masturbating while imagining making love to myself as a woman. Frankly, that notion does not fit my experience at all. My adolescence was the only time in my life when I had a roughly equal number of both male and female friends. I still faced being bullied, but I handled it better than when I was younger. I still preferred the company of girls, though now some of them excited my interest in a sexual manner. I began dating at 15 and had three steady girlfriends across my high school years. None of them ever knew of my crossdressing. I suppose this was the period in my life I felt most comfortable in the gender role I got stuck in at birth.

Living away from home in college my crossdressing increased. It was now easier for me to acquire feminine clothes and to practice crossdressing, though I was always very careful. It was during this time I remember becoming really conscious about things the pros call 'sexual identity' and 'gender identity,' although I don't remember those words being used much when I was in school. I simply grew more aware that I really did not identify well with either gender role. But it was not until I was an adult that I gave the matter any sustained thought.

Q. 30

What is adulthood like for a cross-dresser?

The Short Answer. Adulthood for crossdressers is much like it is for others, except for the complications associated with crossdressing. This answer focuses on the crossdressing behavior, which proves very persistent in adulthood, but which tends to diminish in erotic power over time. A typical course for crossdressing during these years is for it to increase. Research suggests that the adult crossdresser continues to grow into a transgender identity, though this does not necessarily mean progressing from 'transvestite' to 'transsexual' as some people fear. Instead, ordinarily there are prolonged periods of stability in the practice of crossdressing. These may be interrupted or changed by significant life events. In sum, individual variability warns us against trying to apply any predictions about how a given person's life will proceed. What does seem constant is that once established a transgender identity persists much like other gendered identities do and proves as important to self-identity.

The Longer Answer. Adult life is filled with challenges for everyone, whether they crossdress or not. For the crossdresser, the behavior of crossdressing adds particular challenges, but also helps address others. The gender issues associated with crossdressing also raise issues, both in identity and role expression for the crossdresser, and in relationships with others. All of these matters are important, but since dimensions of them are discussed in answers to other questions in this book, the goal in this answer is more modest. Here a short examination of the general course of crossdressing is provided. In addition, a look is given at the question of how frequently crossdressing is practiced during the adult years.

What is the general course of crossdressing?

While it is notoriously difficult to typify the developmental course of people, because individual courses run different, there is some value in seeing how crossdressing behavior develops for many crossdressers. In this regard, the first point to be made is that once established, crossdressing persists. While some people might wish it were otherwise, the experiential reality of crossdressing suggests that this is a behavior not easily resisted by the individual even should they wish to do so, and even though such a wish will likely be fully supported by others. Indeed, fighting the urge carries consequences no less than does complying with it. Assessing the cost either way—crossdressing, or not crossdressing—is important. Transgender therapist Gianna Israel remarks:

> If a person has reoccurring gender questions or a desire to crossdress, these will reappear until one of several things occur. A person can ignore matters and allow self-destructive feelings and poor coping mechanisms to control his or her future. Or, an individual can come to terms with his or her needs and carefully-pace getting questions answered.[519]

One of the most crucial questions most of us are curious about is how crossdressing plays itself out over the course of a person's life. This question has been investigated, with some research focusing on childhood, or adolescence, or adulthood, or transitions from one period to another. With respect to adult experience, psychologist Mary Hogan-Finlay's study of the question whether a "cross-gendered lifestyle" follows a developmental and invariant order finds that it might for many transgendered men. In her sample of 101 "cross-gendered" men (transsexuals and transvestites), Hogan-Finlay concludes that a majority (84%) progress through clearly distinct phases in a predictable order. These men's cross-gendered behavior in adolescence and young adulthood proves more private in expression than is true in the period from the mid-30s through the early-40s when a public expression becomes more likely.[520]

In looking at a number of studies, the situation in adulthood appears to be that despite individual variations some common themes emerge:

- ❑ *Crossdressing is chronic*—though periods where no crossdressing is done may occur, these are almost always self-limiting; this behavior persists across the lifetime.
- ❑ *Crossdressing increases, then stabilizes*—the frequency and extent of crossdressing (both discussed below) generally increase in adulthood until reaching a point of relative stability in practice.
- ❑ *The stability in crossdressing fluctuates*—life circumstances and stresses can and do change the degree of crossdressing practiced.
- ❑ *The actual crossdressing done is generally not the crossdressing desired*—either the frequency or extent—or both—are typically less than what the crossdresser most desires.

As noted in various other answers, the research also consistently shows a change in motivation for many male crossdressers. So-called 'transvestic fetishism,' where the crossdressing is accompanied by sexual arousal, may predominate in adolescence and early adulthood but later subside as a motivational factor. Instead, gender-motivated issues emerge as predominant. This reality was finally recognized by the psychiatric community in its *Diagnostic and Statistical Manual for Mental Disorders* (see the answers to Q. 96, 99).[521]

Returning to Hogan-Finlay's research, she thinks it possible to distinguish a 'cross-gender lifestyle' that is both developmental and largely fixed in its course, with two main age periods. She conducted research involving more than 200 males: 101 non-clinical cross-gender males and an equal number of heterosexual controls. Comparing these two groups demographically, with respect to childhood experiences, and with an eye toward psychological functioning and gender issues, she draws an outline of this cross-gender lifestyle. The first main period, she says, occurs from adolescence through the early 20s. This period is typified by *private* activities. In the next major period, from mid-30s through early 40s, a *public* cross-gender lifestyle emerges. This might be demonstrated in public crossdressing, living in a different gender and/or body modifications (e.g., hormones or sex reassignment surgery).[522]

Hogan-Finlay's subjects are categorized as either transsexuals (N=27), or transvestites (N=64), with the latter group subdivided by whether or not the subjects demonstrate physiological fantasies (e.g., breasts). She does report some differences among these groups, but finds overall that these males develop cross-gender lifestyles mostly in an invariant order (84% of the subjects).[523] However, it is important to recognize that while there may for most crossdressing males be a growing desire to express more publicly their gender identity, this desire varies in intensity, degree of expression, and manner of expression. Thus we must be cautious about drawing too specific conclusions from this research.

Another, more minor point may be pertinent. Many have observed that male crossdressers' interest in clothes is remarkably divided: there is little interest in or attention given to male clothing, but considerable interest and attention toward female garb. Thus Harry Benjamin notes that male transvestites are often miserable when dressed as males and hence show little interest in their appearance, with the result that they often do not dress well and look "shabby."[524] This does not suggest they make passable women when crossdressed, for most do not—and know so. Yet they put far more time and money into choosing feminine clothing.

Lee's Remarks

Once more, let me chime in with my two-cents worth. While I may not always be as mature as I'd like, the calendar says I am middle-aged and all my creditors want me to act like a grown-up. I'd like to point out that while being a transgendered person is central to my life's experience, it is by no means the only thing significant in making me who I am. I sometimes wish we weren't such a sex-obsessed and gender-focused society, which makes being transgendered more powerful and more problematic for me than it might otherwise be. But I've lived my life in such a culture and adapted as well as I can.

So let me address the checklist of 'common themes' that I've been shown. My crossdressing has increased over time, both because I am able to do so and because it pleases me to do so. The former factor seems more significant to me because the desire and pleasure have always been there but the relative freedom has varied with changing circumstances. My kids are grown and I have more personal space in which to crossdress without undue concern over discovery. Plus, quite honestly, I no longer fear discovery like I once did.

All that being said, I still do not crossdress as often as I would like. If I really felt secure enough to always wear what I want to wear, I would seldom if ever be out of feminine dress. My best explanation for why this desire is so strong is my sense that somehow the clothes balance my sexual anatomy so that body and clothes together place me where I feel I belong—in between the only two genders our society permits.

What is the frequency of crossdressing?

There is substantial variety in the frequency with which crossdressers engage in this behavior. Nevertheless, the data from surveys suggest that frequency of crossdressing increases with age. Whether this is a general characteristic or an artifact of the kind of crossdressers who are most likely to participate in surveys and interviews is unknown. It may be that those more invested in the behavior are both more likely to participate in research and desire to crossdress more frequently. That said, what evidence there is consistently suggests that male crossdressers would prefer to crossdress more than they actually do.

But how often do they actually practice crossdressing? Neil Buhrich and Trina Beaumont's study of 222 adult male crossdressers, reported in 1981, finds that about one-third (34%) crossdress more often than weekly, and more than half (57%) have been continuously crossdressed for days or more than a week.[525] Vernon Coleman's 1996 report, based on data obtained from 414 adult British males, finds the respondents would like to crossdress more than six times as long each week as they actually do (12 daytime hours per week on average).[526] Vern and Bonnie Bullough, in research published in 1997, report that 91% of their 372 adult male subjects crossdress to some extent at least once a week.[527]

In a 1999 online survey of over 1,000 male crossdressers (ages ranging 16-76), nearly 90% crossdress at least once a month, with most doing so fairly regularly; only 2% are not actively crossdressing. Frequency reported breaks down as follows:

- ❑ 34% several times a week;
- ❑ 20% daily;
- ❑ 18% several times a month;
- ❑ 12% once a week; and
- ❑ 6% once a month.[528]

Among the respondents to this survey, just over 90% express a desire to increase the frequency of their crossdressing.[529]

This disparate collection of studies cannot be easily collated into a table of meaningful data, but in simplest terms they can be compared as follows:

Table 30.1 Percentage Reporting Crossdressing at Least Weekly

Study	# Subjects	% Crossdressing At Least Weekly
N. Buhrich & T. Beaumont (1981)[530]	222	34% (more than weekly)
V. Coleman (1996)[531]	414	?
B. Bullough & V. Bullough (1997)[532]	372	91%
'Yvonne' (1999)[533]	1,000+	84%

Alongside this desire to crossdress more should be placed time spent getting dressed and observing the results. A notion commoner in the past than today claims crossdressers exhibit narcissism in their crossdressing. Benjamin, responding to the existing literature of his time, comments that the use of the term 'narcissistic' in relation to crossdressers is somewhat misleading; though they can devote considerable time admiring themselves in front of a mirror, or camera, the notion that they—like the mythic Narcissus—are in love with themselves is open to question. Benjamin himself thinks these activities harmless.[534] It also may be queried if such time spent actually is more than others do.

Lee's Remarks

When I am at home, I am almost continually crossdressed, either partially or fully. There have been times when I crossdressed continuously for several days, and as I have confessed already, I would be happy being able to dress however I want, whenever I want, without fear of social reprisals. Given the data I have seen, I rank among those who regularly crossdress.

As an added thought, I find it a little amusing and a little offensive to discover that some people might think I spend hours admiring myself in a mirror when crossdressed. I know what I look like, and I don't crossdress for the sight, but for the way I experience myself when thus dressed.

What is the extent of crossdressing?

The extent of crossdressing also varies. As already described, it tends to become more extensive over time. In adulthood, surveys of male crossdressers indicate a majority prefer and practice complete over partial crossdressing, as the following table shows:

Table 30.2 Preference for Complete Crossdressing

Study	# Subjects	Preference for Complete Crossdressing
V. Prince & P. M. Bentler (1972)[535]	504	85%
Vernon Coleman (1996)[536]	414	77%
R. Docter & V. Prince (1997)[537]	1,032	93%

Those who partially crossdress generally choose feminine underwear worn beneath masculine outerwear. Coleman's respondents overwhelmingly (75%) affirm wearing women's underwear while dressed in ordinary male clothing.[538] Similarly, Buhrich and Beaumont find that 61% wear feminine items while dressed as males.[539]

Research on how often male crossdressers appear fully crossdressed in public has varied rather widely. Buhrich and Beaumont, for example, report nearly two-thirds (65%) of their subjects admit appearing fully crossdressed in public.[540] On the other hand, Prince and Bentler, in their 1972 survey report, calculate a range of between 18%-34% based on responses to a number of questions. They conclude that 18% of their sample have appeared crossdressed in public, with an additional 16% probably having done so.[541] The differences in findings may merely reflect the populations being surveyed in the different studies, though we cannot rule out other factors, such as the possibility that greater public awareness and, perhaps, acceptance has led to more crossdressers being willing to try such an appearance now than in former times.

Lee's Remarks

I have never appeared fully crossdressed in public, though I have been in the company of others who were unaware I was partially crossdressed. So feminine underwear is worn more than feminine outerwear. It is purely a pragmatic matter for me. In a perfect world—by my imagining anyway—I would be socially free to be an in-between gender and display traits or behaviors that society sees as masculine alongside those that are feminine, and without regard to my sexual anatomy. But this world is not that one, so I evade censure (or worse) by presenting as at least mostly masculine when around others.

Q. 31

Does crossdressing lead to a sex-change operation?

The Short Answer. Crossdressing does not lead to sex-change operations. It is not a causal factor in producing a desire to change one's sex assignment. It may accompany such a desire, but that is not the same as producing it. In fact, most crossdressers—by far the majority—do not seek sex reassignment surgery. Those that do are motivated by a conviction that they are living in a wrong-sexed body, not because crossdressing feminized them to the point of wanting a woman's body.

The Longer Answer. Hardly anyone is crass enough to suggest that crossdressing causes feminization leading to seeking sex reassignment surgery. But there are those who think crossdressing is just a signpost along the way to completing life's journey in a body sexed different than the one they started with. For these people, crossdressing reflects 'gender dysphoria' (see answer to Q. 96), with crossdressers starting on a path of limited crossdressing that proceeds to more frequent and complete crossdressing, then feminization through hormones, and eventually seeking sex-reassignment. Like a great many notions in life, this one has just enough coincidence with fact as to make it a dangerous idea.

Not every crossdresser is a transsexual. In fact, only a relatively small percentage of crossdressers are transsexuals. Only transsexuals have the sense of being in the wrong sexed body. Some transsexuals do not crossdress much prior to the treatment regimen leading to sex reassignment surgery. Thus, frequency and completeness of crossdressing is an unreliable predictor of seeking sex reassignment.

A serious misunderstanding of crossdressing lies behind those who believe that everyone who crossdresses either is homosexual (see answer to Q. 30), or desires to be a member of the opposite sex. Fortunately, very little exploration is required to explode such myths. What we will do in the remainder of this question is break down the supposed line of development described above. That hypothesized course is as follows:

- ❏ early sporadic and limited crossdressing gradually gives way to
- ❏ more complete and frequent crossdressing, eventually accompanied by
- ❏ pursuit of feminizing strategies such as the use of hormones and
- ❏ eventual seeking of sex reassignment surgery (SRS).

Throughout it is presupposed that the crossdresser is developing a more complete opposite gender persona because of gender dysphoria.

Why develop an opposite sex gender side?

Let's start with the last idea first. Perhaps the initial thing needing said is that the development of an opposite gender expression in one's self is not bad. Psychological research demonstrates that individuals who stereotypically embrace their assigned gender do more poorly than others who develop a more androgynous self. *Androgyny*—a word combined from the Greek words for male and female—in psychological traits means a blending of masculine and feminine.[542] Carl Jung, the famous Swiss psychiatrist, is one among many who thinks that an important task for healthy psychological development is learning to develop and express the opposite gender side of one's self.[543] So, simply the idea of developing and expressing a feminine side, if you are a man, or a masculine side, if you are a woman, is hardly either radical or disturbed.

If *gender dysphoria*—a sense that gender and sex in oneself don't match the way society expects—is present, that introduces another component that requires attention. Since that is looked at elsewhere (at Q. 96), we won't go into it here at any length. I will say, though, that one of the issues debated about crossdressing concerns to what degree, if at all, gender dysphoria plays a role for many crossdressers. For now, we will leave that matter aside and consider the process of seeking expression of a gender different than the one assigned in infancy regardless of its ultimate motivation.

Transsexuals—like the rest of us—certainly desire congruence between their body and their gender identity. The process they follow is to change their body because that is what feels wrong; their internal gender identity is what feels right. So their process can be said to be one of seeking development of what is a gender persona opposite their assigned one. While some folk regard this as 'unnatural,' giving priority to genitalia, others see it as perfectly 'natural' since the sexual organ that matters most is the brain.

Reports from male crossdressers do show that for many crossdressing expresses a feminine side, or even 'personality' that they regard as valuable and important. But developing this persona does not have to mean that the masculine persona atrophies. Therapist Gianna Israel cautions, "People need to be very careful with their judgments when discussing and exploring gender boundaries and roles. Just as there is nothing wrong with having a healthy en femme persona for a crossdressing male, there is also nothing wrong with having a healthy sense of masculinity."[544]

Does crossdressing always lead to changing sex?

In general, crossdressing typically begins before puberty. In adulthood, perhaps as a response to greater autonomy and ability, crossdressing commonly increases in both extent and frequency. By middle adulthood, few crossdressers feel any desire to diminish or cease their crossdressing. But that does not mean that all—or even most—crossdressers proceed to seek a sex change. Those who do are called transsexuals (see answer to Q. 19), and they constitute a minority of crossdressers. What is more common is the taking of one or more steps to further express the preferred gender. Such steps might range from adding makeup and jewelry to accompany crossdressing, to seeking cosmetic surgery or hormone treatments.

How are genderizing steps pursued?

Although most of what I will discuss here concerns feminizing pursuits, it would be unfair to exclude masculizing pursuits. So, I am using 'genderizing' to refer to efforts to construct a more complete gender identity through strategies aimed at altering the body. In one way, dress does this since our gender identity is not completely separable from what our clothing expresses. But the focus here is on strategies such as the taking of sex hormones or other nonsurgical procedures.

One significant step that requires nothing more than a simple behavior is changing the name by which one is called. Many crossdressers, whether male or female, take a name more appropriate to the gender they are expressing. For crossdressers who are not transsexuals, this name is used when crossdressed. Among transsexuals, a 1971 report based on data obtained from 599 self-designated transsexuals finds nearly half (48%) the males and more than one-third (36%) of the females adopt and use names suited to their preferred gender.[545]

The phenomena of taking sex hormones has been identified as a distinguishing characteristic of a group of male crossdressers known as 'marginal transvestites.'[546] The use of feminizing hormones is for breast development. Virginia Prince and Peter Bentler, in surveying more than 500 male crossdressers, report that only 1-in-20 (5%) are actually taking female hormones. However, half (50%) of the entire group wish to do so. Somewhat less than half (41%) say they definitely do not wish to take them.[547] A 1999 online survey of over 1,000 male crossdressers finds that one-fifth (21%) have taken or are currently taking some form of female hormones, and one-fifth (21%) of these are doing so by a physician's prescription.[548] These latter numbers are similar to what the 1971 report offers about its transsexual subjects: about 20% using hormones.[549]

While a minority use hormones, some pursue activities like hair removal, either through body shaving or electrolysis. The 1999 online survey reports that a majority (60%) remove body hair even when they do not plan on being crossdressed. However, only a small percentage use electrolysis for facial hair (6%) or for body hair elsewhere (5%)[550]

Transsexuals are more likely than other crossdressers to combine techniques as part of a coordinated strategy to achieve more concordance with their felt gender. But even among this group the extent of steps taken varies widely. The 1971 report of 599 transsexuals finds for both males and females that about 1-in-5 (18% of males; 22% of females) take active, coordinated steps using some combination of crossdressing, use of adopted names, hormones, or cohabitation.[551]

How many seek sex reassignment surgery?

How many crossdressers are transsexuals rather than transvestites? In the Prince and Bentler survey reported in 1972, 12% of respondents say they feel they are "a woman trapped in a male body." Not surprisingly, then, an almost identical percentage (14%) express a desire for a sex change operation.[552] Some crossdressers either settle for less extensive surgery, engaging in cosmetic surgery, or employ minor cosmetic surgery as one step in their transitioning process. But the pursuit of cosmetic surgery to appear more feminine seems relatively rare. The 1999 online survey reports just under 3% have experienced such surgery.[553]

A comparative study including 65 male transvestites and 33 transsexuals finds a pronounced difference in respect to desire and behavior to change sex. Less than half of transvestites (47%) have any interest in a sex change, and of those who do only a miniscule number (2%) are favorably inclined toward surgery. In fact, of those who have some interest, nearly half (46%) have looked into the possibility and rejected it. On the other hand, one-quarter (25%) of these men have at one time or another taken sex hormones.[554] In his study of over 1,000 adult British males, physician Vernon Coleman finds that more than three-quarters (77%) say they would not have a sex change operation if the opportunity presented itself.[555]

Lee's Remarks

Wow. This is Lee again, and I'm a little worried about what to say on this subject. I don't want to be misunderstood. I do not experience myself as a female, though I am more comfortable with femininity than masculinity. I do not feel like a woman trapped in a male body; I feel like me trapped in a masculine gender assignment that doesn't fit me and a male body that only sometimes feels okay.

When I consider the supposed 'course' that leads to SRS, I can see myself partway along the path, though I certainly don't think that final destination is an inevitable one. I will admit that the thought of feminizing my body has held some attraction, but only because in a world stuck at one end or the other of masculinity or femininity, the former seems less desirable to me. I'd rather be who I am, but there is a certain appeal to some congruence between sexual anatomy and gender expectations that would allow me to live more freely in the world. Except, I am not at all persuaded that I would find myself anymore at ease as a woman than I am as a man. If masculine male and feminine female are the only choices, I much prefer and better identify with the latter. I suppose all that says, though, is that gender is more important to me than sexual anatomy. And gender is where the problem is for me as a transgendered person. I fit in-between the permissible choices. That is why I crossdress, and why I do not seek to become anatomically female, despite my belief that stuck between two choices that might be the more comfortable fit for me.

Q. 32

Is crossdressing harmful?

The Short Answer. There is no evidence that crossdressing behavior is intrinsically harmful. Some noncrossdressers are upset by the behavior, and some blame the crossdresser for this 'harm.' Yet crossdressing itself is nonviolent. Most of us have trouble seeing how personal upset constitutes being harmed even though the feelings one experiences are unpleasant. This response to crossdressing has been termed an aspect of transphobia—an irrational fear of transgender people. Transphobia *is* harmful, both to the transphobic in diminishing their humanity and to the transgendered against whom it is directed. Some noncrossdressers further claim that crossdressing harms society. This claim is more controversial and the positions taken in respect to it largely reflect personal and cultural values. Some worry that such claims sound suspiciously like those made to support racism, religious bigotry, and other forms of bias, prejudice, and discrimination. Others claim that the gender divide is so important it must be protected from those who violate it—which is especially the judgment made of crossdressers in a two-and-only-two gender scheme. For the crossdresser, this society's mental health community applies a standard that seems applicable to this issue: does crossdressing elicit personal distress in the crossdresser or produce impairment in some important area of functioning? The most likely cause of distress appears to stem from the environment, because of the negative reactions of others, which can impair relationships between a crossdresser and noncrossdressers. In the latter situation, if those who regard crossdressers negatively act in a hostile fashion, very real harm can result. That harm might range from violation of basic human and civil rights with respect to things like housing and employment. Or it can mean aggressive and hostile remarks, or physical violence. On the other hand, with respect to the effects of crossdressing as experienced internally by the crossdresser, evidence supports the contention that the effects are positive. Crossdressers report it is helpful in combating stress and use the behavior for relaxation. As seen earlier (the answer to Q. 27), some psychological testing suggests positive gains when crossdressed. In sum, any harmful effects seem to derive either from acts practiced by those who object to the behavior or from internalized fear, guilt, or shame derived from living in a hostile environment.

The Longer Answer. There are several sides to this question, each of which merits some consideration. These are:

❑ Is crossdressing harmful to the crossdresser?

❑ Is crossdressing harmful to those around the crossdresser?

❑ Is crossdressing harmful to society?

Let us examine each in turn.

Is crossdressing harmful to the crossdresser?

Answering such a simple question is harder than it looks. We must first determine what is meant by harm. Obviously, in terms of direct, physical contact with clothes of the opposite sex, harm in the sense of physical injury is a rather ludicrous notion. The mental health community, within the framework of the DSM model (see the answer to Q. 96), concerns itself with whether an individual experiences significant personal distress and/or impairment in functioning in some important area of life (e.g., work, school, or relationships). How does the crossdresser fare in these respects?

The Mental Health Standard of 'Personal Distress'

Are crossdressers significantly distressed by their crossdressing? Since it is almost always a voluntary behavior, typically associated with significant pleasure and relaxation, to speak about self-directed psychological harm through crossdressing may seem ridiculous. Simply put, crossdressers generally don't complain that the behavior itself produces personal distress.

Of course, some do express distress. On occasion it can appear that crossdressing is like an unwanted obsession—a matter we shall examine more closely in volume 5 (see the answer to Q. 94). The act may elicit positive feelings while being done, accompanied by shame and/or guilt afterwards. Or a mix of positive and negative feelings may occur during and after the behavior. In any event, some crossdressers do exhibit distress, and may turn to therapists for help.

Interestingly, what appears to be the situation in such cases is that the internal distress results from internalized environmental factors such as cultural values and/or the expressed disgust of others. It is not the mere act of crossdressing that arouses negative feelings within the crossdresser. Rather, it is the *meaning* of the experience as filtered through the culture or perceptions of others that occasions the distress. This distress is almost inevitable attached to consequent difficulties in relating to others. Thus it may be most proper to say that when there is distress, it is associated with a specific kind of impairment.

The Mental Health Standard of 'Impairment'

So, let us consider impairment. As seen in the answers to Q. 26-27, crossdressers seem to do at least as well as others in educational and job achievement. They seem at least as smart as others, and much more like others in personality and sexual characteristics than unlike them. Crossdressing is typically done in private, usually in secret, and does not generally intrude on public aspects of a person's life. So where is the impairment?

Let us permit this question to linger for a moment while we sketch a context in which to understand the proposed answer. Let us turn to the possibility that any negative effects do not primarily derive from inside the crossdresser but from the environment. Peggy Rudd, author of a number of books about crossdressing and herself the spouse of a crossdresser, comments early in her book *Crossdressing with Dignity: The Case for Transcending Gender Lines*: "Crossdressing is not harmful, but a fear of it and a lack of understanding can breed prejudice and contempt."[556] The behaviors from others stemming from prejudice and contempt certainly can result in harm—both physical and psychological.

How common is this kind of harm? Unfortunately, according to some research, such harm happens often. Many crossdressers experience harm—and all of it can be viewed as originating in the reactions of others. Croughan and associates indicate that over 95% of their subjects (all adult males) report one or more negative consequences. Among the most common are these:

- ❏ objections by family (57%);
- ❏ interference with social relations with other men (44%);
- ❏ interference with social relations with women (29%);
- ❏ feelings of guilt (21%);
- ❏ divorce (17%); and,
- ❏ loss of friends (16%).[557]

On the other hand, we should not exaggerate the degree of these consequences. Many are minor or limited in duration. Vernon Coleman's research finds that 84% of his subjects (414 adult British males) have not lost a job or a relationship because of their crossdressing. Yet Coleman notes that it is possible the reason for this relatively low incidence is because so many crossdressers labor so hard to keep the behavior secret.[558]

Now we can see the 'impairment' a crossdresser allegedly possesses: interpersonal difficulties connected to crossdressing. The chief contention made by some mental health professionals for treating some crossdressing (specifically 'transvestic fetishism') as a mental disorder is that it results in this kind of impairment. The critical question that then arises is this: *is the impairment in the crossdresser or in the intolerance of others?* The mental health profession is geared to looking at the individual as the source of the presenting problem, whatever it is, and not at society, about which the ordinary therapist thinks he or she can do little. It is easier to see the impairment in someone engaged in socially deviant behavior than to indict the culture as impaired in its values (cf. the answer to Q. 100).

But perhaps the impairment really is in the crossdresser. Maybe the interpersonal difficulties are connected to the crossdressing by virtue of the crossdresser relying more on crossdressing for relational satisfaction than upon satisfying relationships with others. Thus sociologist Taylor Buckner suggests that male crossdressers come to relate to the crossdressed self as to another woman, thus diminishing the need for investing much in a real relationship with another person.[559]

On the other hand, perhaps partners are the ones who reduce their investment in the relationship because of their response to the crossdressing. As we shall see later (the answer to Q. 38), the reactions experienced by partners can be quite varied. Some are very negative. Yet let us return to the matter at hand: does crossdressing necessarily produce impairment in a relationship? Interestingly, some partners of crossdressers report that the crossdresser is more pleasant, relaxed, and easier to relate to when crossdressed. If true, that finding suggests crossdressing can facilitate relating rather than impair it. Richard Docter, for example, finds that nearly two-thirds (63%) of the women he surveyed report that crossdressing adds positive things to a marriage, including increased intimacy, as well as the qualities already mentioned.[560] At best, then, the evidence is mixed. In some cases impairment may occur, but the source of it may be unclear. We should avoid assuming the cause is the crossdressing, since it can prompt either positive or negative relational effects.

Lee's Remarks

This is Lee again and I really hope everyone will hear me clearly: crossdressing is not a problem for me, but it is for you if you let it harm how you feel and relate to those of us who crossdress. In that case, what becomes a problem for me is your response. My concern over what you might do to me because I crossdress is why I keep it secret and is the sole source of any stress I ever have connected with it.

Is crossdressing harmful to those around the crossdresser?

Some people fear that crossdressing, like an infectious disease, is catching. Specifically, they worry that crossdressing behavior by an adult—especially a parent—presents an influential learning model for children, who then are at special risk to grow up transgendered. As seen in answering Q. 22, there is little if any support for this notion. The idea is similar to the concern voiced by many people against allowing homosexuals to adopt children. Despite the compelling body of evidence that children of homosexuals are no more likely to grow up homosexual than anyone else, many people persist in irrational fear. The phenomenon is an aspect of what is called 'homophobia,' and the parallel with other transgendered people is 'transphobia.'

Such phobia is indeed harmful, both to the person who experiences anxiety from having it and to the person against whom aggressive behavior is directed because of it. It would be erroneous, though, to locate the source of the problem in the transgendered person; the problem is the phobia. And it takes many forms. Some people who are in relationships with transgendered people experience this transphobia as a persistent discomfort that they attribute to the willful behavior of the transgendered person. The irrational belief runs something like this: 'If only he/she would choose to be normal (i.e., dress conventionally, or be heterosexual, etc.), then I wouldn't feel uncomfortable.' By locating the source of their anxiety in the transgendered person, they follow an old, familiar path: blame the minority because they are different.

Setting aside the question of how practical or advisable change by the transgendered person is (a matter considered in answering other questions; cf. the answer to Q. 25, 97-98, 100), how is it that we so seldom consider that it is the person with the phobia who needs help to change? The essence of any phobia is an exaggerated anxiety or fear, one all out of proportion to the danger actually posed by the stimulus. What, exactly, is the danger posed by a man wearing panties under his pants? Posing the question reveals the irrationality of the response by the person who claims that a transgendered loved one is hurting them by behavior like crossdressing.

I don't mean, however, to be dismissive of loved one's genuine concerns. Perhaps, for example, there is the prospect of 'people talking,' and saying unkind things, which might elicit embarrassment. Or perhaps the person may feel some shame for being in a relationship with a transgendered person. These are real issues. But who has the problem? In the former instance, the source of the problem resides both in the bigotry of those who ridicule minorities, and in the person who implicitly sides with their bigotry by feeling embarrassment. In the latter situation, the sense of shame is not caused by someone else being transgendered but by the shamed person's feelings about being in relationship to someone who elicits doubts about themselves. In either case the harm is not being generated by the transgendered person; the source of the problem and the need to address it lie elsewhere. These matters we shall return to later (see the answers to Q. 37-39).

Lee's Remarks

As I mentioned earlier, my wife has issues with my crossdressing. Her argument is that my behavior—even though it is almost entirely out of her view and remains secret from others—hurts our relationship. Thus I am hurting her. The solution in her eyes is obvious: I should quit crossdressing and be the masculine male I was intended to be.

Don't think that solution doesn't have some appeal. If I could transform myself to be the kind of man my culture expects of me I have no doubt my life would be easier. That does not mean I think there is anything at all wrong with the way I am, or that I desire to be different. I don't. But I'm not stupid. I know things would be less complicated if I was a conventional man. For that matter, things would be simpler if I was just a conventional woman. Conventional people avoid the kinds of obstacles the rest of us face.

Yet here I am, an unconventional person because our society hasn't figured out what to do with transgendered people. Because I don't fit a simplistic 'masculine male' or 'feminine female' scheme I don't belong—unless *I* change. And of course, I should change because I am the one who is different. Why should the 'normal' folk have to change anything?

Sorry, but I don't buy it. If I am told I hurt someone simply because I am transgendered, and do nothing odder or more transgressive than wear clothes not typical for my anatomical sex, then how is that different from being told I hurt someone because I am left-handed, or because I belong to Church X instead of Church Y? After all, left-handed people can learn to write right-handed, so if they don't do so aren't they just being stubborn? And if your religious beliefs offend me shouldn't you change them to avoid harming me, especially if you care about me? I mean, you are choosing to believe what I find harmful.

Of course, no one anymore makes lefties fake being right-handed. And most of us are willing to let others believe what they will because [a] they aren't going to change on our say so and we can't make them, and [b] few people take beliefs seriously enough to be much concerned by deviant ones anyway. But we aren't quite there yet for the transgendered. I grant that it is ignorance that prompts bias, but it seems to me anyone who professes to care about a transgendered person would at least make an effort to learn about transgenderism and thus overcome their ignorance. In my eyes, it is the ignorance that works the real harm.

Is crossdressing harmful to society?

The line of illogical reasoning identified above is often more than the response of a few individuals. It also has been a response basic in racism, religious persecution, ethnic cleansing, and a number of other social responses in which being different has been a pretext for judgments that the minority person is inferior or evil. Simply being different—whether by virtue of skin color, religious belief or practice, ethnic custom, or crossdressing—is not enough to morally justify harmful acts against the minority, which may include social marginalization or ostracism, discrimination, or physical aggression. For those who feel the transgendered harm society, the burden is on them to demonstrate it factually; the burden is not on the transgendered to prove their innocence.

Not all of us find crossdressing threatening to social order or public decency. But some of us do, labeling it deviant and supporting personal and social methods of control. As detailed in earlier questions (especially question set 1), the expressive system revolving around clothes inevitably involves our values. Those values generate ethical sensibilities and moral judgments (see the answer to Q. 4). If enough people merely acquiesce to a given moral stance—whether they personally agree to it or not—the result may generate anything from informal codes of conduct to laws or other regulations. Thus all of us have a stake in the judgments others make.

When transgendered realities are labeled 'deviant' the tendency may be to focus on the query, 'Why would anyone be that way?' Attention is thus directed at behavior and the individual without questioning why some of us disapprove in the first place. Sociologist David Greenberg, in considering this phenomenon, notes that a significant shift occurred in his discipline in the 1960s when researchers began to ask about reasons for disapproval. Rather than rooting deviance in the individual or act so labeled, as though it were a natural and inevitable fact, this shift uncovered an uncomfortably simple truth: deviance is in the eye of the beholder. As Greenberg points out, with specific reference to homosexuality, but equally applicable to any transgendered reality, it is beliefs that an act or person is "evil, sick, or undesirable—and the corresponding efforts to punish, cure, or prevent it" that make the act or person deviant. "Whether or not these beliefs are true is beside the point."[561]

The judgment some of us make that crossdressing is deviant, and thus intrinsically harmful to society, often stems from the perception that crossdressing threatens the gender divide and that this divide must be maintained or the natural order of things will deteriorate into chaos. Others of us see the threat as more explicitly sexual—crossdressers are viewed as seeking illicit sexual satisfactions through their behavior. In either instance, some of us go a step further by explicitly linking crossdressing to moral turpitude (cf. the answer to Q. 36). Some of us simply find the sight of someone crossdressed emotionally upsetting and believe that no one has the right to offend us by such public display. Those of us thinking along these lines are apt to say, 'Whatever someone does in the privacy of their own home is all right by me, but they shouldn't be out in public.' Further—as the testimony of many crossdressers confirms—even in one's own home a similar restriction may exist, as though by keeping the behavior completely removed from the sight of others stops a contagion from spreading. In this case, though, the 'disease' is simply dis-ease—a feeling of discomfort whose source is projected away from the self and onto the crossdresser.

If we conclude that the bipolar gender divide characteristic of our society is essential to public well-being, we will certainly judge crossdressing harmful. We have considered this issue already (notably in answering Q. 4, 6-7), so we need not treat it at length here. We should remember, however, that the evidence suggests that an insistence on conformity to one or the other of two mutually exclusive gender identities and roles comes at a price. An important question then becomes, 'Is the price we pay for adherence to this rigid divide more harmful to personal and social well-being than the price paid for transgressing it through crossdressing?'

If our concern is about sexual intent by crossdressers, then we need better education. There is no evidence that crossdressers in public exhibit sexually aggressive tendencies or are more likely than others to commit rape. That there are some crossdressing prostitutes is certain, but any objection to them beyond that voiced about other prostitutes amounts to no more than being annoyed about the possibility of being deceived when seeking a service. Apparently, the 'harm' more likely stems from misperceptions of crossdressing than from crossdressers' behavior.

If our concern is that crossdressing offends our sight, then how shall we evaluate that? Is being uncomfortable being harmed? Is the offense to our eyes socially more significant than that posed to our noses by a person who hasn't bathed in a month? We tolerate people coughing and sneezing with infectious illnesses in public, and they pose far more risk to our well-being than a cross-dresser—and are far more common!

For that matter, the irrationality of the logic often used becomes more apparent when we look at some of the things we tolerate with hardly a thought, despite mountains of evidence as to the threat they pose to all of us. For example, we socially approve the consumption of alcohol though we know that use of the drug impairs judgment, alters social functioning, and leads to many kinds of harm, from lowered inhibitions that get people in trouble, to drunk driving, to cirrhosis of the liver. We still at least tolerate smoking in many public venues despite the evidence concerning the health threat of secondhand smoke. Compared to such widespread harms to health and the attendant threats to social order, the very occasional sight of a man in a skirt seems rather insignificant in the scheme of things.

If crossdressing is not demonstrably harmful to the individual (except from the reactions of others), or to others, or to society, then why do some of us still find it threatening? Why does it matter more to us than things like drinking or smoking? I think there are a number of factors involved. First, sex and gender strike closer to home than most things, and crossdressing is unsettling because it clouds matters we want to be crystal clear. Second, many more people publicly drink or smoke than publicly crossdress. It is easier to oppose a minority and to justify oppression because the few hold little power to effectively resist. Some of us find it hard to see any more rational justification for discrimination against crossdressers than against those of a different race.

Though other factors could be named, the point is fairly obvious: perceiving crossdressing as harmful to society is largely irrational. When social order is disturbed in a way that affects the well-being of people, it almost always is because of the hostile reactions of observers and not the behavior of the cross-dresser. Arresting a crossdresser for inciting public unrest thus becomes a way of blaming the victim—not unlike suggesting a woman in a miniskirt invites sexual assault. Perhaps a reevaluation of social values—one that conscientiously looks to reason and evidence—is in order. Some evidence suggests that is happening (see question set 7).

216

Is crossdressing healthy?

Earlier we saw that the harm crossdressers encounter comes not from the behavior itself but from the reactions of others. If crossdressers risk such harm, what motivates them to do so? We could hypothesize that the motivation is pathological—that the desire to crossdress stems from a psychological deficiency. But, as we saw in the research in answering Q. 26-27, crossdressers are almost embarrassingly normal (or above average) in achievement and generally unremarkable in personality characteristics. The crossdressers among us seem no more likely than the rest of us to desire, seek, or need professional intervention for psychological problems.

If the motivation seems not to be pathological, then perhaps it is criminal. Maybe crossdressers engage in the behavior to pursue illicit activities. Yet, if so, the evidence is sparse. Brushes with the law are as likely to be simply for being crossdressed as for doing anything else (see the answer to Q. 36). At no point in history, nor in the present, does there seem to be evidence supportive of concluding that a significant percentage of crossdressing occurs to mask or facilitate criminal activity.

Given the risk of harm from others, and setting aside pathology and criminality as causal explanations, what is going on? Consider motivation in general. What generally moves us to act are benefits that outweigh costs. Whether the rewards are emotional or otherwise, the behavior is sustained over time by the consistent and probably disproportionate degree of good over bad in the experience of the individual. For this possibility there is a goodly amount of evidence.

Let us begin with listing some of the healthy benefits allegedly conferred by crossdressing:

❑ It meets a basic need not otherwise met.
❑ It provides relaxation (a positive stress-reducing response).
❑ It boosts mood and self-confidence.
❑ It enhances interpersonal relating.
❑ It facilitates maximal performance on various tasks.

Let us briefly examine evidence for such claims.

Crossdressing Meets a Basic Need

Peggy Rudd concludes that crossdressing for the crossdresser "is a basic human need."[562] Others express a similar sentiment. That, unlike Rudd, most of these people making this claim are crossdressers should not automatically disqualify its validity. Instead, we would be better served considering what basic need is thus met. In the context of this work that need fits within an experiencing and expressive system centered around dress. Crossdressing uses clothes to experience and express something basic to the person in a way that does not otherwise happen. Exactly what that it is does not have to be the same for every person. What they have in common is both the sense that the need is basic to them and that it is crossdressing that meets it.

Crossdressing Reduces Stress

The successful use of crossdressing to reduce stress and provide pleasant relaxation is well-attested in the testimony of crossdressers. In their research published in 1981, researchers Neil Buhrich and Trina Beaumont report that fully a third of the 222 adult male crossdressers involved in their study say their frequency of crossdressing increases when they feel tense. But this statistic alone probably underestimates the use of crossdressing to relieve tension. When their data is examined it emerges that nearly three-quarters (71%) of the subjects increase the frequency of their crossdressing in response to tension at least some of the time, and only 8% say the frequency decreases because of stress.[563]

In his 1996 study, Vernon Coleman reports that nearly half (48%) of his study's respondents indicate this purpose as the reason (or one of the reasons) for crossdressing. Coleman remarks, "As a physician I would much rather see a man under stress deal with pressure by cross dressing than by taking tranquillisers."[564] He provocatively adds:

> There are, without doubt, other ways in which a man under stress could obtain relief. But most of the available alternatives are likely to be considerably more damaging to him, his family and society in general than dressing up in fancy lingerie. The cross dresser could undoubtedly obtain a similar level of release by taking tranquillisers (likely to become an addictive habit), smoking cigarettes (likely to give him cancer) or drinking himself senseless. Alcohol alters the senses and so makes stress bearable for many. Clothes can affect the senses with a similar result. The difference is that wearing silks and satins won't wreck your liver. Why is the importance of the skin as a sense organ so vastly and consistently underestimated? It is odd that society should, in general, choose to regard alcoholism as a forgivable and understandable consequence of overwork whereas cross dressing remains such a misunderstood remedy that most transvestites make enormous efforts to keep their dressing a secret.[565]

Crossdressing Boosts Mood & Self-confidence

Undoubtedly associated with stress reduction are other benefits often associated with crossdressing: elevation of mood and self-confidence. This idea makes sense in what we have learned about the way men relate to clothes. Some research finds that men rely more than women on clothes to raise their mood and boost their self-confidence.[566] Other research suggests that traditional masculine values lead to signs of psychological distress.[567] Perhaps crossdressing, if it does nothing more than allow temporary respite from the rigors and pressures of masculinity, affords male crossdressers the kind of relief that elicits more positive mood.

To the suggestion that the attainment of these benefits from crossdressing constitutes a cheat, we might respond that even should that premise be granted, the benefits are real and attained without the dubious consequences of more socially accepted ways of boosting mood and/or self-confidence such as by ingestion of nicotine or alcohol. But we need not rely on that defense. Instead we can point out that these benefits occur despite social disapproval of crossdressing, thus attesting to their potency. Further, as we have seen, societal objections are rooted in highly questionable cultural assumptions about gender and sex. Simple appeal to these cultural judgments no longer seems enough to mount a credible contention that the benefits are illusory or illegitimate.

Crossdressing Enhances Interpersonal Relating

We already have seen that the chief justification that may be appealed to for the harmfulness of crossdressing lies in its alleged connection to impaired interpersonal functioning. But we have also seen that at least some research suggests this idea is incorrect. Logically, a relaxed person who experiences a sense of congruence with the self is far more likely to succeed in the challenges of interpersonal relating. Many crossdressers and their partners attest that better relating accompanies the crossdressing and that when the behavior is frustrated interpersonal interactions suffer.

On the other hand, we should not ignore concerns over crossdressing possibly being associated with impaired relational functioning. When we look at this possibility we have to attempt to sort out where the source of the difficulty resides. Does the crossdressed person behave in ways—such as through increased hostility, aggression, or unpleasantness—that make a relationship more difficult? The evidence seems to suggest this is not the case. Indeed, the evidence we have seen (e.g., the answer to Q. 27) indicates that such traits diminish when crossdressed. To date, no reliable pairing of traits and crossdressing have been shown to prompt difficulties.

If the crossdresser's interpersonal behavioral traits improve, but relationships suffer when crossdressing is going on, then what is happening? The crossdressing itself might be implicated as the problem, but only if clothing somehow communicates negative results all-by-itself. Of course, that would be an absurd conclusion; clothes are part of a system that relies on the wearer and the perceiver to determine the outcome of any interaction between them. So if the crossdresser's interpersonal traits improve with crossdressing, then perhaps what is happening is the other person's interpersonal traits are declining with exposure to the crossdressing, or perhaps just knowledge of it.

This possibility helps make sense of what the research reveals: interpersonal functioning in couples where crossdressing occurs depends on how the crossdressing is regarded. We can assume the crossdresser always or almost always views the behavior positively. If the partner concurs, then the outcome will be positive, or at least neutral (i.e., no significant effect). If the partner disapproves, the relational outcome will be negative.

The problem with this understanding, though it may be accurate, lies in the possible application made of it. If we then place all the pressure on the partner for the relational outcome, then all we have accomplished is shifting blame for troubles from the crossdresser to the partner—and that is hardly profitable. The lived reality of any relationship is always negotiated and renegotiated by the parties. The best conclusion we can make is that crossdressing can enhance interpersonal functioning by the crossdresser and thus contribute to a better relationship but such an outcome is not inevitable. The well-being of any relationship likely depends on the values, feelings, and behaviors of both partners. Thus relational success or impairment is better regarded as a function of the relating between the two and not merely the characteristics of just one or the other.

Crossdressing Facilitates Maximal Performance

Crossdressing, as evidenced by various test situations, may actually facilitate the attainment of maximal performance (see the answer to Q. 27). Once more this makes sense if we accept the reasoning that people who feel more relaxed and more themselves are thereby likely to also feel greater confidence, more competent, and perform closer to their actual potential. However, we must again qualify this conclusion by noting that any environment where the crossdressing is negatively evaluated is likely to have an effect on the crossdresser that offsets, perhaps even eliminates, the benefits of crossdressing itself.

Lee's Remarks

I realize I have been rather forceful in my views on this matter of harm. Please allow me to be equally emphatic about the matter of health. Not only am I not harmed by what I choose to wear, such clothes balance me, enriching my experience of myself and allowing me to express—at least to myself—who I know myself to be. If that isn't enough justification for you, then just chalk my satisfaction up to stress relief, because I certainly do feel more relaxed, more confident and capable when crossdressed. For me that makes sense as the result of being congruent with myself. When I have to constantly pretend to be a masculine male it proves very wearying and stressful. When I can just be myself I feel better. I don't see how this makes me different from anyone else, save for the fact that so many others seem to have an irrational interest in not letting me be myself if it doesn't fit their notion of who I 'ought' to be. Like I said before, if that's you, then *you* are the one with a problem.

Q. 33

What is involved in crossdressing?

The Short Answer. Crossdressing as a behavior engages a spectrum of activities. In its broadest sense, 'crossdressing' has been used to refer to any and all activities involving one or another aspect of appearing like a gender other than the one assigned at birth. Thus, 'crossdressing' has been applied at times to a number of things besides clothing *per se*, such as wearing ornamentation, wigs or hairstyles, or makeup. In addition, crossdressing may be partial (i.e., involving only one or a few items), or complete (i.e., involving the entire gendered appearance, at least in terms of clothing). Finally, crossdressing as a transgendered behavior is also sometimes associated with other gender-altering behavior like body shaving, taking sex hormones, or undergoing sex reassignment surgery.

The Longer Answer. By now it should be clear that crossdressing is an amazingly diverse phenomenon. While at its simplest level it is dressing in clothes of a gender different from the one assigned at birth, it is much more than merely that. Because crossdressing fits within the experiencing and expressing system centered around clothes, there are many possibilities for the crossdresser. Exactly what is worn, when, for how long, and for what purpose all are determined by the elements of experience and expression unique to that individual in a particular context of time and place.

What activities constitute crossdressing?

Crossdressing can be conceived as a behavior involving more than clothes. Legal scholar Julie Seaman observes, "Social norms regarding body modification, ornamentation, and covering exist in every known human society. And in every known human society, such norms include gender norms: individuals are expected to adhere to certain sex-differentiated dress and grooming codes."[568] Especially in societies where clothing is not strongly gender differentiated, other items of appearance assume greater gendered significance. If 'dress' is regarded broadly as the constructed appearance one makes through a variety of means, then hair length and style, as well as ornamentation and make-up, fit as much as does clothing.

Hair Length & Style

Hair *length*, historically, enjoys prominence as a gender marker. Long hair traditionally is associated with femininity. In our own society in recent decades this has not been a much-applied standard. That may be because we have such a rich diversity of gender differentiated clothing that relying on hair length is superfluous. Today, both men and women in our society may wear their hair either short or long. Nevertheless, in general practice men continue to wear their hair relatively shorter than women do.

On the other hand, *hairstyles* remain gender differentiated to a greater extent, although here as well some modest changes have taken place in recent decades. Previously, ponytails were seen as feminine; today they tend to be regarded as unisex. But hair done up in a variety of fashion styles still tends to be seen as feminine. As a whole, men are expected to wear their hair—whether long or short—in simpler, unadorned styles. Crossdressers, especially occasional ones, are more likely to employ a wig to create a desired cross-gender hairstyle than to actually attempt to manipulate their own hair. However, this may not be the case where the person is living primarily or entirely in the identity and role of a gender different from the one assigned at birth (e.g., transsexuals).

Ornamentation

A similar explanation to that for hair may pertain to why our contemporary society gives little regard to body piercing for ornamentation. Traditionally, things like earrings were seen as feminine, but that is no longer a strongly endorsed notion. But not many years ago a man with an earring was likely to be seen as more feminine. Today's men in their use of jewelry are more like their forbears of past centuries than of the immediate past decades.

Indeed, archaeological documentation of the use of body ornamentation to distinguish gender may be traceable to Neolithic times.[569] It figures in the Orient as well as in the West.[570] In our own hemisphere, at least as far back as ancient Mesoamerica body ornamentation has been important in gender differentiation.[571] More immediately, for British and American culture, the greater association between body ornamentation and femininity corresponds to the shift in the 18th century toward a more pronounced gender hierarchy, as evident in marriage where the role of man is 'provider and protector' and that of woman is to offer "the innate and passive virtues of beauty and ornamentation."[572] In our own social setting, where women enjoy greater economic leverage, ornamentation—in apparel or otherwise—is relatively diminished (though no one can seriously argue that women are expected to be beautiful and nicely adorned).

Where ornamentation can be used to differentiate genders, it can be incorporated as part of crossdressing. Besides our just mentioned instance of earrings, historians note other examples, especially in ancient times, of crossdressing where a significant marker of gender crossing is non-clothing ornamentation. But we need not look back into the past to see that putting on ornamentation like jewelry remains a common part of male crossdressing.[573] It serves as a contribution to a total effect where presenting as a woman is the goal.

Make-up

Make-up remains an aspect of dress that is strongly gender differentiated in our society. As a general rule, girls and women apply make-up; boys and men do not. As sociologist Richard Ekins puts it, the 'world of make-up' is one of several 'worlds' from which boys and men are largely excluded.[574] That society cares who uses make-up is reflected in codes that may be enforced in schools or workplaces, as well as in broader social disapproval. Legal decisions can enforce these social norms. A 2006 circuit court decision (*Jespersen v. Harrah's Operating Company*) upheld an employer's dismissal of a female employee who refused to adhere to company policy mandating women bartenders wear foundation, blush, and lipstick at work—and forbidding male bartenders from doing the same.[575]

Some scholars distinguish between crossdressing as such and gender *crossover*. The latter is regarded as a modified form of crossdressing, distinguished by its greater social acceptability. Communication scholar Sofie Van Bauwel succinctly declares about gender crossover: "It's about women wearing pants and men using makeup."[576] Though this serves only as an example, the example shows that merely using make-up does not make a male a crossdresser in the manner negatively viewed by society. Another possibility is what has been called *gender fucking*—intentionally contrasting gender elements to make a public statement. So a male might combine masculine clothing with feminine make-up.[577]

Male crossdressers typically find make-up more challenging to master than learning the sizes used for women's clothing and obtaining a good fit. Simply polishing fingernails or toenails is one thing; facial make-up another. Psychiatrist and male crossdresser Richard J. Novic explains:

> At first, my beauty routine took over two hours and usually began with me in my boxershorts shaving my face and chest. I preferred to put my make-up on before my girl clothes so that I kept cool and didn't start to sweat. I always applied concealer and foundation first, then moved on to blush and contour, finished with eyes and lips.
>
> Although most women think of concealer as a little something to cover the dark circles under their eyes, most of us crossdressers see it as the cornerstone of our make-up and the most important trick of the trade.[578]

As Novic indicates, facial make-up is an important aspect of male crossdressing where the individual desires to pass in public as a woman.

As with all other elements of dress, make-up is variously used by crossdressers. While often vitally important in efforts to pass as a different gender, make-up may also be used in private crossdressing. Transgender scholars Richard Ekins and Dave King note that 'gender femalers'—males who adopt gender behaviors associated with women in pursuit of a feminine gender identity—may devote themselves to the study of one or another aspect of socially constructed femininity such as fashion or make-up.[579] Others have noted that male cross-dressers sometimes stand out for their heavy use of make-up.[580]

Clothing

Obviously, in societies like our own clothing is the predominant element in crossdressing. It is uniformly the element people think of whenever the subject comes up. Inasmuch as clothing has been discussed at length in this work (especially in volume 1), no further remark needs to be made here.

How do crossdressers learn these activities?

The question of how crossdressers learn to crossdress can be succinctly answered. Crossdressing is an activity largely mastered through trial-and-error experimentation. Rarely, if ever, is it something initially learned from direct observation of another crossdresser. Occasionally it is taught by a parent who harbors the desire for a child of the opposite sex and so reassigns gender for the child by crossdressing them. However, most individuals probably begin by capitalizing on the availability of garments from nearby members of the opposite sex, typically siblings and parent. With time the reach of available resources expands. Willing partners may provide clothes and instruction. Greater independence and financial means permit individual purchases. Many crossdressers as they grow older also pay attention to members of the opposite sex to see how they wear clothes. They may read magazines, use the internet, or utilize other media such as television and movies. With time and effort they become more aware of what they want and come closer to realizing it.

Lee's Remarks

I don't use jewelry, cosmetics, or wigs (though I have tried one on). As for learning, I definitely fit into the general pattern of learning on my own through trial-and-error. Let me tell you, I have made lots of errors! Learning what sizes and styles work for me has been a never-ending task it seems. Every wrong guess costs money, so I try to be smart about it. I also decided early on to shop where clothes are cheapest until I knew what I was doing. One thing that has been a relief is knowing that merchants don't care who buys what as long as they can pay for it. So many men today buy clothes for women that it really hasn't been an uncomfortable matter for me. In fact, as I've gotten older it has gotten easier. My learning has been mostly through experimentation, but I do observe others and think about what they are wearing, how they are wearing it, and whether that might work for me. I also use the internet and other media, especially magazines, to learn. But inevitably it comes back to trying something to see if it works.

Q. 34

Where do crossdressers find support?

The Short Answer. One of the matters that has most dramatically changed for crossdressers in the last few decades has been the greater opportunity to meet other crossdressers in relative safety. This does not necessarily mean meeting others in public or even in person. For many the anonymity of the internet provides a haven for exploration and contact. For others personal, face-to-face contact is desired. Activism on behalf of and by transgendered people has increased such opportunities and made them safer. This reality encourages transgender people to make their identity known to more people than they might otherwise consider. Today a sizable number of organizations exist to support transgender people, some of them inclusive of all who adopt that term for themselves, and others that cater to particular subgroups. Also important are those organizations that recognize and address noncrossdressers whose lives are inextricably bound to a crossdresser. Finally, there are organizations that work tirelessly on behalf of us all trying to make this a kinder, gentler world, one where everyone is accorded respect and assured equal opportunities in vital areas like housing and employment.

The Longer Answer. Important aspects of being human include the desire to be known as one is and wishes to be, and to congregate with those supportive of this identity. Those of us who are transgendered people are fully human; we long to be known and accepted as we are, rather than merely for the roles thrust upon us or as others wish we were. We also often possess a natural curiosity and yearning to know others like ourselves. Thus these varied motivations contribute to transgendered people and our allies carving out safe places to express transgender realities and to form a community.

Those of us who are not transgendered may find ourselves struggling with opposing feelings about these things. On the one hand, we probably can identify with and even sympathize with the desire to be known as we are and accepted as we are. But the thought that a transgendered friend or loved one might publicly associate with other transgendered people can be unnerving. The sharing of a secret risks its being misused. Moreover, where will *we* fit? If we are not transgendered ourselves, how can we be part of a community of those who are? So we may experience a sense of fear that fuels an opposition to such community.

Accordingly, to answer this question we must address both the resources available to transgendered people and the resources available to non-transgendered folk trying to relate to them. Though these may seem two entirely different matters, there is important common ground. Both tasks begin with a need for understanding the importance and desirability of community.

What is the 'coming out' dilemma transgendered people face?

Transgendered people, by and large, face a stark choice: either accept and conform to gender expectations or endure the punishment that accompanies nonconformity. Research suggests that most transgendered people choose a path that attempts to minimize both choices. By going into the closet and firmly locking the door behind oneself, a transgendered person can remain faithful to the internal imperative to experience and express a transgender reality by keeping it private while allowing it life. At the same time, because it is hidden, social punishment is largely avoided. It is not entirely escaped because we all internalize cultural values, standards, and judgments. Thus the experience and expression of transgender through things like crossdressing still may be complicated by feelings of doubt, guilt, or shame.

Just as importantly, staying in the closet is a survival move that like most survival moves eventually limits growth. The full potential of the transgender identity is no more capable of realization in isolation than is any person's gender identity. It seems reasonable to suggest that the reason so many transgendered people as they grow older—to use the terminology of many mental health professionals—'develop gender dysphoria', or move from 'transvestism' to 'secondary transsexualism,' is because they face the mounting pressure of mortality and the unfulfilled need to be known by someone, *anyone*, as who they really are.

Non-transgendered people need to reckon realistically with this force no less than do transgendered people. Ignoring facts never makes them disappear, and the need to be known can impel people to act out or take unwise risks unless it is consciously acknowledged and responsibly addressed. Somehow, in some manner, the transgendered are likely to eventually insist on finding one person, at least, who can see who they are. In this light a transgendered community has a powerful appeal. Becoming known as one is, and finding acceptance as one is, constitutes a defining moment in self-identity.

Lee's Remarks

I have little I can say on this matter since I have spent my life so deep in the closet that you couldn't prove by me that there are even any other rooms in the house! I have never attended any function where there are other transgendered people doing anything overtly 'transgendered' like crossdressing. Truthfully, I have mixed feelings about doing such a thing. Part of me longs to be among people who would not censure me for being transgendered. The thought is appealing of being able to be openly crossdressed among others who do not view it suspiciously or disapprovingly. On the other hand, I have deeply-rooted anxiety about anyone not transgendered finding out I crossdress and using that knowledge to cause me trouble at work or elsewhere.

This is not a matter of shame over who I am or what I do but what I feel is a legitimate concern about the social consequences that might happen. All that being said, I want to end my remarks on this question by expressing my profound respect and admiration for all those with the courage to be who they are openly even though they know what that might mean in terms of negative consequences. I also admire and respect those who support these transgendered people in being themselves so openly. I wish I had such courage and support.

What resources do transgendered people have?

Often times our resources are limited more by our lack of imagination than by a paucity of help. Transgendered people have an abundance of resources available to assist them in one or another of the various tasks their life experience as transgendered entails. Some of these resources, broadly grouped, include:

- ❑ articles, books, pamphlets and other published materials;
- ❑ internet resources;
- ❑ organizations;
- ❑ professional helpers.

Some brief remarks and examples for each of these resources follow.

Articles, Books, Pamphlets and Other Published Materials

This present work, despite its size and scope, barely scratches the tip of the iceberg that is all published materials relevant to transgender. Many materials are available at no or little cost from organizations such as those described in this answer. Scholarly journals and popular magazines frequently carry articles on one or another aspect of transgender experience. Magazines easily obtainable in bookstores and other places are more likely to offer biographical or autobiographical accounts, or to provide brief and general treatments, in very readable styles, on larger aspects of transgender reality. The principal drawback to this literature is that it is often incomplete or repeats popular misconceptions or contains errors of fact deriving from the writer's limited knowledge. Unfortunately, the same criticism can be made of some writing that is published in scholarly journals. While these publications feature studies and discussions by people who work in the field, sometimes the studies are flawed and sometimes the discussions are one-sided. In all matters it is *caveat emptor*—let the buyer beware. The notes to this volume, and others in the set, offer many publications one might look at, but simply because they are referenced here neither means they are suitable to a given person's needs nor that I concur with them in part or in whole. However, it cannot hurt to look at a wide range of materials, at least sampling a variety of perspectives and topics.

Internet Resources

Therapist Arlene Istar Lev claims, "the main reason for the increase in information about transgenderism can be attributed to two sources—the burgeoning transgender liberation movement and the technological explosion of the internet."[581] The two forces are clearly intertwined, but perhaps no other force has been more instrumental in combating social isolation and promoting a sense of community among the transgendered than the internet.[582] This vast system of information and communication affords varying levels of contact. A transgendered person can remain completely anonymous or disclose the self in varying degrees. The internet can be used to collect information both academic and personal. That information may range from learning more about what being transgendered means to finding out where other transgendered people can be met or where needed services can be obtained. The web also can be utilized to make educational, political, or individual statements. In short, the internet is a versatile tool.

The name 'World Wide Web' is apt, too. Around the world, in disparate societies, transgendered people connect through internet organizations and chat rooms. These can be valuable support to the transgendered. For example, a qualitative study of the internet Brazilian Crossdressers Club (BCC), oriented to adult male crossdressers, finds it highly organized with members active in providing support to one another. The researchers conclude that the internet provides a good environment for people to meet who otherwise would be unlikely to do so given the stigma male crossdressing carries in that society.[583]

But where does one start? Perhaps most people who are interested in using the internet to learn more about transgender or to find resources start by using a search engine such as that provided by Google. But on a given day, simply entering the term 'transgender' yields nearly 7 *million* returns. 'Crossdressing,' perhaps surprisingly, yields significantly fewer, but still more than a million. 'Transsexual,' which would seem to be a very specific term, brings nearly 6 million returns. In sum, any of the more common terms is likely to produce far more possibilities than a person could ever get through and there is no assurance the top 10 or 20 will be what one needs.

Another option is to use a published resource such as *The Harvey Milk Institute Guide to Lesbian, Gay, Bisexual, Transgender, and Queer Internet Research*, published in 2002.[584] Unfortunately, as anyone experienced with the Web knows, strands change, and come and go, frequently. While a resource like this is more likely to point toward reliable and relatively stable internet sites, they cannot guarantee that. Websites also offer help, including providing book lists, such as that offered by the GENDYS Network.[585] A very comprehensive source on the web is A GLBTQ Education Internet Resources website.[586] But these examples are just that: examples. In the end, there is no substitute to exploring to discover what best meets one's own needs.

What organizations exist to support transgendered people?

There is no exaggeration involved in saying that the venues for transgender people to meet other transgender folk have explosively multiplied over the last few decades. This volume is inadequate to the task of naming them all, let alone describing them. But some small sampling of various organizations can show the outline of resources available. Our focus here is both on organizations operating in the United States (though they may have a reach wider than that or there may be parallel organizations found in other societies), and on crossdressers. In the answers dealing with other places in the world there are mentions of organizations found within those societies. In very real respects the cumulative effect of these organizations around the world, especially in making use of resources such as the World Wide Web, have created a global transgender community.

Looking at a number of organizations can prove useful. There is always room to quibble over where to begin and what to include, but in this case the answer to the first matter seems reasonably clear. One organization ranks first in historical importance and ongoing influence for many transgendered people, especially those for whom crossdressing is important: the 'Society for the Second Self,' or more simply and popularly, Tri-Ess.

Tri-Ess

The first thing to know about Tri-Ess is the story of its origin. That story is rooted in the experience of perhaps the single most significant figure in the transgender community in North America in the last century—Virginia Prince (see the answer to Q. 49). At the beginning of the 1960s, Prince began publishing *Transvestia*, a magazine aimed at a male crossdressing audience. Some of the subscribers to this publication formed the core in 1961 for the 'Hose and Heels Club' in Los Angeles.[587]

About 1962 this club evolved into a national phenomenon. Prince called his movement either 'Foundation for Full Personality Expression,' or 'Feminine Personality Expression,' or 'Freedom of Personality Expression' (FPE, or 'Phi Pi Epsilon').[588] The target group was heterosexual male crossdressers; neither homosexuals nor transsexuals were included in its reach. Overseas chapters formed in Europe and in 1967 Virginia Prince visited 37 cities in 8 European countries. A British branch in 1966 formed itself around the name 'Beaumont Society.' After a few years, in the mid-1970s, FPE was joined to the "Ma'mselle Society" led by Carol Beecroft. The new entity was named the 'Society for the Second Self' (SSS), or popularly, 'Tri-Sigma'—changed under threat of a lawsuit by the sorority Sigma Sigma Sigma to today's 'Tri-Ess.' Leaders such as Jane Ellen Fairfax and Mary Francis continued and extended its work. Growth was steady throughout the 1980s and Prince remained actively involved.[589]

In 1987 Tri-Ess gained national attention after several members of one chapter appeared as guests on the *Donahue Show*. By the decade's end a board of directors had been established, some reorganizing transpired, and a vision statement was articulated. A significant change during this period was recognition and inclusion of spouses and partners of crossdressers as equal members. In the 1990s, Tri-Ess ratified the Gender Bill of Rights (see the answer to Q. 36), and became a recognized nonprofit organization. By the time the new millennium was underway, Tri-Ess had continued to diversify what it offers and to establish its own domain on the World Wide Web.[590]

A characterization of the organization can be offered by consideration of its name and motto. With time, the three 'S's of Tri-Ess have undergone change in meaning. Fairfax writes that the organization's Board of Governance designated three 'S' words as a motto: 'Support, Serenity, Service.' Support comes from the acceptance and encouragement of other crossdressers. That support generates internal serenity—a peace with one's self, accompanied by a sense of pride. This eventually leads to a desire to give back by offering service to others.[591]

The philosophy of Tri-Ess is also captured in the twin bill of rights the organization posts. One, authored by Jane Ellen Fairfax, is a Crossdressers' Bill of Rights. The dozen rights affirm: (1) an expectation of acceptance by spouses, (2) interaction with them about crossdressing, (3) reasonable rights to crossgender expression; (4) communication, negotiation and compromise by both spouses, especially about expression and telling one's children; (5) freedom from guilt; (6-7) membership in support groups, both for oneself and for one's spouse; (8) freedom from discrimination; (9) dignity and respect from others; (10) permission from others before personal items are borrowed; (11) personal time and personal growth; and (12) to contribute positively to others while expressing one's gender.[592]

Parallel to this is a Wives' Bill of Rights, authored by Frances Fairfax. Its dozen rights affirm: (1) knowing about a husband's crossdressing; (2) open and honest spousal communication with negotiation and compromise on both sides; (3) patience by the crossdressing spouse; (4) the crossdressing spouse as a man even though he explores his femininity; (5) consensus over body alterations by either partner; (6-7) membership in support groups, both for oneself and for one's spouse; (8) not being mocked or demeaned by others; (9) not being pressured to attend meetings anywhere that pose a security risk; (10) permission from others before personal items are borrowed; (11) personal time and personal growth; and (12) an expectation that gender organizations and conventions support and promote such rights in their policies and programs.[593]

AEGIS

Some organizations exist to disseminate educational information. One such is the American Educational Gender Information Service (AEGIS). It was founded by noted educator Dallas Denny in 1990 and achieved tax exempt status in 1994. As the name specifies, the organizational aim has been to provide gender information to educate the public about transgender and transsexual issues. A membership newsletter (*AEGIS News*), the periodical *Chrysalis: The Journal of Transgressive Gender Identities*, and *The Transgender Treatment Bulletin* are among its various publications. Among its leadership are some of the foremost names in transgender study and support, including Gianna Israel, a counselor who specializes in transgender issues, and JoAnn Roberts, who was instrumental in the creation of the widely adopted *International Gender Bill of Rights* (see the answer to Q. 36). Presently AEGIS is part of Gender Education and Advocacy (GEA).[594]

GenderPAC

One way in which transgendered people and their supporters have been assertive is in the formation of activist groups to promote political and legal changes. Among such groups, the Gender Public Advocacy Coalition (GenderPAC) may claim pride of place as the first significant effort. Founded in 1995 as a coalition of like-minded organizations, and incorporated in 1999, it is a nonprofit human rights organization headquartered in Washington, D.C. It maintains a website at which its opening statement about the organization proclaims it "works to ensure that classrooms, communities, and workplaces are safe for everyone to learn, grow, and succeed—whether or not they meet expectations for masculinity and femininity."[595] Presently, the Executive Director is Riki Wilchins, well-known for her writings on gender and queer theory.

IFGE

Another important educational resource is The International Foundation for Gender Education (IFGE), founded in 1987 by Merissa Sherrill Lynn, also founder of the Tiffany Club (1977)[596] and a transgender pioneer in the United States. IFGE is headquartered in Waltham, Massachusetts and maintains an active and extensive website on the internet (IFGE Transgender Tapestry). At that website, in answering the question, 'What is IFGE?' the purpose is stated as "overcoming the intolerance of transvestism and transsexualism brought about by widespread ignorance." However, the answer also notes an expansion of consciousness within the organization has led to a rededication to educating toward the "emancipation of all people from restrictive gender norms."[597]

The 'About' page on the IFGE website notes that the organization is *not* a support group. Rather, IFGE provides information and serves as a clearinghouse for materials related to anything considered transgressive of our society's established gender norms. Five values of the organization are listed on this page: individual uniqueness and dignity; personal wholeness; respect for human diversity; freedom from society's arbitrarily assigned gender definitions; and respect, acceptance, enforcement, and protection of gender-related human and civil rights for all.[598]

NCTE

The National Center for Transgender Equality (NCTE) is a nonprofit organization headquartered in Washington, D.C. Founded in 2003 by transgender activists, the NCTE's brief website Mission statement declares that it is "a national social justice organization devoted to ending discrimination and violence against transgender people through education and advocacy on national issues of importance to transgender people."[599] The NCTE website provides news updates, resources, and materials on specific issues (e.g., discrimination, hate crimes, health), among other things.

TOPS & T-COPS

Organizations may be larger or smaller in their intended service scope. One targeted group served by a transgender support organization was TOPS: Transgendered Officers Protect and Serve. This organization's target population is transgendered people serving the public's safety as police officers, firemen, or military personnel. It was founded by Anthony (Tony) Barreto-Neto, a FtM postoperative transsexual police officer. Publicity over the organization from its feature on ABC's news program *20/20* generated some hostility toward Barreto-Neto, including shots fired at his house. Some of the ill will stemmed from fellow officers and led to Barreto-Neto's resignation. He filed a lawsuit in 2002 alleging his departure resulted from intentional efforts made to force him from the police force because of being transgendered.[600] Barreto-Neto won this lawsuit in 2004 in a settlement awarding him $90,000, and requiring the police department to enact a formal policy of nondiscrimination against transgendered people as well as carry out employee training on transgender issues.[601] Unfortunately, TOPS did not endure. Barreto-Neto himself became a member of a new organization: T-COPS.

The Transgender Community of Police and Sheriffs (T-COPS) is a peer support network open to transgender people in law enforcement. The T-COPS website's 'Welcome' page identifies the network's purpose as providing information, education, support, and networking opportunities to transsexual officers. The network itself was born out of research conducted by Tom Whetstone, a faculty member of the Southern Police Institute at the University of Louisville, concerning transsexual law enforcement officers. From the folk brought together by this research, Julie Marin initiated a Yahoo Group in late 2002. At the time of this volume, the group was actively looking at ways to expand and formalize its services.[602]

As this last entry indicates, change is a constant. Most transgender organizations are young; an 'old' organization is one only 30-40 years old. Many do not survive, at least under their original name. Some join hands and become a new, stronger entity. Others simply disappear. They vary widely in purpose and reach, in membership and in success. But in the diversity and multiplicity of such organizations there are resources and opportunities for anyone seeking information, support, or opportunities for service.

What help is available for non-transgendered partners, family, and friends?

Non-transgendered partners, family members, and friends also have resources, though those specifically designed to address issues associated with transgender are too few and too inaccessible to prove of much help to many. To some extent, those in relationships with transgendered people—especially life-partners—experience the kind of isolation common to transgender experience in our culture. While we soon will turn our attention to partners of crossdressers (Q. 38) and to their families and friends (Q. 39), a few brief remarks on resources are pertinent here.

Tri-Ess

Already we have seen some organizations, like Tri-Ess, are family-oriented and offer resources and support not only for the crossdresser but also for loved ones. Local chapters meet in places around the country for those who wish to meet others face-to-face. For those not desiring that manner of support, various chapters of Tri-Ess also maintain websites and offer resource materials for spouses, partners, and loved ones of crossdressers. But these, while highly visible, are hardly the only sources for help.

PFLAG

Another well-known nonprofit organization with a national reach is 'Parents, Families, and Friends of Lesbians and Gays (PFLAG). Although the name suggests an interest only in people defined by homosexual orientation, the organization's Vision Statement immediately makes clear that transgender persons and their family and friends are included. PFLAG can claim some 200,000 members and supporter, with local affiliates in 500 communities, making it the largest grassroots-based family organization of its kind.[603]

FPC

Family Pride Coalition (FPC) is another nonprofit organization with a national scope. It began in 1979 when a group of gay fathers banded together to form the 'Gay Fathers Coalition.' Lesbian moms were included in 1986, leading to a change in name to 'Gay and Lesbian Parents Coalition International' (GLPCI). The organization under this name spawned, in 1990, 'Children of Lesbians and Gays Everywhere' (COLAGE), which became an independent organization in 1999. The current name for FPC was adopted in 1998. Headquartered in Washington, D.C., FPC has about 200 membership-based LGBT parenting groups and some 35,000 supporters. Its website lists as its 'Strategic Objectives' three primary areas of labor: advocacy, education, and support.[604]

SSN

Straight Spouse Network (SSN) operates an international support system with 74 support groups in the United States and 7 abroad. A nonprofit organization, its 'Welcome' page at its website declares that SSN "provides personal, confidential support and information to heterosexual spouses/partners, current or former, of gay, lesbian, bisexual or transgender mates and mixed-orientation couples for constructively resolving coming-out problems." Its 'Our Mission' statement offers three goals: reaching out, healing, and building bridges. The last of these includes not only building bridges between partners, but also collaborating with professional and community organizations to foster understanding at the levels of couples, families, and communities.[605]

Published Materials (Books & Internet)

Some individuals prefer not to meet face-to-face with others, at least not now. For them, reading materials or the relative anonymity of the internet may be better choices. In addition to the resources available through the World Wide Web, a few examples of which will be offered presently, there are print materials that offer information from different perspectives.

In this volume, the answers to Q. 38-39 cover some of the research related to partners and families of crossdressers. Another kind of resource many partners may find valuable are accounts by others who are partners of a crossdresser. Probably the best-known example of this sort is the book *My Husband Betty*, by Helen Boyd.[606] This account of living with a crossdressing husband was followed years later by a second book, *She's Not the Man I Married: My Life with a Transgender Husband.*[607] Together these two books offer an extended look at a particular relationship, supplemented by educational information. A variant of this approach is offered by psychologist Virginia Erhardt, whose book *Head Over Heels* presents the stories of some 30 women, covering a spectrum of different situations, experiences, and outcomes.[608]

CrossDressersWives.com

The World Wide Web offers information and access targeted to spouses and other significant others. One such is CrossDressersWives.com. This internet site has a Mission Statement which begins by stating the site's intent to provide a safe environment for sharing anonymously personal experiences. The site explicitly declares it is *not* intended either to 'out' crossdressers or to bash them. The goal, rather, is to help support partners, provide them information, and validate their experiences. Among features of the website, in addition to the stories contributed by partners, are an online survey and forum, a FAQs page and education page with some statistics (without notation of their sources), links to resources, a Bill of Rights, and other materials.[609]

Laura's Playground

Laura Amato's website (Laura's Playground) provides an even fuller example of internet help in a site originated by an individual active in the transgender community.[610] Begun in 2004, by 2007 nearly three dozen volunteers had been enlisted to serve as moderators; some of these have some training in working with others, notably as youth suicide prevention counselors.[611] Among the various resources offered at the website, one offers 'Support for Significant Others and Family.' Included are articles, information on various books, support links and forums, lists of local support groups and of gender therapists, and an online chatroom.[612]

Other Resources & Simple Guidelines

More limited internet-based resources also exist. At the time of this writing, CDWSOS was the name for an email-based support group open only to genetic women whose significant other is a male crossdresser.[613] This kind of limited contact, easily controlled by the individual, may prove a good first step in reaching out to tell one's own story.

Many other resources might be named and described, but for those interested a better course of action probably is to conduct a personal search. In this manner one can acquire a firmer sense of alternatives. If conducting a web search, use specific terms indicating what best fits or is most important. For example, a spouse of a preoperative transsexual male might try entering as search terms 'spouse, wives of male transsexuals' or 'partner support for wives of transsexuals.' Searching the internet can be time consuming and frustrating, but there is no substitute for experience to become adept at it.

Q. 35

Are all crossdressers homosexual?

The Short Answer. Many people believe that all crossdressers are homosexual. They are incorrect. There are homosexual crossdressers, but they are the minority of those who crossdress. There has been an unfortunate tendency to automatically link gender variance with homosexuality. This byproduct of the medicalization of sex thus lumps together anyone who is different from the culture's ideal of heterosexual masculinity and femininity expressed in gender-conforming ways. In this manner, all crossdressers are presumed at least latently homosexual because they do not conform to gender expectations. If they are different in one way (gender), it is easy to imagine them different in another (sexual orientation) as well. Unfortunately, those individuals who are transsexual are especially likely to be labeled as homosexual because many people insist that anatomical sex, rather than gender identity, is what matters in determining sexual orientation. The reasoning is that since one always remains genetically the same sex, and sex can be used to determine sexual orientation, then a genetic male, even if altered by hormones and surgery to appear female, remains 'really' male. Thus such a person professing a desire for a male sexual partner must be homosexual. This way of reasoning, which prioritizes sex over gender, has been challenged in recent years. In an alternative to the view just described, gender can be seen as what determines sexual orientation. A genetic male who experiences the self as female, and alters the body accordingly, should be regarded as a woman. The desire for a male sexual partner then can be seen as heterosexual. Most crossdressers, however, are not transsexuals. They do not see their body sex as wrong. Nor do most of them desire to have sexual relations with others whose bodies are like their own. They regard themselves as males and, for example, see themselves both as men and as persons with a feminine side, or as men who also have a separate feminine identity. If they see themselves as heterosexual because they desire sexual relations with those who have female bodies, then such a self-identification may be established on either basis described above. Obviously, this matter can be confusing and *has* created confusion. This seems especially unfortunate because sexual orientation has been made inordinately important in a way that places stress on all of us.

The Longer Answer. One of the more persistent myths about crossdressers is that they are all homosexual. Yet the association between crossdressing and homosexuality is not accidental or arbitrary; it reflects powerful cultural forces at work in history (see the answer to Q. 91). Psychologist Darryl Hill observes that it was not until the latter half of the 20th century that gender nonconformity finally became conceptually distinguished from homosexuality, at least in some circles.[614] Marjorie Garber is quite correct in remarking that, "the history of transvestism and the history of homosexuality constantly interact and intertwine, both willingly and unwillingly."[615] Cultural anthropologist Jason Cromwell, following the lead of historian Vern Bullough, does not find this surprising since transvestism, as well as transsexualism, were both embedded for so long within the category of homosexuality.[616] The legacy of this history is an entanglement of truths, half-truths, and outright lies that complicate comprehension of both crossdressing and homosexuality.

Undoubtedly this common belief is largely a remnant from the days when the best-known and most widely held explanation for male crossdressers was the psychoanalytic hypothesis that all crossdressers are either outright homosexuals or latent ones.[617] Although this idea enjoyed early popularity, some of the most prominent sexologists of the 20th century, like Alfred Kinsey and Harry Benjamin, were among those who criticized it.[618] While this hypothesis has been long disproved, the notion lingers in the popular consciousness. As we have seen, the facts show that there are distinct groups of people who crossdress, including children and adults, males and females. If all crossdressers are divided into two groups, strictly by whether they identify their sexual orientation as 'heterosexual' or 'homosexual,' the former group is by far the largest.

Are transsexuals homosexual?

Having said that, we must still acknowledge that the waters have been made murkier when transsexual individuals are discussed. With this group a persistent problem occurs because of the different ways people regard the relationship between sex and gender. For those who insist that anatomical sex determines gender designation, a transsexual person born male is likely to be referred to as a man by others regardless of gender presentation. Even after sex reassignment surgery (SRS) the individual may be regarded by these folk as essentially male. Thus, when a male-to-female (MtF) post-operative transsexual expresses a sexual desire for men they are viewed as having a homosexual orientation.

By now we should know better. In the lived world of personal and social experience gender is far more determinative of identity and behavior than is anatomical sex. Simple respect suggests addressing and treating people in accordance with their gender presentation. As Gianna Israel puts it, "If a male-born person consistently dresses as a woman, and that person identifies as female, chances are that person wishes to be treated as a woman."[619] In such situations we ought to treat others as we would ourselves wish to be treated. In this light, a MtF transsexual desiring male sexual partners is heterosexual.

At the same time, we need also to be aware that sexual orientation itself may not be as fixed as is popularly believed. A common definition for sexual orientation is "a fixed erotic attraction." But we would do well to modify this definition by adding a word: "sexual orientation is a *relatively* fixed erotic attraction." As Israel, whose professional work is as a therapist working with transgender persons, observes, a majority of transsexual clients explore their sexual orientation during their transition period from one sex to the other and some do redefine it.[620] However, we should note that this redefinition frequently only occurs to fit other people's notions. For example, those who regard sexual orientation as a matter of anatomical presentation will see a biological male who sexually desired women before SRS as heterosexual. That same desire postoperatively will be regarded as homosexual. But where gender identity is recognized as determining sexual orientation that particular person has always been homosexual—a woman desiring other women.

How many crossdressers are homosexual?

With these things in mind let us return to the broader question. Transsexuals make up a small proportion of the total population of those who crossdress. As in other matters, most of the research in recent decades has only examined men. The following table illustrates what a variety of studies have found for adult male crossdressers:

Table 35.1 Sexual Orientation

Study	# Subjects	Heterosexual
V. Prince & P. M. Bentler (1972)[621]	504	89%
Bullough, Bullough, & Smith (1983)[622]	65	82%
R. Docter (1988)[623]	110	97%
R. Schott (1995)[624]	85	92%
V. Coleman (1996)[625]	414	80%
B. Bullough & V. Bullough (1997)[626]	372	68%
R. Docter & V. Prince (1997)[627]	1,032	87%
'Yvonne' (1999)[628]	1,159	80%

Some of the reports listed in this Table allow the research subjects to respond by identifying "bisexual" as a choice. Thus, for example, in Schott's mixed group of transvestites and transsexuals, 32% use the term bisexual—though he notes that most of those using this term are probably heterosexuals with one or more 'experimental encounters' with other men.[629] Similarly, Bullough and Bullough's 1997 report allows for both "bisexual" (10%) and "sex not a part of my life now" (20%).[630] Docter handles this matter by differentiating between degrees of heterosexual exclusiveness and permitting for the response "bisexual."[631]

How many homosexuals crossdress?

Of course, the question about how many crossdressers are homosexual only addresses one side of the coin. We may also want to know how many homosexuals are crossdressers. This question is not often asked, perhaps because the vast majority of attention scholars pay to crossdressers is directed at transvestites and transsexuals. In one respect, the question may be no more pertinent than asking how many in the general population crossdress. That is because much crossdressing by homosexuals is transient and situation-dependent; rather than serving some gender-identity purpose it is purposeful performance. This kind of crossdressing by homosexuals we call 'drag.'

Why do some homosexuals crossdress?

Drag, together with a history of psychoanalytical imputation of homosexuality to crossdressers, is why so many people so strongly link homosexuality and crossdressing (cf. the answer to Q. 17). Yet drag is a distinctive form of crossdressing, done for different reasons and pursued in a different manner. Roselle Pineda offers this succinct explanation: "The politics of drag lies in the idea that drag doesn't over simplistically imitate the traditional gender roles (as in the case of transvestism), but it subverts these traditional roles by parodying them. It creates a whole new language by firstly, exaggerating and carnivalising these rules/roles, and secondly, by presenting a visibility to absence."[632] Drag may be entertaining, but it can also be shocking; either way its performance challenges, subverts, and destabilizes prevailing gender role expectations in a conscious manner while simultaneously proclaiming pride. Drag is a way to demonstrate a lack of shame over being homosexual. By confronting social stereotypes in such a visible manner the person in drag says, in effect, 'I know what you think about me, and I'll give you an act you'll never forget! But you'll also go away knowing it was just an act.' Drag successfully capitalizes on a negative stereotype to refute ignorance while championing being different.

Many homosexuals engage in drag at one time or another, but many never do so. As noted above, it may be misleading to ask how many homosexuals crossdress if we think that doing drag is equivalent to the kind of crossdressing done by transgender heterosexuals. Instead, it may be more like the crossdressing occasionally done by heterosexual noncrossdressers at festivals or parties. Yet it seems best to reserve a special and distinct place for drag. In the end, it is no more possible to accurately determine how many homosexuals crossdress than it is to determine how many heterosexuals do so.

Question Set 5:
How are transgender realities regarded by others?

Although most crossdressers keep their crossdressing largely, if not entirely secret, the sheer vastness of the phenomenon ensures that it receives plenty of attention from others. Thus, crossdressing is something perceived and evaluated—by family, friends, and strangers—in many different ways. Societies sometimes take a public interest in it by enacting codes regulating dress, though these tend to be imperfectly and often capriciously enforced. The questions in this set look at the perceptions of noncrossdressers, both in terms of the wider public and also within the sphere of the family and friends of crossdressers.

In this question set the answers generally operate within the context of American society in the United States. The situation in other cultures is discussed to some extent in the material of Question Set 7 (Volume 3, Q. 51-60). In those answers are some indication of the legal status and public perception of transgendered people and crossdressing in various societies. In the current set of answers there is only brief consideration of broad international matters, a topic still evolving on the world stage.

The first two answers (to Q. 56-57) examine broader social issues. First, we shall examine legal and policy matters. Though explicit laws against transgender behaviors like crossdressing have largely disappeared and are typically not enforced even where they remain in legal codes, such laws are only part of the legal picture. Other legal matters, of great pertinence, involve basic human rights. Concerns over discrimination and violence remain real. The answer to Q. 57 examines why the matters in Q. 56 remain vital through examining public attitudes and the experience of transgender people in public. This answer finds that violence in many forms remains a serious problem, and perhaps especially so for transgender youth.

The next two answers (to Q. 58-59) are more narrowly focused. The former considers the partners of crossdressers. This often neglected and historically underserved population merits close attention. So, too, do the other family members (and even friends) of transgender people—the subjects of Q. 59. There are as many responses to transgender behavior as there are people, yet certain issues emerge as fairly common. These require consideration.

The question set, and this volume, ends with asking why society tolerates crossdressing. Of course, 'tolerance' is a relative term. As answers leading up to this one show, much intolerance and violence persist. Yet in the sense of society not making a concerted effort to eradicate crossdressing, and in fact generally treating it with mild disapproval, indifference, or partial sanction, the eruptions of violence and the incidences of discrimination more and more appear the work of a minority and the vestiges of a disappearing era. If this is the case—and it is admittedly debatable—it is worth pausing at the end of this volume to reconsider what society's response is, and why.

Q. 36

What is the legal status of crossdress-
ers?

The Short Answer. Transgendered people have had a checkered history with the law, especially when practicing behaviors like crossdressing. This fact is not due to greater engagement in different forms of law-breaking than other people, but because transgender behavior itself was against some laws. Cross-dressing was often illegal in the past, though sanctions against it in the United States were typically mild. Moreover, past and present, restrictions commonly have been overlooked, only partially enforced, or allowed to have exceptions. Today there are few outright prohibitions of crossdressing although a variety of other laws are used to curb public crossdressing. However prosecuted, cases based merely on an individual appearing in public crossdressed are today routinely thrown out of court. Other issues have emerged as prominent. Discrimination against transgendered people in the workplace remains a problem despite antidiscrimination measures becoming more common. Housing discrimination also persists. Identity recognition is an issue for some, and various places handle the matter differently. The most serious issue remains violence against transgender people. Efforts to extend hate crime legislation protection to the transgendered has met with varying success. The legal picture continues to develop in our society, but to this point it can be reasonably said that most progress has occurred at local levels. The federal government, rather than leading the way, has lagged behind in many matters.

The Longer Answer. In the United States in recent decades there slowly has grown momentum for what some term a Transgender Civil Rights Movement. Like the historic civil rights movements before it, this one has advanced along multiple fronts: education, activism, court challenges, and changes in laws and policies. Although this answer provides merely a brief overview, one important resource (which became available too late for full consideration in this volume), with much more information, appeared in 2007: *Transgender Rights*, published by the University of Minnesota Press. This edited volume includes contributions from activists and legal experts alike. Of particular interest to us in light of this question, seven chapters are devoted to legal issues, and cover not only this country but other societies, too.[633] While this volume may be the first comprehensive work of its kind, as this answer shows there are a number of published resources documenting or commenting in one fashion or another on the legal issues, court cases, and policy changes transpiring in the U.S. and abroad.

Since crossdressing in relation to the law has inescapably been connected to issues of sex and gender, we must begin by framing a context. That context entails numerous elements, but we shall focus on two in establishing a general background: the philosophical context in for legal reasoning and the relation of dress to law.

Cultural Ideas & Legal Reasoning

Famed sexologist John Money (whose work is summarized in answering Q. 95) once analyzed how secular law about sexual matters developed in Western societies. Money contends that secular law followed the lead of Medieval canon law. That body based itself on a notion of 'natural law.' Sexual behavior in conformity with what the theologians considered 'natural' could then also be described as 'normal.' Anything deviating was thus 'abnormal.' But, Money points out, this ignores what people actually do. In the world of statistics, 'normal' is what people, on average, do. In following the concept of natural law, secular authorities were substituting theological judgments for empirical facts.[634]

This manner of reasoning for the creation, interpretation, and enforcement of laws has persisted. In the United States, as in other nations, laws reflect cultural values. Those values, with regard to human sexual behavior, are largely but not entirely rooted in the natural law concept Money describes. Other influences include various ideas about sacred law and, to a lesser extent, other cultural values. From the beginning, the U.S. has experienced crossdressers in its midst and faced the question of what, if anything, to do about them. Anti-crossdressing laws extend back in American history to at least the end of the 17th century.[635] Still, in the growing young nation there seemed enough room to allow a few individuals to go their own cross gender way as long as they remained largely apart from mainstream society.

That situation changed with time. The nation faced the challenge of civil war and in the post-war setting, the newly reaffirmed United States experienced something new in its cities. Yale law professor William Eskridge observes that crossdressers and homosexuals became more visible as subcultures in American cities. This prompted new laws, including anti-crossdressing ordinances, which at first were principally aimed at women.[636] Such ordinances proliferated and in time targeted crossdressing men. By mid-20th century, there were many such local laws. At the same time, beginning in the late 19th century and extending into the early 20th century, an important movement was underway to change the perception of cross-gender people and bring them out from under criminal penalties. The people involved in this movement were medical and mental health professionals.

When mental health experts largely succeeded in getting civil authorities to re-conceive of unconventional sexual behaviors as psychological disorders rather than criminal acts (cf. answer to Q. 91), they left in place the foundational reasoning that such behaviors are deviant. They may have changed the penalty, but they did not change the charge. Because of this, even as some laws were being discarded, others were being broadened to permit a continued sanction of oppressive acts by duly appointed officials. Thus sexual minorities, and cross-dressers, found themselves still harassed by police officers. But now they were as likely to be remanded for psychological treatment as to face criminal punishment. In either instance, the social judgment remained the same: these folk were deviant because their behavior did not conform to the majority population's standards of conduct and the general cultural conception of what constitutes 'natural' law.

As cultural values have changed, so have social mores and legal codes. But such changes are rarely rapid. Public attitudes tend to conserve what is perceived as 'tradition' and so some resistance is typical. Where sex and gender are involved the degree of resistance is likely to be greater and the time for change longer. Because crossdressing is connected to sex and gender in the public mind, doubts, hesitations, and opposition are expectable—and such have a long history in the United States. Indeed, in a 1997 report, the Gender Public Advocacy Coalition (GenderPAC) expresses the belief that incidents of transgender people running afoul of gender-based laws or ordinances remain common.[637]

Dress and U. S. Law

Freedom in dress expression has always been a limited right. In U.S. society, legal cases involving alleged violations associated with dress have ranged from wearing the American flag, to inappropriate use of military uniforms, to wearing nothing at all. But contemporary judges often prove sensitive to how social values may reflect changes from the intent of the original legislation. In fact, they often rule that legal sanctions have been improperly applied.[638]

The law in our society reflects a commonly held—but sometimes erroneous—judgment that we can reliably infer a person's attitude or intent from what they wear.[639] This has particularly been studied with reference to sexual assault cases, where the belief that a victim's manner of dress is a factor in what happens remains disturbingly common.[640] A similar process may be involved in assaults on those perceived as crossdressing—a transgression of cultural gender conventions that aggressors may use as justification for their behavior. Such individuals may even see themselves as upholding the law, for there is a history of statutes forbidding crossdressing, which has sometimes been viewed as a civil disturbance threatening social order and peace.

However, it may be best to view anti-crossdressing legal enactments along the lines described in the late 1980s by Sister Mary Elizabeth, a noted activist and legal expert on the legal aspects associated with transsexualism in the United States. Sr. Elizabeth terms crossdressing a "status offense"—legal breaches that can only be committed by individuals assigned that status. It is recognition that a society opposes a certain specific group; only crossdressers can be tried for crossdressing. Theoretically, the group is comprised of all people distinguished by wearing clothes associated with a different gender than the wearer's culturally assigned one. But, as Sr. Elizabeth points out, laws that either directly or indirectly can be applied to crossdressers are done so principally against males presenting as women, not females crossdressed as men.[641]

For the most part, laws in the United States specifically forbidding crossdressing have been discarded. But we need not go far back in time to see them in operation. Less than a half century ago, large states like California, Texas, and New York still had laws with reference to such behavior, and many cities and towns had codes prohibiting it—and enforced those codes. Remarkably, in less than a half century we have witnessed significant changes.

Related policies and regulations also have undergone change. In the 1960s, Virginia Prince was able to successfully lobby the United States Postal Service to change its regulations so that material on crossdressing would no longer be considered pornography and thus could be mailed—a tremendous boon both for connecting crossdressers with one another and for educating the public. As a general rule, most legal action taken against crossdressers today comes about when law enforcement officers apply other ordinances to public crossdressing. Such enforcement practices have been challenged repeatedly. Many of them have been either largely or entirely discontinued, though some officers continue to harass transgender people in public. Progress has been made; the need for progress remains. In order to understand the present it is instructive to examine history.

What have been legal issues pertinent to crossdressing?

In the past, some of the areas of law bearing on crossdressers have been the following:

- ❑ *Anticrossdressing laws*—specific regulations prohibiting crossdressing.
- ❑ *Antimasquerading laws*—local ordinances against disguises; these have often been applied against crossdressing.
- ❑ *Antidiscrimination law*—this probably has been the most significant area of law, especially with regard to employment and housing.
- ❑ *Disorderly conduct laws*—these have often been used as a pretext for arresting homosexuals and crossdressers.
- ❑ *Identity recognition issues*—the legal transition from one gender identity to another has been a significant issue for transsexuals.

- ❑ *Moral turpitude legal concept*—this concept provides a catch-all provision that makes possible legal charges based on social value standards.

- ❑ *Use of public restrooms*—a matter most of us take for granted and give no thought to is an issue of substantial practical concern for many crossdressers.

- ❑ *Vagrancy laws*—historically such ordinances have been used to harass or arrest crossdressers in public.

To the above list might be added other laws, such as prohibitions against 'annoying persons,'[642] or that prohibit 'lewd dress,'[643] that reportedly have been used against crossdressers. Each item above requires some elaboration.

Anticrossdressing Laws

As mentioned earlier, anti-crossdressing ordinances belong to the class known as 'status offences.' In short, any member of this group (crossdressers) is guilty simply by virtue of belonging to the group, regardless of other behavior. Such laws in the U.S. have been used against both male and female crossdressers. According to Georgetown University Law Professor William Eskridge, Jr., New York once utilized a 'three-piece' rule to determine violations: all persons must wear at least three pieces of clothing deemed appropriate to that individual's biological sex.[644]

Eskridge offers as an example of the kind of ordinance typical in many municipalities between 1946-1961 the following from the 1956 Miami Ordinance 5521: "It is unlawful for a person in any place, whether publicly or privately owned, in the city to be found in a state of nudity or in a dress not customarily worn by his or her sex . . . ."[645] Such an ordinance is sweeping; even private crossdressing is illegal. Another, more limited example of a local ordinance is this one, enacted in 1967: "No person shall appear in any street or public place in the city in a state of nudity or in a dress not belonging to his sex."[646]

In one guise or another, anticrossdressing provisions persisted in major cities at least through the 1980s, as reflected in court cases of the time.[647] Greater awareness and recognition of transgender conditions, particularly transsexualism, have helped change social attitudes and facilitate legal changes. But from a legal perspective fundamental ideas intrinsic to our society have been especially instrumental. Attorney Arlene Zarembka, who was involved in a case that led to the dismissal of the anticrossdressing ordinance in St. Louis in 1985, observes that *tolerance of individual differences* is fundamental to a successful democracy. She cites approvingly an 8th Circuit Court of Appeals ruling declaring that the freedom to govern one's personal appearance "ranks high on the spectrum of our societal values" and enjoys constitutional protection under the Fourteenth Amendment's due process clause.[648] Persuaded by sound legal reasoning based on the precepts of constitutional law, courts increasingly dismissed cases brought under anticrossdressing ordinances—and cities increasingly removed them from their codes.

Such laws now have become rare in our society. In the United States, at the end of the 20th century, Ariadne Kane could declare, "most states do not have statutes that specifically prohibit the practice of CD/CG presentation in public."[649] Where such prohibitions persist, they tend to be at the level of local municipalities. Existing regulations are less often enforced than in the past. In most places the existing laws are either ignored or, when attention is called to them, repealed. Those few cases that are prosecuted are generally dismissed.

Antimasquerading Laws

While laws explicitly forbidding crossdressing are now rare in modern Western societies, other laws are often used to discourage public crossdressing. Among these are so-called antimasquerading laws. These are commonly conjoined with other statutes such as vagrancy laws. In his 1959 review of transvestism, British psychiatrist Narcyz Lukianowicz notes a 1938 legal article on masquerading indicating the belief that crossdressing *per se* constitutes insufficient grounds for criminal charges but can be construed as evidence of criminal intent, and a man masquerading as a woman may incur suspicion under the Vagrancy Act of 1898. He also observes that "a similar attitude prevails in other countries, where the legislature is based on English legal concepts"—such as the United States.[650]

These laws have been used against all segments of the wider transgendered community, including gays, lesbians, transsexuals, and transvestites. New York City's anti-mask law has, since 1965, said that a person is guilty of loitering if said person is "masked or in any manner disguised by unusual or unnatural attire or facial alteration" unless this masquerade is in connection with a masquerade party or like entertainment. In the past, this language was used to convict male crossdressers.[651] Another example, offered by Houston attorney Phyllis Randolph Frye, is the now repealed (as of August 12, 1980) Code of Ordinances §28-42.4 for that municipality, which forbade a person appearing in public dressed with the intent to disguise his or her sex as that of the opposite sex. Frye observes that after much attention through lobbying and numerous court battles, most of these ordinances have been repealed or at least actively ignored.[652]

Antidiscrimination Issues

Discrimination against transgendered people is common. In some cases this discrimination is both legal and justified by appeal to a mental health standard that regards transgender realities such as transvestism and transsexualism as mental disorders. Thus, for example, the U. S. military prohibits enlistment of transgendered people—explicitly including transvestites and transsexuals.[653] The policy reads, in part: "The causes for rejection for appointment, enlistment, or induction are transsexualism, transvestism, voyeurism, and other paraphilias (302)."[654]

Discrimination in employment settings has been common. Crossdressing, even when done in private and away from the place of employment has resulted in dismissal—an action upheld in a U.S. District Court.[655] From the mid-1970s through the mid-1980s, a series of lawsuits in federal court consistently determined that Title VII legislation—which protects against discrimination based on sex—was not applicable to the transgendered. This was particularly deleterious to transsexuals, even post-operative transsexuals, who were ruled not protected by the federal act because Title VII did not consider change-of-sex discrimination.[656]

However, in January, 2001, an Ohio case brought in U.S. district court against United Consumers Financial Services (UCFS) by a person referred to as 'Mrs. Doubtfire' successfully utilized Title VII protection. The individual had worked only 10 days as a temporary employee when, after a complaint by a fellow employee that a man dressed as a woman was using the ladies restroom, 'Mrs. Doubtfire' was questioned by management about her gender. UCFS sought dismissal of the suit on the grounds that Title VII offered no protection in such a case. But Judge Kathleen McDonald O'Malley rejected that motion, pointing to the U.S. Supreme decision in *Price Waterhouse v. Hopkins* (1989). UCFS then reached a satisfactory settlement with the plaintiff.[657]

The *Price Waterhouse v. Hopkins* case is notable for clarifying the place of gender under Title VII. In the case, Ann Hopkins, a senior manager at Price Waterhouse, came under consideration for partnership. Rather than being offered a partnership, or denied one, the matter was held for reconsideration the following year. But the next year she was not reproposed. Hopkins resigned and sued on the basis of sex discrimination under Title VII protection. Evidence was brought forward showing that partner comments about her gender presentation—specifically, that she acted too masculine and should change her interpersonal behavior so as to be less abrasive and more feminine in dress and manner—played a pivotal role in the partners' decision.

In its judgment the U.S. Supreme Court offered in the majority opinion that in a suit brought under Title VII, when an individual demonstrates that gender served a motivating part in an employment decision, the employer is liable unless it can provide by a preponderance of evidence that the same decision would have been made on legitimate grounds apart from consideration of gender. The key is the degree to which an issue of gender is at play. If it provides the motivation for an action that would not have occurred on other grounds, then discrimination under Title VII has occurred.[658]

Suits brought under Title VII have been a steady reality for decades. Although the federal government has been largely inactive, states, and especially cities, have not. From the late 1970s forward a number of local jurisdictions have amended their codes to extend protection to the transgendered. These changes are considered later.

Disorderly Conduct Laws

Disorderly conduct laws offer latitude for law enforcement that has been used on occasion to harass or arrest crossdressers. R. V. Shervin, in 1954, notes that in the U.S. a 'wide and broad' disorderly conduct statute has been used to arrest crossdressers instead of laws specifically forbidding wearing the clothes of the opposite sex.[659] Since what constitutes disorderly conduct can be what a law enforcement official construes it in a given situation, crossdressers in public who attract attention could find themselves subject to such ordinances.

Identity Recognition Issues

Some crossdressers are not crossdressing in their own eyes, because they are dressing consistent with a stable gender identity and occupying a stable gender role. But because of the disagreement between their dress and their biological sex others often view them as crossdressed. So transsexuals are at special risk. They commonly find that legal change from one gender identity to another is not a simple, straightforward matter. The treatment process typically outpaces the legal. The end result is that a postoperative transsexual may run into problems because forms of legal identification (e.g., birth certificate, driver's license) reflect information at variance with the public gender presentation. Moving local jurisdictions to expedite the legal process of identity recognition to better match the progress of treatment has been an area of special challenge.

In this regard, the State of California has been more progressive than most in providing legal provisions helpful to the transgendered community. The Department of Motor Vehicles (DMV) instituted changes so that pre-operative transsexuals living in the gender identity and role they would possess postoperatively could hold a license with that name and gender on it.[660] This provides important protection against potential misconstruing of intent concerning their appearance and manner of dress.

Moral Turpitude Legal Concept

'Moral turpitude' is a concept in the law with a long history. It figures in federal law (e.g., immigration law), state law, and local codes. The definition of the Supreme Court of North Carolina, in 1917, is typical: "[A]ct[s] of baseness, vileness, or depravity in the private and social duties that a man owes to his fellowman or to society in general."[661] This definition was reaffirmed by the state Supreme Court in 1986.[662]

The essential logic of the concept is plain: it provides a moral foundation for legal action to uphold social values. It is flexible in that it need not be bound to specific acts; what a society values may change over time and moral standards fluctuate. This basis is well-articulated in a 2001 Ohio disciplinary action against an attorney: "We have held that acts of moral turpitude 'must be measured against the accepted standards of morality, honesty, and justice prevailing upon the community's collective conscience.'"[663] It is up to judicial or administrative bodies to interpret this 'collective conscience.'

Authorities may apply certain subsidiary notions to sharpen the concept of moral turpitude and bring whole classes of offense potentially under its reach. For example, in South Carolina the state Supreme Court, in *State v. Harrison*, reasoned that any crime with an element of fraud is a crime of moral turpitude.[664] Conceivably crossdressing could be held moral turpitude under South Carolina law based on being a fraudulent presentation (based on biological sex). Similar situations may pose legal risks for crossdressers in other jurisdictions.

While legal codes including moral turpitude commonly define the concept, they generally offer no list of specific behaviors. Because the concept refers to behaviors judged by a society to be intrinsically or inherently immoral, it is an umbrella capable of covering a wide and diverse range of acts. Among the kinds of acts that have been considered examples of moral turpitude are aggravated assault, domestic violence, child abuse, kidnapping and murder. The concept has also been applied to driving while intoxicated (DWI), fraud, counterfeiting and tax evasion. Acts not considered examples of moral turpitude include simple assault, carrying a concealed weapon, disorderly conduct, contributing to the delinquency of a minor, tax evasion and traffic violations.

Sexual behaviors also have often come under its reach, including adultery and oral sex. Not surprisingly, then, the concept has also been applied to crossdressing. In this manner, crossdressing becomes conceptually linked to crimes involving serious physical harm, psychological trauma, and/or severe economic consequence.

Michael Okun, an attorney, and John Rubin, an academic specialist in criminal law, writing with reference to employment and licensing consequences point out some of the difficulties in the concept:

> The uncertainty about the term's meaning is magnified by the different contexts in which it is used. Thus one who falsely accuses another of a crime of moral turpitude may be sued for slander. In a criminal prosecution, a misdemeanor may be elevated to a felony if the crime is "infamous"—that is, if it involves moral turpitude. At one time a witness's credibility could be impeached by conviction of a crime involving moral turpitude, though not by other criminal convictions. Finally, several court cases have interpreted occupational licensing statutes that authorize revocation or denial of a license for conviction of a crime of moral turpitude.[665]

This concept may be the most dangerous of all legal devices that can be used against crossdressers. By its very nature it is dependent on social values and standards. To successfully challenge any charges brought with this element involved the crossdresser must appeal to changes in community values sufficient for the crossdressing to be viewed as morally inoffensive. Since the concept is highly unlikely to disappear, those who crossdress in public must rely on public tolerance making itself felt in the judicial system.

Use of Public Restrooms

A persistent problem for crossdressers has been local ordinances that forbid the use of restroom facilities designated strictly along lines of anatomical presentation and not gender expression.[666] While this poses an inconvenience for public outings, it is more significant as a workplace issue. Employers often follow a rubric known as the 'Principle of Least Astonishment.' This means that restroom use follows appearance; a person presenting as a female should use the women's restroom, and a person presenting as a male should use the men's restroom. On June 20th, 2002, a federal court decision affirmed the right of employers to follow this rubric. If other employees complain the employer can offer the complainant an accommodation.[667]

Vagrancy Laws

A common way to utilize legal authority to control public crossdressing has been through vagrancy laws. In 1966, Harry Benjamin pointed to the New York State Code of Criminal Procedure, Section 887, Subdivision 7, as an example of an old vagrancy law (even then more than a century old), that read much like the antimasquerading laws discussed above. It forbade any change in facial or body appearance intended to disguise personal identity. This law was used against crossdressers in public—a far cry from the original intent of the law.[668]

These ordinances generally prohibit idle wandering or disorderly conduct— both broad notions that can be used against crossdressers. In fact, vagrancy laws are sometimes struck down because they are too broad. Without specific guidelines, vagrancy laws offer too much discretion to law enforcement officers and intrude upon the basic liberties championed in our society.

Because a crossdressing presentation can be confusing to onlookers a person so dressed may become the object of attention—and suspicion. Where the person has been successfully 'passing' as a member of the opposite sex, but some event causes the biological identity to become known, special suspicion may be aroused as to the intent of the 'disguise.' It is easy to see how antimasquerading and vagrancy ordinances can become combined and then have the concept of moral turpitude added on.

How often do crossdressers run into trouble with the law?

Problems by crossdressers with one or another law because of this behavior do occur. For example, a study published in 1971, involving 599 self-identified transsexual respondents to a survey, discloses that 23% of the males and 15% of the females report having encountered problems with law enforcement. The authors of this study note, though, that these percentages are low given the extent of crossdressing practiced and the then common habit of arrests made for impersonation.[669] Social tolerance has grown since then, but problems persist.

Croughan and associates, in a 1981 report of interviews conducted with 70 crossdressing adult males, find that 6 of them (8.5%) report having been treated for their crossdressing as a result of pressure from the courts. Nearly a quarter (23%) of their subjects experienced arrest for crossdressing.[670] On the other hand, in a more tolerant society, Vernon Coleman's results from 414 adult British males finds only 4% have ever been in trouble because of their crossdressing.[671]

What has been the legal situation for transsexuals?

A substantial part of the legal history with regard to crossdressers concerns transsexuals (cf. the answer to Q. 19).[672] One of the experts on legal considerations with regard to transsexuals, Sister Mary Elizabeth, observes that it is no more likely a transsexual will encounter problems with law enforcement than anyone else, with two exceptions, both of them tied to the preoperative status when anatomical sexual characteristics do not match gender presentation:

❑ the transsexual may have sexual contacts regarded as homosexual by law enforcement, prosecutors, or the court; and, more seriously,

❑ the transsexual's public appearance may be viewed as crossdressing and occasion problems with ordinances used against crossdressers.[673]

A common experience has been arrest for impersonation.[674]

But until the 20th century, merely being transsexual was problematic. Seeking legal changes in status after sex reassignment surgery has produced some notable cases. Examining one may help reveal the kinds of legal issues historically involved.

The Case of Arlette-Irène Leber (1945)

Arguably one of the most important court cases occurred in the mid-1940s. Swiss native Arlette-Irène Leber, born Arnold-Lèon in 1912, had undergone sex-reassignment surgeries that were completed in 1942. Subsequently, Leber petitioned a Cantonal Court for 'rectification of civic status.'[675] The legal basis for the petition became that an error had been made in designating Leber a man. The court accepted this as providing grounds to hear the petition. The case went to trial midway through 1945.

The court's decision notes the following: "The fate of Leber's petition depends on whether or not the alleged discrepancy really exists and whether Leber is really a woman entered in the register as a man. In other words, is the petitioner a man or a woman?"[676]

In answering this question, the Court reasons as follows:

The sex of an individual is determined in the first place by his physical make-up; but in addition to this physical element there exists a psychic element which differs entirely in men and women. In the case in question, Leber has - or had - the body of a man and the psyche of a woman. The coexistence of these two elements in the same individual has provoked in him serious psychic disequilibrium, preventing his normal social adaptation.[677]

The court notes that Leber had first received psychiatric treatment aimed at making the male element predominant in Leber's psyche. That effort failed. Hence, in the interest of establishing 'psychic equilibrium,' the therapeutic response had been sex reassignment surgeries. The court remarks: "The legality of this surgical procedure could not be seriously challenged once it was regarded as a therapeutic measure. . . ."[678]

The court observes that the chief objection that can be brought against Leber's petition is that Leber is an 'invert' (homosexual). However, reasons the court, this objection can only be valid in the case of an invert known as a 'psychosexual hermaphrodite'—one who remains male despite having 'a female mind.' Leber's situation, the court determines, is that of a 'constitutional invert':

> [T]he feminine sentiments of constitutional inverts are deeply inherent and are independent of all outside influences; they make their appearance at an early age and are so strong that will-power is incapable of controlling them. The subject is driven to transvestism because he cannot bear masculine garments and feels at ease only when dressed as a woman. But his feminine make-up manifests itself above all in a marked aversion for his male organs.[679]

The court finds itself inclined to regard the psychic element as at least equal to the physical element, noting that mind as well as body determines an individual's sex. The court sensibly reasons: "When there is discord between body and mind, one must see which of these two elements predominates. Leber, being neither a perfect man nor a perfect woman, must be placed in the category of human beings which he most resembles."[680]

Accordingly, the court grants the petition. As a matter of law, then, Leber 'becomes' a woman from that day forward. The court specifically regards this decision as both in Leber's interest and in the best interest of 'public order and morality.' The court also refrains from either putting Leber under supervision or preventing any future contracting of marriage, ruling that both are outside its competence.

Legal Issues Remaining

There have been a number of other notable cases involving transsexuals, which are outside the scope of this volume. Although transsexuals are able to obtain medical services (e.g., hormonal therapy and sex reassignment surgery) in the United States, they remain faced with problems associated with their gender identity. Recognition of the legitimacy of change from permanent assignment in one gender to permanent assignment in another has been slow in coming. This creates the practical awkwardness, inconvenience, and occasionally danger accompanying disagreement between gender presentation and declarations on legal documents. Some of these issues are touched upon in the review of the changes occurring in our society, to which we shall turn shortly.

Finally, it would be remiss not to observe here that transsexuals continue to face special obstacles and remain in need of specific (not special) consideration related to those obstacles. In particular, discrimination in employment and housing (discussed below) remain problem areas, though more and more legal codes are changing to extend protection so that the transgendered enjoy rights and liberties equal to those taken for granted by other members of society. To date, somewhat more than a dozen countries have legalized sex reassignment surgery.[681]

What has been happening nationally?

In the United States there have been significant changes with respect to law and policies vis-à-vis transgendered people. For some of us these changes appear both too slow and incomplete; for others of us they seem a headlong rush into social disintegration. But they are occurring. While it is beyond the scope of this volume to examine all of them—or even any of them in depth—some description of some changes should be illustrative of what is happening.

Historically, the U.S. federal government has exhibited reluctance to enact specific protection of transgendered people, whether in hate crime legislation or antidiscrimination laws. Each of these areas merits some consideration, beginning with federal protection through hate crime legislation.

Federal Hate Crime Legislation

Historically, since 1968 federal law has specifically provided legal authority to investigate and prosecute crimes based upon race, color, national origin, or religious bias. But crimes based on hatred of a person because of their gender, gender identity, or sexual orientation have not been covered. In this respect, the federal government has followed, rather than led, as local governments and states have extended legal protection to people in these classes. However, there long have been elected officials who have sought to amend federal legislation.

For example, in late May, 2005, one such effort, H.R. 2662, 'Local Law Enforcement Hate Crimes Prevention Act of 2005' was introduced into the U.S. House of Representatives. The section of this bill entitled 'Prohibition of Certain Hate Crime Acts' specifies acts previously covered in federal legislation and adds new protected classes, including sexual orientation and gender identity. Later in the bill 'gender identity' is defined as "actual or perceived gender-related characteristics."[682] At the same time the Senate considered S. 1145, 'Local Law Enforcement Enhancement Act of 2005,' introduced by Senator Ted Kennedy of Massachusetts.[683] This legislation experienced the same fate as its predecessors: it was not successful.

However, in the Spring of 2007, the 'Local Law Enforcement Hate Crimes Prevention Act' (H. R. 1592) passed the House of Representatives by a vote of 237-180. Enjoying bipartisan support, with more than 100 cosigners of the legislation introduced by John Conyers (a Democrat) and Mark Kirk (a Republican), the Act already had been endorsed by 230 law enforcement, civil rights, civic and religious organizations. Polls showed support by nearly three-quarters (73%) of the American public. The Act facilitates federal assistance to local law enforcement efforts when hate crimes are based on race, color, national origin, religion, disability, gender, gender identity, or sexual orientation. It also authorizes the federal government to intervene when local authorities are unable or unwilling to act.[684]

At the same time the House was dealing with this issue, the Senate was considering its own bill, under the name 'Matthew Shepard Act' (S. 1105).[685] Introduced by Senator Ted Kennedy (Democrat), with 43 cosponsors, it was read twice and referred in April, 2007 to the Senate Judiciary Committee. Meanwhile, in response to the House's passing of H. R. 1592, President Bush's office released a 'Statement of Administration Policy.' That document declares the President's belief that the Act is "unnecessary and constitutionally questionable."[686] The President promised to veto such legislation if passed by Congress.

IRS Ruling

While legislative initiatives grind slowly forward, other problems at the federal level also persist. For example, an Internal Revenue Service (IRS) examiner ruled on a tax case that no deduction can be taken for the expense of sex reassignment surgery (SRS) because it is cosmetic rather than medically necessary (see Tax Code, 26 USC §213). The individual in question, Rhiannon O'Donnabhain, had completed SRS in 2001. The IRS decision prompted the Gay & Lesbian Advocates & Defenders (GLAD) organization to represent O'Donnabhain in an appeal of the ruling. The IRS Appeals Officer overturned the earlier decision, concluding that the SRS was medically necessary.[687] However, that was not the end of the matter. The IRS then set forward, in 2005, a ruling setting as a principle that SRS could not be deducted because it is cosmetic surgery (Chief Counsel Advice #200603025).[688] That led to a GLAD petition in United States Tax Court in the Spring of 2006 requesting a redetermination.[689] Final disposition in this matter was undetermined at the time of this writing.

National Events in Antidiscrimination & Employment Law

Only a few brief remarks need be made in this section since the material following specifies various actions taken by state and municipal governments. First and foremost, despite legal strides, employment discrimination continues to be a problem for many transgender people, especially those perceived as crossdressers. For example, a heterosexual crossdresser was fired from his job after 21 years of employment, ostensibly because he crossdressed away from the job. A federal court in 1999 upheld the employer's decision.[690] All too many examples like this one remain to remind us that where the reach of law does not extend a leveling hand the land remains uneven.

Antidiscrimination legislation specifically including gays and lesbians remains far ahead of protection extended for transsexuals, transvestites and other members of the transgendered community.[691] But some state and municipal governments have acted by extending protection to crossdressers. The provisions are varied and unequal, but they indicate a growing awareness on the part of government officials that public attitudes have been changing. Still, controversy often attends the enactment of new legislation.

Changes at the State Level

A number of states have addressed issues of sexual orientation, sometimes defined so as to include gender identity and role, as the following table indicates:

Table 36.1 Examples of State Changes Enacting Legal Protections

State	Year	Nature of Change (Area)
California	1998	Legislative (Hate Crimes)
	2003	Legislative (Discrimination)
Colorado	1990	Executive Order (Discrimination)
Connecticut	1991	Legislative (Discrimination)
Delaware	2001	Executive Order (Discrimination)
Hawaii	2003	Legislative (Hate Crimes)
Illinois	2005	Legislative (Discrimination)
Indiana	2001	Legislative (Discrimination)
Kentucky	2003	Executive Order (Discrimination)
Maine	2005	Legislative (Discrimination)
Maryland	2001	Legislative (Discrimination)
Massachusetts	1989	Legislative (Discrimination)
Michigan	2003	Executive Order (Discrimination)
Minnesota	1992	Legislative (Hate Crimes)
Missouri	1999	Legislative (Hate Crimes)
Nevada	1999	Legislative (Discrimination)
New Hampshire	1997	Legislative (Discrimination)
New Jersey	1991	Legislative (Discrimination)
New Mexico	2003	Legislative (Hate Crimes; Discrimination)
New York	2000	Legislative (Hate Crimes)
Oregon	2003	Legislative (Discrimination)
Pennsylvania	2002	Legislative (Hate Crimes)
	2003	Executive Order (Discrimination)

Rhode Island	2001	Legislative (Discrimination)
Vermont	1992, 1999 2007	Legislative (Discrimination) Legislative (Hate Crimes) Legislative (Discrimination based on gender identity)
Washington	1985 2006	Executive Order (Discrimination) Legislative (Discrimination)

Minnesota pioneered in acknowledging the need to provide specific recognition of the transgender community in the interest of upholding basic human rights. In 1992, the legislature added a paragraph to amend the law with respect to hate crimes to include "having or being perceived as having a self-image or identity not traditionally associated with one's biological maleness or femaleness."[692] A number of other states have followed suit. In 1999, Vermont amended its hate crime statute to add "gender identity" to the classes listed.[693] In 2007, the state passed legislation and the governor signed into law specific protection against discrimination in banking, employment, housing, education, health care, and public accommodations based on gender identity or gender-related characteristics.[694]

Also in 1999, Missouri added "sexual orientation" to the categories protected, but defined it so as to include "having a self-image or identity not traditionally associated with one's gender."[695] That procedure—to use the phrase 'sexual orientation,' but define it so as to include other transgender realities besides homosexuality—has become increasingly popular. In 2003, Hawaii's amended statute used the phrase "gender identity or expression."[696] New Mexico, that same year, adopted similar language.[697] Maine's law, which recognizes and protects the transgendered explicitly, went into effect at the end of 2005.[698] In early 2006, culminating efforts begun in 1977, Washington State enacted specific protection for gay and lesbian people, and became the 7th state to explicitly protect the transgendered. The legislation (House Bill 2661) bars discrimination in housing, employment and health insurance practices, as well as affirming the right to the "full enjoyment" of public accommodations and facilities.[699]

As seen earlier, California has been a leader in addressing transgender issues. In 1998 California law amended its hate crime legislation by adding 'gender' to the protected classes and defining it in a way similar to other states enacting such legislation:

> "Gender" means the victim's actual sex or the defendant's perception of the victim's sex, and includes the defendant's perception of the victim's identity, appearance, or behavior, whether or not that identity, appearance, or behavior is different from that traditionally associated with the victim's sex at birth.[700]

This California Penal Code's definition of 'gender' is also referenced in the State's 2003 antidiscrimination legislation. But not all proposed bills find passage. This legislation was followed in 2000 with an enactment—'Vital Records: Change of Sex'—in reference to court procedures to be followed when transsexuals present themselves for legal recognition of their new sex status; it was vetoed by the governor.[701]

Various states also have acted to combat employment discrimination. This has been notable especially in the arena of state employment and contract awards. While discrimination against the transgendered in the workplace has not been eliminated, there have been changes offering more protection. Some of these have come about by Executive Orders issued by state governors. On May 20, 2003, Kentucky Governor Paul Patton issued an Executive Order forbidding discrimination against state employees based on gender identity or sexual orientation.[702] A little more than two months later, on July 30, 2003, Pennsylvania Governor Ed Rendell signed an Executive Order banning discrimination against state employees based on either their gender identity or gender expression.[703]

State legislative bodies also have considered or acted upon proposed legislation with reference to gender issues. On April 22, 2003, California's Assembly passed AB 196 in the House. It then moved through the Senate and was signed into law by the governor on July 31, 2003. The law extends existing nondiscrimination provisions to cover transgender (or 'gender variant') individuals, including transvestites and transsexuals.[704]

In the State of Oregon, transsexuals have employment protection, albeit under the notion that transsexualism constitutes a 'disability.'[705] Under Oregon administrative rules: "[A]n employer may not refuse to hire or promote or bar or discharge from employment or discriminate in compensation, terms, conditions or privileges of employment because a person is transsexual when the person is otherwise qualified."[706]

As the above examples make clear, not all regions of the country are equally represented in the changes occurring. The South and the Midwest remain areas where change lags behind. However, irrespective of what a state government may or may not be doing, local cities may be active in promoting change.

Changes at the Municipal Level

From the 1990s forward, various city governments have enacted antidiscrimination provisions with regard to gender expression or sexual orientation.[707] These are sometimes met with controversy. For example, in 1992 Cincinnati, Ohio, passed a Human Rights Ordinance making it illegal for either private property owners or employers within the city's jurisdiction to discriminate on the basis of race, gender, religion, marital status, age, disability status, HIV status, sexual orientation, national and ethnic origin, or Appalachian regional origin. This initiated a storm lasting years and going all the way to the U.S. Supreme Court. The ordinance did not stand as written.[708]

Nevertheless, according to the International Foundation for Gender Education (IFGE), by the Spring of 2004 some 71 municipalities in the U.S. had added gender identity as a protected class in their human rights ordinances.[709] An instructive and well-known example is that passed in 1998 in New Orleans, Louisiana. The city passed an ordinance to prohibit discrimination based on either sexual orientation or gender expression. 'Gender identity' is defined as follows by the ordinance:

> Gender identification is the actual or perceived condition, status or acts of:
> (1) Identifying emotionally or psychologically with the sex other than one's biological or legal sex at birth, whether or not there has been a physical change of the organs of sex;
> (2) Presenting and/or holding oneself out to the public as a member of the biological sex that was not one's biological or legal sex at birth;
> (3) Lawfully displaying physical characteristics and/or behavioral characteristics and/or expressions which are widely perceived as being more appropriate to the biological or legal sex other than one's biological sex at birth, as when a male is perceived as feminine or a female is perceived as masculine; and/or
> (4) Being physically and/or behaviorally androgynous.[710]

It is perhaps worth noting that New Orleans explicitly states that homosexuality, transvestism, and transsexualism (among other conditions) "shall not be considered disabilities."[711] Crossdressing is specifically mentioned in the ordinance. A distinction is made between the dress of transsexuals and others who might be perceived as crossdressing:

> Nothing in this Chapter shall prohibit an employer from prohibiting cross-dressing in the work place or while an employee is acting in the course and scope of his or her employment. For purposes of this section, a person shall be deemed to be acting in the scope of his or her employment if he or she would be deemed to be in the scope and course of his employment for the purpose of determining eligibility for worker's compensation. For purposes of this section, "Cross-dressing" shall mean the wearing of clothing, cosmetics, footwear and/or other accouterments generally deemed or perceived as inappropriate to the gender that was one's biological or legal gender at birth and/or generally deemed or perceived as more appropriate to the gender that was not one's biological or legal gender at birth. "Cross-dressing" shall not be deemed to include the regular wearing of clothing, cosmetics, footwear and or other accouterments which is appropriate to the gender

other than his or her biological or legal gender at birth with which an employee or applicant identifies if the employee or applicant provides the employer with the written statement of a licensed doctor or other health care professional certifying that the employee or applicant presents the characteristics of gender identification disorder or another similar status or condition and that the employee or applicant intends prospectively to attire and conduct himself or herself for the foreseeable future in the employee's employment and workplace or workplaces in the manner appropriate for persons of the gender with which he or she identifies.[712]

Other cities also are addressing gender expression and discrimination. The following table provides examples (current as of the writing of this volume) from select major cities in different regions of the United States:

Table 36.2 Gender Identity Awareness in Selected Municipal Codes

City (State)	Excerpted Phrasing from the Code
Atlanta (GA)[713]	". . . gender identity . . ."
Boston (MA)[714]	". . . sex, gender identity or expression . . ."
Chicago (IL)[715]	". . . sex, gender identity . . ."
Iowa City (IA)[716]	". . . gender identity . . ."
Los Angeles (CA)[717]	". . . sexual orientation . . ."
Minneapolis (MN)[718]	". . . affectional preference . . ."
Santa Cruz (NM)[719]	". . . sex, gender, sexual orientation . . ."
Seattle (WA)[720]	". . . sexual orientation, gender identity . . ."

Increasingly, local jurisdictions are becoming more inclusive in legal protection against discriminatory practices in employment, housing, and other matters. Clearly, the times are changing. Yet just as clearly significant obstacles remain for crossdressers. There remains much latitude for law enforcement officers to harass or arrest crossdressers in public, even if a judge later throws out the matter. There remain difficulties in the workplace, particularly over policies with regard to the use of restrooms. In short, there is still a significant distance to go before crossdressers enjoy all the same protections and liberties of other citizens.[721]

What is happening internationally?

Despite continuing challenges, for transgendered people there have also been some positive signs, not only in this nation but also elsewhere. The international community has demonstrated increased awareness of and concern for transgendered people. Although a report to the General Assembly of the United Nations in 2001 notes that sexual minorities are disproportionately subjected to torture and other forms of ill-treatment, both before and since the U.N. has acted to curtail such violations of basic human rights and discrimination against this population. For example, in 1994 the U.N. Human Rights Commission ruled that sexual orientation held protected status against discrimination under the provisions of Articles 2 and 26 of the International Covenant on Civil and Political Rights.

In 2003, Brazil introduced to the 59th session of the U.N. Commission on Human Rights a resolution on 'Human Rights and Sexual Orientation.' It was supported by the European Union's Parliament. Controversy over the matter brought about its postponement to the 60th session in 2004, where discussion found Human Rights Watch urging adoption of a resolution calling for U.N. member nations to promote and protect the basic human rights and fundamental freedoms of all persons without regard to their sexual orientation or gender identity.[722] On the first day of the 61st session (March 14th, 2005) the Canadian Minister of Foreign Affairs explicitly referenced the need of attention to fighting discrimination based on sexual orientation and gender identity.[723]

To date, however, explicit protection of the transgendered (including gays and lesbians), remains rare. The U.N. has made stands, such as the affirmation of its Working Group on Arbitrary Detention that such arrests of people (e.g., homosexuals simply because they are homosexual) violates fundamental human rights.[724] But the U.N.'s role remains subordinate to what individual nation states determine for themselves, which is often contrary to the principles they agree to abide by as members of that body.

The courts have been instrumental in safeguarding basic human rights. For example, in 2002 the European Court of Human Rights in the case of *Christine Goodwin vs. the United Kingdom* ruled the U.K.'s practices of not altering birth certificates to reflect a post-operative transsexual's new status and denial of their right to marry in their new gender were violations of the European Convention on Human Rights (articles 8 and 12).[725] This court, according to a report issued in 2007, also "has been interpreting Article 12 provisions with increasing flexibility, tending to allow marriages of transsexuals."[726]

Only a handful of nations have enacted laws to protect sexual minorities from discrimination:

Table 36.3 Examples of Changes Enacting Legal Protections[727]

Country	Code	Area(s)
Australia	Human Rights & Equality Commission Act	Employment
Canada	Human Rights Act	Employment, Housing, Services
Denmark	Penal Code	Employment
Ecuador	Constitution	General protection
Finland	Penal Code	Employment, Services, Access to public meetings
France	Penal Code	Employment
Iceland	Penal Code	Access to goods and services
Ireland	Employment Discrimination Law; Prohibition of Incitement to Hatred Act	Employment; Speech
Israel	Parliamentary Act	Employment, Anti-defamation
Luxembourg	Parliamentary Act	General protection
Netherlands	Penal Code	Employment, Education, Services
New Zealand	Human Rights Act	Employment, Education, Services, Housing, etc.
Norway	Penal Code	Access to goods, services, public meetings; prohibitis hate speech
Slovenia	Penal Code	General protection
South Africa	Constitution	General protection
Spain	Penal Code	Employment, Housing, Public Services, etc.
	Identity Documents (2007)	Name change
Sweden	Parliamentary Acts	Employment
Switzerland	Constitution	General protection
United Kingdom	Gender Recognition Act of 2004	Permits transsexuals legal right to live in acquired sex and gender

Despite the paucity of their numbers, though, the general trend appears to be toward increasing awareness and protection.

What is the International Bill of Gender Rights?

One significant development has been the creation of a document that has proved to function as a model for many groups and organizations, with many adopting it outrightly. At the beginning of the 1990s, working independently and without knowledge of each other's efforts, two women initiated action to craft a gender 'Bill of Rights.' In Pennsylvania, JoAnn Roberts, an author on crossdressing and a cofounder of the Renaissance Transgender Association (1987), wrote such a document and began circulating it.[728] In New York, Sharon Stuart, a former Judge Advocate General (JAG) officer, published a proposal for such a document in the newsletter for the International Foundation for Gender Education (IFGE). In 1992, the International Conference on Transgender Law and Employment Policy (ICTLEP) had its first annual meeting. Subsequently, Stuart began drafting a formal Gender Bill of Rights that utilized both her own earlier proposal and the work of Roberts.[729]

In 1993, the *International Bill of Gender Rights* (IBGR) was drafted in committee and adopted at the 2nd annual ICTLEP. This was reviewed, amended, and adopted with revisions at the annual meetings in the next few years. The IGBR affirms the primacy of individual self-determination, independent of biological or social factors. It also affirms the resolution that neither Human nor Civil Rights shall be denied in consequence of such choices. Ten 'gender rights' are enumerated in the version of July 4, 1996:

1. The Right to Define Gender Identity.
2. The Right to Free Expression of Gender Identity.
3. The Right to Secure and Retain Employment and to Receive Just Compensation.
4. The Right of Access to Gendered Space and Participation in Gendered Activities.
5. The Right to Control and Change One's Own Body.
6. The Right to Competent Medical and Professional Care.
7. The Right to Freedom from Involuntary Psychiatric Diagnosis or Treatment.
8. The Right to Sexual Expression.
9. The Right to Form Committed, Loving Relationships and Enter into Marital Contracts.
10. The Right to Conceive, Bear, or Adopt Children; The Right to Nurture and Have Custody of Children and to Exercise Parental Capacity.[730]

Though the IBGR has no force of law on its own, it serves as a model for legislative bodies and as a guide to individual organizations and persons.

The IBGR has been only one product of the ICTLEP, which Houston attorney Phyllis Randolph Frye founded in 1992. Annual meetings, held in various cities, feature presentations from politicians, lawyers, judges, and academic scholars on issues relevant to the name continued for six years, through 1997. The proceedings and various other documents have been published. Many materials are available on the internet. With a sense that many of its objectives had been achieved, especially the realization of legal movements at both national and grassroots levels, the organization went into stasis.[731]

Today efforts continue to shape laws and policies aimed at securing a better world for us all.

Q. 37

How are crossdressers treated in public?

The Short Answer. If we exclude women dressed in mannish styles, or popular and well-known entertainers—both groups generally enjoying public approval—the remainder of crossdressers, mainly men, whether heterosexual or homosexual, meet a decidedly mixed reaction in public. A good deal of the time it is relatively indifferent, but it can also be negative, even aggressively hostile. The stakes are even higher for transgender children and youth, whose identity and safety are more vulnerable because of developmental and environmental issues. We should not be surprised that so many transgender people in our social climate choose to keep their transgender reality hidden as much as possible. Indeed, we are more justified being surprised at the increasing willingness of transgender people to make their identities public and to actively press for basic legal protections. Such activities carry risks. Transphobia and homophobia expose transgender people to verbal and physical harassment and violence. Even when aggression does not occur, more passive social resistance in the form of bias, prejudice, and discrimination in matters such as employment and housing may occur. Transgender children and youth daily manage realistic fears for their safety in the nation's schools. Yet there are indications that when members of the general public are educated about crossdressing and other transgender realities their tolerance increases. Indeed, we may be witnessing a shift in public attitudes toward greater tolerance, if not wholehearted acceptance. People's anxieties often flow from unexamined assumptions, inherited biases, and ignorance. When reason and evidence are presented most of us demonstrate some willingness to reconsider our position. With regard to transgender realities, women are generally more open to such education and change than are men, though both genders show shifts in thinking when accurate information is offered. How pronounced or enduring apparent changes will prove remains to be seen.

The Longer Answer. Writing in 1970, sociologist H. Taylor Buckner observes that crossdressing does not appear to be a major social problem; it is, he claims, mostly an issue for crossdressers and their partners. Buckner notes that in five years of careful watching of news and publications he has seen no "hor-ror stories" with reference to transvestites. In fact, he feels that the reason the crossdresser is kept out of "the institutional order of society" is because the problem of crossdressing has never risen to the level of public discussion where "transvestite" might become a respectable role in its own right.[732]

Has this situation, some 40 years later, changed? Is crossdressing now at the level of public discussion that transgender people might attain 'respectability'—accepted as occupying a respectable identity and gender role that is *sui generis*? Despite the increased visibility—and often more enlightened conversation—on crossdressing, we scarcely can declare that such a pronounced shift has oc-curred. Indeed, we can doubt that society at large has yet to reckon sufficiently with transgender realities such that this possibility can as yet even be glimpsed. As long as crossdressers stay largely out of public view this kind of discussion is likely to stay muted. So it is a reasonable question, given the potential gain the group might make should *all* its members go public, to ask why so many cross-dressers keep their crossdressing hidden.

Why do so many crossdressers stay 'in the closet'?

Plenty of evidence over the last several decades suggests that there are per-fectly rational reasons for why so many crossdressers keep their behavior a closely guarded secret. In common parlance, they remain 'in the closet.' Most crossdressers are unwilling to risk the social response they might face if they made their crossdressing behavior public. Some learned in childhood that their behavior should be kept secret. As adults they are aware of the stereotypes and myths held about crossdressers, even by loved ones. Few are willing to face the potential harm that can result from a hostile response to their behavior.

Surveys of adult male crossdressers consistently find that a majority do not venture out in public while crossdressed, as the following table shows:

Table 37.1 Percent of Adult Male Crossdressers Reporting Public Crossdressing

Study	# Subjects	Crossdressed in Public
V. Prince & P. M. Bentler (1972)[733]	504	18-34%
V. Coleman (1996)[734]	414	47%
R. Docter & V. Prince (1997)[735]	1,032	14% frequently; 48% occasionally
Yvonne (1999)[736]	1,178	50%

It should also be borne in mind that those crossdressers who participate in research are the ones most likely to be public about their crossdressing to oth-ers. Presumably, those most secretive are not thereby represented by these subjects and thus the actual percentage of crossdressing men who appear in public is likely to be lower—perhaps much lower—than these figures suggest.

In fact, report after report of research affirms the keen concern crossdressers have to keep their behavior secret. More than 40 years ago, the article on transvestism in the *Encyclopedia of Sexual Behavior* estimated that more than 90% of crossdressing is done in secret.[737] Coleman's 1996 report found that more than two-thirds (69%) of respondents acknowledged a fear of being found out.[738] There is no reason to doubt the accuracy of such findings.

Why are crossdressers so reticent if they both enjoy the experience and see nothing wrong with it? Peggy Rudd, wife of a crossdresser and author of several books on the subject, offers this explanation: "Crossdressers are secretive, largely because they have not been able to crash through the preconceived ideas of society that tend to stereotype people as distinctly masculine or feminine."[739] Certainly she is correct for many crossdressers—but not all. Most have little interest in being social crusaders, no matter how much they might yearn for the same degree of freedom and acceptance others enjoy. Instead, they choose secrecy as the most practical route to minimizing risk while maximizing gain.

We must also distinguish between the degree of total secrecy, where no one is let in on what is going on, and relative secrecy where one or more others are trusted with the secret. While a small minority of crossdressers publicly out themselves, a perhaps surprising number venture to share their secret with at least one other person. As would be expected, this is most often a significant other—a spouse or other intimate companion.

The large-scale study of male crossdressers released in 1972 by Prince and Bentler finds that more than half (58%) have told someone about their crossdressing. Among those who are or have been married, four-fifths (80%) have spouses (or ex-spouses) who know. Only 7% have confined their secret to just one other person; if they tell at all, it is a secret likely shared with more than one individual. Perhaps surprisingly, the vast majority of recipients of this secret (91%) are either neutral (35%) or accepting (56%); less than one-in-ten (9%) prove antagonistic. Not surprisingly, women are far more accepting than men (77% to 23%).[740]

Data like that just cited might make us wonder at the reluctance of crossdressers to let themselves be seen. Apparently, few people respond with rejection or hostility. Yet this situation needs closer scrutiny. First, we must recall that a crossdresser's experience of gender socialization growing up emphasizes the need to appear as gender conforming. Adult messages in mainstream society reinforce these early messages. Further, we must consider the data offered a moment ago in the light that most crossdressers are both cautious and highly selective in disclosing their secret. In other words, they do their best to ensure that the reaction they receive will not be punitive or rejecting. Seen in that light, the numbers look less happy—only slightly more than half of those selected to be told prove accepting. If this is true for those carefully chosen for the news, what might be expected from the general public?

What are people's attitudes toward the transgendered?

Social work professionals Mary Boes and Katherine van Wormer, at the beginning of the 21st century, remind us that, "the most extreme forms of discrimination, including ridicule and violence, are reserved for transgendered persons . . . ."[741] Though they speak with specific reference to transsexuals, to some degree the observation is pertinent for all who crossdress, especially when they do so in public, and for transgender people in general. Yet this reality is not the whole reality. Both attitudes and laws have been changing in recent years. The complexity of the social situation in the United States—and elsewhere—makes the following question pertinent: Are we on our way to a society where transgender people are accorded respect for the unique reality they embody? The evidence needed to answer such a question is mixed.

To understand how transgender people—especially those most visible by virtue of crossdressing—are received in society we must look underneath polite public behavior to the attitudes people hold. As we shall see, the evidence is mixed as to how far transgendered people have come in gaining a measure of respect or acceptance from the wider public. Quite clearly there are those who, though outside the transgender community, welcome its members as valued within the wider social fabric. Just as obviously, there persist others whose behavior marginalizes or ostracizes the transgendered.

With regard to the latter, attorney and activist Phyllis Randolph Frye notes a salient point about their perception:

> Today, most activists in the transgender community and many activists in the lesbian, gay male and bisexual community agree that people who hate, despise, feel ashamed of, preach from the pulpits against, or otherwise act in a disparaging manner toward transgenders, lesbians, gay men and bisexuals simply do not distinguish among the categories of queers. In the struggle to stay employed, maintain family relationships, stay out of jail, stay with children or adopt children and not be verbally abused by people who wield some form of holy writ, all transgenders, lesbians, gay men and bisexuals are labeled as being queer.[742]

It is legitimate to wonder if this lack of discernment regarding distinctions among transgender people also is widespread among those who are not hostile. Do most people perceive subgroups among the gender-different? If so, do they recognize these differences as important ones? Are some transgender groups accorded more respect or receive greater acceptance? The answers to such questions contribute to the attitudes and behaviors people show one another.

In our culture, differences have been found in the perceptions of men and women toward transgender behaviors and people. In general, women are more tolerant. Social psychologist Gregory Herek advances the provocative notion that heterosexual males in American society are culturally constructed homophobic as an important aspect of their heterosexual masculinity. In short, to be an American heterosexual male means identifying oneself as not homosexual and as not feminine. Intolerance or hostility toward other males who display homosexual or feminine identity or behavior has become part of self-affirmation for heterosexual males. Further, such a construction lessens the likelihood of such men interacting with gay men, which might challenge their preconceived attitudes.[743]

Similarly, we have speculated earlier (in the answer to Q. 22) that the construction of masculine identity in our culture may also predispose men toward transphobia. If, as research suggests, men rely more on clothes for self-expression, including as gendered beings,[744] then the stakes are raised by males who dress like women. As researchers Stephen Gould and Barbara Stern phrase it, "That fashion conscious men are more gender conscious suggests that these men connect fashion with their self-identity and internalized maleness, their concept of what it means to be a man."[745]

If there are men-women differences in perception, there are also signs of differences among men with respect to sexual orientation. Some research has been conducted to see how some male members of the transgender community vary in their perceptions of gender-different behavior of others in comparison to gender-conforming males. In a 1997 study, John Moulton III reports research contrasting two groups of young men. One is comprised of 45 heterosexual males, the other of a like number of homosexual males. The question the study asks is whether these groups vary in their attitudes toward crossdressing males, both heterosexual and homosexual, and non-crossdressing homosexual males. Using story vignettes where the principal character is presented in three different 'gender-discordant' conditions (homosexual crossdresser or non-crossdresser, or heterosexual crossdresser), the subjects of both groups in the studies are evaluated for their tolerance toward the story character. As hypothesized, the homosexual males prove more tolerant of all three gender-discordant conditions than their heterosexual counterparts. However, the gay men view the non-crossdressing gay character as more masculine than either the gay or straight crossdresser. The heterosexual subjects make no such distinction.[746] This research supports the idea that differences in perception toward crossdressers exist between the transgender community and the wider public, but that they also differ even among transgender groups.

Some argue that, historically, those who look or act differently generally do not fare well in public, regardless of the cause of their 'differentness.' It seems not to matter overly much whether the difference places anyone at health risk either (see answer to Q. 32). Many people, for example, still shun those visibly mentally retarded as though the condition is infectious. So it should come as no surprise that crossdressers in public are likely to fetch some negative reactions—unless, of course, they succeed in passing as a member of the opposite sex. If so, the only danger they then face is the consequences of exposure—and that danger can be substantial, as cases like that of Tina Brandon/Brandon Teena show.[747]

Crossdressing, especially by males, often engages strong feelings in others. In a society where some of the sexual and gender lines are both rigidly and narrowly drawn, crossdressing constitutes for some a challenge they decide must be met not only forcefully, but perhaps also with physical force. As Viviane Namaster comments, "Given the cultural coding of gender into a binary framework, a high incidence of violence directed against TS/TG people is not surprising."[748] Perhaps not surprising, but certainly irrational and definitely not what we as a society want to uphold.

How common is public hostility?

Homophobia & Transphobia

Before looking at the limited information that exists on crimes against transgender people *because* they are transgendered, let us consider a couple preliminary matters. First, the Connecticut TransAdvocacy Coalition suggests we recognize the existence of 'transphobia.' They distinguish this from 'homophobia' as follows: "Homophobia is an irrational fear of gays, lesbians and bisexuals based upon their sexual orientation. However, Transphobia results from a fear of one's Transgressing the societal Gender binaries of Masculine and Feminine [TransGender]."[749] The very unfamiliarity of the term in contrast with the well-known term 'homophobia' suggests how little attention has been given to negative social reactions to transgender people. Yet Gregory Herek's claim that "prejudice against men who display feminine behavior is nearly as common as prejudice against homosexuality in our society"[750] is hard to dispute. In this climate it is inescapable that crimes against transgendered people motivated by repulsion of their transgendered status are significantly underreported.

Hate Crimes

Second, we must be able to see that crimes committed against transgender people *because* they are transgender are no different in their nature than like crimes committed against homosexuals because they are homosexual, or against racial groups because of their race, or against Muslims because of their religion. These crimes are hate crimes.[751] To date, though, federal legislation on hate crimes only recognizes crimes motivated by race, religion, national origin or color. Nor does this seem likely to change in the immediate future since the present administration under President George W. Bush opposes amending the law. So, from a federal legal standpoint, crimes against transgendered people motivated by the fact the victim is transgendered may be hateful, but they are

272

not legally hate crimes meriting federal law enforcement involvement. The lack of recognition of such crimes as hate crimes has carried with it at least two very unfortunate consequences:

❑ there has been little incentive to collect data on a national level substantiating the extent of the problem; and,

❑ there remain no specific national provisions to protect potential victims or to punish perpetrators motivated by their hate of transgendered people.

It is against this backdrop we must view the relative lack of information we can review. Nevertheless, there are some data we need to recognize—and with an increasing number of states amending their hate crimes statutes to protect the transgendered (see the answer to Q. 36), more data is forthcoming.

In a study published in 1997 by the Gender Public Advocacy Coalition (GenderPAC),[752] a serious incidence of violence against transgendered people becomes apparent. The study utilizes a questionnaire designed to assess transgendered people's lifetime experiences with violence. The questionnaire is not randomly distributed—infeasible given the nature of the target population—but distributed through events, volunteers, and the internet. In a 12 month period, 402 cases collected from respondents yield disturbing information. The data from these cases finds that well over half (59.5%) report having been a victim of harassment or violence. Other highlights of the study are:

❑ Verbal abuse is the most common adverse act; over half (56%) of the cases involve such an incident just within the previous year.

❑ Assault, either with a weapon (10%) or without one (19%) has occurred at least once in nearly a third (29.6%) of cases.

❑ Being followed or stalked has occurred at least once in nearly a quarter (23%) of the cases.

❑ Robbery is involved in about 1-in-7 (14%) of the cases.

❑ Rape or attempted rape has happened in about 1-in-8 (13%) of the cases.[753]

While most of us will deplore such acts (and all of us *should*), we are likely to interpret these events as the actions of a fringe or criminal element—certainly not folk like ourselves. Yet one of the more sobering indicators that such acts are tacitly accepted by our society comes from another finding of this study: law enforcement officers and facilities are not uncommonly implicated in adverse incidents (e.g., nearly 8% of the cases involved an unjustified arrest).[754] Moreover, the authors of the study remind us that acts of violence against transgendered people elicits little outcry from the public, occasions little study, and to date has produced inconsistent and often partial legislative movement to provide protection.[755]

A 1999 online survey of more than a thousand male crossdressers reveals that a substantial minority either have personally experienced public harassment or know someone who has. Specifically, more than 1-in-10 (13%) have been confronted either by law enforcement or security while crossdressed, about 1-in-6 (16%) have been either verbally abused or physically assaulted while cross-dressed in public, and 1-in-4 (25%) personally know someone who has been either verbally abused or physically assaulted while crossdressed in public.[756] Similarly, a 1992 study of transsexuals in London finds that more than half (52%) of the male-to-female (MtF) transsexuals involved in the research have been physically assaulted.[757]

Why do male crossdressers, in particular, receive such responses? Obviously, they transgress a social norm, but at least superficially that seems harmless enough—it is just clothing after all! But people see a gender statement being made, and perhaps a sexual one as well. They apply cultural filters to interpret the behavior and then may act out the resulting personal judgment. As seen elsewhere in this work, crossdressing by men presents a different challenge than that undertaken by women (who fought these same battles for public tolerance for a long time). As Kelly Kleiman in the Chicago-Kent Law Review reminds us: "[W]omen who dress as men are dressing up, seeking power, privilege, or even just protective camouflage from male violence; while men dressing as women are dressing down."[758]

The crossdressing man may be viewed by others as voluntarily lowering his social status and becoming weak, inviting disdain and censure at best, and violence at worst. In fact, those who perpetrate the hostility typically believe it is warranted and place responsibility for what happens on the crossdressing victim. But who is really responsible for the treatment those who crossdress in public generally receive? Do crossdressers invite the scorn, ridicule, and sometimes worse behavior they receive? Therapist Gianna Israel comments, "the problems transgender men and women face are not one necessarily of self-creation, but primarily originate from others' opinions and judgments."[759]

Indeed, crossdressing men are not the only ones who meet opposition. The 1992 study of London transsexuals referred to above also finds that 43% of the female-to-male (FtM) transsexuals have been physically assaulted.[760] While it might seem that crossdressing males face a greater risk, the risk for crossdressing females is also significant—and no statistical comparison matters when you are the individual who has experienced a beating.

Experience of Children & Adolescents

If adults are vulnerable, children and adolescents are even more so. A study of 'School Climate' conducted in the fall of 1999 by the Gay, Lesbian, and Straight Education Network (GLSEN) returned responses from 496 lesbian, gay, bisexual and transgender students in 32 states. Survey results reveal more than 90% of these students have been subject to homophobic remarks, most often from other students (94.4% of those reporting such remarks), but frequently enough from faculty and staff, too (36.6%). Nearly two-thirds (61%) have experienced verbal harassment, almost half (46.5%) sexual harassment, and more than a quarter (27.6%) physical harassment, including physical assault. No wonder, then, 41.7% report not feeling safe at school.[761] The *SIECUS Report* covering this study notes that, "transgender kids probably suffer even more harassment and discrimination than lesbian, gay, or bisexual students."[762]

GLSEN's survey for 2001 had an even wider reach: 904 LGBT youth from 48 states and the District of Columbia. Of these, 4.3% self-identify as transgender or other gender identity; 95.7% regard themselves as identifying at one of the two gender poles (though their sexual orientation places them under 'transgender' in the widest sense of the term—see the answer to Q. 20). Their school experience has been marked by exposure to homophobic or transphobic behavior. Nearly all of them (94%) hear homophobic comments (e.g., 'You're so gay'), or labels (e.g., 'Faggot,' 'Dyke'), often or frequently, and nearly a quarter (23.6%) hear such remarks from faculty or school staff.[763]

Such behavior by others fosters a hostile environment. In such an environment anxiety and fear over personal safety arise. In probing issues of safety at school pertinent to this population the survey finds that these youth "most commonly reported that they felt unsafe in their school because of their sexual orientation or their gender expression; with over two-thirds of youth (68.6%) reporting that they felt unsafe in their school because of sexual orientation and almost half reporting they felt unsafe because of their gender expression (45.7%)."[764] Their fear is rational, as shown by the numbers:

Table 37.2 Experience of LGBT Youth in School[765]

Behavior	Total % Experienc-ing	Experienced Rarely or Sometimes	Experienced Often or Frequently
Verbal Harassment (re: sexual orientation)	83.3%	43.3%	40%
Verbal Harassment (re: gender expression)	67.5%	39.4%	28.1%
Physical Harassment (re: sexual orientation)	41.9%	27%	15%
Physical Harassment (re: gender expression)	31.3%	21%	10.4%
Physical Assault (re: sexual orientation)	21.1%	15.3%	6.7%
Physical Assault (re: gender expression)	13.7%	8.2%	5.5%

Apart from experiences such as those listed above, transgender students suffer in other ways. School attendance is impacted by their fear. GLSEN's survey finds such fear motivates nearly a third of the students to skip class at least once in the past month (31.9%) and to miss at least one entire day of school in the past month (20.8%).[766] Even when they are present they may be more likely than other students to refrain from participation in school events such as dances (where they might be afraid to bring a same-sex or same-gender partner), or classroom discussions (e.g., on LGBT issues). No wonder, then, that many transgender students choose not to be 'out' about their gender identity or sexual orientation because such things being publicly known increases their level of risk.[767]

Educator Linda McCarthy asks some hard questions: how will educators address issues affecting transgender youth in school settings? Or will they respond at all? Are professional educators willing to educate themselves on the issues accompanying nonnormative gender expression? Are school administrators willing to shoulder responsibilities to support transgender youth? Finally, can educators take seriously and speak out against gender oppression, as they do for racism and sexism?[768] The answers remain unknown in too many schools.

McCarthy points out that even in schools where efforts are being made, such as those offering GLBT (Gay, Lesbian, Bisexual, Transgender) education or support, the 'T' is treated in cursory fashion, if at all. For all practical purposes, GLBT means GLB.[769] As long as transgender children and adolescents remain invisible even within the community they are identified as a part of, things are unlikely to improve very much for them.

Are attitudes changing?

The safety and well-being of transgender children, youth, and adults—like that of any minority group—depends on the sufferance of the majority. In that respect, legal reforms often alert and shape public behavior in the hope that attitudinal shifts will follow. We need to consider a moment the interrelationships among laws or policies, public behavior, and private attitudes. To do this, let us begin with a couple of plausible scenarios: settings where transgender realities like crossdressing are forbidden, and those where they are protected.

In the first, where ordinances or policies prohibit public crossdressing, the message is clear: those who do so are wrong and merit punishment. In this situation most of the public is likely to hold an attitude mirroring the law or policy. Coercive and punitive acts become justified to discourage transgender behavior—and negative attitudes flourish. This is why even where an organization may believe it has compelling reasons to forbid crossdressing it must be explicit in justifying the prohibition and accompany it with education. Otherwise, the policy itself fosters a sense that transgender behavior is wrong and the people who do it are bad.

But what of situations where people know the law does *not* forbid public crossdressing and that, in fact, crossdressers are explicitly recognized as a class meriting protection from acts against them based on their gender identity or sexual orientation? Most behavior, even if colored by rejection or hostility, will seek to remain generally within the law. A sizable number of folk, though, skirt the law or violate it in small ways, or harbor attitudes at variance from the correct behavior they feel impelled to show publicly. Only a small minority ever act out more extreme responses. But this number would be substantially smaller if not for some aggressors sensing a tacit approval of their acts by many others.

Accordingly, a corrective response to negative public reactions, whether in behavior or attitude must be twofold: legal and educational. We have examined legal responses (the last question), so here we will focus on education. While we shall elaborate a little later on research about its effects with reference to attitudes concerning transgender realities, a preliminary remark or two are in place here. First, no teaching is value-free; the best teaching believes that accurate and honest conveyance of facts will reinforce the desirability of basic human values such as respect and tolerance. Educators need not feel compelled to push any agenda other than adhering to reason and evidence.

Second, historically educational efforts concerning transgender realities have progressively encouraged a socially more tolerant stance. For example, the long struggle of women to win the right to change what is deemed acceptable gender dress is evidence of how gender crossing behavior can come to be re-evaluated to the benefit of society. More accepting attitudes toward female crossdressing first meant less enforcement of laws against the behavior and finally abandonment of such statutes. Anticrossdressing ordinances, once drafted largely with women in mind, became relics of the past. Fewer and fewer places retain laws against crossdressing and even those that do widely ignore them—though crossdressing men may still be the exception. As attitudes change, laws against a behavior like crossdressing are first ignored, then repealed, and at last change to afford protection for those who engage in a behavior now seen as harmless at worst. This transition is where our society seems to presently be.

Some recent evidence suggests that the American public may be becoming more tolerant of the transgender community—or at least more willing to protect their basic human and civil rights. For example, as noted in the last answer, about three-quarters of Americans surveyed support broadening federal hate crime legislation to include protection for transgender people. Some legislative changes aimed at ensuring transgender folk the same rights and protections (not more) that other citizens possess now is in place (see the answer to Q. 36). In various states around the country (e.g., California, Florida, New York, and Texas), inclusionary safe schools legislation has been introduced.[770] These acts offer one indication of trends in attitudinal shifts.

Public attitudes have been probed by survey and interview research, too. A national poll commissioned by the Human Rights Commission, conducted with 800 randomly selected registered voters and 6 focus groups, and reported at the end of the Summer of 2002, reveals the following:

❑ more than three-quarters (77%) think transgendered children should be permitted to attend public schools;

- more than two-thirds (70%) are familiar with the term 'transgender';
- more than two-thirds (68%) support hate-crime laws inclusive of protection for transgendered people;
- more than two-thirds (67%) agree that it is possible for a person to be born of one biological sex but psychologically identify as a member of another sex;
- almost two-thirds (61%) agree to the need for legal protection from discrimination for members of the transgendered community; but,
- more than half (57%) incorrectly assume that present laws already protect transgendered people from being fired because of their transgender status; and,
- half (50%) agree that a transgendered adult should be allowed to hold a job teaching in a high school.[771]

Of course, these findings tell only part of the story. The same study finds that more than half (60%) do not agree that a transgendered adult should be allowed to hold a job teaching in an elementary school, serve as a scout master, or work in day care.[772] And in the nations schools the experience of transgender youth shows improvement in some respects (e.g., intervention by faculty and staff increased), but not in others (e.g., harassment and violence also increased).[773]

What is most worrisome for the transgender community is that some of the positive impression people reflect in the survey might be the result of a misapprehension of what it means to be transgendered. When provided a description of a 'transgender person,'[774] the percent of those who regard transgender people unfavorably rises by nearly a third, and rises by more than a quarter among those who regard transgenderism as "morally wrong."[775]

What is the value of education on transgender realities?

Yet the answer is not to hide facts from people. As gender historian Elizabeth Reis puts it, "Transgender is out of the closet, and it should be in the classroom as well."[776] And it should be seen by all of us as relevant, for as Reis points out, issues of gender identity and self-presentation affect us all—including those of us who see ourselves fitting neatly into a dominant gender.[777] Education—the presentation of reason and evidence in an open and balanced manner—can and does have a positive effect. That does not make it easy. We have seen already how educators themselves can be part of the problem. Increasingly, they are trying to be part of the solution.

A 2002 study reported in the *College Student Journal* finds that when college undergraduates are directly exposed to crossdressers and able to interact with them in a classroom setting, their discomfort with crossdressing diminishes. The study reports results gathered in 37 classes over a period from 1989-2002. During that time, students enrolled in human sexuality courses were exposed to crossdressing members of The Society for the Second Self (Tri-Ess), an organization offering support for crossdressers. Prior to meeting their guests, the students read information about crossdressing and formulated questions to ask. Participating Tri-Ess members provided autobiographical sketches and then students were encouraged to ask their questions. Afterward, the students were provided an opportunity through interviews and discussions to appraise what they had learned. Results obtained show widespread reduction of discomfort.[778]

However, not everyone may be affected equally by interactions with crossdressers. In a study reported in 2004, scholars Cindi Ceglian and Nancy Lyons examine whether an individual's gender type might affect the level of comfort with crossdressed men. A total of 157 undergraduate students (117 female; 40 male) were administered the Bem Sex Role Inventory (BSRI), which uses 60 characteristics to gender type a person as 'feminine,' 'masculine,' or 'gender-neutral' (i.e., androgynous). They also were tested with regard to their degree of comfort with crossdressing. After this testing, the students were exposed to two male crossdressers, who interacted with the students in a classroom setting. Then the students' levels of comfort were again measured. All three gender type groups show increased levels of comfort (or decreased levels of discomfort) after interacting with the crossdressers. The greatest degree of change proves to be among the male students, who initially were more negative than the female students, but whose scores become similar to those of the women after interacting with the crossdressing men.[779]

Especially in the case of transgender children and adolescents, more than education is needed. Formal policies against discrimination and harassment based on sexual orientation and/or gender identity are needed, with a firm commitment to enforcement of them. A 1999 *SIECUS Report* on sexual harassment points out that school districts permitted to develop their own policies are free to add such matters, and emphasizes that because provisions about sexual orientation do not cover gender identity that the latter should be expressly incorporated. The report also mentions that such action is important in light of the possibility of schools losing federal funding for failure to do enough to protect sexual minorities. Such policies need to extend to everyone within the school—students, faculty, staff, and administration.[780]

So, if we return to Buckner's observations cited at the beginning of our answer, we may well ask what all this means today. Most observers of the situation will concur that crossdressing is a more visible phenomenon now than it was in 1970. Increasing numbers of crossdressers have gone public, often through the relatively safe forum of the internet. Public awareness—and discussion—seem more pronounced than ever. In this climate there are both accepting and rejecting responses offered by non-crossdressers. The 'problem' of crossdressing is now being debated in a more vigorous way than at perhaps any other time in history. Whether or not the eventual result will be the according to transgender people a 'publicly sanctioned role' remains to be seen.

Q. 38

How do partners handle the crossdressing of their Significant Others?

The Short Answer. There is no one way individuals respond to a crossdressing partner. Reactions run the range from permanent rejection to public celebration. Most people, and most partners, find themselves somewhere in-between. Many share some common fears and concerns, and all quickly learn the paramount value of solid information. Knowledge is power—the power to cope with an unusual situation. Those relating to crossdressers (or to any transgender individual) occupy one or another of four basic statuses, each differentiated in two forms. For some partners their initial location in a particular status represents just the first phase, or stage, in a developmental process. While that process may be toward a better relationship, sometimes it is merely toward a redefined one, and sometimes it results in the ending of the relationship, either for a time or forever. Just as it is inappropriate to mandate how transgender people must be and relate, so it is inappropriate to mandate how their partners must be and relate, save for one universal mandate that ought to apply to us all—according to every person a basic dignity and respect.

The Longer Answer. Although not all crossdressers are involved in intimate relationships, many are. Intimate relationships pose challenges for as long as they endure. One such challenge is a crossdressing partner. Responses to such a partner are inevitably individualistic, but reflect the weight of cultural values as well as personal factors such as previous experiences and personality. No one sentence can summarize how a partner *will* respond, nor can anyone fairly say how someone *ought* to respond, save the caveat that all of us should be accorded respect and civil behavior.

What we know about partners and their responses comes from a variety of sources. First, crossdressers often recount their experience of what happens when a partner discovers their behavior. Second, much of what is known about the partners of crossdressers come from the partners themselves. There is a rich literature of first hand accounts, much of it accompanied by advice to others facing this situation. Finally, there is data acquired from social science research.

Though there has not been an abundance of such work, it is valuable as an alternative source that is likely more objective and more representative than what individual accounts can offer.[781]

How do partners respond?

Let's begin with a foundation. Research has consistently found that most crossdressing men are heterosexual and married.[782] That means spouses who may or may not know about their husband's behavior. Either way can be problematic, but much more so when behavior attempted to be kept secret becomes exposed. How do such marriages persist? There are probably as many answers as there are couples—and, of course, some don't survive, though the crossdressing may or may not be the cause or a significant factor.

In 1978, J. L. McCary, citing earlier research, offers one possible explanation: "Many transvestites are married and have masculine interests and hobbies; they are able to make successful marital adjustment due to the fact that crossdressing takes place only intermittingly . . . ."[783] Unfortunately, such a remark begs both the inference that the behavior remains largely or entirely secretive and that marriage means constraint or the relationship won't survive. In some cases this proves true, but not in all. The reality is more complex. But how can we know what that reality is? What is it like to have a crossdressing partner?

Response Statuses

Let us begin by proposing four basic response statuses, as follows:

❑ *Rejection*—the partner refuses to tolerate the transgender behavior:
  o *transient*—the partner's rejection is temporary and passes; or,
  o *permanent*—the partner's rejection persists.
❑ *Tolerance*—the partner puts up with at least some crossdressing:
  o *partial*—the partner agrees to endure some crossdressing, though without approval; or,
  o *complete*—the partner endures all crossdressing, but without approval.
❑ *Acceptance*—the partner favorably receives transgender behavior:
  o *conditional*—the partner's favor is conditioned in one respect or another; or,
  o *unconditional*—the partner's favor sets no conditions.
❑ *Celebration*—the partner supports and encourages transgender behavior:
  o *private*—the support and encouragement is qualified by a practical desire to keep the transgender behavior limited in exposure to others; or,
  o *public*—the support and encouragement extends to a willingness or desire to let others know that transgender behavior is good and welcomed.

The first and most important thing to remember in considering these statuses is this: each reflects a partner's response to transgender *behavior*. In other words, what is in view are the things done that cross gender lines, such as crossdressing. These statuses are not described in terms of how a partner responds to a transgender *identity*. We might expect that in most if not all cases these would be the same. However, most people find the idea of an internal identity more elusive than visible acts. A partner might, for example, in principle tolerate the notion that someone has a transgender identity but find the actual expression of that intolerable. Most of us find it easier to set aside from our conscious attention or judgment what is going on inside someone else as long as it doesn't dictate behavior we disapprove of. For these reasons all the following remarks have to do with partner responses to visible transgender behavior.

As pictured, each response status may take one or another of two basic forms. As a continuum, blurring at the boundaries of each status may occur, and they are permeable, with movement from one to another always a possibility. For some partners there may occur movement that constitutes what might be viewed as developmental progression. In such cases the partner, or others, sees the change in statuses as reflecting purposeful, directional movement. So, for example, a partner may begin in initial shock by expressing rejection. Put formally, we might say they reside in 'the status of rejection, transient type.' After the shock wears off, they may move to tolerance and, eventually, acceptance. A few embrace celebration.

Rejection may be transient or permanent. If it begins as transient—typically in a culturally conditioned shock response to an unexpected disclosure or discovery[784]—it may move either to permanent rejection or to some form of tolerance. It is hard to imagine transient rejection persisting very long. Likewise, it is difficult to imagine a person moving from transient rejection immediately to acceptance or celebration. Transient rejection serves as a status that simultaneously accomplishes at least three distinct ends: it expresses a ready-made cultural vehicle of response to transgender (one requiring no particular thought or preparation to use), it thus discharges the initial feeling and anxiety, and it fills time while the person sorts things out.

Transient rejection may lead to permanent rejection. The partner may concur with a negative social judgment, be unable to overcome strong negative feelings in one's own self, or simply find it too overwhelming a reality to want to cope with. In such instances, separation and ending of the relationship are almost inevitable. The qualifier 'almost' is applicable because the partner may issue an ultimatum, such as the crossdresser seeking therapy or voluntarily ending transgender behavior, which may save the relationship, at least for a time. Of course, transient rejection may also give way to tolerance.

Tolerance may be partial or complete. Tolerance, whether partial or complete, is characterized by endurance without approval. The partner agrees to the continuance of the behavior but offers neither sanction nor favor. In partial tolerance the partner draws limits with respect to the behavior that will be endured. That might mean the kind of crossdressing suffered (e.g., unseen under outerwear), and/or when it is permitted (e.g., only when the crossdresser is alone). Perhaps most tolerance is partial. Probably less often complete tolerance is offered, where the partner makes no attempt to set limits but endures whatever the transgender person does. In the latter case, depending upon how much internal adjustment the partner can make, the movement may be to rejection or to acceptance.

Acceptance may be conditional or unconditional. What differentiates acceptance from tolerance is that acceptance does not endure what is not favored, but rather receives the transgender behavior favorably. Where tolerance grants the transgender person the formal right to be who they are, at least to some extent, acceptance views being transgender as all right—different, perhaps, but not less human, nor mentally disordered, nor sinful or shameful. The qualitative difference between tolerance and acceptance is significant. A partner's internal feeling state is different.

In light of these remarks, it may seem illogical to speak of 'conditional' acceptance. But favor need not be unconditional and often in life is not. For example, a parent may show favor to a child's school behavior as long as it is compliant to school rules and successful in academic performance. In such a case, the parent's favor is conditioned; some degree of getting into trouble or bringing home poor grades may be tolerated, but it isn't accepted. Similarly, conditional acceptance of transgender behavior means favorably receiving some kinds of behavior and/or all behavior—but only at certain times or in certain contexts. For instance, a partner may think it a good thing for the crossdresser to be crossdressed, but not agree that it needs to be public. Thus a condition is set on the favorable reception.

Unconditional acceptance offers a favorable reception no matter the kind, degree, timing, or context of the transgender behavior. This kind of acceptance is harder for many partners to offer. Often what limits their acceptance is one or another fear, which we shall examine shortly. Of course, it is possible for a partner to move from partial to complete acceptance. But it is also possible to withdraw acceptance if some unforeseen, undesired outcome is the result. As with any other status, this one need not prove permanent. Some partners may change their feelings or perceptions and move from acceptance to tolerance. Others may move to celebration.

Anecdotal evidence and survey evidence alike suggests that the rarest status is *celebration*. This status may take either a private or a public form. In private celebration the partner offers full support and encouragement of transgender behavior, but desires for it to remain a private matter. This wish is not motivated by duplicity or shame, but by an appraisal that to be public would be unacceptably risky or dangerous. Public celebration means the partner not only supports and approves transgender behavior, but wishes that to be publicly known. Some such partners become active in efforts to educate the wider public or to change public policy and law to ensure equal treatment for all people.

Hopefully, reviewing these statuses raises the question as to what factors make it most likely a partner will occupy a particular status at a given time. To answer such a query requires examining several other matters. We will begin with certain themes that emerge from the research on partners.

Response Themes

Various sources suggest certain themes, such as the following:

❑ *Knowledge is power*—partners who acquire credible knowledge are more likely to understand transgender behavior and make informed decisions as to how to respond.

❑ *Secrecy is dangerous*—a partner kept in the dark stays in the dark, and one thrown suddenly into the light of a secret exposed well into a relationship is unlikely to make a favorable response.

❑ *Personal values and self-knowledge are critical*—a partner's personal values about identity, relationships, gender and sexuality will all influence a response to transgender behavior; when self-knowledge on these matters is weak, more difficulty in responding is likely.

First, as in most matters, *knowledge is power*. The more a crossdressing partner knows, the better the predicted outcome. Yet most partners—like most other members of the general public—know little, if anything, about crossdressing before finding themselves in relationship with a crossdresser. Richard Docter, in interviews with 21 wives of crossdressers, finds the vast majority (85%) either have little or misleading information prior to learning about their husband's behavior.[785]

Second, *secrecy is dangerous*. Secrets prevent equality and mutuality in a relationship. To equalize power in the relationship and promote trust there must be both an absence of secrets between the couple and reliable, factual information about crossdressing. Beyond understanding crossdressing, it is crucial for partners to also understand themselves. One aspect of this is being armed with knowledge about the group to which they belong—partners of crossdressers—so that they can combat a sense of isolation and resist the myths they may encounter.

Third, *personal values and self-knowledge are critical*; partners exposed to transgender behavior are especially confronted by the need to re-examine matters most of us take for granted without much examination even though they are so important to our identity and relationships. This offers an opportunity for change and growth. Those partners who are in close touch with their own values, who know themselves, are more likely to make choices they are confident about. Depending on how much they already value things like openness, tolerance, or acceptance, they may be more or less likely to reject transgender behavior. For example, a person who already champions acceptance of racial and religious diversity is more likely to accept transgender realities than someone who believes in rigid separation of groups with different characteristics. Personality qualities such as openness to experience also play a role. Self-knowledge matters, but is most likely to assist in responses keeping a relationship alive when the knowledge is accompanied by desires to learn more and to grow.

These themes merge at a starkly basic level: partners are faced with a choice—stay in the relationship, or leave. Making the best decision is largely predicated on how the themes described above come together. A relationship without secrets, where both parties seek understanding, and where each understands the self and is open to the other has a good prospect for continuing and growing. On an individual level, no less than for the transgendered person, the partner's success hinges on healthy personal values, resolving value conflicts within themselves, facing beliefs that may be erroneous, confronting fears, and exercising personal power. Just as much is at stake for the crossdresser, so also much is at stake for the partner.

Achieving Acceptance

For many partners the critical decision after a period of initial shock is whether to move to permanent rejection or to tolerance with the hope of someday being able to achieve acceptance. Of course, some choose tolerance with a different hope—that they will succeed in persuading the crossdresser to stop crossdressing. We will return to that idea shortly, but here we will take a moment to consider how a partner might move from tolerance to acceptance.

Obviously, the initial obstacle is the strong feeling that may be engaged. Let us consider two aspects to this. First, a partner's feelings complicate matters for the crossdresser. Understandably, the crossdresser will be affected by the rejection. Though there are any number of ways a response might occur, we might do well to remember that since crossdressing often is employed to reduce stress, increased stress may prompt *more*, not less crossdressing. Psychiatrist John Bancroft (director of the Kinsey Institute) says his impression from clients is that early in a relationship crossdressing may diminish. However, he goes on to remark, "When problems arise in the relationship or marriage, particularly sexual difficulties, the urge to cross-dress returns and over a number of years may fluctuate as the success of the marital relationship varies."[786]

Second, feelings complicate matters for the partner, too. Many of us permit our feelings great power over our decision-making. Certainly feelings matter. They are a source of information. At the same time, they are only *one* source of information. Prizing feelings above other facts can lead to poor outcomes. Strong feelings may seem compelling merely because they are strong. Yet even strong feelings have trouble sustaining themselves for long and have to be actively renewed by certain thoughts to keep their intensity. This process means that interrupting one's thoughts, or changing them, can rob a feeling of much of its power. In fact, changing one's *mind* about something can change one's *heart* as well. If a partner desires to achieve acceptance, then strong feelings must be challenged. But how does this happen?

First, and foremost, the above themes must be engaged. A conviction that knowledge is power, and that such power can be achieved, is essential. Without a sense of control that comes from understanding rather than manipulating the environment to control exposure a genuine balance and health in the relationship will not happen. To attain such understanding means not merely knowing about crossdressing and other transgender realities pertinent to the situation, but specifically knowing about the partner's experience and expression of these. In other words, to overcome secrecy and keep open channels both parties must engage in disclosure and in questioning. Partners need to feel free to ask whatever they like and to express their fears (to which we will soon turn). When these things take place, a reexamination of personal values may find shifts based on new knowledge and the trust encouraged by disclosures freely given and received. One sign of health and growth in any individual is a willingness to reexamine personal beliefs, challenge exposed stereotypes, and develop more humane values. In the relational climate being described here, this should go on in *both* parties.

It may appear that the above, truthful though it might be, remains too general to be as helpful as what a partner desires. Therefore, let us add to it some rather specific suggestions. Psychological science has found that upsetting stimuli diminish in their power the more we are exposed to them. For example, people with a morbid anxiety of spiders can overcome that through calculated exposure to spiders where their experience slowly erodes the irrational fear that something bad will happen. They *habituate* to the stimuli. Our bodies aren't built to stay in highly aroused states of anxiety and after a period of exposure, when nothing bad happens except our anxiety, the anxiety diminishes. This same idea can be put into practice dealing with crossdressing.

A partner can either choose what is called 'flooding'—a sudden and full exposure to the crossdressing—or 'progressive' exposure. In the latter, which seems most often a better choice, exposure to the crossdressing proceeds in an orderly fashion. The following steps might be helpful:
1. Start slowly by reading about crossdressing without bothering to look at pictures of crossdressed individuals.
2. After anxiety over the subject diminishes to a tolerable level, talk to one's crossdressing partner about what crossdressing means to him (or her). Do this when the person is not crossdressed. Ask questions.[787]
3. After achieving enough comfort about the subject that anxiety is manageable when doing so, move on to visual material. Start by gaining permission to look at the crossdressing partner's outerwear. This can be done with or without discussion. But it should start without the clothes being looked at being worn at the time.
4. Next (or as an alternative), go on the internet and look at pictures of ordinary people crossdressed. Be warned: many of the images (particularly of 'she-males') are designed to be sexually explicit. Since these are

likely to be upsetting, choose search terms carefully. For example, if you have Mozilla's Firefox search engine, select Google images and then use the 'Preferences' option to filter content in order to avoid sexually explicit images. Next, enter in the search box 'crossdresser photos.' With filtering in place this should result in a selection of thumbnail photos of mostly ordinary people in different styles of dress. Selecting a thumbnail will result in going to the webpage where the photo is posted. In this manner control is retained of what one looks at (and even anxiety-provoking photos will initially display as small).

5. After becoming accustomed to seeing pictures of other people cross-dressed, try exposure to one's partner when crossdressed. In order to maximize a sense of control over one's feelings in an anxiety-provoking situation, perhaps this can be done by selecting in advance what the partner will wear. Stay with the exposure, while talking to the cross-dressed partner, long enough for the initial anxiety to diminish in strength.

6. Repeated, planned, and controlled exposures will rob anxiety of its power. Once that is reduced significantly, or eliminated, the crossdressing stimuli may be seen in new light.

Partners may never grasp emotionally what crossdressing means to a loved one. But if they can defeat the power of anxiety elicited by crossdressing then they have a chance to construct something more positive than mere tolerance. Since acceptance means coming to value in some degree the behavior, and not feeling negatively about it, time, patience, and empathy (imaginatively putting one's self in the other person's place and trying to feel what they feel) are all needed. Winning acceptance in one's self, if chosen as a goal, is worth taking time and effort to achieve. But in addition to some of the kinds of things just discussed, there are other factors meriting attention.

In what follows, I have attempted to draw on the existing literature to address many of the matters useful in coping with a crossdressing partner. Because I anticipate that more of those partners reading this book are—at least for now—choosing to remain with the crossdresser, more attention is given to that open and ongoing choice than to the decision to leave.

How needed is knowledge?

The need for accurate information emerges as the most fundamental requirement for partners of crossdressers to cope with their situation. Of course, among the kinds of information useful to a partner are reliable facts about transgender people, including ideas about why they are the way they are, and how they are like or different from other people. But it needs to also include reliable facts about other partners of transgender people, including the unique challenges they face in a disapproving society. Other types of knowledge may be useful, too, like what we know regarding families with transgender members.

However, the necessary information really starts with knowing the behavior exists—and knowing sooner rather than later. The famous sexologist Harry Benjamin puts it bluntly: "No transvestite should ever marry a girl without telling her of his peculiarity beforehand."[788] Psychiatrist George Brown finds this most basic of information plays a critical role. When discovery of crossdressing is delayed it can lead to profound feelings of betrayal and lost trust.[789]

Secrecy is the principal obstacle. Most crossdressers adopt this secrecy in childhood, and relinquishing it in adulthood isn't easy. But often, necessary things in life are not easy—and this is one of the necessary things for anyone hopeful a long-term relationship will be built and sustained on trust. The facts in this matter are relatively straightforward: [1] most crossdressing men don't tell before a committed relationship exists and [2] most partners eventually find out about the behavior.

The following table illustrates the basics, reaffirmed in study after study:

Table 38.1 Partner Awareness of Crossdressing

Study	Number of subjects	% of partners knowing about the crossdressing	% of partners knowing before marriage
Prince & Bentler (1972)[790]	504	80%	28%
Lind (1978-1980)[791]	43	100%	30%
Wise, Dupkin & Meyer (1980)[792]	18	100%	28%
Docter (1988)[793]	35	100%	29%
Coleman (1996)[794]	414	74%	unreported
Docter & Prince (1997)[795]	1032	83%	33%
Yvonne (1999)[796]	897	76%	34%
Forge (2002)[797]	101	88%	unreported

Not telling and then being found out diminishes the likelihood of a supportive partner; those told, suggests one study, are much more likely to be supportive (65%) than those who find out otherwise (44%).[798]

Why wouldn't a crossdresser tell the most significant person in his or her life? Consider this: Betty Ann Lind reports that when asked if they would have still married knowing of the crossdressing beforehand, virtually all partners say, "I don't know."[799] Perhaps such a conclusion is why crossdressers are unlikely to confess their behavior until the relationship is well-established by a commitment of marriage. Then the partner may be asked—implicitly if not explicitly—

to help keep the secret. One wife, who only found out about her husband's crossdressing after 24 years of marriage, speaks to a reality many partners know:

> What I thought was a good stable life was blown up, into pieces. We talked for hours, and to this day, I really can't remember all that we said. But I do remember that I just wanted to run away, but my husband held on to me tightly. Before we left the motel, there was one rule that we can never break. And that is, that none of our family or friends will ever know about this.[800]

Obviously, as witnessed in the pain of the woman above, the entrance of crossdressing into a relationship can be a matter of great gravity. The very fact that her partner has held a secret most of his life bears testimony to the power behind it. But it also hints that this is a matter about which knowledge may be hard to acquire—and that seeking it may come at a risk. To whom can the partner turn? Transgender pioneer Virginia Prince writes in the Foreword to *The Crossdresser and His Wife*:

> A wife who has the motivation for a truly happy marriage will want to put whatever effort is necessary into it; but where understanding is required she is helpless without some information and knowledge to base it on. All transvestic husbands try to impart this knowledge but wives tend to discredit their explanations as rationalizations and self serving.[801]

If true, where does that leave the partner? Many are too embarrassed by behavior they do not understand to seek knowledge in public venues like bookstores or libraries. Even less acceptable would be talking to someone; though confused and uncertain most partners of crossdressers still are careful to guard 'the secret.' So, whether distrustful or not of whatever explanations the crossdresser may offer (and such explanations are often sparse and vague), there seems little else to rely upon. And that can create problems.

Helen Boyd, in writing about her experiences being married to a crossdresser, is candid about the added burden those like herself carry. She notes that in our culture women are socialized to accommodate men and their eccentricities. But crossdressing by a spouse pushes beyond normal bounds. This sets up new challenges and every partner discovers in the process the extent of their own limits. Still, in Boyd's experience, the vast majority of partners of male crossdressers rise to the challenge.[802]

But for success in any relationship, initial knowledge alone is not enough. There remains the need for ongoing dialog between the crossdresser and the spouse. In their booklet *He, She, We, They* a group of partners of male crossdressers emphasize that one theme repeatedly emerges from a questionnaire administered to partners of crossdressers: *talk*. And they meant more than confront; answers included terms like 'discuss,' 'negotiate,' 'compromise,' and 'keep on working on it.' Negative reactions need to be balanced by positive input.[803]

What about counseling and/or support groups?

There may be considerable shock following discovery. The questionnaire that provided data for the booklet *He, She, We, They* finds a range of emotional responses. They include feeling stress, anger, fear, uncertainty and rejection. But they also include feelings of acceptance, understanding, and love.[804] There is no 'right' or 'wrong' way to feel; one feels what one feels. It is the *behavior* that follows the feeling that proves decisive for what happens to the relationship.

Some individuals turn to counselors for help. While finding the right counselor is a challenging task at any time, finding one well-educated on transgender issues can be particularly challenging. Some therapists are not only hostile to crossdressers, but unsympathetic to their partners. It is always a good idea to be straightforward at the start in asking about the counselor's educational background, especially with regard to any training on transgender issues. It also is only fair to find out immediately what, if any, biases the counselor may hold toward transgender people.

In terms of counseling issues, psychotherapist Kathleen Cairns notes that the range of adjustment partners make to the situation of crossdressing is very wide, with those going to a therapist because of their unhappiness over the crossdressing only a subgroup of the whole.[805] Thus an initial task for the therapist is understanding how the partner has coped with the situation. In some instances, the coping mechanisms used have been unproductive, including hostility, depression, and alcohol abuse. So another important therapeutic task is increasing understanding of the partner's behavior and finding better ways to cope.[806]

Cairns recommends attention to the following issues and tasks in the process of counseling a client who identifies a partner's crossdressing as the source of her or his unhappiness:

- ❑ *Vocabulary*—the therapist needs to discover, and follow, the choice preferred to describe the crossdresser's behavior (e.g., 'transvestism,' or the more commonly preferred 'crossdressing').
- ❑ *Fact-based reassurance*—clients commonly present with fears based on misinformation (e.g., their loved one is gay; crossdressing will be inherited by their children), which a therapist can correct with accurate information.
- ❑ *Candidness*—therapists must avoid reinforcing client hopes that will likely prove unfulfilled (e.g., that the crossdresser can be cured, or the situation will remain stable), or offering certain answers where uncertainty is more realistic (e.g., speculation on the outcome if the children are told about the crossdressing, or if the crossdresser's behavior is discovered by others).
- ❑ *Support of emotional expression*—clients need the safety to feel what they feel (e.g., grief, disgust, betrayal) and convey that in the coun-

seling process; resolution of unhappiness or of marital problems is unlikely without permitting such release.

❑ *Reckoning of consequences*—the crossdressing by the loved one may mean for the client a number of felt consequences such as a sense of a loss of freedom and social isolation; feelings may develop into resentment over what crossdressing is perceived to be doing (e.g., taking away time and money from the family).

❑ *Patience*—adjustment that leads to staying together with relief from the unhappiness may take considerable time; early exposure through support groups to others whose acceptance of crossdressing is greater may generate despair in the client so such exposure is best used toward the end of therapy.[807]

Some couples also seek counseling together. An online survey in 1999 reports that almost 15% of respondents who have been married, are married, or are in a relationship try marriage counseling. Perhaps surprisingly, only 39% of respondents say it is the wife who suggests they go to counseling; it proves about as likely to be a mutual decision (40%). While almost three-quarters (72%) feel their counselor is accepting of crossdressing, most (62%) do not find the counseling helpful, and four-fifths (80%) go less than a year.[808]

For partners of crossdressers, transgender therapist Gianna Israel offers the following advice:

> Encouraging a spouse to view differences in people as a positive characteristic can be an asset to any relationship. While not every significant other likes the idea that their husband (or wife) crossdresses, they often benefit from this person's sensitivity and willingness to understand other's needs. Finally, in a broader educational view, many people do not understand that crossdressing provides a healthy emotional release for those who do so. People do not crossdress to destroy other people's lives or bring devastation into their own. They crossdress because it fulfills an inner need that nothing else can fulfill.[809]

Yet, as accurate at Israel's advice may be, we would be wrong to dismiss partners who turn away from their loved one's crossdressing as 'weak' or 'faithless.' As Annie Woodhouse warns, it can be too easy to 'blame the victim.'[810] In reality, *both* crossdresser and partner are victims of an inflexible gender system, social ignorance, and a fear of intolerance from others. What may prove decisive in the struggle to adjust and manage the situation is finding connection with each other and with others facing these issues. Support for the partner can be a potent assist in dealing with living with a crossdresser. Support groups can help a partner overcome the profound alienation and isolation that follows discovery of crossdressing.[811] Generally, partners do not actively seek a crossdresser; they suddenly discover that is whom they have. How they handle the knowledge reflects a variety of personal factors. It is time we turn to some of these.

What are some characteristics of partners of crossdressers ?

George Brown, in perhaps the largest study of its kind, gathered data from 106 women over a six year span. Instruments used in his research to accumulate information include a questionnaire and interviews with three-quarters of the women. Although nearly 75% are married to their crossdressing husband at the time of the research, all are involved at present with crossdressing men. They range in age from 19-69 years old. Their relationships range in duration from 2 weeks to 46 years (average length of 13.1 years). Most (60%) did not find out about the crossdressing behavior until they had been in the relationship for some time.[812]

In comparison to the general population, these women are:

- ❏ more likely to be a first-born child;
- ❏ more likely to be childless;
- ❏ more likely to be slightly overweight, and,
- ❏ more likely to hold at least a 2 year college degree.[813]

On the other hand, these women are *not* more likely to abuse alcohol[814]— apparently, a crossdressing partner does not drive a woman to drink!

Nor are women who are in relationships with crossdressers suffering from character flaws.[815] Brown's study addresses earlier speculation that crossdressers' partners are women suffering from low self-esteem and high dependency.[816] Instead, he finds such traits are not general characteristics of such women.[817] Similarly, Richard Docter does not find this to be true of the group of 21 spouses he interviewed and tracked over four years.[818] Brown proposes instead the following view: "An alternative hypothesis to deficient self-esteem would be that these women have high levels of openness, a personality trait that fosters novel ideas and rejection of rigid stereotypes."[819]

On the other hand, in a smaller study featuring interviews with five women with crossdressing spouses, feminist Annie Woodhouse reports rather less openness and rather more endorsing of conventional expectations. She identifies as a common theme among these five "their attachment to traditional notions of gender roles and appearance."[820] Since these women are relatively negative toward crossdressing, it seems likely that this attachment to convention complicates how accepting they can be.

In a far larger study, researchers Vern Bullough and Thomas Weinberg explore the area of the female partner's self-esteem. They interviewed 70 women married to a crossdressing husband. They report a correlation between adjustment to the crossdressing and self-esteem. Women with high self-esteem rate their marriages as happier than do those with low self-esteem. Among these women, a feeling of control over their own life is critical; those who feel such control possess higher self-esteem. But women with lower self-esteem do not feel such power, worry over public exposure, and tend to view themselves as failures in their role as wives.[821]

Which partners leave?

Clearly, some partners decide that crossdressing behavior pushes past the limits of their tolerance. They choose to end the relationship. Transgender therapist Gianna Israel observes, "Introduction of crossdressing and gender issues into the family has often been the catalyst for parents separating or divorcing. Simply put, in many circumstances it is difficult to maintain a marriage commitment which does not fulfill both adult parties' needs."[822]

How many choose this path? The answer is impossible to know for the same reason that these people often do not seek information: they find the matter too shameful to discuss. Thus it remains a matter of pure speculation how many people placed in this situation choose escape rather than trying to work through whatever difficulties they identify.

On the other hand, there is some knowledge that clues us in as to how common a reaction leaving might be. Brown's study finds that even among those who choose to remain in a committed relationship with a crossdresser, many have entertained thoughts of leaving. In fact, Brown finds that nearly one-third (32%) have "seriously considered" separation or divorce based "wholly, or substantially, on his cross-gender interests/activities."[823] Clearly, many women find the crossdressing of their partner a serious obstacle, at least initially.

Which partners remain?

Among those who choose to stay—often even despite their doubts, fears, and misgivings—there remains a range of acceptance of the partner's behavior. Although meanings of 'accept' vary from one study to another, and while some research is based on the perception of crossdressers rather than their partners, the following table shows that many partners who stay with their crossdressing men do achieve some kind of acceptance:

Table 38.2 Partner Acceptance of Crossdressing

Study	#	Who reported	Accepting/ Supportive	Midway Responses	Non-accepting
Prince & Bentler (1972)[824]	504	men	23% "completely accepting"	57%	20% "completely rejecting"
Talamini (1982)[825]	50	wives	60%	--	40%
Docter (1988)[826]	35	wives	43%	20%	37%

Brown (1994)[827]	106	wives	39% "high ac-ceptors"	25% "moderate acceptors"	19% "low accep-tors"
Coleman (1996)[828]	414	men	43%	--	57%
Docter & Prince (1997)[829]	1032	men	28% "completely accepting"	47%	19% "completely rejecting"
Yvonne (1999)[830]	691	men	59% (19% "completely accepting")		41% (14% "completely rejecting")

Interestingly, in Brown's study 44% of the women think they should be *more* accepting; only 8% believe they are too accepting.[831]

Perhaps remarkably, given the social stigma, more than one-fifth (22%) of the women in Brown's study think they would support their partner if he sought to pursue further feminizing, such as by estrogen treatment or sex reassignment surgery.[832] Of course, almost all (96%) of these women do not believe the partner will ever seek sex reassignment surgery.[833]

In contrast to those who choose to leave, those who choose to remain occasionally are very vocal about why and how they do so. This has produced a body of material recounting the experience of living with a crossdresser. As might be expected, women living with crossdressing men write the bulk of this material.[834] These accounts can be very useful to others—if they can access them. Inasmuch as that is often problematic, I have decided to draw on some of these writings both to illustrate common issues and possible responses, and to point the way to sources for further research.

Many partners find ways to integrate a partner's crossdressing behavior into the total fabric of the relationship. Among the most noted writers about cross-dressing is one such partner: Peggy Rudd. In the Introduction to one of her books she writes:

> For nine years I have been married to a crossdresser, a man who enjoys wearing women's clothing. In the case of my husband it is frequently my clothing that is worn. Does that seem strange to you? I must admit that it was difficult for me to comprehend this most unusual practice. There was a time when I wished that some morning I would wake up and the whole crossdressing situation would be gone forever.
>
> Today the expression, 'Clothes don't make the man,' has a new meaning for us. My husband is as loveable in my clothes as in his. In fact he seems to be a more complete person when

the feminine side of his personality is openly expressed by wearing feminine clothes. For me acceptance and understanding have been accomplished by reading, interacting with others who crossdress, and being sensitive to my husband and his needs. . . .[835]

Echoing this positive sentiment is Rachel Miller, who points to an unexpected plus that relationship to a male crossdresser may entail. She contends, "Women are disappointed in relationships where men are reluctant to engage in intimacy. As a group, transvestites tend to be more sensitive than typical males."[836]

What are some beliefs partners may hold?

Various beliefs may complicate the relationship a partner has with a crossdresser. Among such beliefs might be the following:

- ❑ My partner can be cured of his crossdressing.
- ❑ I'll never be able to be more accepting or tolerant than I am now.
- ❑ My partner can be cured of his crossdressing.

A relatively common belief a partner may have concerns the possibility the crossdresser may cease crossdressing. Lind's interviews report that the majority of crossdressers' wives who know about the crossdressing before marriage think that marriage will cure it.[837] Brown's study finds that 25% of the women initially believe a 'cure' might be found for the crossdressing. This belief dissipates over time for almost all of them.[838] Once more knowledge is essential (see the answer to question 95); understanding both the nature and prognosis for crossdressing can help alleviate negative feelings by a partner concerning any self-reproach for being unable to get a loved one to stop crossdressing.

'I'll never be able to be more accepting or tolerant than I am now.' Imagine being well into a committed relationship and discovering something that causes you to question if you have ever really known the person you are with. That is exactly the situation many women find themselves in. In the midst of the shocked surprise it can scarcely be wondered that they may say, 'I'll never be able to be more accepting or tolerant than I am now.' And right now they may not be very accepting!

Yet time dulls the effects of surprise and heals many wounds. Human beings have a marvelous ability to habituate to all kinds of situations without a permanent decrease in their levels of happiness or satisfaction.[839] Indeed, Brown reports in his research that partners of crossdressers frequently do become more accepting over time. He writes:

[M]any women develop very different views/attitudes towards cross-dressing, likely due in part to the dispelling of myths and misinformation, reassessment of the relationship, and broader participation in CD social activities. . . . [T]he overall trend observed was for greater acceptance over time, assuming that the woman obtained accurate information and access to other women living in similar circumstances.[840] For partners who want their relationship to survive, such finds are reassuring.

What are some fears partners may have?

Some of the fears partners of crossdressers may encounter may be phrased in these queries:

❑ Is my partner homosexual?
❑ Will my partner want to go all the way and change his/her sex?
❑ What if others find out?
❑ What does it say about me that I am in such a relationship?
❑ Does my partner expect me to help him in his/her crossdressing?

Each of these fears merits a response.

Is my partner homosexual?

Janet Davies and Ellen Janosik warn nursing students that, "Some wives who discover that their husbands are transvestites mistakenly assume that their husbands are homosexual."[841] Of course, many people erroneously assume that a male crossdresser is homosexual—including not a few uninformed health providers. It should be no surprise, then, that a spouse might at least wonder about the matter. But, as we saw earlier (see the answers to Q. 26, 35) most crossdressers identify themselves as heterosexual, and this is especially true among those who are married. Indeed, the classic survey of more than 500 male crossdressers published in 1972 reports 89% characterize their sexual orientation as heterosexual.[842] A 1997 study patterned on this earlier research, but utilizing more than twice the pool of subjects, finds an almost identical rate: 87%.[843] A 1983 study finds that 82% of transvestite men say they are more sexually attracted to women.[844] In sum, research consistently finds a heterosexual orientation for most crossdressers.

Will my partner want to go all the way and change his/her sex?

Perhaps the greatest fear a partner of a crossdresser might experience is that the crossdressing is just a stop along the way to a sex change operation. Indeed, a common joke in the transgendered community asks, 'What is the difference between a transvestite and a transsexual?' The answer: 'About two years—or maybe one.' But while it might be correct to say that all transsexuals crossdress, it is neither logical nor factual to reverse the equation and claim that all crossdressers are transsexual. As seen above, this fear is actually rare—the vast majority of women do not think their partners will seek sex reassignment surgery. But for those who do have such a fear, it is no less real for being uncommon.

Helen Boyd is frank about the fear engendered by the thought of a crossdressing partner wanting to do more than just change clothes. What if a partner wants also to change sex? Is crossdressing just a 'slippery slope' to sexual reassignment? Though in her looking into the matter she encountered arguments that transvestism and transsexualism are completely separate realities, she also found evidence that sometimes crossdressers who initially seem to be transvestites ultimately pursue sex changes. Hence, such fear is not completely unfounded.[845]

On the other hand, it should not be exaggerated. A comparative study including 65 male transvestites and 33 transsexuals reports a pronounced difference in respect to desire and behavior to change sex. Less than half of transvestites (47%) hold any interest in a sex change, and of those who do only a miniscule number (2%) are actually favorably inclined toward surgery. In fact, of those who have some interest, nearly half (46%) have looked into the possibility and rejected it. On the other hand, one-quarter (25%) of these men have at one time or another taken sex hormones.[846] In his study of over 400 adult British males, physician Vernon Coleman finds that more than three-quarters (77%) say they would not have a sex change operation even if the opportunity presented itself.[847]

Finally, it should be noted that some women choose to be with partners who are transsexuals. Some remain with a marriage partner even after the husband has undergone sex reassignment surgery.[848] Others are content to be married to 'penisless men.' A Canadian study of 41 female-to-male (FtM) transsexuals (ages 18-63), and 21 female partners, finds them in stable and long-term relationships. In fact, in many cases the FtM seeks a partner who already has children so as to fulfill a desire to be a parent.[849] In the range of human experience and relationships, some people are capable of finding satisfaction in situations that others find unimaginable.

What if others find out?

The fear of discovery may be simply fear of being embarrassed (if crossdressing is seen as shameful), or fear of being harmed by others. Such harm can range from isolation to violence. Interestingly, Peggy Rudd, herself partner to a crossdresser, finds in her research with 850 crossdressers that their greatest fear is over the potential harm that might come to their loved ones.[850] If nothing else, then, this is one fear the parties are likely to have in common.

Docter discovered the most commonly mentioned fear among his survey subjects is having the husband's crossdressing discovered by a visitor. Yet, while nearly three-quarters (71%) of the wives mention this fear, its average weighting on a 7 point scale (0 being "no problem"; 6 being a "very great problem") is only a 3.7—midway between "a moderate problem—not especially difficult," and "a difficult problem."[851] Indeed, it may be that the underlying concern is not what others will think of the husband, but of the woman living with him. This leads to the next fear.

What does it say about me that I am in such a relationship?

One fear a partner might have is that being in a relationship with a cross-dresser might indicate that she herself is homosexual. In truth, gender identity therapist Deborah Feinbloom speculates that some female partners of cross-dressers may be latent homosexuals, unable to consciously acknowledge lesbian tendencies but able to act on them through relationship with a male cross-dresser.[852] Moreover, therapists Sally Hunt and Terri Main, in interviews with four wives of transvestites and transsexuals, do find sexual orientation confusion among the wives of transvestites, but not the spouses of transsexuals.[853] Yet Brown's study finds that women married to crossdressers are *not* more likely than other women to have engaged in a homosexual experience.[854] Other research seems to indicate the same. This fear, then, appears unfounded for the majority of partners.

On the other hand, a partner's fears may not be so specific. They may have general doubts about their sexuality or sexual identity.[855] Or, their concerns may not have anything to do with sexuality but rather be of a more ambiguous nature and attached to vague worries about what others might think and say should the word get out. Annie Woodhouse writes:

> Given the stigma attached to transvestism, wives often fear that this will rub off on them, along the lines of, 'Well, they'll think I'm stupid/weak/pathetic/perverted to want to stay with him.' Thus it becomes difficult for women to find out about the little support that does exist, and this difficulty is intensified by their fear of ridicule and censure.[856]

The partners of crossdressers who provided answers to the questionnaire for the booklet *He, She, We, They* also have concerns about exposure. The authors write:

> Very few, if any, partners when presented with this question could give a positive answer. The majority of partners experienced feelings ranging from simple reluctance to mortification. The thought of family and friends discovering the secret is absolutely frightening. The fear of ridicule and rejection could become reality. This is something that should be thoroughly discussed between the cross-dresser and his partner and it is not to be taken lightly.[857]

Bullough and Weinberg find in their interviews with 70 spousal partners that such fears accompany low self-esteem and a lack of feeling control over one's own life.[858] Perhaps while this may be more generally or especially true for partners already low in self-esteem, this kind of fear can touch even the most self-assured. In an ideal world, such women might find the freedom to embrace their own inherent worth and value without regard for what others think. But in this world, with all its pettiness and judgments, a fear like this can be well-founded.

So why would any woman find herself in a relationship with a crossdressing man? And being found in one, risking hostile judgments from others, why would she stay? Docter hypothesizes that the following four traits characterize the kind of man a women who marries a crossdresser is looking for:

- [ ] a good provider;
- [ ] an undemanding sexual partner;
- [ ] conventional in attitudes; and,
- [ ] both controlled and cautious in relationships.

But, he contends, since she is herself likely to be sexually reserved and conventional in her thinking, the discovery of her husband's crossdressing constitutes a significant shock—and challenge.[859]

Rather differently, in summing up what he discovers among his subjects, Brown offers the following speculation:

> These women may therefore be attracted to partners who have increased capacities for soothing and other "traditionally feminine" interpersonal characteristics, e.g., warmth, tenderness, understanding, and empathy. Women married to CD mates often report that those features are very attractive to them and are present in their husbands, at least during the time they engage in CD activities . . . .[860]

This echoes pioneering sexologist Havelock Ellis' observation that a crossdressing man more often than not is "most tenderly and sympathetically devoted to his wife," and excels in bringing a refined and sensitive nature to the relationship.[861] In short, then, like the rest of us, partners generally stay because the benefits outweigh the risks and potential costs.

Does my partner expect me to help him in his/her crossdressing?

Partners of crossdressers are no different from the rest of us in respect to a healthy caution about the different and the unknown. Faced with crossdressing, shock may be followed by doubt and concern. If a loved one has revealed this behavior—or been caught in it—does this now mean it has to become a part of everyday life for the partner? Or does crossdressing go back into the closet? In short, has a line been crossed that cannot be undone and which forever alters the relationship?

There are no uniform or universal answers to such questions. Every relationship is unique. What works for one couple can prove disastrous for another. The reality is that responses range across the spectrum. Some crossdressers do go back into the closet and the couple pretends what was discovered never happened. Other couples agree that the crossdresser's business is personal and the partner wants to neither know about it or participate in it—a form of tolerance without acceptance. Still others accept it into the relationship in some form and to some degree. This may be either very limited or more extensive. There are even couples where the crossdresser's partner actively joins in clothes shopping and appears in public with the crossdresser while he or she is crossdressed.

Like so many other matters in a relationship, crossdressing may be a behavior where negotiation needs to occur. Indeed, it often does. Practically, though, this often just means what a partner is willing to put up with; the degree to which they will 'permit' the behavior. Prince and Bentler's 1972 survey results reveal that husbands report varying degrees of "permissiveness" by their spouses: 12% allow crossdressing only at home but are willing to witness it, while 21% permit crossdressing as long as they don't have to see it.[862] The 1999 online survey reports that 11% of partners can accept the crossdressing, but don't want to see it. Another 9% accept it as long as it is at home. A fraction more than 5% are willing to go out in public with the crossdressed partner.[863] Coleman's 1996 report finds that nearly two-thirds (63%) of his respondents do not have partners willing to help them choose makeup, clothes or other items.[864]

Docter discovers in his survey that of the 26 problems identified by spouses, the one with the most weight concerns the husband's desire for his wife to assist him in crossdressing or makeup. Yet while this problem attains an average weighting as "difficult," it is only reported by 20% of the wives. In fact, the problem with the next closest weighting—reported by 40% of the spouse— concerns how difficult the husband is to live with when blocked from crossdressing![865] Clearly, navigating the waters of how much involvement a partner might take in a spouse's crossdressing is a matter of avoiding the Scylla of uncomfortable over-involvement and the Charybdis of a self-defeating opposition.

What happens to the sexual relationship?

Of course, to this point we have danced around an issue—and often a fear—central to a long term, intimate relationship: the sexual relating. Helen Boyd, not only partner to a crossdresser but an avid student of partner issues, observes her finding that often crossdressers still keep some important secrets after their crossdressing becomes known. In her view, the most likely candidate for such a secret concerns their sexuality. Specifically, they don't own up to an erotic element in crossdressing.[866]

On the other hand, one problem in our sex-obsessed culture is interpreting *any* pleasurable association with crossdressing as sexual in nature. For many crossdressers there is a general sense of well-being and specific pleasure in being crossdressed. That can carry over in a sexual setting to erotic pleasure. The one feeling merges into the other. Of course, partners may be oblivious to this fact.

Still, Boyd may be right that many are motivated by a fear of being perceived as fetishists. In our culture it is difficult to admit being aroused by wearing clothes and *not* thereby being branded a pervert. But such a characterization oversimplifies the matter for most crossdressers. Even noncrossdressers typically are aroused by sexy clothing, and some try on a lover's lingerie as part of occasional sexual play. For crossdressers, being crossdressed may enhance the sexual experience for another reason—it allows participating in the most intimate connection with another person in a manner that best facilitates the experience and expression of themselves as a gendered and sexual being.

What separates sexual fetishism from nonfetishistic sexual behavior is whether the stimulus is *necessary* and *sufficient*. If the partner is inconsequential because it is being crossdressed that matters, then transvestic fetishism is present. What may muddy the waters, though, is a situation where the crossdresser insists on crossdressing during sexual relations, but still desires such relations with the partner. In this case it may seem the crossdressing is necessary but not sufficient. Investigation into *why* this is important to the crossdresser can be beneficial. If it is because the crossdresser desires to be crossdressed in order to be fully self-realized, then it stands to reason that apart from this condition the crossdresser may still be able to sexually perform, still love and desire the partner, but remain to some degree sexually unfulfilled.

Clearly this poses an issue both parties must grapple with. In some instances the crossdresser may be open to compromise, crossdressing on some occasions of lovemaking and refraining at other times, or limiting what is worn, or submitting to a partner's approval of clothing. But compromise and negotiation require both parties. Some partners may be willing; others may be reluctant or refuse to do so. Therapist Arlene Istar Lev points out what some may see as an uncomfortable truth, but others will celebrate: partners vary in their flexibility in adjusting to their sexual relationship after learning their lover is a transgender person. Lev acknowledges some people have little flexibility when it comes to sexual desire; others find ease in dealing with their lover's reality.[867]

One thing is reasonably sure: while a few relationhips can move from having been sexual to being nonsexual, most that go that route do not endure. If the parties desire to pursue a successful sexual relationship, honest conversation and negotiation seem indispensable. If the needs of either party are entirely set aside, a festering dissatisfaction is likely to erode the relationship. For some partners this may be or become the chief obstacle in keeping the relationship, and it is beyond the scope of this brief coverage to do more than encourage the basic human instinct to strive together in truth and in love.

What are the outcomes in relationships?

Outcomes in relationships with crossdressers are as varied as in any other relationship. As I tell my graduate students in counseling: People enter relationships for all kinds of reasons, stay in relationships for all kinds of relationships, and leave relationships for all kinds of reasons.

Not surprisingly, crossdressers who can be characterized as 'distressed' over their behavior may be in marriages more at risk. This may be because distressed crossdressers tend, as a group, to score on psychological tests in ways that might indicate more problematic personality functioning (cf. answer to Q. 27). Such individuals may be more prone to an interpersonal style that is abrasive, self-centered, disagreeable, and even hostile.[868] One study of partners of such crossdressing men find the wives are also prone to problems. In 1980, psychiatrist Thomas Wise and colleagues reported on 18 such partners, 6 of whom had been interviewed, with data on the others coming from "chart review." More than a third (44%) of these women had received psychiatric treatment and as a group all of them are characterized by the researchers as "moral masochists"—women who suffer for suffering's sake, with high dependency needs and a tendency to use "hysterical defenses" (e.g., repression or denial) to cope with the crossdressing. In such cases, marital therapy proves generally unsuccessful.[869]

Yet such relationships may be at the extreme low end of relational outcomes. The 1999 online survey of male crossdressers finds that on a scale of 0-10, with 10 being a perfect score, the average rating of the quality of relationship with their spouse or significant other is 7.6, with more than three-quarters (78%) offering a rating of 7 or higher, and almost one-fifth (18%) rating it as a perfect 10.[870] Docter reports that nearly two-thirds (63%) of the wives he surveyed respond affirmatively to the query whether crossdressing has added anything positive to the marriage. The most common kinds of remarks concern:

❑ Crossdressing enhances closeness between the couple.

❑ The crossdressed spouse is more affectionate and considerate.

❑ The crossdressed spouse displays increased ability in intimacy, including sexual involvement.

❑ The crossdressed spouse enjoys a better mood.[871]

On the other hand, a similar proportion (66%) of the spouses surveyed by Docter remark about ways crossdressing detracts from their marriage. The kinds of comments likely here concern the following:

❑ The wife fears discovery of her husband's secret, with all that might entail, including loss of job, friends, status, and damage to his relationship with the kids.

❑ The wife feels the sexual relationship is diminished.[872]

Docter also identifies three broad patterns of marital adjustment he observes among couples with a crossdressing husband. In most instances, a mixing of patterns is embraced. And, of course, Docter is careful to add that simply managing crossdressing is not the determinant of overall marital success. Though Docter labels each pattern as a 'game,' I prefer to discuss them as patterns of movement and power. The four he discusses can be summarized in terms of movement and power as follows:

❑ *Mutual movement away from each other and subsequent holding of power.* Docter characterizes this 'game' as one of isolation where the crossdressing is simply ignored.

❑ *Mutual movement toward each other and sharing of power.* Docter describes this 'game' as one where the partners work together for personal growth.

❑ *Unilateral movement past each other with a retention of power.* Docter highlights this as a 'game' where each partner pretends openness and communication but practice denial and gradually end up distant from one another.

❑ *Unilateral movement of the husband to subordinate himself to his partner.* Docter speaks of this 'game' as one where the husband acts like a child dependent on his mother.[873]

Of course, other patterns are possible, too. The wife, for example, may unilaterally submit to her partner. The point is, these 'games' can help or hurt. I think the keys are whether the couple are moving together and toward one another with an honest desire to equalize their investment in the relationship (which is the basis of relational power).

I think it important to acknowledge that those who experience unsatisfactory outcomes in their relationships to crossdressers tend to be less public about it than others. This is no surprise—most people prefer not to go into depth about what they view as failed relationships. Likewise, those who find the relationship troubled often prefer to keep the difficulties private. Accordingly, there is relatively more material about those who have adjusted to life with a crossdressing partner and found it a positive experience.

After dealing with a mix of feelings stemming from 24 years of secrecy by her husband concerning his crossdressing, one woman came to terms enough with the situation to be able to write as follows:

> People who have known us for a long time, have noticed a difference. Our children tell people that their parents are on a second honeymoon. It is really great. I have never been so happy in all ways . . . .
>
> When I am out shopping for clothes, I find myself looking for something for Michelle as well. We even laugh about me looking for a shirt for my husband.
>
> With all this, you may wonder if I have forgiven my husband for the lies and betrayal. Not completely, as the hurt is very deep. There are times it comes to the surface, and I try to deal with it a little at a time until it is at rest. I don't dwell on it, as it would eat me alive. Hopefully, someday it will be all gone. I do however understand why he didn't tell me until now. Our love we have is very special and we are not about to give it up .
> . . .
>
> There are more positives, than negatives in this situation. Just enjoy each other and do it together. It does get easier. Keep in mind, respect for each other plays a big part in your life together, and there is always a reason for things happening in your lives.[874]

Q. 39

How does crossdressing affect families?

The Short Answer. Families, like individuals, have distinct personalities. No one rule can be laid down about how a crossdressing member will affect the family. Some family members may be more accepting, others more rejecting. The same statuses described for partner reactions in the last answer pertain here as well. Like any unusual and misunderstood behavior, crossdressing prompts responses that create a challenge for any family. In too many families the rejection by one or more members divides, even breaks, the family. Fortunately, in some such cases the damage, though real, is overcome and the family heals. Often the most significant issues surround disclosure: deciding *if* anyone should know, and if so, *who* should be told about the transgender reality, *when* they should be informed, and *how* it should happen.

The Longer Answer. "'Our child' is a line that every transgender child longs to hear from his or her parent," write social workers Gerald Mallon and Teresa DeCrescenzo.[875] But transgender specialist Gianna Israel plainly states a more common and painful reality: "Family rejection is the most pervasive and damaging phenomenon transgender persons face. This includes partial exclusion to outright rejection."[876]

What lies at the root of one family member rejecting another? Israel observes, "Generally most rejection occurs when the informed party cannot traverse the gap between their gender experiences and yours."[877] She notes how, ironically, the transgender person often becomes caretaker to other family members, helping them manage their shock and distress, at the very time when the transgender individual may need support the most.[878]

Since Q. 38 examines how partners respond to crossdressing, here we will consider other family (parents, siblings, and others), with a chief focus on children. But before examining relationships with particular family members, we will do well to begin by considering the process of *disclosure*. Of course, transgender realities are sometimes discovered unintentionally by others, and sometimes purposely revealed. In either instance a process is initiated in which the transgender experience is in some manner articulated, most often to those who receive it with some difficulty whether because of ignorance or because of sharing in common cultural prejudices. This process, then, is a weighty matter and by its very significance a fragile one.

How can self-disclosure well proceed?

None of us can control how others will respond to our experiences or our words. At best we can hope to present ourselves well and hope to receive a fair, full, and open hearing. At best, then, things will go well enough that some measure of understanding is attained and with it acceptance and support that allow the relationship to grow and be healthy. Without any certain assurance that self-disclosure will gain a ready hearing and win acceptance, transgender individuals are understandably reluctant to share with others a self-reality so important to themselves. This may lead to profound feelings of alienation from loved ones, anxiety over involuntary discovery, and a mounting pressure to be 'out' to others.

Positive results from self-disclosure may be maximized by the presence of certain key elements that may be remembered as the '3 Ps':

❑ *Preparation*—self-disclosure is likely to go better when careful thought has been given to what should be revealed, to whom, and when.

❑ *Patience*—self-disclosure that proceeds all at once in a rush is more likely to overwhelm others and generate a less positive response.

❑ *Process*—self-disclosure will probably require parceling information into manageable bits over a lengthy period with time for others to digest and respond to what they are learning.

Israel recommends that disclosures use very basic terms and emphasize that the person disclosing does not have all the answers but is also exploring what this transgender reality means. Additionally, Israel warns that gradually revealing information is especially important where a dramatic disclosure puts the person at risk of being put out of the home. She points out that if nothing else this approach provides time for the individual to make alternative living arrangements if it becomes clear that the process is not going well.[879]

Should children be told?

One of the hardest questions a transgender person's family faces is whether the children should be told. Research suggests that most children don't know.[880] Interestingly, a 1999 online survey of male crossdressers reports that children not living at home are more likely to know (25% to 13%), but less likely to be supportive (32% to 45%) than those residing with the crossdresser.[881] Psychiatrist George Brown, in his study of female partners of male crossdressers, finds that among the families who have children (either hers or his), one-third know about the crossdressing behavior. In most instances this knowledge is not through chance discovery, but by the children having been told.[882] Similarly, John Talamini offers that slightly more than a third (37%) of his sample of couples with children have told their children about dad's crossdressing, though in only a single instance had the crossdressing been observed by the kids.[883]

Outcomes of Telling

Is telling a good idea? One might argue that the answer depends on the outcome, but since that is only known after the fact it is not a terribly helpful suggestion. So what have been outcomes? In Talamini's study, apparently no negative outcomes followed from the children being informed. None of them adopted the behavior or demonstrated cross-gender identity or role problems.[884] Similarly, Israel thinks it a myth that telling young children will do them harm, such as prompting development of confused ideas about sex and gender. If anything, observes Israel, younger children generally handle the news better than adolescents.[885]

On the other hand, Brown's study reports that three mothers relate how their young sons (school-age) have "spontaneously cross-dressed on more than one occasion without assistance or overt encouragement from either parent."[886] In seeking to understand this, Brown draws upon previous research and indicates several possible explanations:

❏ The behavior might mark the onset of gender identity disorder of childhood.

❏ The behavior could indicate early transvestism.

❏ The behavior might be the first indication of a homosexual orientation.

❏ The behavior might be the boy's attempt at identifying with his father.

❏ The behavior might reflect a normal incidence rate for such behavior in the general population.

Brown himself opts as the most likely explanation "that such behavior represents a short-lived identification phase."[887]

Perhaps the point of such a list, though, is that there are so many possibilities. Brown's own caution is meritorious in adopting a sensible 'normal' explanation when sufficient evidence for diagnosing 'abnormality' is not present. So, should children be told? Harry Benjamin, in his 1966 *The Transsexual Phenomenon*, expresses his belief that children should be "protected" from learning of their father's crossdressing because of potential damage to their development. He feels sons are at particular risk since the boy's identification with his father might suffer irreparable damage.[888] Two decades later, Richard Docter likewise argues that being open and honest runs a risk for younger children that may exceed the benefits.[889] This general view still appears to be the majority opinion on the question.

However, we have seen that little if any empirical evidence exists that harm actually occurs. In fact, the fear of harm itself may be the most damaging result. If the decision is made to tell the children, Israel believes it should be a fairly straightforward process. She recommends keeping the following in mind:

- ❏ In the face of anything new and different in the family children need to be reminded they are loved and accepted unconditionally.
- ❏ They also need reassurances things will be okay.
- ❏ They need help to learn that a parent being different is about the parent, not themselves.
- ❏ They may need help in facing harassment from others, especially bullying peers.[890]

Unfortunately, revelation of a parent's transgender reality may come about because the parents have decided to separate or divorce. This decision raises the stakes for the whole family, and most particularly for the children.

How do other family members respond?

Those who think they know us because of long familiarity through a family of origin are especially likely to have trouble adjusting to the discovery that a family member lives within a transgender reality. Setting aside preconceived notions is difficult for anyone, but particularly for family members, and especially for parents. They may respond with disbelief and the disclaimer, "We didn't raise our child to be like this!" They may experience grief alongside shock as they comprehend their own hopes and desires for the child no longer seem to fit.

The online survey in 1999, mentioned earlier, sought to assess how supportive family might be. Respondents were more than 1,000 male crossdressers (ages 16-76). Of these men, 539 are married to spouses who know of their crossdressing. The survey finds that in marriages where the spouse is supportive, other family members who know of the crossdressing are more likely to be supportive. However, with regard to parents, in no instance—whether the wife is supportive or not—are a majority supportive.

A substantial difference is found among siblings: a spouse's support is correlated with twice the likelihood that siblings will be supportive, too. Even more pronounced is the correlation with supportiveness among extended family. When the crossdresser's spouse is supportive, extended family members are more than four times more likely to be supportive. However, it must be noted that most family members do not know about the crossdressing, with parents being more likely to know than siblings, who are more likely to know than extended family.[891]

Families, like individuals, have habits and boundaries. The safety and comfort of the familiar is stripped away by discovery of transgender realities. To make a successful transition to a new family identity, one where the transgender person has a place, requires adjustments of perception and behavior alike. Some families are unwilling to expend the effort to make such changes. For these families it proves easier to discard 'the stranger' the transgender person appears to have become. For those families most bound to cultural conventions such as adherence to the rigid pairing of anatomical sex and gender, the mismatch they perceive in a family member is hard enough. But if that person then attempts to eliminate the mismatch by changing body sex rather than gender presentation, the family may regard the act as crossing a line that puts the transgender person out of the family.[892] In fact, the way other family members are likely to cope with the situation is by justifying their behavior as a legitimate response to the 'outrageous decisions' of the 'transgressor.' In short, they interpret the transgender person as the one leaving the family rather than as themselves casting the person out.

Who is family?

When transgender individuals find themselves cast off from family, most move from mourning the loss to efforts to construct a new family. In this regard, we may legitimately ask who constitutes a family anyway. The idea that family is a matter of biological relations persists despite decreasing relevance. The fact is that many of us find our sense of family—bonds of respect, affection, and loyalty—among a group of people who may include only a few, and perhaps none of those to whom we are genetically related. Among transgendered people, no less than among any of us, family are the people who love, support, and welcome us any time and always. And no less than anyone else, transgendered people need family, seek family, and build family as best they can. Even a single such other person can make a family happen—and prove to be the difference in how the challenges of life will be met.

Some adopt a broad understanding of family and thus identify the people of their church, or support group, or closest friends as 'family.' Others seek out and form new intimate bonds, finding housemates, roommates, or spouses. Being different appears to encourage and elicit creativity simply to survive and adapt, and transgender people as a group seem to have an abundant supply of creativity. This resource serves them well in identifying different people to be in a family with, or crafting a different way to be in a family. One way or another, many find a path to end isolation or estrangement.

Q. 40

Why does society tolerate crossdressing?

The Short Answer. To end this volume we venture an important question—one we have touched on at points and to which we shall return later in the work: if transgender realities, as often alleged, are bad for society, then why does society put up with them? The ubiquity of crossdressing, for example, hardly explains why it has not been dealt with more harshly than it has if, in fact, it is as dire a threat to social order as some have proclaimed. Regardless of negative pronouncements found in cultures more rigid in their ideas about gender, the reality has been that transgender realities like crossdressing have generally been tolerated without widespread or severe sanctions. At least three possibilities suggest themselves to explain the general social response. First, perhaps what tolerance exists occurs because of a certain collective resignation attendant on the recognition that no matter what one thinks of transgender people, or crossdressing behavior, these realities are here to stay. Or, perhaps it is because even when transgender behavior is viewed negatively it is not seen as overly serious. In this view, transgender realities may not be good, but they also aren't going to be the end of civilization, so why get too worked up over them? Finally, perhaps something like crossdressing provides an important social safety valve. In this perspective, although transgender realities like crossdressing are not particularly desirable, they are necessary. They serve a limited, but useful function: they allow the pressure built up by gender pressure to be discharged in a socially controlled fashion. All three of these possibilities presume that society negatively judges transgender realities. For our society, for some time, this has been a fair characterization. It remains fair even though social tolerance has spread. We still cannot speak of our society as being an 'accepting' one.

The Longer Answer. There is no single, uniform response cultures offer to the reality of crossdressing. In this answer our focus shall be restricted to our own society—the United States early in the 21ˢᵗ century. That society is more tolerant of transgender realities than perhaps at any other time in its history. But it can scarcely be called an 'accepting' society, where transgender identities, homosexual orientations, and crossdressing behavior are received favorably. A widespread negative valuation persists and, at best, we can only judge our present society as grudgingly tolerant.

Transgender realities historically have been denied, minimized, marginalized, legislated against, socially censored in most contexts, and relatively tolerant of hostility against transgender people. In short, they have consistently been deemed undesirable—a detriment to society. And yet, here we are, at a time of greater tolerance than ever. Why, if transgender realities are not good for society does society put up with them?

At least three broad possibilities suggest themselves:

- ❑ Perhaps tolerance exists because nothing can be done.
- ❑ Perhaps tolerance exists because transgender realities aren't serious enough to exert more effort to get rid of them.
- ❑ Perhaps tolerance exists because transgender has a useful, if limited, social function.

All three possibilities presume a social appraisal of transgender that is at best neutral. In reality, social attitudes seem more mildly rejecting than neutral. But civic behavior has become increasingly—if grudgingly—tolerant.

Why can't something be done about transgender?

A possible explanation for the social tolerance that exists may be a certain collective resignation. Perhaps as a whole our people recognize that no matter what one thinks of transgender people, or crossdressing behavior, these realities are here to stay. After all, most everyone has enough sense of history to know that ours has been filled with negative views about transgender people, that laws have been passed against some transgender behaviors, and that policies and practices commonly keep transgender people away from the rest of the population. And yet . . . here they are. Not only do they refuse to go away, they actually seem to be here more than ever before!

Of course, there remain some who are dedicated to the suppression of transgender realities. Some not only wish them eradicated, but cling to the hope that end will one day come to pass. Many persist in seeing transgender realities as signs of mental disorder and think that the answer is to put transgender people on drugs, or in therapy (see the answers to Q. 97-98). Others go further, still desiring to criminalize transgender behaviors, whether same-sex relations or crossdressing. A few even look to a new eugenics to someday identify whatever genes might contribute to transgender and modify them. A very few have gone so far as to offer that perhaps parents, knowing the destiny of the organism while still *in utero* might opt to abort it.[893]

The vast majority of us, though, appear to have come to some uneasy peace with transgender realities. In a world drawn closer together by modern technology we are more aware than any previous generation of how common such re-alities are around the world. Our fascination with them suggests something inside ourselves that makes us reluctant to completely abolish them. An easier, safer course is a resignation to putting up with them because they cannot be done away with.

Perhaps that is why we endure crossdressing. One of the more remarkable observations we can make about it is how tolerated it generally is even in those cultures most hostile to it. Unlike, for example, racial differences or the treatment that homosexuals have sometimes been subjected to, crossdressers have for the most part met with little harsh repression by societies.[894] Ours certainly fits that pattern. No jury has ever sentenced someone to death because of crossdressing—though too many have died because particular individuals have acted as judge, jury, and executioner. But such individual instances of violence, though they do speak to something in society that lets them happen, cannot be claimed to typify our society's response.

The problem with thinking that society tolerates transgender realities simply because of resignation is that it too much diminishes a critical fact: in our society gender matters very much. So while many may indeed be resigned to suffering what they don't think can be changed or eliminated, perhaps there is another, better answer for society at large.

Is it worth the effort to discourage something like cross-dressing?

Maybe too much is made of the significance of transgender realities. Civilization has not been ended by their presence, nor does it seem likely to be. Given how much effort it takes to push it underground—and the futility of trying to eradicate it—perhaps the most rational course is to tolerate it and largely leave it alone. In fact, in a society that champions as its primary social values personal freedom, a right to privacy, and social justice, to mount a concerted effort against people based on their identity, or what they do in private, or on a passive and harmless activity like crossdressing clearly means acting against these primary values. Frankly, it seems un-American to deprive others of the rights we cling to for ourselves and advocate for everyone. In short, maybe the best action is no action: live and let live.

This may indeed be the attitude of a fair number of people. On the other hand, as we have been documenting throughout the first two volumes of this work, *gender matters*. In our society—perhaps the most rigid in its interpretation and application of Western gender ideas—gender is very important to personal identity and to relationships. Given the two-and-only-two gender scheme our society has adhered to, the existence of transgender realities poses a problem. At best these realities constitute a serious challenge to rethink gender; at worst they offer a serious threat to identity and relationships.

What are we to do then? Perhaps the sensible course is to keep a watchful eye on transgender realities and put up enough resistance to keep their display from getting out of hand. Rather than push a strong agenda of controls, maybe simple disapproval, mild resistance, and insistence on a few key matters (e.g., no same-sex marriages, or adherence to established standards of care before authorization for sex reassignment surgery) will be enough. After all, making a stand on a few items is both more likely to succeed and less likely to be seen as irrational homophobia and transphobia. Moreover, in letting transgender people make strides in areas deemed less consequential, they may prove less likely to insist on things the larger society does not wish to grant them.

We could argue that this actually has been the course society follows. Most of us don't care about a number of things that concern transgender people and so it is easy enough to support—or at least not vigorously oppose—their efforts to get them. If we are transgender, this is certainly better than nothing, but worrisome in how it smacks of tokenism. The issues that the majority still get up in arms over suggest that, at heart, nontransgender people remain unwilling to see us as equal. Whichever population we belong to, this compromise course ultimately feels unsatisfactory.

Another problem with it is that really doesn't solve the dilemma of how to handle the essential challenge posed by transgender to our dominant gender scheme. At best, this course can only be a stopgap one. How long can a society continue to try having it both ways—denying the legitimacy of transgender as a gender alternative while according transgender people legal recognition and a measure of social tolerance? Eventually, our society's culture must either change its gender scheme, or snap back and renew opposition to transgender realities. At present the former of these seems to be happening. But we cannot afford to relax vigilance if we think this an admirable goal.

Is there a positive social function provided by crossdressing?

There is a third possibility. Maybe the best explanation for social tolerance is an implicit recognition that transgender realities serve a useful, if limited, social function. So perhaps our society tolerates crossdressing as well as it does not merely because it seems a relatively harmless violation of cultural gender norms, but because of a largely unconscious sense of a valuable role this behavior provides. Historian and philosopher Ivan Illich, in his study entitled *Gender* observes such a thing in Western societies with regard to 'travesty'—a rich term denoting disguise through altered dress or appearance so as to ridicule:

> Almost everywhere transvestism is ritualized into a seasonal participatory event. Carnivals from Sicily to Scandinavia have throughout the ages demanded that women play men, men play women, and men play women who play men. It has

been argued that such "travesties" were occasionally used to inflame political passion. Especially during the eighteenth century, in fact, these traditional reversals became the occasion for ridiculing the "process of civilization" resented by the crowd; they became a tactic for resisting the teacher and the cleric. Recent studies on the cultural features of laughter, fairs, mummery, and riots rightly highlight the political uses to which travesty has been put in protecting the moral economy, the gendered existence of the crowds. These gender turnarounds also served to lampoon, thus keeping in check the relative domination of one gender: Putting women occasionally, publicly, and festively on top was a way of ridiculing men without seriously undermining their dominance. Inversely, in a Mexican village that is still today riddled by the fear of witches, the dance of men in drag as hags pursuing pre-adolescent boys dressed up as coyotes triggers an annual day-long celebration of laughter, putting simmering anguish in its proper place. [1]

But the mild and occasional ridicule, accompanied by laughter that discharges anxiety, is not the only function of travesty that Illich recognizes. He sees a "deeper function" in magical and religious rituals where the pattern is meant to preserve the gender line by reversing public perspective about its shape. Alongside this function may be a magical one in some cultures where the reversal of gender keeps guardian demons satisfied and thus away from daily human affairs. So, for Illich, crossdressing travesties ultimately reflect "the rootedness of gender in the deepest mystical experiences."[895]

Anthropologist Victor Turner warns that the "public liminality" of Carnival ought not be viewed merely as a social safety valve, an avenue for cultural catharsis. Its perceived danger from social authorities stems from its community function of weighing in the scales the prevailing social structure—and sometimes finding it wanting. The forms found in Carnival represent new possibilities. Thus, the ambiguity of such festivals is their ability to both uphold and criticize the existing order and its values.[896]

Such scholars affirm a place for a transgender reality like crossdressing in the broader social fabric. But we need not stop with the role of festivals that sanction for a time cross gender behaviors. As we have glimpsed in materials gleaned from history and other societies, transgender people play important roles in the spiritual, religious, mediating and healing roles embraced by humanity. Seen as advantageously positioned both vertically (between mortals and deity) and horizontally (between men and women), transgender people are often valued for doing what others cannot or will not do.

In our next volumes we shall given increased attention to these possibilities.

Notes

Please note: works cited more than once in this volume are given in full citation the first time they appear in any chapter (i.e., answer to a question).

Introduction to Question Set 2

[1] No matter what course one takes in defining 'crossdressing' or 'crossdresser' there will be legitimate grounds for complaint. The adopted definitions are pragmatic in the sense that they reflect the common conception of most people in our culture. Accepting, for the sake of argument, that such a definition is workable, we shall see where it leads us.

Q. 11 Notes

[2] My own calculations are that worldwide about 6% (+/-2%) of the population fits within the parameters generally set for transgender, the largest portion of which are crossdressers; this figure includes both males and females.

[3] Richard Ekins, *Male Femaling. A Grounded Theory Approach to Cross-Dressing and Sex-Changing.* (N. Y.: Routledge, 1997), p. 11.

[4] In the Spring of 2005, Pakistani security agents, dressed in women's *burqas*, were able to capture a prominent Al Qaeda figure, Abu Faraj Al-Libbi. See Michael Isikoff & Mark Hosenball, "Got Him. Now What?" *Newsweek*, pp. 24-27 (2005, May 16). Several months later, Israeli defense forces suspected a group of Palestinian gunmen disguised themselves as women to gain access to a mosque under siege by Israeli forces. The operatives inside had asked local women to come and act as a human shield; the gunmen used the opportunity to enter the mosque. See Josh Brannon, "Gunmen May Have Dressed as Women in Mosque Raid," *The Jerusalem Post* (2006, Nov. 3). Accessed online at http://www.jpost.com/servlet/Satellite?cid=1162378318370&pagename=JPost/JP Article/ShowFull.

[5] A survey of more than 100 University of Pittsburgh undergraduates in serious, committed relationships finds that nearly three-quarters (72%) of the female students have slept in or with their partner's clothing. More than a quarter (27%) of male students own up to the same behavior. Sharon S. Blake, "Scent of a Partner," *Pitt Chronicle* (2004, May 10). Accessed online at http://www.umc.pitt.edu/media/ pcc040510/partner_scent.html.

[6] Albert D. Klassen, Colin J. Williams, & Eugene E. Levitt, *Sex and Morality in the U. S.*, H. J. O'Gorman, Ed. (Middletown, CT: Wesleyan Univ. Press, 1989), p. 383.

[7] Ibid. The number of people responding to the question was 3,007 (1,544 female; 1,464 male). Response choices were "Never," "Rarely," "Sometimes," and "Often." The latter three choices thus represent at least an occasional preference. In each of these three choices the percent of females selecting the response is greater than the percent of males: "Rarely" (6.5% to 1.2%), "Sometimes" (6.2% to 0.2%), "Often" (3.3% to 0.1%).

[8] Ibid. While the percentages are very low for both males and females, the proportional difference at least reflects the similar manifold likelihood that women actually appear in male-like clothing (however it may have been altered to be feminine).

[9] Richard L. Schott, "The Childhood and Family Dynamics of Transvestites," *Archives of Sexual Behavior, 24* (no. 3), 309-328 (1995).

[10] D. G. Brown, "Transvestism and sex-role inversion," in A. Ellis & A. Abarbanel (Eds.), *The Encyclopedia of Sexual Behavior, vol. 2.* (N. Y.: Hawthorne Books, 1961).

[11] J. L. McCary, *Human Sexuality* (3rd ed.). (N. Y.: Van Nosstrand, 1978).

[12] W. B. Arndt, *Gender Disorders and the Paraphilias* (Madison, WI: International Universities Press, 1991). Arndt estimates up to 1 million, which in a population of 247 million is less than .5%.

[13] Samuel S. Janus & Cynthia L. Janus, *Janus Report on Sexual Behavior* (N. Y.: John Wiley & Sons, 1993), p. 120f. Interestingly, more people report never having heard of crossdressing (14% of men; 17% of women)—figures scarcely believable even in the early 1990s, but perhaps explained by the nature of the question put to them, which concerns crossdressing as one among a number of 'sexual practices.' The respondents may have been aware of crossdressing, but may not have connected it to a 'sexual practice.'

[14] Vernon Coleman, *Men in Dresses: A Study in Transvestism/Crossdressing.* (Chilton Designs Publishers, 1996). A European Medical School Journal Special Report. Accessed online at http://www. vernoncoleman.com/downloads/mid.htm. See opening section entitled 'Transvestism: A 20th Century Social Phenomenon.' In the research, conducted in 1995, 414 men completed questionnaires; over 600 others were involved in written communications. Coleman also notes that some authorities have estimated half (50%) of all men have either partially or completely crossdressed at some point.

[15] Lynn Conway, *How Frequently Does Transsexualism Occur?* (2001-2002). Accessed online at http://ai.eecs.umich.edu/people/conway/TS/TSprevalence.html. For more on Conway, see footnotes at the answer to question 19. Conway writes that "most conservative estimates are in the range of 2% to 5% of all adult males engage in routine crossdressing (1:50 to 1:20)."

[16] Niklas Langström & Kenneth J. Zucker, "Transvestic Fetishism in the General Population: Prevalence and Correlates," *Journal of Sex & Marital Therapy, 31* (no. 1), 87-95 (2005).

[17] Mariette P. Allen, *Transformations: Crossdressers and Those Who Love Them.* (N. Y.: E. P. Dutton, 1989).

[18] Neil McConaghy, "Sexual Deviation," in A. Bellack, M. Hersen, and A. Kazdin (Eds.), *International handbook of Behavior Modification and Therapy* (N. Y.: Plenum Press, 1982). See chapter 22.

Q. 12 Notes

[19] Josh White, "Abu Ghraib Tactics Were First Used at Guantanamo," *Washington Post* (2005, July 14). Accessed online at washingtonpost.com at http://www.washingtonpost.com/wp-dyn/content/article/ 2005/07/13/AR2005071302380.html.

[20] Vernon Coleman, *Men in Dresses: A Study in Transvestism/Crossdressing* (European Medical Journal. Chilton Designs Publishers, 1996). Accessed online at http://www.vernoncoleman.com/ downloads/mid.htm. See §2, 'Why Do Men Crossdress?'

[21] Gianna E. Israel, "Tired of Transgender?" *Gianna Israel Gender Library* (2001). Accessed online at http://www.firelily.com/gender/gianna/tired.html.

[22] See, especially, G. G. Bolich, *Conversing on Gender. A Primer for Entering Dialog* (Raleigh, NC: Psyche's Press, 2007), pp. 24, 154-172.

[23] For more on Butler's ideas, see volume 1, Q. 5, pp. 124-125.

[24] My view thus varies from those who, like consultant Lisa Maurer ("Transgressing Sex and Gender," p. 16), conceive of gender expression as necessarily congruent with gender experience.

[25] The bulk of this material is reproduced from Bolich, *Conversing on Gender*, pp. 160-161.

[26] Diane Reay, "'Spice Girls', 'Nice Girls', 'Girlies', and 'Tomboys': Gender Discourses, Girls' Cultures and Femininities in the Primary Classroom," *Gender and Education, 13* (no. 2), 153-166 (2001), p. 161f.

[27] George A. Kelly, *The Psychology of Personal Constructs*, 2 vols. (N. Y.: Norton, 1955). Also see his *A Theory of Personality: The Psychology of Personal Constructs* (N. Y.: Norton, 1963).

[28] In a society like our own, crossdressing is of necessity a cross-gender activity, because only two genders are granted legitimacy. In settings where a 'third gender' is admitted, the so-called 'crossdressing' is intended to reflect a gender other than masculinity or femininity by using dress elements associated with one or both of these predominant genders (because those are what are readily available as tools for expression).

Q. 13 Notes

[29] "The Governor's Mission," *The New York Times* (1886, June 19), pg. 1, recounts, "Exactly 200 years ago Gov. Edmond Andros, so it is recorded, 'came from New-York to the colony of Massachusetts and brought some bad men with him. He was finally arrested by the outraged people of the colony and had nearly escaped in female clothes, but that his cavalry boots showed him off.'" Cf. Mary Caroline Crawford, *St. Boltoph's Town. An Account of Old Boston in Colonial Days* (L. C. Page & Co., 1908), ch. 9. Accessed online at http://www.kellscraft.com/StBoltophTown/StBoltophTown09.html.

[30] *Harper's Weekly* noted in its report that "The captors report that he hastily put on one of his wife's dresses and started for the woods, closely followed by our men, who at first thought him a woman, but seeing his boots while he was running, they suspected his sex at once." See "Capture of Davis," *Harper's Weekly, IX* (no. 439), p. 1 (1865, May 27). Accessed online at http://www.sonofthesouth.net/leefoundation/civil-war/1865/jefferson-davis-capture.htm. This incident is considered further in the answer to Q. 47.

[31] Ellen Sherman, "The Real Truth About Crossdressing," *Selfhelp Magazine* (1998, May 28), accessed online at http://www.selfhelpmagazine.com/articles/sex/xdress.html. *Selfhelp Magazine* is one of the oldest online mental health websites, featuring articles by mental health professionals and advanced students.

[32] Amy Alkon, "Who Wears the Panties in the Family?" [Bring It: The Advice Goddess column], *Herald News* (Passaic County, NJ) (2006, Apr. 7), p. D09.

[33] Sheila Jeffries, "Heterosexuality and the Desire for Gender," in D. Richardson (Ed.), *Theorizing Heterosexuality. Telling It Straight* (Phila.: Open University Press, 1996), p. 83.

Q. 14 Notes

[34] Harry Brierley, *Transvestism. A Handbook with Case Studies for Psychologists, Psychiatrists and Counselors* (Oxford: Pergamon Press, 1979), p. 223. Brierley, by the way, casts no negative judgment about this—he is simply stating facts.

[35] Peggy Rudd, *My Husband Wears My Clothes.* (Katy, TX: PM Publishers, 1990), p. 2.

[36] Vern LeRoy Bullough & Bonnie Bullough, *Cross Dressing, Sex, and Gender* (Phila.: Univ. of Pennsylvania Press, 1993), p. 307.

[37] Oyeronke Oyewumi, "Discourse on Gender: Historical Contingency and the Ethics of Intellectual Work," *West Africa Review, 3* (no. 2) (2002). Accessed online at http://www.westafricareview. com/vol3.2/owomoyela.html.

[38] H. S. Barahel, "Female Transvestism and Homosexuality," *Psychiatric Quarterly, 27* (no. 3), 390-438 (1953).

[39] Samuel S. Janus & Cynthia L. Janus, *Janus Report on Sexual Behavior* (N. Y.: John Wiley & Sons, 1993), p. 120f.

[40] Ibid.

[41] Havelock Ellis, "Eonism and Other Supplementary Studies," vol. 2, pp. 1-110 in H. Ellis, *Studies in the Psychology of Sex,* 2 vols. (N. Y.: Random House reprint of 1941-1942; original work published 1905-1928), p. 36.

[42] Cf. Jason Cromwell, *Transmen and FTMs. Identities, Bodies, Genders, and Sexualities* (Chicago: Univ. ofChicago Press, 1999), p. 62.

[43] John D'Emilio & Estelle B. Freedman, *Intimate Matters. A History of Sexuality in America* (N. Y.: Harper & Row, 1988), p. 124.

[44] Richard von Krafft-Ebing, *Psychopathia Sexualis. A Medico-Forensic Study,* 12th ed. (N. Y.: Pioneer Publications, 1939/1947; original work published 1886), p.609.

[45] Shasta Turner, "Disordered Subjects: Female Cross-Dressing and Sumptuary Regulation in Early Modern England," (1998). Accessed online at http://www. major-weather.com/projects/000040.html. A version of this paper was originally presented as part of the 1998 Huntington Library Graduate Seminars in Early Modern British History.

[46] Cromwell, p. 63.

[47] See the answer to Q. 48 for Tipton's story.

[48] "Authorities: Mother Abducted Children. Then Posed as Father," *Shelby Star* (2006, Mar. 28), p. 12A.

[49] To the claim that women throughout history have faced similar situations where they have been denied their children and may have resorted to extreme actions, I would answer that seems entirely plausible to me. However, history offers little evidence of crossdressing in such instances and, strictly speaking, the child custody cases of today are a relatively recent development that has facilitated the possibility of such acts. In short, the juxtaposition of crossdressing with this social setting has a thoroughly contemporary feel.

[50] Arlene Istar Lev, *Transgender Emergence: Therapeutic Guidelines for Working with Gender-Variant People and Their Families* (N. Y.: Haworth Clinical Press, 2004), p. 141.

[51] For more on the situation with the DSM model, see question set 12, especially the answer to Q. 96.

[52] Emil A. Gutheil, "Analysis of a Case of Transvestism," in Wilhelm Stekel, *Sexual Aberrations: The Phenomena of Fetishism in Relation to Sex,* 2 vols. (New York: Liveright, 1930), vol. 2, pp. 281–318. For more on this case, see the answer to Q. 95.

[53] Lawrence S. Kubie, "The Drive to Become Both Sexes," *Psychoanalytic Quarterly, 43* (no. 3), 349-426 (1974), p. 354.

[54] Robert J. Stoller, "Transvestism in Women," *Archives of Sexual Behavior, 11* (no. 2), 99-115 (1982).

[55] Lorraine Gamman & Merja Makinen, *Female Fetishism* (Washington Square, NY: NY Univ. Press, 1994), p. 68. Gamman and Makinen (pp. 68ff.) also comment on

'Vogueing,' a practice found in various sexual subcultures and involving both male and female crossdressing.

[56] Ira B. Pauly, "Female Transsexualism: Part 1," *Archives of Sexual Behavior, 3* (no. 6), 487-507 (1974), p. 487.

[57] Cf. the discussion on this matter in Claudine Griggs, *S/he. Changing Sex and Changing Clothes* (N. Y.: Berg, 1998); see especially p. 124.

[58] See, for example, Anke A. Ehrhardt, G. Grisanti, & E. A. McCauley, "Female to Male Transsexuals Compared to Lesbians: Behavioral Patterns of Childhood and Adolescent Development," *Archives of Sexual Behavior, 8* (no. 6), 481-490 (1979). This study found that 80% of its 15 FtM transsexuals had crossdressed in childhood.

[59] Pauly, p. 499 and p. 500, Table IX.

[60] Colette Chiland, *Transsexualism: Illusion and Reality*, translated by P. Slotkin (Middletown, CT: Wesleyan Univ. Press, 2003), p. 117.

[61] Pauly, p. 500.

Q. 15 Notes

[62] Kimberly K. Powlishta, "The Effect of Target Age on the Activation of Gender Stereotypes," *Sex Roles, 42* (nos. 3-4), 271-282 (2000).

[63] It seems telling to note that a study of third-sixth grade children's identification with television characters finds that while boys uniformly want to be like male characters, girls almost a third of the time (30%) also name male characters. See Byron Reeves & M. Mark Miller, "A Multidimensional Measure of Children's Identification with Television Characters," *Journal of Broadcasting, 22* (no. 1), 71-86 (1978). It might be argued that television 30 years ago offered fewer desirable female characters for girls to identify with, and that society today is more accepting of strong female presentations in activities previously reserved for males. However, it still seems likely that girls soon understand masculine privilege remains a force to be reckoned with, like it or not.

[64] D. B. Carter & L. A. McCloskey, "Peers and Maintenance of Sex-Typed Behavior: The Development of Children's Concepts of Cross-Gender Behavior in Their Peers," *Social Cognition, 2*, 294-314 (1984). This same duality is found among adults; see the discussion in the section, "Are Attitudes Changing?" in the answer to Q. 37.

[65] Gary D. Levy, Marianne G. Taylor, & Susan A. Gelman, "Traditional and Evaluative Aspects of Flexibility in Gender Roles, Social Conventions, Moral Rules, and Physical Laws," *Child Development, 66* (no. 2), 515-531 (1995); quote is from p. 528.

[66] M. S. MacGillivray & J. D. Wilson, "Clothing and Appearance Among Early, Middle and Late Adolescents," *Clothing & Textiles Research Journal, 15* (no. 1), 43-49 (1997). This study examined 478 6th, 9th, and 12th grade students (representing early, middle, and late adolescence).

[67] Richard Ekins writes with regard to boys that, "any observer of child's play may note male femaling behaviors." ['Male femaling' refers to ways biological males 'female' behaviorally; see the answer to Q. 95 for details.] *Male Femaling. A Grounded Theory Approach to Cross-Dressing and Sex-Changing* (N. Y.: Routledge, 1997), p. 61.

[68] Harry Bakwin, "Transvestism in Children," *Journal of Pediatrics, 56* (no. 2), 294-298 (1960).

[69] Richard Green, "One-Hundred Ten Feminine and Masculine Boys: Behavioral Contrasts and Demographic Similarities," *Archives of Sexual Behavior, 5* (no. 5), 425-446 (1976), p. 425. For more on Green's work, see the answer to Q. 95.

[70] Ibid, p. 434f.

[71] Ibid, p. 425.

[72] Ibid, pp. 434-444. On the wish to be a girl, the Bulloughs uncover a related finding in their research with adult male crossdressers who recall their childhoods to answer survey items. Nearly three-quarters (70%) confess to having envied girls. See Bonnie Bullough & Vern Bullough, ""Men Who Cross-Dress: A Survey," in B. Bullough, V. L. Bullough, & J. Elias (Eds.), *Gender Blending*, pp. 174-188 (Amherst, NY: Prometheus Books, 1997), p. 181, Table 2.

[73] Arnold van Gennep, *The Rites of Passage*, translated by M. Vizedom & G. Caffee (Chicago: Univ. of Chicago Press, 1960 translation of 1909 work).

[74] See David D. Leitao, "The Perils of Leukippos: Initiatory Transvestism and Male Gender Ideology in the Ekdusia at Phaistos," *Classical Antiquity, 14*, 130-163 (1995).

Q. 16 Notes

[75] Claudine Griggs, *S/he. Changing Sex and Changing Clothes* (N. Y.: Berg, 1998), p. 124.

[76] Kate Davy, "Fe/Male Impersonation: The Discourse of Camp," in M. Meyer (Ed.), *The Politics and Poetics of Camp*, pp. 130-148 (N. Y.: Routledge, 1994), p. 133. More provocatively, Davy goes on to contend that, "Male impersonation has no such familiar institutionalized history in which women impersonating men say something about women. Both female and male impersonation foreground the male voice and, either way, women are erased."

[77] Florence King, "The Misanthrope's Corner—Cleaning Files: Items on People for the Ethical Treatment of Animals, Lesbianism, etc.," [column] *National Review* (2002, June 17).

[78] Helen Bode, "Is Drag Subversive of Binary Gender Norms?" *Dialogue, 1* (no. 3), 19-26 (2003), pp. 21-22.

[79] Ivan Illich, *Gender* (N. Y.: Pantheon Books, 1982), p. 146. For more on Illich's ideas, see the answer to Q. 40.

[80] Some exploration of the role of crossdressing and its connection to social anxiety has been done by scholars with reference to the theater. Please see the answer to Q. 44.

Q. 17 Notes

[81] See the U.S. Decennial Census, 2000. A convenient summary of the data with reference to homosexuals may be found in Rodger Doyle, "Gay and Lesbian Census," *Scientific American, 292* (no. 3), 28. Cf. Gary J. Gates & Jason Ost, *The Gay and Lesbian Atlas* (Washington, D. C.: Urban Institute Press, 2004).

[82] Based on the available evidence, it would appear that the entirety of the homosexual 'lifetsyle' is the object of their erotic attraction. Abundant research has established that in demographics, in relational attitudes and patterns, in sexual habits, likes and dislikes, and in all other areas of living, homosexuals are far more like heterosexuals than unlike them. It seems incredible to conclude on a single difference an entire 'lifestyle,' which suggests that the term is merely a rhetorical device to separate the homosexual population, hold them at a distance, and make them an undesired 'other.' A parallel experience happens with other transgender people. With regard to transsexualism, noted novelist and MtF transsexual Jennifer Finney Boylan remarks:

> What it's emphatically *not* is a "lifestyle," any more than being
> male or female is a lifestyle. When I imagine a person with a lifestyle,

I see a millionaire playboy named Chip who likes to race yachts, or an accountant, perhaps, who dresses up in a suit of armor on the weekends.

Being transgendered isn't like that. Gender is many things, but one thing it is surely not is a *hobby*. Being female is not something you do because its clever or postmodern, or because you're a deluded, deranged narcissist.

(Jennifer Finney Boylan, *She's Not There. A Life in Two Genders* (N. Y.: Broadway Books, 2003), p. 22.)

[83] I encounter this tactic frequently among students who piously proclaim that they would never condemn a homosexual although they personally don't 'agree' with the 'preference' of 'that lifestyle.' They fail to see the moral condemnation in their words. It becomes a way to have their cake and eat it too—they can make plain their moral disapproval without overtly being critical. This kind of speaking is what garners the name 'hypocrite.' Cf. the answers to Q. 73-74 in volume 4.

[84] For more on the (il)logic of such thinking, see the answer to Q. 8.

[85] Ben Sifuentes-Jauregui, *Transvestism, Masculinity, and Latin American Literature: Genders Share Flesh* (N. Y.: Palgrave, 2002), p. 220 n. 61.

[86] Despite the number of studies done on the subject an exact estimate of how many people are homosexual has remained elusive. Rodger Doyle, based on the 2000 Census, extrapolates the percentages in the U.S. to be 2.5% (gay males) and 1.2% (lesbian females). But Doyle notes that research shows the percentages of those claiming same-sex sexual desire are virtually identical: 7.7% (male) and 7.5% (female). Even Kinsey's famous figure of 10% has been misunderstood; he ranged the matter along a continuum, recognizing that while 37% of his male respondents acknowledged at least one same-sex sexual encounter, only 4% reported *exclusive* same-sex sexual contact. The 10% figure was derived based on reported male behavior during any three year period between ages 16-55. See Alfred C. Kinsey, Wardell B. Pomeroy, & Clyde E. Martin, *Sexual Behavior in the Human Male* (Phila.: W. B. Saunders, 1948). Cf. S. M. Rogers & C. F. Turner, "Male-Male Sexual Contact in the U.S.A.: Findings from Five Sample Surveys, 1970-1990," *Journal of Sex Research*, 28, 491-519 (1991).

[87] The incidence of crossdressing among heterosexual males is far better documented than among gay males. It may be that gay males are more likely to use crossdressing as a means of public expression, but less likely to do so regularly or for other purposes.

[88] One matter we will leave aside is the question of transsexual crossdressers who identify as homosexual. This is for two reasons. First, transsexualism is the subject of its own question (Q. 19). Second, the question of sexual orientation with reference to transsexuals is murky. Is a male-to-female (MtF) transsexual who is attracted to women homosexual or heterosexual? Those who rely on genetic sex argue that such a MtF transsexual is heterosexual because the attraction is to a different biological (=genetic) sex. Others argue that such reasoning is superficial, even ridiculous. They contend that this MtF's attraction is homosexual since the MtF's post-operative body and gender identification are female. There are even some who claims that the orientation changes by virtue of the pre- or post-operative status. Pre-operatively, the MtF attracted to

women is heterosexual; post-operatively, the MtF has become homosexual. In light of this mess, we shall leave the matter largely aside though it is addressed in the main text.

[89] Ethel S. Person & Lionel Ovesey, "Homosexual Cross-Dressers," *Journal of the American Academy of Psychoanalysis and Dynamic Psychiatry, 12* (no. 2), 167-186 (1984).

[90] Gay men may feel pressures both explicit and implicit to at least occasionally crossdress. Moreover, given the bind society places them in through stereotyping, their reasons for crossdressing may not always be fully clear even to themselves. Cf. Keith E. McNeal, "Behind the Make-Up: Gender Ambivalence and the Double-Bind of Gay Selfhood in Drag Performance," *Ethos, 27* (no. 3), 344-378.

[91] While the origin of the term stems from the practice of crossdressed males in theater, the word itself does not seem to have originated as an acronym, despite the popular interpretation of it as "*Dr*essed *a*s a *g*irl."

[92] Kelly Kleiman, "Drag=Blackface," *Chicago-Kent Law Review, 75*, 669-686 (2000), p. 681 Available online at http://lawreview.kentlaw. edu/articles/75-3/AFTERMACRO Kleiman.pdf.

[93] Esther Newton, *Mother Camp: Female Impersonators in America* (Chicago: Univ. of Chicago Press, 1972), p. 64. More provocatively, Newton also claims, "professional drag queens are . . . professional homosexuals; they represent the stigma of the gay world" (p. 3).

[94] Quoted in Don Romesburg, "The Politics of Drag: June 15, 1977—From the Advocate Archives—Brief Article," *The Advocate* (2003, April 1). Accessed online at http://articles.findarticles.com/p/articles/mi_m1589/is_2003_April_1/ai_100111733.

[95] Amanda Lock Swarr, "Moffies, Artists, and Queens: Race and the Production of South African Gay Male Drag," in S. P. Schacht & L. Underwood (Eds.), *The Drag Queen Anthology. The Absolutely Fabulous But Flawlessly Customary World of Female Impersonators*, pp.73-89 (Binghamton, NY: Haworth Press, 2004), p. 75.

[96] Roselle Pineda, "Undressing Dresses," *Women in Action*, no. 3 (2002). Accessed online at http://www.isiswomen.org/pub/wia/wia302/undress.htm.

[97] Steven P. Schacht, "Four Renditions of Doing Female Drag: Feminine Appearing Conceptual Variations of a Masculine Theme," *Gendered Sexualities, 6*, 157-180 (2002).

[98] Adrian Gillan, "Outspoken Crossdressers," *OutUK* (2000-2004). Accessed online at http://www.outuk.com/index.html?http://www.outuk.com/outback/features. html.

[99] Lorraine Gamman & Merja Makinen, *Female Fetishism* (Washington Square, NY: New York Univ. Press, 1994), p. 63.

[100] This is clearly meant to parallel the idea of 'drag' meaning 'dressed as a girl.'

[101] Steven P. Schacht, "Lesbian Drag Kings and the Feminine Embodiment of the Masculine," *Journal of Homosexuality, 43* (no. 4), 75-98 (2002). Cf. Del LaGrace Volcano & Judith 'Jack' Halberstam, *The Drag King Book* (London: Serpent's Tail Press, 1999).

[102] Helen Bode, "Is Drag Subversive of Binary Gender Norms?" *Dialogue, 1* (no. 3), 19-26 (2003), p. 23. Bode, a college undergraduate student at the time the article was published, confuses gender and sex at times but makes some instructive observations about Drag Kings.

[103] Gamman & Makinen, p. 67f. The authors characterize this latter practice as indebted to 'protest' and 'resistance' rather than merely to sexual fetishism.

[104] Ibid, p. 68.

105 For a fine review of how this matter was viewed by mental health scholars in the late 19th-early 20th centuries, see John Matlock, "Masquerading Women, Pathologized Men: Cross-Dressing, Fetishism, and the Theory of Perversion, 1882-1935," in E. Apter & W. Pietz (Eds.), *Fetishism in Cultural Discourse*, pp. 31-61 (Ithaca, NY: Cornell Univ. Press, 1993).

106 There are numerous sources for such stories. A brief collection may be found in Jason Cromwell, *Transmen and FTMs. Identities, Bodies, Genders, and Sexualities* (Chicago: Univ. of Chicago Press, 1999), pp. 72-74.

107 Gamman & Makinen, p. 67. The authors cite the 1991 case brought against an 18 year old girl who was alleged to have disguised herself as a boy in order to seduce two 17 year old girls. Convicted and sentenced to six years imprisonment, the case was overturned on appeal.

108 See the answer to Q. 14 for discussion of this matter. In the psychiatric literature see, for example, Emil A. Gutheil, "Analysis of a Case of Transvestism," in Wilhelm Stekel, *Sexual Aberrations: The Phenomena of Fetishism in Relation to Sex*, 2 vols. (New York: Liveright, 1930), vol. 2, pp. 281–318. Original work, "Analyse eines Falles von Transvestimus," published in 1923. This case is described in the answer to Q. 95. Also see Robert J. Stoller, "Transvestism in Women," *Archives of Sexual Behavior, 11* (no. 2), 99-115 (1982). Cf. the answer to Q. 88.

109 Gamman & Makinen, p. 68. Also see Carole-Anne Tyler, "Boys Will Be Girls: The Politics Of Gay Drag," in D. Fuss, (Ed.) *Inside/ Out. Lesbian Theories, Gay Theories*, pp. 32-71 (N. Y.: Routledge, 1991).

Q. 18 Notes

110 Ben Sifuentes-Jauregui, *Transvestism, Masculinity, and Latin American Literature: Genders Share Flesh* (N. Y.: Palgrave, 2002), p. 2.

111 Magnus Hirschfeld, *Transvestites: The Erotic Urge to Cross-Dress*. Tr. Michael A. Lombardi-Nash. (Prometheus Books, 1991; original work published 1910.) For a brief summary of this work and of Hirschfeld's career, see the answer to Q. 95.

112 This view persists, though it has far fewer advocates. Because it worked its way into the popular consciousness it still exercises disproportionate influence.

113 Havelock Ellis, "Eonism and Other Supplementary Studies," vol. 2, pp. 1-110 in H. Ellis, *Studies in the Psychology of Sex*, 2 vols. (N. Y.: Random House reprint of 1941-1942; original work published 1905-1928). For more on Ellis' ideas, see the answer to Q. 95.

114 Robert Stoller, *Observing the Erotic Imagination* (New Haven, CT: Yale Univ. Press, 1985), p. 176. For more on Stoller's views, see the answer to Q. 95.

115 Andrea Cornwall, "Gendered Identities and Gender Ambiguity Among Travestis in Salvador, Brazil," in A. Cornwall & N. Lindisfarne (Eds.), *Dislocating Masculinity: Comparative Ethnographies*, pp. 111-132 (N. Y.: Routledge, 1993), p. 112.

116 Devor, H. (1993). "Toward a Taxonomy of Gendered Sexuality." *Journal of Psychology and Human Sexuality*, 6(1): 23-55. For the example, cf. Devor's Figure 4.

117 Hirschfeld, *Transvestites: The Erotic Urge to Cross-Dress*. The patterns are delineated in the answer to Q. 95.

118 Havelock Ellis, "Eonism and Other Supplementary Studies," vol. 2, pp. 1-110 in H. Ellis, *Studies in the Psychology of Sex*, 2 vols. (N. Y.: Random House reprint of 1941-1942; original work published 1905-1928), p. 36.

[119] N. Lukianowicz, "Survey of Various Aspects of Transvestism in the Light of Our Present Knowledge," *Journal of Nervous and Mental Disease, 128* (no. 1), 36-64 (1959), pp. 43-50.

[120] Harry Benjamin, *The Transsexual Phenomenon* (N.Y.: The Julian Press, 1966), Table 2, 'Sex Orientation Scale'. This book has been reprinted on the Symposion.com website as an IJT Electronic Book. Accessed online at http://www.symposion.com/ ijt/benjamin/index.htm.

[121] Neil Buhrich & Neil McConaghy, "The Clinical Syndromes of Femmiphilic Transvestism," *Archives of Sexual Behavior, 6* (no. 5), 397-412 (1977). The distinction between the two groups they identify among the 34 subjects is the same as indicated in a latter study led by Buhrich; see following note.

[122] Neil Buhrich & Neil McConaghy, "Three Clinically Discrete Categories of Fetishistic Transvestism," *Archives of Sexual Behavior, 8* (no. 2), 151-157 (1979). Cf. Neil Buhrich & Neil McConaghy, "The Discrete Syndromes of Transvestism and Transsexualism," *Archives of Sexual Behavior, 6* (no. 6), 483-495. For more on the work of Buhrich and McConaghy, see the answer to Q. 95.

[123] Neil Buhrich & Trina Beaumont, "Comparison of Transvestism in Australia and America," *Archives of Sexual Behavior, 10* (no. 3), 269-279 (1981). Their latter group today is commonly called 'transsexuals' (see the answer to Q. 19).

[124] Richard F. Docter, *Transvestites and Transsexuals: Toward a Theory of Cross-Gender Behavior.* (N. Y.: Plenum Press, 1988), pp. 11-36. For more on Docter's research and theory, see the answer to Q. 95.

[125] Richard Ekins, *Male Femaling. A Grounded Theory Approach to Cross-Dressing and Sex-Changing* (N. Y.: Routledge, 1997), pp. 54-58 for summaries. Further information can be found in the answer to Q. 95.

[126] The broader implications of the debate between essentialists and others, as well as the many dimensions of the dialog, can be pursued by reading G. G. Bolich, *Conversing On Gender. A Primer for Entering Dialog* (Raleigh: Psyche's Press, 2007).

Q. 19 Notes

[127] Judith Shapiro, "Transsexualism: Reflections on the Persistence of Gender and the Mutability of Sex," in J. Epstein & K. Straub (Eds.), *The Cultural Politics of Gender Ambiguity*, pp. 248-279 (N. Y.: Routledge, 1991), p. 248.

[128] Arndt describes a case in the literature reported in 1830 of a man having "the delusion of being a woman." See William B. Arndt, Jr., *Gender Disorders and the Paraphilias* (Madison, WI: International Universities Press, 1991), p. 113.

[129] Magnus Hirschfeld, "Die intersexuelle Konstitution," *Jahrbuch für Sexuelle Zwischenstufen, 23*, 3-27 (1923).

[130] David O. Caulfield, *Questions and Answers on the Sex Life and Sexual Problems of Transsexuals* (Girard, KS: Haldeman-Julius, 1950).

[131] Harry Benjamin, *The Transsexual Phenomenon* (N. Y.: Julian Press, 1966), and "Transvestism and Transsexualism in the Male and Female," *Journal of Sexual Research, 3*, 107-127. Also see his earlier works: "Transvestism & Transsexualism," *International Journal of Sexology, 7*, 12-14 (1953); "Transsexualism and Transvestism," *Journal of Sex Research, 5* (no. 2), 13; "Transsexualism and Transvestism as Psychosomatic and Somatopsychic Syndromes," *American Journal of Psychotherapy, 8*, 219-230 (1954).

[132] Friedemann Pfäfflin, "Sex Reassignment, Harry Benjamin, and Some European Roots," *The International Journal of Transgenderism, 1* (no. 2) (1997, Nov.-Dec.). Accessed online at http://www.symposion.com/ijt/ijtc0202.htm. Pfäfflin writes that Benjamin had visited Hirschfeld's institute in 1926, met him in Vienna in 1929, helped prepare Hirschfeld's journey to the United States in 1930, and hosted Hirschfeld lectures at his own apartment.

[133] *Diagnostic and Statistical Manual of Mental Disorders, 4th edition* (Washington, D.C.: American Psychiatric Association, 1994), p. 535. Cf. *Diagnostic and Statistical Manual of Mental Disorders, 4th edition, Text Revision* (Washington, D.C.: American Psychiatric Association, 2000), p. 579.

[134] Richard A. Carroll, "Assessment and Treatment of Gender Dysphoria," in S. R. Leiblum & R. C. Rosen (Eds.), *Principles and Practice of Sex Therapy*, 3rd ed., pp. 368-397 (N. Y.: Guilford, 2000), p. 369.

[135] Ray Blanchard, "Transsexualism," in A. E. Kazdin, *Encyclopedia of Psychology*, vol. 8, pp. 116-118. (N. Y.: Oxford Univ. Press, 2000), p. 117.

[136] Richard A. Carroll, "Assessment and Treatment of Gender Dysphoria," in S. R. Leiblum & R. C. Rosen (Eds.), *Principles and Practice of Sex Therapy*, 3rd ed., pp. 368-397 (N. Y.: Guilford, 2000), p. 369.

[137] Ibid.

[138] Philip Wilson, Clare Sharp, & Susan Carr, "The Prevalence of Gender Dysphoria in Scotland: A Primary Care Study," *British Journal of General Practice, 49*, 991-992 (1999).

[139] T. Sorensen & P. Hertoft, "Sexmodifying Operations on Transsexuals in Denmark in the Period 1950-1977," *Acta Psychiatrica Scandinavia, 61* (no. 1), 56-66 (1980).

[140] J. Hoenig & J. C. Kenna, "The Prevalence of Transsexualism in England Wales," *British Journal of Psychology, 124*, 181-190 (1974).

[141] Cordula Weitze & Susanne Osburg, "Transsexualism in Germany: Emperical Data on Epidemiology and Application of the German Transsexuals' Act During Its First Ten Years," *Archives of Sexual Behavior, 25* (no. 4), 409-425 (1996).

[142] P. L. Eklund, L. J. Gooren, & P. D. Bezemer, "Prevalence of Transsexualism in the Netherlands," *British Journal of Psychiatry, 152*, 638-640 (1988). In 1980, figures presented had been 1-in-45,000 for males and 1-in-200,000 for females.

[143] P. J. Van Kesteren, L. J. Gooren, & J. A. Megens, "An Epidemiological and Demographic Study of Transsexuals in the Netherlands," *Archives of Sexual Behavior, 25* (no. 4), 589-600 (1996).

[144] Wilson, Sharp, & Carr, p. 991.

[145] W. F. Soi, "The Prevalence of Transsexualism in Singapore," *Acta Psychiatrica Scandinavia, 78* (no. 4), 501-504 (1988). The previous figures were 1-in-25,000 for MtF transsexuals (1977), and 1-in-36,000 for FtM transsexuals (1980).

[146] Jan Walinder, *Transsexualism: A Study of Forty-three Cases* (Goteborg: Scandinavian University Books, 1967).

[147] Stig-Eric Olsson & Anders R. Möller, "On the Incidence and Sex Ratio of Transsexualism in Sweden, 1972-2002," *Archives of Sexual Behavior, 32* (no. 4), 381-386 (2003).

[148] Ira B. Pauly, "Female Transsexualism: Part 1," *Archives of Sexual Behavior, 3* (no. 6), 487-507 (1974), p. 493.

[149] Aude Michel, Christian Mormont, & J. J. Legros, "A Psycho-Endocrinological Overview of Transsexualism," *European Journal of Endocrinology, 145,* 365-376 (2001), p. 368, Table 1. Accessed online at http://www.eje.org/eje/145/0365/1450365.pdf.

[150] Harry Benjamin, *The Transsexual Phenomenon* (N.Y.: The Julian Press, 1966), chapter 9, "Legal Aspects in Transvestism and Transsexualism." This book has been reprinted on the Symposion.com website as an IJT Electronic Book. Accessed online at http://www.symposion.com/ijt/benjamin/index.htm.

[151] Jan Wilander, "Transsexualism: Definition, Prevalence and Sex Distribution," *Acta Psychiatrica Scandinavica 44* (Supplement 203), 255-258 (1968).

[152] Jon K. Meyer, Norman J. Knorr, & Dietrich Blumer, "Characterization of a Self-Designated Transsexual Population," *Archives of Sexual Behavior, 1* (no. 3), 219-230 (1971), p. 220.

[153] Michel, Mormont, & Legros, p. 368, Table 1.

[154] John Sik-Nin Ko, "Research and Discussion Paper: A Descriptive Study of Sexual Dysfunction and Gender Identity Clinic in the University of Hong Kong Psychiatric Unit, 1991-2001." Extracts from a dissertation submitted as part of the Part III Fellowship Examination for the Hong Kong College of Psychiatrists. Accessed online at http://web.hku.hk/~sjwinter/TransgenderASIA/ paper_qmh_evaluation.htm.

[155] P. J. Van Kesteren, L. J. Gooren, & J. L. Megens, "An Epidemiological and Demographic Study of Transsexuals in The Netherlands," *Archives of Sexual Behavior, 25,* 589-600. Between two-thirds and three-quarters (67-78%) of transsexual adults report this discrepant feeling having first surfaced in childhood.

[156] W. F. Tsoi, "Developmental Profile of 200 Male and 100 Female Transsexuals in Singapore," *Archives of Sexual Behavior, 25* (no. 6), 595-605 (1990).

[157] Virginia Prince & P. M. Bentler, "Survey of 504 Cases of Transvestism," *Psychological Reports, 31,* 903-917 (1972), p. 910.

[158] American Psychiatric Association, *Diagnostic and Statistical Manual of Mental Disorders, 4th ed., Text Revision* (Washington, D. C.: American Psychiatric Association, 2000), p. 581. For the history of this condition in the DSM model, see the answer to Q. 96; for criticisms that have been directed against this model, see the answer to Q. 99.

[159] Blanchard's views are more fully set out in the answer to Q. 95. See Ray Blanchard, "Transsexualism," in A. E. Kazdin, *Encyclopedia of Psychology*, vol. 8, pp. 116-118. (N. Y.: Oxford Univ. Press, 2000).

[160] The most controversial of Blanchard's ideas is his concept of *autogynephilia*—a crossdressing male's 'love of himself as a woman.' This idea has proven deeply divisive within the transgender community, though the DSM model (with Blanchard and allies on the committee for revising this section) incorporated it into the Text Revision of the 4th edition (2000). I think the term is more often than not misleading. When I listen to crossdressing males what I hear might be better labeled 'auto*auto*philia'—'love of oneself as oneself'—a deeply felt sense of a self liberated through crossdressing, and not as sexually focused as Blanchard appears to suggest.

[161] J. Paul Federoff, 'The Case *Against* Publicly Funded Transsexual Surgery,' pp. 1-3, in Ray Blanchard & J. Paul Federoff, "The Case For and Against Publicly Funded Transsexual Surgery," *Psychiatry Rounds, 4* (no. 2), 1-6 (2000), p. 1f..

[162] Michel, Mormont, & Legros, pp. 366-367. Also see my discussion in the answers to Q. 21-22.

[163] Noelle Howey, *Dress Codes. Of Three Girlhoods—My Mother's, My Father's, and Mine* (N. Y.: Picador USA, 2002), p. 175.

[164] Sally Hines, "What's the difference? Bringing Particularity to Queer Studies of Transgender," *Journal of Gender Studies*, 15 (no. 1), 49-66 (2006), p. 59.

[165] Meyer, Knorr, & Blumer, p. 226. Cf. Figure 6. They later write that one-third crossdressed "most of the time" (p. 229).

[166] Ko, 'Results' section.

[167] Anke A. Ehrhardt, G. Grisanti, & E. A. McCauley, "Female to Male Transsexuals Compared to Lesbians: Behavioral Patterns of Childhood and Adolescent Development," *Archives of Sexual Behavior*, 8 (no. 6), 481-490 (1979).

[168] W. F. Tsoi, "Developmental Profile of 200 Male and 100 Female Transsexuals in Singapore," *Archives of Sexual Behavior*, 19 (no. 6), 595-605 (1990), p. 595.

[169] Andrew Sharpe, "From Functionality to Aesthetics: The Architecture of Transgender Jurisprudence," *Murdoch University Electronic Journal of Law*, 8 (no. 1) (2001), accessed online at http://www.murdoch.edu.au/elaw/issues/v8n1/sharpe81nf.html. Also see Andrew Sharpe, "English Transgender Law Reform and the Spectre of Corbett," *Feminist Legal Studies*, 10 (no. 1), 65-89 (2002). Cf. Andrew Sharpe, "One Step Beyond: The New Zealand Judiciary and Transgender Law Reform," *Alternative Law Journal*, 26 (no. 3), 130-135 (2001). Also cf. Andrew N. Sharpe, *Transgender Jurisprudence: Dysphoric Bodies of Law* (London: Cavendish, 2002).

[170] Ibid, §11.

[171] Ibid, §§17-24.

[172] The medical advances needed to accomplish a successful transition from one sex to another involved both endocrinology—Harry Benjamin's field—and surgery. With respect to the latter, techniques learned during the First World War proved crucial, as illustrated in Pagan Kennedy's *The First Man-Made Man. The Story of Two Sex Changes, One Love Affair, and a Twentieth-Century Medical Revolution* (N. Y.: Bloomsbury, 2007).

[173] Benjamin, chapter 10, "The Female Transsexual." Accessed online at http://www.symposion.com/ijt/benjamin/chap_10.htm.

[174] Magnus Hirschfeld, *Sexuelle Zwischenstufen. Sexualpathologie. 2. Tiel* (Bonn: Marcus & Webers, 1918).

[175] Friedemann Pfäfflin, "Sex Reassignment, Harry Benjamin, and Some European Roots," *The International Journal of Transgenderism*, 1 (no. 2) (1997, Nov.-Dec.). Accessed online at http://www.symposion.com/ijt/ijtc0202.htm. Cf. Felix Abraham, "Genitalumwandlung an zwei maenlichen transvestiten," *Zietschrift für Sexualwissenschaft*, 18, 223-226 (1931); see the translation, "Genital Reassignment on Two Male Transvestites," *The International Journal of Transgenderism*, 2 (no. 1) (1998, Jan.-Mar.), accessed online at http://www.symposion.com/ijt/ijtc0302.htm.

[176] In addition to Einer Wegener/Lili Elbe, a MtF transsexual whose story is presented in the answer, others include the FtM transsexuals Zdenka Koubkova/Zdenek Koubkov (1935) and Elvira de Brujin/Willy de Brujin (1937). Pioneering SRS involved both genetic males and females.

[177] Lili Elbe, *Ein Mensch wechselt sein Geschlecht. Eine Lebensbeichte* (Dresden: Carl Reissner, 1932). Her autobiography appeared in English shortly thereafter: Niels Hoyer (Ed.), *Man into Woman* (London: Jarrods, 1933). "Niels Hoyer" is a pseudonym for

Ernst Ludwig Hathorn Jacobson. Also see David Ebershoff, *Danish Girl* (N. Y.: Penguin Books, 2000), a novel based on Elbe's life.

[178] Niels Hoyer (Ed.), *Man into Woman* (London: Jarrods, 1933). While the basic facts of Elbe's story are easily ascertained, the account is sensationalistic in tone and rather unreliable for accurate details. While still legally a man, Wegener, a successful painter, had been married to the noted Danish Art Deco painter Greta Wegener (formerly Greta Waud), who remained with her husband throughout his transition. In this transitional period, prior to the surgeries, Wegener/Elbe was a favorite model for Greta; the paintings of Lili were popular and perhaps contributed to the 1920s image of the 'ideal woman.' After surgery, Elbe had her marriage annulled and accepted an offer of marriage. Greta soon remarried, to a mutual friend. Lili Elbe's death was reputed to be heart problems as a result of complications from her surgeries.

[179] The information on Dillon comes from Pagan Kennedy's *The First Man-Made Man* and other published sources. On the internet, see the material (including a brief video) at Transgenderzone.com, accessed online at http://www.transgenderzone.com/features/michaeldillon.htm.

[180] Jennifer Finney Boylan, *She's Not There. A Life in Two Genders* (N. Y.: Broadway Books, 2003), p. 245.

[181] Jan Morris, *Conundrum* (N. Y.: Harcourt Brace Jovanovich, 1974, reissued 2006 by Random House), p. 143.

[182] The biographical material on Morris comes from a variety of sources, but most especially, Caroline Frost, *Jan Morris: A Profile* [Documentaries], on the BBC Four website accessed online at http://www.bbc.co.uk/bbcfour/documentaries/profile/profile_jan_morris.shtml. The BBC Documentary was first broadcast in March, 2002.

[183] Susan Stryker, *Christine Jorgensen: A Personal Autobiography* (S. F.: Cleiss Press, 2000 reprint of 1967 ed.).

[184] Ibid. (Dustjacket back cover.)

[185] Michelle Ingrassia, "In 1952, She Was a Scandal: When George Jorgensen Decided to Change His Name—and His Body—the Nation Wasn't Quite Ready," *Newsday* (1989, May 5). Accessed online at http://www.transhistory.org/history/ TH_New Clip_Christine1.html.

[186] Renee Richards with John Ames, *Second Serve* (N. Y.: Stein and Day, 1983).

[187] Susan Birrell & Cheryl L. Cole, "Double Fault: Renee Richards and the Construction and Naturalization of Difference," *Sociology of Sport Journal*, 7 (no. 1), 1-21 (1990). Reprinted in S. Birrell & C. L. Cole (Eds.), *Women, Sport, and Culture*, pp. 373-397 (Champaign, IL: Human Kinetics, 1994). The argument mounted in court by Richards' opponents was that an unfair competitive advantage was gained by virtue of having had before surgery development and training as a male tennis player.

[188] Cindy Shmerier, "Regrets, She's Had a Few" [interview with Renee Richards], *Tennis, 35* (no. 2), 31-32 (1999, Mar.).

[189] Information drawn from Jayne County with Rupert Smith, *Man Enough to Be a Woman* (N. Y.: Serpent's Tail, 1995). Also see Jayne Wayne's website, accessed online at http://www.jaynecounty.com/.

[190] "Government Policy Concerning Transsexual People," *Department for Constitutional Affairs*. Accessed online at http://www.dca.gov.uk/constitution/transsex/ policy.htm.

Q. 20 Notes

[191] Dallas Denny, "Transgender in the United States: A Brief Discussion," *SIECUS Report, 28* (no. 1), 8-13 (1999, Oct./Nov.), p. 9.

[192] Walter O. Bockting, "From Construction to Context: Gender Through the Eyes of the Transgendered," *SIECUS Report, 28* (no. 1), 3-7 (1999, Oct./Nov.), p. 3.

[193] Richard A. Carroll, "Assessment and Treatment of Gender Dysphoria," in S. R. Leiblum & R. C. Rosen (Eds.), *Principles and Practice of Sex Therapy,* 3rd ed., pp. 368-397 (N. Y.: Guilford, 2000), p. 370. This is preferable to the succinct but misleading phrase suggested by activist writer Leslie Feinberg, who writes, "trans*gender* people traverse, bridge, or blur the *sex* they were assigned at birth." I dislike the commingling of the terms sex and gender in this fashion; the 'traversing, bridging, or blurring' is primarily of gender assignment, though it may often also encompass sex assignment (cf. the answer to Q. 5). See Leslie Feinberg, *Transgender Warriors: Making History from Joan of Arc to Dennis Rodman* (Boston: Beacon Press, 1996), p. x.

[194] *GenderPAC. First National Survey of TransGender Violence* (GenderPAC, 1997), p. 3. Accessed online at http://hatecrime.transadvocacy.com/documents/TransViolence %20Survey%20Results.pdf.

[195] B. Thom & K. More, "Welcome to the Festival," in *The Second International Transgender Film and Video Festival* (London: Alchemy Festival Productions, 1998), cited in Richard Ekins & Dave King, "Transgendering, Migrating and Love of Oneself as a Woman: A Contribution to a Sociology of Autogynephilia," *The International Journal of Transgenderism, 5* (no. 3) (2001), accessed online at http://www.symposion.com/ijt/ijtvo05no03_01.htm.

[196] My list is similar to that offered by Bockting (p. 3), except that I include the intersexed and he separates transgenderists from transvestites.

[197] Patricia Gagne & Richard Tewksbury, "Conformity Pressures and Gender Resistance Among Transgendered Individuals," *Social Problems, 45* (no. 1), 81-101 (1998), p. 100.

[198] Denny, p. 8.

[199] See Kittiwut Jod Taywaditep, "Marginalization Among the Marginalized: Gay Men's Anti-Effeminacy Attitudes," *Journal of Homosexuality, 42* (no. 1), 1-28 (2001).

[200] Virginia Prince, "Seventy Years in the Trenches of the Gender Wars," in B. Bullough, V. L. Bullough, & J. Elias (Eds.), *Gender Blending,* pp. 469-476 (Amherherst, NY: Prometheus Books, 1997), p. 469.

[201] Richard F. Docter, *Transvestites and Transsexuals: Toward a Theory of Cross-Gender Behavior.* (N. Y.: Plenum Press, 1988). Cf. Richard F. Docter, "Dimensions of Transvestism and Transsexualism," *Journal of Psychology & Human Sexuality, 5* (no. 1), 15-37 (1993).

[202] Bonnie Bullough & Vern Bullough, ""Men Who Cross-Dress: A Survey," in B. Bullough, V. L. Bullough, & J. Elias (Eds.), *Gender Blending,* pp. 174-188 (Amherst, NY: Prometheus Books, 1997), p. 184.

[203] Randolph Trumbach, "The Third-Gender in Twentieth Century America [A Review of George Chauncey's *Gay New York*]," *Journal of Social History, 30* (no. 2), 497-501 (1996).

[204] Will Roscoe, *Changing Ones: Third and Fourth Genders in Native America* (N. Y.: St. Martin's Press, 1998), p. 210.

[205] Ingrid M. Sell, "Third Gender: A Qualitative Study of the Experience of Individuals Who Identify as Being Neither Man Nor Woman," *The Psychotherapy Patient, 13* (nos. 1-2), 131-145 (2004), pp. 139-140.

[206] Ibid, pp. 140-142; quote is from p. 142.

[207] Yvonne, "Who We Are," *Yvonne's Place for Crossdressers* (1999). Accessed online at http://www.yvonnesplace.net/index2.html. There were 1,212 respondents on this matter. Other choices endorsed ranged from 'man' (8%), to 'bi-gendered' (6%), to 'gender enhanced male' (5%), to 'gender gifted' (3%), to 'she-male' (3%), to 'androgynous' (2%). Interestingly, as noted by Elizabeth Reitz Mullenix, the label 'she-male' was used in the 19th century to criticize members of the Women's Movement who wore dress defined as masculine. See Elizabeth Reitz Mullenix, "Private Women/Public Acts: Petticoat Government and the Performance of Resistance," *The Drama Review, 46* (no. 1), 104-117 (2002), p. 110.

[208] Lynne Carroll, Paula J. Gilroy, and Jo Ryan, "Counseling Transgendered, Transsexual, and Gender-Variant Clients," *Journal of Counseling & Development, 80* (no. 2), 131-139 (2002), p. 131. A few other terms include 'gender blender,' 'gender free,' 'shemales,' and 'GEM—gender enhanced male.'

[209] Ana Mariella Bacigalupo, "The Struggle for Mapuche Shamans' Masculinity: Colonial Politics of Gender, Sexuality, and Power in Southern Chile," *Ethnohistory, 51* (no. 3), 489-533 (2004), p. 514. Bacigalupo prefers the term 'co-gendered,' though even that term does not work equally well for the different groups she describes. She credits Barbara Tedlock for her notion of 'co-gendered'; see Barbara Tedlock, "Recognizing and Celebrating the Feminine in Shamanic Heritage," in M. Hoppal (Ed.), *Rediscovery of Shamanic Heritage*, pp. 297-316 (Budapest: Akademiai Kiado).

Introduction to Question Set 3

[210] Richard F. Docter, Transvestites and Transsexuals: Toward a Theory of Cross-Gender Behavior. (N. Y.: Plenum Press, 1988), Preface.

Q. 21 Notes

[211] Cf. Havelock Ellis, "Eonism and Other Supplementary Studies," vol. 2, pp. 1-110 in H. Ellis, *Studies in the Psychology of Sex*, 2 vols. (N. Y.: Random House reprint of 1941-1942; original work published 1905-1928), vol. 2, pp. 32, 110. For more on Ellis' views, see the answer to Q. 95. Also see Christina Hamburger & Georg K. Stürup, "Transvestism. Hormonal, Psychiatric, and Surgical Treatment," *Journal of the American Medical Association, 152* (no. 5), 391-396 (1953). The authors appeal to Hirschfeld's contention for 'constitutional factors' being operative. They focus on what we today refer to as transsexualism, about which they say, "It is probable that physical factors play a decisive role . . ." (p. 392).

[212] Jason Cromwell, *Transmen and Ftms: Identities, Bodies, Genders, and Sexualities* (Urbana: Univ. of Illinois Press, 1999), p. 128.

[213] Lawrence S. Kubie, "The Drive to Become Both Sexes," *Psychoanalytic Quarterly, 43* (no. 3), 349-426 (1974), p. 354.

[214] See, for example, *The Nature of the Child* §20, a 4th century B.C.E. treatise that speculates that "the reason that those who are made eunuchs while they are still children neither become pubescent nor grow hair on their chins, but are hairless over their whole body, is that no passage is opened for the sperm, and therefore the epidermis does not become porous anywhere on the body . . . ." See I. M. Lonie (Translator), "Embryology

and Anatomy," in G. E. R. Lloyd (Ed.), *Hippocratic Writings*, pp. 315-353 (N. Y.: Penguin Books, 1983 reprint of 1978 ed.), p. 333.

[215] Douglas T. Kenrick & Carol L. Luce, "An Evolutionary Life-History Model of Gender Differences and Similarities," in T. Eckes (Ed.), *The Developmental Social Psychology of Gender*, pp. 35-64 (Mahwah, NJ: Lawrence Erlbaum, 2000), p. 37.

[216] Myra Hird claims that non-linear biology "provides a growing catalogue of homosexual, transgender, and non-reproductive heterosexual behavior in animals. . . ." See Myra J. Hird, "Naturally Queer," *Feminist Theory, 5* (no. 1), 85-89 (2004), p. 87. On homosexuality in animals see the massive study (752 pages) done by Bruce Bagemihl, *Biological Exuberance: Animal Homosexuality and Natural Diversity* (N. Y.: St.Martin's Press, 1999). A list of more than 450 species in which homosexual behavior has been documented is found in Jonah Lehrer, "The Effeminate Sheep & Other Problems with Darwinian Sexual Selection," *Seed, 2* (no. 5), 52-57 (2006), p. 56. More than 200 of these species are mammalian.

[217] Joan Roughgarden, *Evolution's Rainbow. Diversity, Gender, and Sexuality in Nature and People* (Berkeley: Univ. of California Press, 2004), p. 14.

[218] Joan Roughgarden, "Evolution and the Embodiment of Gender," *GLQ: A Journal of Lesbian and Gay Studies, 10*, 287-291 (2004), p. 288. Cf. *Evolution's Rainbow*, chapter 1 (pp. 13ff.).

[219] Ibid. Cf. *Evolution's Rainbow*, chapter 3 (pp. 30ff.).

[220] Ibid. On multiple genders in animal species, see *Evolution's Rainbow*, chapter 6 (pp. 75ff.).

[221] Ibid, p. 290. On 'masculine females' see *Evolution's Rainbow*, chapter 7 (pp. 106ff.); on 'feminine females' see chapters 6-7 (pp. 83-113). In nature some species permit changes in sex, as in protogynous hermaphroditic fish such as the Nassau grouper, where all young are female and when the need for a male arises the largest female in a harem is transformed through hormonal changes into a larger male. See Kenrick & Luce, p. 43.

[222] Bagemihl, p. 38.

[223] Robert T. Mason & David Crews, "Female Mimicry in Garter Snakes," *Nature, 316*, p. 59 (1985). Also part of *Science Frontiers Online* (no. 41, Sept.-Oct., 1985), accessed online at http://www.science-frontiers.com/sf041/sf041p07.htm. Also see, R. Shine, B. Phillips, H. Waye, M. LeMaster & R. T. Mason,"Benefits of Female Mimicry in Snakes," *Nature, 414* (2001), 267. Cf. R. Shine, P. Harlow, M. P. Lemaster, I. T. Moore, & R. T. Mason, "The Transvestite Serpent: Why Do Male Garter Snakes Court (Some) Other Males?" *Animal Behaviour, 59* (no. 2), 349-359 (2000).

[224] Bagemihl, p. 38.

[225] W. T. Wcislo, "Transvestism Hypothesis: A Cross-Sex Source of Morphological Variation for the Evolution of Parasitism among Sweat Bees (Hymenoptera: Halictidae)?" *Annals of the Entomological Society of America 92* (1999), 239-242.

[226] C. Clarke, F. M. M. Clarke, S. C. Collins, A. C. L. Gill, & J. R. G. Turner, "Male-Like Females, Mimicry and Transvestism in Butterflies (Lepidoptera: Papilionidae)," *Systematic Entomology, 10* (1985), 257-283. Cf. S. E. Cook, J. G. Vernon, M. Bateson, & T. Guilford, "Mate Choice in the Polymorphic African Swallowtail Butterfly, *Papilio dardanus*: Male-like Females May Avoid Sexual Harassment. *Animal Behavior, 47*, 389-397 (1994).

[227] K. Peschke, "Male Aggression, Female Mimicry and Female Choice in the Rove Beetle, *Aleochara curtula* (Coleoptera, Staphylinidae)," *Ethology, 75*, 265-284 (1987). Cf. A. Forsyth & J. Alcock, "Female Mimicry and Resource Defense Polygyny by Males of a Tropical Rove Beetle, *Leistotrophus versicolor* (Coleoptera: Staphylinidae)," *Behavioral Ecology and Sociobiology, 26* (no. 5), 325-330 (1990).

[228] D. Scott, "Sexual Mimicry Regulates the Attractiveness of Mated *Drosophila melanogaster*Ffemales. *Proceedings of the National Academy of Sciences, USA 83*, 8429-8433 (1986).

[229] J. Godwin, D. Crews, & R. R. Warner, "Behavioural Sex Change in the Absence of Gonads in a Coral Reef Fish," *Processions Royal Society of London B 263*, 1683-1688 (1996). Also see Mark D. Norman, Julian Finn, & Tom Tregenza, "Female Impersonation as an Alternative Reproductive Strategy in Giant Cuttlefish," *Proceedings of the Royal Society Biological Sciences Series B, 266*, 1347-1349 (1999).

[230] N. E. Langmore & A. T. D. Bennett, "Strategic Concealment of Sexual Identity in an Estrildid Finch. *Proceedings of the Royal Society Biological Sciences Series B, 266*, 543-550 (1999).

[231] Mason & Crews.

[232] The case of the Serengetti spotted hyena is discussed in the text; see M. L. East, H. Hofer, & Wolfgang Wickler, "The Erect 'Penis' Is a Flag of Submission in a Female-Dominated Society: Greetings in Serengeti Spotted Hyenas. *Behavioral Ecology and Sociobiology, 33*, 355-370 (1993)..

[233] See, for example, Glenn-Peter Sætre & Tore Slagsvold, "The Significance of Female Mimicry in Male Contests," *The American Naturalist, 171* (no. 6), 981-995 (1996). This article nicely details some of the general arguments and data for sexual mimicry done by males in a variety of species.

[234] Bagemihl, p. 38.

[235] Mason & Crews, p. 59.

[236] Hillary Mayell, "Female-Mimicking Male Snakes Are Out to Get Warm, Study Says," *National Geographic News* (2001, Nov. 15). Accessed online at http://news.nationalgeographic.com/news/2001/11/ 1115_snakemating.html. Mason and Shine's work was published in the Nov. 15, 2001 issue of *Nature*.

[237] East, Hofer & Wickler. Cf. Martin M. Muller & Richard Wrangham, "Sexual Mimicry in Hyenas," *The Quarterly Review of Biology, 77* (no. 1), 3-16 (2002). Muller & Wrangham suggest the sexual mimicry provides a measure of protection from aggression by other females.

[238] John H. Crook, "Sexual Selection, Dimorphism, and Social Organization in the Primates," in Bernard Campbell (Ed.), *Sexual Selection and the Descent of Man 1871-1971*, pp. 231-281 (Chicago: Aldine, 1972); see p. 245.

[239] Andreas Paul, "Sexual Selection and Mate Choice," *International Journal of Primatology, 23* (no. 4), 877-904 (2002), p. 880, Table 1.

[240] Wolfgang Wickler, *Emancipated Sexual Signals in Primates* (nd.). Accessed online at http://www.mpi-seewiesen.mpg.de/~knauer/wickler/sose3.html. Cf. Wolfgang Wickler, "Socio-Sexual Signals and Their Intra-Specific Imitation Among Primates," in D. Morris (Ed.), *Primate Ethology*, pp. 69-147 (London: Weidenfeld & Nicolson, 1967).

[241] Kenrick & Luce, p. 40.

²⁴² Such seems to be the case, for example, among Lazuli buntings, where dull plumage in a SY male's first breeding season reduces aggression from older ASY males, presumably by signaling a less competitive status. See Vincent R. Muehter, Erick Greene, & Laurene Ratcliffe, "Delayed Plumage Maturation in Lazuli Buntings: Tests of the Female Mimicry and Status Signalling Hypotheses," *Behavioral Ecology and Sociobiology*, 41 (no. 4) 281-290 (1997).

²⁴³ Of course, the 'feminine' male walks a dangerous course, for too effeminate an appearance can itself generate aggression by other males.

²⁴⁴ For an introduction to attachment theory, see John Bowlby, *A Secure Base. Parent-Child Attachment and Healthy Human Development* (N. Y.: Basic Books, 1988). Bowlby's major work was a trilogy on attachment and loss, of which the final volume may be especially pertinent; see John Bowlby, *Attachment and Loss, vol. 3: Loss* (N. Y.: Basic Books, 1980).

²⁴⁵ Object relations theorist Donald Winnicott observes that children use objects (e.g., a favorite blanket) as concrete substitutes for the temporary absence of a parent. Such an object is transitional in that it helps the child move from complete dependence on the actual proximity of the parent to independence from the physical presence of the parent because the parent has become an internalized object. See D. W. Winnicott, *Human Nature* (N. Y.: Schocken Books, 1988), pp. 106-107; also see D. W. Winnicott, "The Fate of the Transitional Object," in C. Winnicott, R. Shepherd, & M. Davis (Eds.), *Psycho-Analytic Explorations*, pp. 53-58 (Cambridge: Harvard Univ. Press, 1989).

²⁴⁶ Such incidents have been self-reported in surveys of crossdressing males in the United States, but the behavior has also been reported in other cultures, which supports the notion of a biological mechanism at work. For one such instance in another culture, see Susan Sered, *Women of the Sacred Groves. Divine Priestesses of Okinawa* (N. Y.: Oxford Univ. Press, 1999).

²⁴⁷ Examples can be found in Japanese *No* drama; see Royall Tyler (Ed. & Trans.), *Nō Dramas* (N. Y.: Penguin Books, 1992), p. 188. For more on *No* drama and crossdressing, see the answer to Q. 44.

²⁴⁸ For more on Shakespeare's use of crossdressing and its use generally in the theater, see the answer to Q. 44.

²⁴⁹ Such commercials feature either men or women. In one, for example, a man dons his absent lover's dress. In another a woman wears her absent lover's shirt and boxers.

²⁵⁰ In children, for instance, many professionals talk about tactile defensiveness, "a pattern of observable behavioural and emotional responses, which are aversive, negative and out of proportion, to certain types of tactile stimuli that most people would find to be non-painful." Sidney Chu, *Tactile Defensiveness. Information for Parents and Professionals* (1999), p. 1. Accessed online at http://www.dyspraxiafoundation.org.uk/dyspraxia-information/PDFfiles/Tactile%20Defensiveness.pdf.

²⁵¹ Ibid, p. 2. Chu recommends (p. 5) permitting the child to avoid irritating substances and to wear clothes with the fabric they find soothing. The National Autistic Society likewise notes the role of the tactile system and how some children refuse to wear certain clothes because they dislike the texture or pressure on their skin; they similarly recommend allowing such children to wear clothing they find comfortable. See *The Sensory World of the Autistic Spectrum* published on the United Kingdoms' National Autis-

tic Society website, accessed online at http://www.nas.org.uk/nas/jsp/ polopoly.jsp?d= 299&a= 3766&view=print.

252 Patricia Gail Williams, Anna Mary Allard, & Lonnie Sears, "Case Study: Cross-gender Preoccupations in Two Male Children with Autism," *Journal of Autism & Developmental Disorders, 26* (no. 6), 635-642 (1996).

253 Richard W. Smith, "Is Biology Destiny? Or Is It Culture? (A New Look at Transvestism and Homosexuality)," *Counseling Psychologist, 5* (no. 1), 90-91 (1975).

254 Glenn D. Wilson, "An Ethological Approach to Sexual Deviation," in G. D. Wilson (Ed.), *Variant Sexuality: Research and Theory*, pp. 84-115 (London: Croom Helm, 1987). Cf. the ideas of John Money (see answer to Q. 95).

255 George H. Wiedeman, "Transvestism (Correspondence)," *Journal of the American Medical Association, 152* (no. 12), 1167 (1953).

256 Phoebe Dewing, Tao Shi, Steve Horvathm & Eric Vilain, "Sexually Dimorphic Gene Expression in Mouse Brain Precedes Gonadal Differentiation," *Molecular Brain Research, 118*, 92-90 (2003). The researchers' aim was to test the hypothesis that by directly inducing sexually dimorphic patterns of neural development in the subject mice brains they could influence the sexual differences between male and female brains.

257 G. J. De Vries, E. F. Rissman, R. B. Simerly, L. Y. Yang, E. M. Scordalakes, C. J. Auger, A. Swain, R. Lovell-Badge, P. S. Burgoyne, & A. P. Arnold, "A Model System for Study of Sex Chromosome Effects on Sexually Dimorphic Neural and Behavioral Traits," *Journal of Neuroscience, 22* (no. 20), 9005-9014 (2002).

258 For more information on intersex conditions, see the website of the Intersex Society of North America, especially their FAQ webpage, accessed online at http://www.isna.org/faq/.

259 John Bancroft, "Biological Factors in Human Sexuality," *The Journal of Sex Research, 39* (no. 1), 15-21 (2002), p. 15. Cf. Kenneth Zucker, "Intersexuality and Gender Identity Differentiation," *Annual Review of Sex Research, 10*, 1-69 (1999).

260 Dean Hamer *et al.*, "A Linkage Between DNA Markers on the X Chromosome and Male Sexual Orientation," *Science, 261*, 321-327 (1993). Also see Dean Hamer & Peter Copeland, *The Science of Desire: The Search for the Gay Gene and the Biology of Behavior* (N. Y.: Simon & Schuster, 1994).

261 Brian S. Mustanski, Michael G. DuPree, Caroline M. Nievergelt, Sven Brocklandt, Nicholas J. Schork, & Dean H. Hamer, "A Genomewide Scan of Male Sexual Orientation," *Human Genetics, 116* (no. 4), 272-278 (2005).

262 Studies have found differences in various behaviors suggestive of a 'hard-wired,' or innate biological difference between homosexual and heterosexual men. These include physiologically mediated differences in PET scan findings for response to pheromones, response preferences to the smell of sweat, and involuntary startle response. See, for example, Ivanka Savic, Hans Berglund, & Per Lindström, "Brain Response to Putative Pheromones in Homosexual Men," *Proceedings of the National Academy of Sciences, 102*, 7356-7361 (2005).

263 For a thorough examination of many possible ties between intersex conditions and transgender, see Robert W. Jasinski, "Gynecomastia: An Occasional Marker for M2F Transgenderism?" *The Journal of Gender Speculation, 1* (no. 1) (2004). Accessed online at http://www.geocities.com/gmapop04. 'Gynecomastia' (literally, 'women breasts') is the medical term for unusually large breasts in males.

[264] H. F. L. Meyer-Bahlburg, R. S. Gruen, M. I. New, J. J. Bell, A. Morishima, Y. Bueno, & S. W. Baker, "Gender Change from Female to Male in Classical Congenital Adrenal Hyperplasia," *Hormones and Behavior, 30*, 319-332 (1996). Also see K.J. Zucker, S. J. Bradley, G. Oliver, *et al.*, "Psychosexual Development of Women with Congenital Adrenal Hyperplasia," *Hormones and Behavior, 30*, 300-318 (1996). Cf. F.M. E. Slijper, "Androgens and Gender Role Behavior in Girls with Congenital Adrenal Hyperplasia," *Progress in Brain Research, 61*, 417-422 (1984).

[265] Richard Green, "Family Cooccurrence of 'Gender Dysphoria': Ten Sibling or Parent-Child Pairs," *Archives of Sexual Behavior, 29* (no. 5), 499-507 (2000), p. 504.

[266] Neil Buhrich, "A Case of Familial Heterosexual Transvestism," *Acta Psychiatrica Scandinavica 55* (no. 3), 199-201 (1977).

[267] J. Arcelus & W. P. Bouman, "Case Reports: Gender Identity Disorder in a Child with a Family History of Cross-Dressing," *Sexual and Relationship Therapy, 15* (no. 4), 407-411 (2000).

[268] Peter R. Joyce & Les Ding, "Transsexual Sister," *Australian and New Zealand Journal of Psychiatry, 19* (no. 2), 188-189 (1985).

[269] Green, pp. 500-504. Cf. Robert J. Stoller & Howard J. Baker, "Two Male Transsexuals in One Family," *Archives of Sexual Behavior, 2* (no. 4), 323-328 (1973). Also cf. Robert F. Sabalis, Allen Frances, Susan N. Appenzeller, & Willie B. Mosely, "The Three Sisters: Transsexual Male Siblings," *American Journal of Psychiatry, 131* (no. 8), 907-909 (1974). Also cf. Embry A. McKee, Howard B. Roback, & Marc H. Hollender, "Transsexualism in Two Male Triplets," *American Journal of Psychiatry, 133* (no. 3), 334-337 (1976).

[270] Jack L. Croughan, Marcel Saghir, Rose Cohen, & Eli Robins, "A Comparison of Treated and Untreated Male Crossdressers," *Archives of Sexual Behavior, 10* (no. 6), 515-528 (1981), Table VII (and discussion accompanying it).

[271] J.-N. Zhou, M. A. Hofman, L. J. Gooren, & D. F. Swaab, "A Sex Difference in the Human Brain and Its Relation to Transsexuality," *Nature, 378*, 68-70 (1995), p.68. The article is reprinted online by *The International Transgender Journal,1* (no. 1) (1997, July-Sept.), accessed online at http://www.symposion.com/ijt/ijtc0106.htm.

[272] Ibid, pp. 69-70. Cf. W. C. Chung, G. J. De Vries, & D. F. Swaab, "Sexual Differentiation of the Bed Nucleus of the Stria Terminalis in Humans May Extend Into Adulthood," *Journal of Neuroscience, 22*, 1027-1033 (2002), which records research indicating that the significant difference found between male and female brains only becomes apparent in adulthood, suggesting that sexual differentiation of the brain continues into adulthood. The authors pointedly caution that, "the lack of marked sexual differentiation of the BSTc volume in our study before birth and in childhood certainly does not rule out early gonadal steroid effects on BSTc functions" (p. 1032).

[273] Frank P. M. Kruijver, Jiang-Ning Zhou, Chris W. Pool, Michael A. Hofman, Louis J. G. Gooren, & Dick F. Swaab, "Male-to-Female Transsexuals Have Female Neuron Numbers in the Central Subdivision of the Bed Nucleus of the Stria Terminalis," *The Journal of Clinical Endocrinology & Metabolism, 85* (no. 5), 2034-2041 (2000).

[274] Ibid, p. 2036. Subsequent research also has found an indication of higher somatostatin receptor density in the temporal and frontal cerebral cortex. See Robert Pichler, Wilhelmine Maschek, Carmen Crespillo, Isabel Esteva, & Federico Soriguer, "Is There a

Gender Difference of Somatostatin-Receptor Density in the Human Brain?" *Neuroendocrinology Letters, 23* (nos. 5/6), 440-441 (2002).

[275] Ibid, p. 2039.

[276] John Money, *Love & Love Sickness. The Science of Sex, Gender Difference, and Pair Bonding* (Baltimore: Johns Hopkins Univ. Press, 1980), p. 32. I must add, however, that Money also regards this hypothesis, though "scientifically legitimate," as remaining "largely science-fictional with regard to proof" (p. 32)—a statement true enough at the end of the 1970s, but not so more than 30 years later.

A number of studies have investigated the effects by sex hormones on the developing brain. See, for example, G. Dörner, F. Götz, W. Rohde, A. Plagemann, R. Lindner, H. Peters, & Z. Ghanaati, "Genetic and Epigenetic Effects on Sexual Brain Organization Mediated by Sex Hormones," *Neuroendocrinology Letters, 22* (nos. 5/6), 403-409 (2001).

[277] Harry Benjamin, *The Transsexual Phenomenon* (N.Y.: The Julian Press, 1966). This book has been reprinted on the Symposion.com website as an IJT Electronic Book. Accessed online at http://www.symposion.com/ijt/benjamin/index.htm. For a summary of this important volume see the answer to Q. 95.

[278] M. Philbert, "Male Transsexualism: An Endocrine Study," *Archives of Sexual Behavior, 1* (no. 1), 91-93 (1971), p. 92.

[279] John Money, *Gay, Straight, and In-Between: The Sexology of Erotic Attraction* (N. Y.: Oxford Univ. Press, 1988). Brief quote from p. 87. For more on Money's work, see the answer to Q. 95.

[280] John M. W. Bradford, "The Neurobiology, Neuropharmacology, and Pharmacological Treatment of the Paraphilias and Compulsive Sexual Behavior," *Canadian Journal of Psychiatry, 46* (no. 1), 26-34 (2001). An "In Review" article. Accessed online at http://www.cpa-apc.org/Publications/Archives/CJP/2001/Feb/Inreview.asp or at http://www.cpa-apc.org/Publications/Archives/ CJP/2001/ Feb/Feb2001.asp. Cf. the "Letter to the Editor" in response to this article, by David Haslam, Susan Adams, & Toba Oloruntoba, "Re: The Neurobiology, Neuropharmacology, and Pharmacological Treatment of the Paraphilias and Compulsive Sexual Behavior," *Canadian Journal of Psychiatry, 46* (no. 6), 559 (2001). This is available as a PDF accessed online at http://www.cpa-apc.org/Publications/ Archives/CJP/ 2001/August/PDF/letters.pdf.

[281] Geert J. De Vries, *Sexual Differentiation of the Brain.* Faculty webpage at The Molecular and Cellular Biology Graduate Program at the University of Massachusetts at Amherst. Accessed online at http://www.bio.umass.edu/mcb/faculty/devries.html.

De Vries also has called attention to the role played by sex differences in the brain for *preventing* some sex differences in function and behavior. See Geert J. De Vries, "Minireview: Sex Differences in Adult and Developing Brains: Compensation, Compensation, Compensation," *Endocrinology, 145* (no. 3), 1063-1068 (2004); cf. G. J. De Vries & P. A. Boyle, "Double Duty for Sex Differences in the Brain," *Behavioral Brain Research, 92* (no. 2), 205-213 (1998).

[282] June M. Reinisch, M. Ziemba-Davis, & S. A. Sanders, "Hormonal Contributions to Sexually Dimorphic Behavioral Development in Humans," *Psychoneuroendocrinology, 16* (no. 1-3), 213-278 (1991). The data on prenatal exposure to synthetic estrogen in this review was derived primarily from individuals exposed to diethylstilbestrol (DES), which has been much studied for its effects on humans. The effect of DES in humans

has been debated vigorously. For the argument that prenatal DES exposure has *not* been demonstrated to lead to behavioral masculinization or defeminization, see J. D. Lish, H. F. Meyer-Bahlburg, A. A. Ehrhardt, B. G. Travis, & N. P. Veridiano, "Prenatal Exposure to Diethylstilbestrol (DES): Childhood Play Behavior and Adult Gender-Role Behavior in Women," *Archives of Sexual Behavior, 21* (no. 5), 423-441 (1992).

[283] A. N. Elias & L. J. Valenta, "Are All Males Equal? Anatomic and Functional Basis for Sexual Orientation in Males," *Medical Hypotheses, 39* (no. 1), 85-87 (1992).

[284] Robert M. Boyar & James Aiman, "The 24-hour Secretory Pattern of LH and the Response to LHRH in Transsexual Men," *Archives of Sexual Behavior, 11* (no. 2), 157-169 (1982). In contrast between MtF transsexuals and FtM transsexuals, it should be noted that a 1989 study of FtM transsexuals compared to heterosexual females finds no significant differences in LH serum concentrations or pulsatile release characteristics. See T. Spinder, J. J. Spijkstra, L. J. Gooren, & C. W. Burger, "Pulsatile Luteinizing Hormone Release and Ovarian Steroid Levels in Female-to-Male Transsexuals Compared to Heterosexual Women," *Psychoneuroendocrinology, 14* (nos. 1-2), 97-102 (1989).

[285] G. Dörner, W. Rohde, G. Schott, & G. Schnabl, "On the LH Response to Oestrogen and LH-RH in Transsexual Men," *Experimental and Clinical Endocrinology, 82* (no. 3), 257-267 (1983). This result is presumably because of prenatal exposure to different than normal hormonal levels. However, the study's results have not been replicated, thus casting some doubt as to their reliability.

[286] M. Giusti, M. R. Falivene, A. Carraro, C. M. Cuttica, S. Valenti, & G. Giordano, "The Effect of Non-Steroidal Antiandrogen Flutamide on Luteinizing Hormone Pulsatile Secretion in Male-to-Female Transsexuals," *Journal of Endocrinological Investigation, 18* (no. 6), 420-426 (1995).

[287] Vin Tangpricha, Stanley H. Ducharme, Thomas W. Barber, & Stuart R. Chipkin, "Endocrinologic Treatment of Gender Identity Disorder," *Endocrine Practice, 9* (no. 1), 12-21 (2003).

[288] Jasinski; see section entitled, 'Estrogen Excess Disorders.'

[289] Money, p. 85.

[290] Richard C. Pillard & James D. Weinrich, "The Periodic Table Model of the Gender Transpositions: Part I. A Theory Based on Masculinization and Defeminization of the Brain," *The Journal of Sex Research, 23*, 425-454 (1987).

[291] Ibid. See especially pp. 435-438.

[292] Jean D. Wilson, "The Role of Androgens in Male Gender Role Behavior," *Endocrine Reviews, 20* (no. 5), 726-737 (1999). Accessed online at http://edrv. endojournals.org/cgi/content/full/20/5/726#SEC4. Quote is from §6, 'Discussion.'

[293] Gilbert Herdt & Martha McClintock, "Rethinking Puberty: The Development of Sexual Attraction," *Current Developments in Psychological Science, 5* (no. 6), 178-183 (1996). The authors' research suggests that among American children, at least, a new way of thinking about their bodies, gender roles, and others emerges between ages 9-11.

[294] Gilbert Herdt & Martha McClintock, "The Magical Age of 10," *Archives of Sexual Behavior, 29* (no. 6), 587-606 (2000). The authors are explicit in distinguishing sexual attraction from sexual orientation, and childhood sexual subjectivity from adult sexual subjectivity.

[295] Scott P. Kerlin, *The Presence of Gender Dysphoria, Transsexualism, and Disorders of Sexual Differentiation in Males Prenatally Exposed to Diethylstilbestrol: Initial Evidence from a 5-*

Year Study (2004). Paper presented at the 6th Annual E-Hormone Conference, New Orleans, Oct. 27-30, 2004. Found at the TransAdvocate.org website, accessed online at http://www.antijen.org/transadvocate/id33.html.

[296] Martin P. Kafka, "A Monoamine Hypothesis for the Pathophysiology of Paraphilic Disorders. *Archives of Sexual Behavior, 26* (no. 4), 343-358 (1997).

[297] This contention is a prominent focus in the answers to Q. 2-3. For more on the concept of boundaries in relation to human psychology, see G. G. Bolich, *Serving Human Experience: The Boundary Metaphor* (Ann Arbor, MI: Docteral dissertation for the Union Institute, 1993).

[298] This paragraph and the following three are reproduced verbatim from the answer to Q. 2. To see evidence concerning the physiological and psychological effects of dress that answer should be consulted.

[299] Martin Daly & Margo Wilson, *Sex, Evolution, and Behavior*, 2nd ed. (Boston: PWS Publishers, 1983), p. 267.

[300] Tom Boelstorff, "Playing Back the Nation: Waria, Indonesian Transvestites," *Cultural Anthropology, 19* (no. 2), 159-195 (2004), p. 170.

Q. 22 Notes

[301] Richard L. Schott, "The Childhood and Family Dynamics of Transvestites," *Archives of Sexual Behavior, 24* (no. 3), 309-327 (1995), p. 318, Table III, shows only a little more than one-fourth (27%) endorsed family/environmental factor as the major influence on their crossdressing. Almost as many (21%) believe genetic or internal factors are the major influence. Other endorsed views include the sensuality or erotic appeal of feminine items (22%) or emotional factors, such as gaining attention, feeling happy, or experiencing excitement (6%); fully one-in-six (17%) simply don't know. However, Schott, in the discussion of his Table V, also indicates that when these crossdressers are separated into 3 distinct groups ('nuclear transvestites,' 'marginal transvestites,' and 'transsexuals') the percentages change. Where 80% of transsexuals believe the major influence is genetic or internal, only 5% of the nuclear transvestites believe this. On the other hand, more than two-thirds of nuclear transvestites adopt as the major influence either family/environmental factor (34%), or the appeal of feminine garb (37%), neither of which enjoy much support by transsexuals.

[302] Thomas N. Wise & Jon K. Meyer, "Transvestism: Previous Findings and New Areas for Inquiry," *Journal of Sex & Marital Therapy, 6* (no. 2), 116-128 (1980).

[303] On the possible involvement of other kin, see Ellen Hale, Chester W. Schmidt, & Jon K. Meyer, "The Role of Grandmothers in Transsexualism," *American Journal of Psychiatry, 137* (no. 4), 497-498 (1980). This article looks at 27 transsexual subjects for whom a grandmother (generally the maternal grandmother) served an important parental role. It finds that this figure's attitudes and behaviors contribute to the development of transsexualism. Encouragement of crossdressing by the child is specifically indicated as an example of the grandmother's contributing behavior.

[304] Ralph R. Greenson, "A Transvestite Boy and a Hypothesis," *International Journal of Psychoanalysis, 47*, 306-403 (1966); Greenson follows the case of a 5 ½ year old boy, with a lack of a loving father and a mother who wished him to be feminine; the child was described earlier in Robert J. Stoller, "The Mother's Contribution to Infantile Transvestic Behavior," *International Journal of Psychoanalysis, 47*, 384-395 (1966).

305 Hedy Francesconi, "Transvestitismus beim Mann (Male Transvestism)," *Psyche Zeitschrift für Psychoanalyse und ihre Anwendungen, 38*, 801-816 (1984).

306 Marianne Leuzinger-Bohleber, "Transvestitische Symptombildung. Klinischer Beitrag zur Atiologie, Psychodynamik und Analysierbarkeit transvestitischer Patienten. (Transvestite Syndrome Formation: A Clinical Contribution Concerning the Etiology, Dynamics, and Analyzability of Transvestite Patients)," *Psyche Zeitschrift für Psychoanalyse und ihre Anwendungen, 38* (no. 9), 817-845 (1984). This case study is built on a five year analysis that finds the etiology of the crossdressing in traumas suffered both during separation-individuation and during the Oedipal phase of development.

307 Robert L. Munroe & Ruth H. Munroe, "Male Transvestism and Subsistence Economy," *The Journal of Social Psychology, 103*, 307-308 (1977).

308 Ibid. The Munroes do not contend that all male transvestism is explained by this hypothesis. Indeed, they note at the end of their brief report that where differentiation between the roles for men and women is small there may also be male transvestism.

309 Jason Schnittker, "Gender and Reactions to Psychological Problems: An Examination of Social Tolerance and Perceived Dangerousness," *Journal of Social Behaviors, 41* (no. 2), 224-240 (2000).

310 Carol Lynn Martin, "Attitudes and Expectations About Children with Nontraditional and Traditional Gender Roles," *Sex Roles, 22* (nos. 3/4), 151-165 (1990).

311 Lisa Hinkelman & Darcy Haag Granello, "Biological Sex, Adherence to Traditional Gender Roles, and Attitudes Toward Persons with Mental Illness: An Exploratory Investigation," *Journal of Mental Health Counseling, 25* (no. 4), 259-270 (2003). Importantly, evidence suggests that those with higher self-esteem are less likely to endorse such hypergender attitudes. For example, a study published in 1999 involving more than 500 college-aged women from four different ethnic groups (Korean, Singaporean, African-American and Caucasian-American) finds a correlation between high self-esteem and non-traditional attitudes toward gender roles as well as positive body image. See S. J. Lennon, N. A. Rudd, B. Sloan, & J. S. Kim, "Attitudes Toward Gender Roles, Self-Esteem, and Body Image: Application of a model," *Clothing & Textiles Research Journal, 17* (no. 4), 191-202 (1999).

312 Ibid, p. 267.

313 Manuel X. Zamarripa, Bruce E. Wampold, & Erik Gregory, "Male Gender Role Conflict, Depression, and Anxiety: Clarification and Generalizability to Women," *Journal of Counseling Psychology, 50* (no. 3), 333-338 (2003), p. 333. Cf. J. M. O'Neil, "Patterns of Gender Role Conflict and Strain: Sexism and Fear of Femininity in Men's Lives," *Personnel and Guidance Journal, 60*, 203-210 (1981).

314 Ibid, pp. 336-338. On the role homophobia plays in the construction of Western masculinity, see David Plummer, *One of the Boys: Masculinity, Homophobia, and Modern Manhood* (Binghamton, NY: Haworth Press, 1999).

315 Although crossdressing may provide relief from the male gender role, some worry that it does so in such a way as to reinforce our culture's gender stereotypes. This reinforcement happens when crossdressers dress and enact a female gender stereotype that has little relation to the reality of life as a woman. Such a gender role emphasizes women as soft, passive, yielding, and preoccupied with makeup, appearance, and shopping. On this problem, see Vern Bullough, "Transvestism, Women & Politics," *En Femme, #16* (1990, Jan./Feb.). Accessed online at http://www.cdspub.com/eftwp.html.

[316] N. Lukianowicz, "Two Cases of Transvestism," *Psychiatric Quarterly, 34*, 517-537 (1960).

[317] Cf. A. P. Sidhar, "Transvestism," *Samiksa, 32* (no. 4), 87-94 (1978), who presents a case wherein he finds the central dynamic the response of the crossdressing male to a powerful 'phallic' mother.

[318] Jon K. Meyer, Norman J. Knorr, & Dietrich Blumer, "Characterization of a Self-Designated Transsexual Population," *Archives of Sexual Behavior, 1* (no. 3), 219-230 (1971), p. 224.

[319] J. Spensley & J. T. Barter, "The Adolescent Transvestite on a Psychiatric Service: Family Patterns," *Archives of Sexual Behavior, 1* (no. 4), 347-356 (1971).

[320] Robert J. Stoller, "Fathers of Transsexual Children," *Journal of the American Psychoanalytic Association, 27* (no. 4), 837-866 (1979).

[321] Michael D. Newcomb, "The Role of Perceived Relative Parent Personality in the Development of Heterosexuals, Homosexuals, and Transvestites," *Archives of Sexual Behavior, 14* (no. 2), 147-164 (1985).

[322] Susan J. Bradley, "Gender Disorders in Childhood: A Formulation," in B. W. Steiner (Ed.), *Gender Dysphoria*, pp. 175-188 (N. Y.: Plenum Press, 1985).

[323] Kenneth J. Zucker and Ray Blanchard, "Transvestic Fetishism: Psychopathology and Theory," in D. Laws & W. O'Donahue (Eds.), *Handbook of Sexual Deviance: Theory & Application*, chapter 14, pp. 253-279 (N. Y.: Guilford Press, 1997).

[324] Kenneth J. Zucker & Susan J. Bradley, *Gender Identity Disorder and Psychosexual Problems in Children and Adolescents* (N. Y.: Plenum Press, 1995). Cf. Kenneth J. Zucker & Susan J. Bradley, "Gender Identity Disorders and Transvestic Fetishes," in S. D. Netherton, D. Holmes, & C. E. Walker (Eds.), *Child and Adolescent Psychological Disorders: A Comprehensive Textbook*, chapter 18 (Oxford: Oxford Univ. Press, 1999).

[325] Ibid, p. 262.

[326] Ibid.

[327] Ira B. Pauly, "Female Transsexualism: Part 1," *Archives of Sexual Behavior, 3* (no. 6), 487-507 (1974), p. 496.

[328] Vern Bullough, Bonnie Bullough, & Richard Smith, "A Comparative Study of Male Transvestites, Male to Female Transsexuals, and Male Homosexuals," *The Journal of Sex Research, 19* (no. 3), 238-257 (1983).

[329] M. D. Newcomb, "The Role of Perceived Relative Parent Personality in the Development of Heterosexuals, Homosexuals, and Transvestites," *Archives of Sexual Behavior, 14*, 147-164 (1985), p. 160.

[330] The connection between wish and crossdressing can be viewed without reference to the parents by focusing on the individual crossdresser. Certainly many historical examples show crossdressing as an activity pursued in fulfillment of a wish to be a different gender, or to participate in gender-specific activities otherwise not available. But the connection also extends beyond crossdressing. Dress has often been used in pursuit of wish fulfillment with reference to social class; by donning the apparel of a class different than one's own a person imaginatively joined that class. A dramatic example of dress reflecting wish is the yearning symbolically shown in women's dress after the ravages of the plague when pillows extended the midriff to produce the image of pregnancy. Cf. Susan Kaiser, *The Social Psychology of Clothing: Symbolic Appearances in Context* (N. Y.: Macmillan, 1985), p. 67.

[331] Cf. the report of Stone, who notes that 82% of 126 respondents in his study indicated it was the mother who first made them wear particular clothes. Gregory P. Stone, "Appearance and the Self," in M. E. Roach & J. B. Eicher (Eds.), *Dress, Adornment, and the Social Order*, pp. 216-245 (N. Y.: John Wiley & Sons, 1965), p. 234f.

[332] Ibid, p. 235.

[333] Albert D. Klassen, Colin J. Williams, & Eugene E. Levitt, *Sex and Morality in the U. S.*, H. J. O'Gorman, Ed. (Middletown, CT: Wesleyan Univ. Press, 1989), p. 382.

[334] Ibid.

[335] Ibid. For first the father, and then the mother, the question was asked, "How old were you by the time (he/she) no longer treated you this way (or felt this way)?"
With regard to the father's sign that he would have preferred the child be of the opposite sex in how he wanted the child to dress the figures are:

Age at which this ended	Male	Female
12-15	21.4%	28.6%
16-19	14.3%	24.5%
20 or older	14.3%	12.2%

With regard to the mother's sign that she would have preferred the child be of the opposite sex in how she wanted the child to dress the figures are:

Age at which this ended	Male	Female
12-15	17.9%	15%
16-19	20.5%	30%
20 or older	5.1%	25%

[336] Neil Buhrich & Trina Beaumont, "Comparison of Transvestism in Australia and America," *Archives of Sexual Behavior*, 10 (no. 3), 269-279 (1981). Percentage compiled from data reported in Table 1. 'Characteristics of Feminine Gender Identity.' Such wishes were recalled as even more frequent *after* age 12 (39% between 12-18; 35% after age 19).

[337] Pauly, p. 496f.

[338] Neil Buhrich & Neil McConaghy, "Parental Relationships During Childhood in Homosexuality, Transvestism, and Transsexualism," *Australian and New Zealand Journal of Psychiatry*, 12 (no. 2), 103-108 (1978).

[339] Jim B. Tucker & H. H. Jurgen Keil, "Can Cultural Beliefs Cause a Gender Identity Disorder?" *Journal of Psychology & Human Sexuality*, 13 (no. 2), 21-30 (2001).

[340] Ian Stevenson, "The Southeast Asian Interpretation of Gender Dysphoria: An Illustrative Case Report," *Journal of Nervous and Mental Disease*, 165 (no. 3), 201-205 (1977).

[341] David J. Krueger, "Symptom Passing in a Transvestite Father and Three Sons," *American Journal of Psychiatry*, 135 (no. 6), 739-742.

[342] H. Taylor Buckner, "The Transvestic Career Path," *Psychiatry*, 33 (no. 3), 381-389 (1970). Buckner also notes other less likely possibilities: that the boy acts out the role of his mother, or identifying with a mother or sister and dressing so as to reinforce

this identity, or from valuing his mother, who may encourage his feminization. Accessed online at http://www.tbuckner.com/TRANSVES.HTM.

[343] Ibid, esp. pp. 384-385.

[344] Albert C. Kinsey, Wardell B. Pomeroy, Clyde E. Martin, & Paul H. Gebhard, *Sexual Behavior in the Human Female* (Philadelphia: W. B. Saunders, 1953), p. 681. For more on Kinsey, see the answer to Q. 95.

[345] Ibid, p. 643. See the discussion in Joanne Meyerowitz, "Sex Research at the Borders of Gender: Transvestites, Transsexuals, and Alfred C. Kinsey," *Bulletin of the History of Medicine, 75*, 72-90 (2001), pp. 86-87.

[346] John Money, "Puberty: Psychology and Sexology," *British Journal of Sexual Medicine, 42-44* (1987, February), p. 43. For more on Money's views, see the answer to Q. 95.

[347] Anna Freud, "Assessment of Pathology in Childhood, Part II," in A. Freud, *The Writings of Anna Freud, Vol. V: Research at the Hampstead Child-Therapy Clinic and Other Papers 1956-1965*, pp. 38-52 (N. Y.: International Universities Press, 1969).

[348] Ibid, p. 57

[349] Ibid.

[350] Anna Freud, *Normality and Pathology in Childhood: Assessments of Development* (N.Y.: International Universities Press, 1965), p. 173.

[351] Peter M. Bentler, "A Typology of Transsexualism: Gender Identity Theory and Data," *Archives of Sexual Behavior, 5* (no. 6), 567-584 (1976).

Q. 23 Notes

[352] American Psychiatric Association, *Diagnostic and Statistical Manual of Mental Disorders, 4th ed., Text Revision* (Washington, D. C.: American Psychiatric Association, 2000), p. 579.

[353] Richard L. Schott, "The Childhood and Family Dynamics of Transvestites," *Archives of Sexual Behavior, 24* (no. 3), 309-327 (1995), p. 316.

[354] Kenneth J. Zucker & Susan J. Bradley, *Gender Identity Disorder and Psychosexual Problems in Children and Adolescents* (N. Y.: Guilford Press, 1995).

[355] Janet Thompson, "Transvestism: An Empirical Study," *International Journal of Sexology, 4*, 216-219 (1951).

[356] Vern Bullough, Bonnie Bullough, & Richard Smith, "A Comparative Study of Male Transvestites, Male to Female Transsexuals, and Male Homosexuals," *The Journal of Sex Research, 19* (no. 3), 238-257 (1983), p. 255.

Q. 24 Notes

[357] See, for example, the incidental remark by John Money, *Lovemaps: Clinical Concepts of Sexual/Erotic Health and Pathology, Paraphilia, and Gender Transposition in Childhood, Adolescence, and Maturity.* (N. Y.: Irvington, 1986), p. 210. Money suggests that child abuse and attendant dissociation "could be etiologically important."

[358] Anette Kersting, Michael Reutemann, Ursula Gast, Patricia Ohrmann, Thomas Suslow, Nikolaus Michael, & Volker Arolt, "Dissociative Disorders and Traumatic Childhood Experiences in Transsexuals," *Journal of Nervous & Mental Disease, 191* (no. 3), 182-189 (2003).

[359] Comic novelist John Irving uses Jack, the semi-autobiographical protagonist of one of his novels, to at least speculate on such an association. Jack is repeatedly molested by girls and women as a child and grows up to become a famous actor who spe-

cializes in sexually ambiguous, crossdressed characters. See John Irving, *Until I Meet You* (N. Y.: Random House, 2005).

[360] Holly Devor, "Transsexualism, Dissociation, and Child Abuse: An Initial Discussion Based on Nonclinical Data," *Journal of Psychology & Human Sexuality, 6* (no. 3), 49-72 (1994).

[361] National Clearinghouse on Child Abuse and Neglect Information. *Child Maltreatment 2002: Summary of Key Findings.* Accessed online at http://nccanch.acf.hhs.gov/ pubs/factsheets/canstats.cfm.

[362] Niklas Langström & Kenneth J. Zucker, "Transvestic Fetishism in the General Population: Prevalence and Correlates," *Journal of Sex & Marital Therapy, 31* (no. 1), 87-95 (2005). See especially Table 1 (p. 90) and the remarks on p. 92f.

[363] Yvonne, "Who We Are," *Yvonne's Place for Crossdressers* (1999). Accessed online at http://www.yvonnesplace.net/index2.html. This survey makes no pretence at being scientific, and has some admitted methodological flaws, so results should be held loosely. There were 944 respondents on this matter. The question can also be asked whether there were others who had experienced abuse who chose not to report it for the survey.

[364] Lin Fraser, "Observations About Transgendered People." Presentation to ETVC San Francisco, August 11, 1990, edited by R. Schneider. Accessed online at *GenderWeb.org* at http://www.genderweb.org/experien/ obstg.html.

Q. 25 Notes

[365] Jack L. Croughan, Marcel Saghir, Rose Cohen, & Eli Robins, "A Comparison of Treated and Untreated Male Crossdressers," *Archives of Sexual Behavior, 10* (no. 6), 515-528 (1981), p. 522.

[366] This has been a consistent finding. In addition to the aforementioned work by Croughan, Saghir, Cohen, & Robins, see, for example, Neil Buhrich, (1978). "Motivation for Crossdressing in Heterosexual Transvestism," *Acta Psychiatrica Scandinavica, 57,* 145-152 (1978).

[367] Harry Benjamin, *The Transsexual Phenomenon* (N.Y.: The Julian Press, 1966), chapter 6, "Nonsurgical Management of Transsexualism." This book has been reprinted on the Symposion.com website as an IJT Electronic Book. Accessed online at http://www.symposion.com/ijt/benjamin/index.htm.

[368] John M. W. Bradford, "The Neurobiology, Neuropharmacology and Pharmacological Treatment of the Paraphilias and Compulsive Sexual Behavior," *Canadian Journal of Psychiatry, 46,* 77-85 (2001), p. 77. Accessed online at http://www.cpa-apc.org/Publications/Archives/CJP/2001/Feb/Feb2001.asp.

[369] Ibid.

[370] Benjamin J. Saddock & Virginia A. Saddock, *Kaplan & Sadock's Pocket Handbook of Psychiatric Drug Treatment,* 3rd ed. (Phila.: Lippincott Williams & Wilkins, 2001), pp. 193.

[371] C. H. N. Abdo, A. Hounie, M. de T. Scanavino, & E. C. Miguel, "Case Report: OCD and Transvestism: Is There a Relationship?" *Acta Psychiatrica Scandinavica, 103,* 471-473 (2001), p. 472.

[372] Peter M. Bentler & Virginia Prince, "Personality Characteristics of Male Transvestites, III," *Journal of Abnormal Psychology, 74,* 140-143 (1969), pp. 141-142; quote is from p. 141. Also see Peter M. Bentler & Virginia Prince, "Psychiatric Symptomatology in Transvestites," *Journal of Clinical Psychology, 26,* 434-435 (1970).

[373] Letter of Alfred Kinsey to Harry Benjamin dated November 27, 1953. Quoted in Meyerowitz, p. 86. Cf. his remarks in Harry Benjamin, *The Transsexual Phenomenon* (N.Y.: The Julian Press, 1966), chapter 3, " The Transvestite in Older and Newer Aspects." This book has been reprinted on the Symposion.com website as an IJT Electronic Book. Accessed online at http://www.symposion.com/ijt/ benjamin/index.htm. For more on Benjamin's views, see the answer to Q. 95.

[374] Janet Thompson, "Transvestism: An Empirical Study," *International Journal of Sexology, 4*, 216-219 (1951).

[375] As we saw in answering Q. 5, Judith Butler proposes we view gender as something we *do* rather than as something we *are*. She has talked about dressing in 'drag' as a 'transgressive performance' that offers the positive possibility of helping us rethink gender categories. As Butler writes elsewhere, "the transvestite's gender is as fully real as anyone whose performance complies with social expectations" —the difference lies not with gender *per se* but with our social expectations about gender. Crossdressers choose a gender performance both unusual and at variance with the majority of performances being enacted by people day-by-day. See Judith Butler, "Performative Acts and Gender Constitution: An Essay in Phenomenology and Feminist Theory," in Sue-Ellen Case (Ed.), *Performing Feminisms: Feminist Critical Theory and Theatre* (Baltimore: John Hopkins Univ. Press, 1990), p. 278. Some have suggested that male crossdressers should be referred to as GEMs—gender enhanced males. While perhaps offered tongue-in-cheek, the term fits a notion of performative gender.

[376] This way of looking at things is not new. Nearly two millennia ago Rabbi Jose said, "The hermaphrodite is a creature *sui generis*, and the Sages did not determine whether he is a male or a female" (Yebamoth 83a in the Talmud).

Q. 26 Notes

[377] A desire that has often appeared to be motivated by the covert agenda of establishing that such heterosexual men are not *really* heterosexual, but either latent homosexuals, bisexuals, or *autogynephilic*—men in love with themselves as women (a controversial idea examined elsewhere).

[378] One important study that sought to compare/contrast the clinical and nonclinical crossdressing populations was reported in 1981, using interviews with 70 adult males (34 having received treatment). A person was placed into the 'treated group' if he had ever been seen by a physician, counselor or mental health professional in connection with his crossdressing. The results of this study are incorporated in this answer and elsewhere in this book. See Jack L. Croughan, Marcel Saghir, Rose Cohen, & Eli Robins, "A Comparison of Treated and Untreated Male Crossdressers," *Archives of Sexual Behavior, 10* (no. 6), 515-528 (1981).

[379] Virginia Prince & Peter M. Bentler, "Survey of 504 Cases of Transvestism," *Psychological Reports, 31*, 903-917 (1972), p. 911. Another quarter (26%) were second born.

[380] Richard L. Schott, "The Childhood and Family Dynamics of Transvestites," *Archives of Sexual Behavior, 24* (no. 3), 309-327 (1995), p. 314. Schott used a random sample drawn from a group of self-identified crossdressers (84% transvestites; 16% transsexuals). He obtained usable surveys from 85 men, with data drawn from 44 male graduate students used for a comparison group. Among the crossdressers, more than half are either firstborn (40%) or only (19%) children, and nearly three-quarters (74%) are firstborn sons. Schott points out that these numbers are substantial and significant com-

pared to national population norms, where families with firstborn males are just 25% of the total and male only families just 6%.

[381] Yvonne, "Who We Are," *Yvonne's Place for Crossdressers* (1999). Accessed online at http://www.yvonnesplace.net/index2.html. This survey was available online in 1999 and solicited voluntary responses, which were submitted by email. Altogether, 1,316 people responded, though not every person responded to every survey item.

[382] Richard F. Docter, *Transvestites and Transsexuals: Toward a Theory of Cross-Gender Behavior* (N. Y.: Plenum Press, 1988).

[383] Richard F. Docter & Virginia Prince, "Transvestism: A Survey of 1032 Cross-Dressers," *Archives of Sexual Behavior, 26* (no. 6), 589-605 (1997), Table I.

[384] Prince & Bentler, p. 911.

[385] Neil Buhrich & Neil McConaghy, "Parental Relationships During Childhood in Homosexuality, Transvestism, and Transsexualism," *Australian and New Zealand Journal of Psychiatry, 12* (no. 2), 103-108 (1978).

[386] Schott, p. 314f. Table II shows that 86% of crossdressing sons evaluate their relationship with the mother as 'very positive' (45%), 'fairly positive' (31%), or 'neutral' (10%). Schott, in his discussion of Table VI (p. 320), notes that 'nuclear transvestites' report the most positive relationship with the mother.

[387] M. D. Newcomb, "The Role of Perceived Relative Parent Personality in the Development of Heterosexuals, Homosexuals, and Transvestites," *Archives of Sexual Behavior, 14*, 147-164 (1985), p. 160.

[388] Schott, p. 317, Table II.

[389] Bonnie Bullough & Vern Bullough, ""Men Who Cross-Dress: A Survey," in B. Bullough, V. L. Bullough, & J. Elias (Eds.), *Gender Blending*, pp. 174-188 (Amherst, NY: Prometheus Books, 1997), pp. 179-180, report that 93% of their subjects remembered being afraid of being caught, though almost two-thirds (65%) also said that being caught resulted either in not being a problem or being a minor one.

[390] Schott, p. 317.

[391] Vern Bullough, Bonnie Bullough, & Richard Smith, "A Comparative Study of Male Transvestites, Male to Female Transsexuals, and Male Homosexuals," *The Journal of Sex Research, 19* (no. 3), 238-257 (1983), p. 248, Table 6. This was a comparative study; transvestites were less likely to characterize their childhood as "happy" compared to a noncrossdressing group (38% to 60%). Other numbers, though were less different: "unhappy" (23% to 19%) and "mixed" (39% to 21%). Interestingly, transvestites were more likely to characterize their childhoods as "happy" than were transsexual males (38% to 16%), and less likely to describe it as "unhappy" (23% to 50%). The group most frequently calling their childhood "happy" was homosexual men (64%).

This research conscientiously separated itself from the treatment process and gathered its data from the point of view of the subjects rather than clinicians' impressions (see p. 239).

[392] Bullough & Bullough, p. 181, Table 2.

[393] Ibid, p. 180.

[394] Prince & Bentler, p. 906, Table 1. This figure represents a number in excess of the educational attainment of the general male population of the mid-1960s as indicated by census reports.

[395] Croughan, Saghir, Cohen, & Robins, Table I. The figures reported in my answer are compiled from their data, which reports percentages for the 2 groups being compared. A quarter (25%) had completed college, and 11% had graduated from a professional or graduate school.

[396] Docter, p. 126.

[397] Docter & Prince, Table I.

[398] Yvonne, Table on 'Education' in 'Education, Profession and Income' subsection, in Demographics section.

[399] Richard F. Docter & James S. Fleming, "Measures of Transgender Behavior," *Archives of Sexual Behavior, 30* (no. 3), 255-271 (2001). The 73% was extrapolated from their report that 90% of the 516 subjects had at least an A.A. degree, and of that number 19% earned an A.A., 44% a B.A. or B.S., 26% a Masters degree, and 11% a doctorate. Thus some 464 subjects had degrees, some 88 of them the A.A., leaving 376 with a bachelors degree or higher. The 516 subjects were all male, with 88% identified as 'transvestite' and 12% as 'transsexual.' The transvestite group was all periodic crossdressers who dressed fully as women; partial crossdressers were not included.

[400] Bullough, Bullough, & Smith, p. 250, Table 7.

[401] Croughan, Saghir, Cohen, & Robins, Table II (and discussion following). The finding that 90% started with partial crossdressing agrees with the finding by Docter (p. 134) that 92% of his subjects initially crossdressed only partially.

[402] Schott, p. 317. Schott notes that 19% were ambivalent and 14% experienced crossdressing with negative feelings because of guilt, shame, or a sense of being crazy.

[403] Prince & Bentler, p. 907.

[404] Bullough, Bullough, & Smith, pp. 252-254, especially Tables 11-12. Vernon Coleman speculates that one reason crossdressing is so often kept secret is because it is "particularly common" among successful males in business, the services, and professions—occupations where exposure may carry the highest price. See Vernon Coleman, (1996). *Men in Dresses: A Study in Transvestism/Crossdressing*, §2, 'Why Do Men Crossdress?' European Medical Journal. Chilton Designs Publishers. Accessed online at http://www. vernoncoleman.com/downloads/mid.htm.

[405] Docter, 1988, p. 126, which reports above average occupational status for the subjects of his sample, and Docter & Prince, Table I. Similarly, the 1981 report by Croughan, Saghir, Cohen, & Robins showed 64% of their subjects in skilled or professional/managerial positions (see Table I).

[406] Jon K. Meyer, Norman J. Knorr, & Dietrich Blumer, "Characterization of a Self-Designated Transsexual Population," *Archives of Sexual Behavior, 1* (no. 3), 219-230 (1971), p. 222.

[407] Ingrid M. Sell, "Third Gender: A Qualitative Study of the Experience of Individuals Who Identify as Being Neither Man Nor Woman," *The Psychotherapy Patient, 13* (nos. 1-2), 131-145 (2004), p. 140.

[408] Meyer, Knorr, & Blumer, pp. 224-225. Percentages calculated from data offered on males and females, and from Table II.

[409] Prince & Bentler, p. 912; cf. p. 906, Table 1; almost two-thirds (64%) were presently married.

[410] Croughan, Saghir, Cohen, & Robins, Table I; 56% were currently married. The figures reported in my answer are compiled from their data, which reports percentages for the 2 groups being compared.

[411] Docter, p. 125; data on children from p. 169.

[412] Docter & Prince, Table I; 60% were currently married.

[413] Yvonne, Table on 'Marital Status and Children' in Demographics section.

[414] Docter & Fleming, 'Demographic and Identifying Data,' p. 258.

[415] Meyer, Knorr, & Blumer, p. 225. Percentages calculated from data offered on males and females.

[416] Prince & Bentler, p. 907.

[417] Docter, p. 125.

[418] Meyer, Knorr, & Blumer, p. 226. Percentages calculated from data provided in Table III.

[419] Prince & Bentler, p. 907.

[420] Croughan, Saghir, Cohen, & Robins, Table I. The figures reported in my Table are compiled from their data, which reports percentages for the two groups being compared.

[421] Docter & Prince, Table I.

[422] Yvonne, Table on 'Religious Affiliation' in subsection 'Matters of Religion,' in Demographics section. Based on 1,189 respondents, of whom 84% said they were participants, but only 19% were active participants.

[423] Sell, pp. 140-142; quote is from p. 142.

[424] Mariette P. Allen, *Transformations: Crossdressers and Those Who Love Them.* (N. Y.: E. P. Dutton, 1989).

[425] Docter & Prince, Table II; the other 20% felt that crossdressing just meant being themselves in different clothes.

[426] Yvonne, 1999. This finding was based on 1,205 respondents.

[427] Neil Buhrich, "Motivation for Cross-Dressing in Heterosexual Transvestism," *Acta Psychiatrica Scandinavica, 57* (no. 2), 145-152 (1978).

[428] Prince & Bentler, p. 908.

[429] Croughan, Saghir, Cohen, & Robins, p. 518.

[430] Ibid. In this group of 11 subjects motivated by relational pressures, almost two-thirds (64%) were at the request of a spouse; the rest were evenly divided between requests by parents or by friends.

[431] Yvonne, 1999. This information was obtained from 658 respondents.

[432] Prince & Bentler, p. 909.

[433] Neil Buhrich & Trina Beaumont, "Comparison of Transvestism in Australia and America," *Archives of Sexual Behavior, 10* (no. 3), 269-279 (1981). Percentages compiled from data reported in Table 1. 'Characteristics of Feminine Gender Identity.'

[434] Docter & Prince, Table III. Interestingly, of those who expressed a preference for one gender identity or another, more preferred the feminine self (28%) than preferred the masculine self (11%).

[435] Buhrich & Beaumont, Table I data used to compute percentages.

[436] Bullough, Bullough, & Smith, p. 251, Table 9.

[437] Meyer, Knorr, & Blumer, p. 226.

[438] Prince & Bentler, pp. 913-916. Similarly, the 1999 online survey found 90% of respondents would like to crossdress more frequently than they currently do (Yvonne, 1999). Other studies with reference to this matter include the following:

With regard to individual items, H. Taylor Buckner's data, preserved by Benjamin, found in a survey of 262 crossdressing males that the most popular items worn during intercourse were nightgown (26%) and panties (22%), followed by stockings (16%) and high heels (10%), though 16% dressed in full costume. See Harry Benjamin, *The Transsexual Phenomenon* (N.Y.: The Julian Press, 1966), chapter 3, " The Transvestite in Older and Newer Aspects," n. 3. This book has been reprinted on the Symposion.com website as an IJT Electronic Book. Accessed online at http://www.symposion.com /ijt/benjamin/index.htm. For more on Benjamin's views, see the answer to Q. 95.

Also with reference to individual items, Coleman found that about half (45%) of his respondents said they slept in a nightie and three-quarters (75%) used feminine underwear (bra and/or panties) under male outerwear. See Vernon Coleman, (1996). *Men in Dresses: A Study in Transvestism/ Crossdressing.* European Medical Journal. Chilton Designs Publishers, §8, 'Bra and Panties Beneath the Suit: The Number of Crossdressers Who Wear Women's Underwear When Dressed in Ordinary Male Clothes.'and §8, 'Crossdressing: Nighttime Wear.' Accessed online at http://www.vernoncoleman.com/ downloads/ mid.htm.

[439] Docter & Prince, Table II and following discussion. They note that factors such as age and affiliation with a crossdressing organization may influence the high percentage expressing a preference for complete crossdressing. They also remark that only about a quarter of the subjects ever engaged in public activities (e.g., eating in restaurants) while crossdressed.

The results from the 1972 and 1997 survey reports can be contrasted somewhat to those found among respondents to the 1999 online survey. Without specifying what it meant to go out in public while crossdressed, fully half (50%) answered they had. On the other hand, only little more than half (52%) engaged in crossdressing to the point of wearing a wig and makeup along with women's clothes. Three-quarters (75%) had purged at some point, with 23% having done so within the previous 12 months (Yvonne, 1999).

[440] Prince & Bentler, p. 915.

Q. 27 Notes

[441] Gianna E. Israel, "Impact on Children." *Gianna Israel Gender Library* (1997). Accessed online at http://www.firelily.com/gender/gianna/impact.children.html.

[442] H. Taylor Buckner, "The Transvestic Career Path," *Psychiatry, 33* (no. 3), 381-389 (1970), p. 381. Accessed online at http://www.tbuckner.com/TRANSVES.HTM.

[443] Thomas N. Wise & Jon K. Meyer, "Transvestism: Previous Findings and New Areas for Inquiry," *Journal of Sex & Marital Therapy, 6* (no. 2), 116-128 (1980).

[444] Neil Buhrich & Trina Beaumont, "Comparison of Transvestism in Australia and America," *Archives of Sexual Behavior, 10* (no. 3), 269-279 (1981).

[445] Peter M. Bentler, "A Typology of Transsexualism: Gender Identity Theory and Data," *Archives of Sexual Behavior, 5* (no. 6), 567-584 (1976).

[446] George R. Brown, Thomas N. Wise, Paul T. Costa, Jr., Jeffrey H. Herbst, Peter J. Fagan, & Chester W. Schmidt, "Personality Characteristics and Sexual Functioning of

188 Cross-Dressing Men," *The Journal of Nervous and Mental Disorders 184*, 265-273 (1996), p. 265.

[447] Peter M. Bentler, R. W. Sherman, & Virginia Prince, "Personality Characteristics of Male Transvestites," *Journal of Clinical Psychology, 26*, 287-291 (1970); quote is from p. 290.

[448] Evelyn F. Hill, "A Comparison of Three Psychological Testings of a Transsexual," *Journal of Personality Assessment, 44* (no. 1), 52-100 (1980).

[449] Michael Fleming, David Jones, & Jack Simons, "Preliminary Results of Rorschach Protocols of Pre and Post Operative Transsexuals," *Journal of Clinical Psychology, 38* (no. 2), 408-415 (1982); quote is from p. 414.

[450] F. S. Morgenstern, J. F. Pearce, & W. L. Rees, "Predicting the Outcomes of Behavior Therapy by Psychological Tests," *Behavior Research and Therapy, 2*, 191-200 (1965).

[451] Peter M. Bentler & Virginia Prince, "Personality Characteristics of Male Transvestites, III," *Journal of Abnormal Psychology, 74*, 140-143 (1969), pp. 141-142; quote is from p. 141.

[452] Ibid, pp. 142-143; quote is from p. 142.

[453] Peter M. Bentler & Virginia Prince, "Psychiatric Symptomatology in Transvestites," *Journal of Clinical Psychology, 26*, 434-435 (1970).

[454] William T. Tsushima & Danny Wedding, "MMPI Results of Male Candidates for Transsexual Surgery," *Journal of Personality Assessment, 43* (no. 4), 385-387 (1979). Cf. Howard B. Roback, *et al.*, "Psychopathology in Female Sex-Change Applicants and Two Help-Seeking Controls," *Journal of Abnormal Psychology, 85* (no. 4), 430-432 (1976).

[455] Donald S. Strassberg, H. B. Roback, J. Cunningham, E. A. McKee, & P. Larson, "Psychopathology in Self-Identified Female-to-Male Transsexuals, Homosexuals, and Heterosexuals," *Archives of Sexual Behavior, 8* (no. 6), 491-496 (1979). Intelligence and personality tests also were used to compare 15 FtM transsexuals and 15 lesbians. Tests used were the WAIS, DAP, Embedded Figures Test (EFT), Bem Sex Role Inventory (BSRI), and Guilford-Zimmerman Temperament Survey (GZTS). The groups prove comparable on the WAIS and EFT, but different on the others. See Elizabeth F. McCauley & Anke A. Ehrhardt, "Role Expectations and Definitions: A Comparison of Female Transsexuals and Lesbians," *Journal of Homosexuality, 3* (no. 2), 137-147 (1977). Also cf. H. B. Roback, D. S. Strassberg, E. A. McKee, & J. Cunningham, "Self-Concept and Psychological Adjustment Differences Between Self-Identified Male Transsexuals and Male Homosexuals," *Journal of Homosexuality, 3* (no. 1), 15-20 (1977).

[456] D. Daniel Hunt, John E. Carr, & John L. Hampson, "Cognitive Correlates of Biologic Sex and Gender Identity in Transsexualism," *Archives of Sexual Behavior, 10* (no. 1), 65-77 (1981). It is worth noting that a Czechoslovakian assessment of 64 transsexuals and 18 homosexuals finds above average IQ scores for most subjects. See *Ceskoslovenska Psychiatriae, 71* (nos. 2-3), 131-136 (1975).

[457] Thomas N. Wise, Peter J. Fagan, Chester W. Schmidt, Yula Ponticas, & Paul T. Costa, "Personality and Sexual Functioning of Transvestitic Fetishists and Other Paraphilics," *Journal of Nervous and Mental Disease, 179* (no. 11), 694-698 (1991).

[458] Ibid.

[459] Chris C. Gosselin & Sybil B. Eysenck, "The Transvestite 'Double Image': A Preliminary Report," *Personality and Individual Differences, 1* (no. 2), 172-173 (1980).

[460] Chris C. Gosselin & Glen D. Wilson, *Sexual Variations: Fetishism, Transvestism and Sadomasochism* (N. Y.: Simon & Schuster, 1980). Cf. Glen D. Wilson & Chris C. Gosselin, "Personality Characteristics of Fetishists, Transvestites, and Sadomasochists," *Personality and Individual Differences, 1*, 289-295 (1980).

[461] Mary T. Hogan-Finlay, *Development of the Cross-Gender Lifestyle and Comparison of Cross-Gendered Men with Heterosexual Controls*. Ph.D. dissertation. (Carleton University, 1995).

[462] Brown, *et al.*, pp. 265-267.

[463] Ibid, p. 267f.

[464] Ibid.

[465] Ira B. Pauly & Thomas W. Lindgren, "Body Image and Gender Identity," *Journal of Homosexuality, 2* (no. 2), 133-142 (1977). Cf. Ira B. Pauly, "A Body Image Scale for Evaluating Transsexuals," *Archives of Sexual Behavior, 4* (no. 6), 639-656 (1975).

[466] Ibid.

[467] Brown, *et al.*, p. 271.

[468] Kurt Freund, Betty W. Steiner, & S. Chan, "Two Types of Cross Gender Identity," *Archives of Sexual Behavior, 11* (no. 1), 49-63 (1982).

[469] Peter Ackroyd, *Dressing Up: Transvestism and Drag. The History of an Obsession* (N. Y.: Simon & Schuster, 1979).

[470] Richard Green, M. Fuller, & B. Rutley, "It-Scale for Children and Draw-a-Person Test: 30 Feminine vs. 25 Masculine Boys," *Journal of Personality Assessment, 36*, 349-352 (1972). The "feminine boys" are significantly more likely to draw a female figure first on the DAP. Also cf. M. Grotjahn, "Transvestic Fantasy Expressed in a Drawing," *Psychoanalytic Quarterly, 17*, 340 (1948).

[471] Neil Buhrich & Neil McConaghy, "Tests of Gender Feelings and Behavior in Homosexuality, Transvestism, and Transsexualism," *Journal of Clinical Psychology, 35* (no. 1), 187-191 (1979).

[472] Michael Fleming, et al, "The Use of an Animal Drawing Test in the Assessment and Disposition of Transsexualism," *Journal of Clinical Psychology, 38* (no. 2), 420-424 (1982).

[473] Peter J. Fagan, Thomas N. Wise, Leonard R. Derogatis, & Chester W. Schmidt, "Distressed Transvestites," *Journal of Nervous and Mental Disease, 176* (no. 10), 626-632 (1988), pp. 628, 631.

[474] Leonard R. Derogatis, Jon K. Meyer, & Noelia Vazquez, "A Psychological Profile of the Transsexual: I. The Male," *Journal of Nervous and Mental Disease, 166* (no. 4), 234-254 (1978). The pronounced identification with the feminine gender role, even to a somewhat extreme stereotyped notion of it, was underscored by the results obtained in a study reported in 1974. In the comparative study, the 17 MtF transsexuals more strongly endorse middle class sexual conservatism (as measured on a 64 item Masculinity-Femininity Scale) than do either 17 heterosexual men or 17 heterosexual women. See Thomas Kando, "Males, Females, and Transsexuals: A Comparative Study of Sexual Conservatism," *Journal of Homosexuality, 1* (no. 1), 45-64 (1974).

[475] Candice Skrapec & K. R. MacKenzie, "Psychological Self-Perception in Male Transsexuals, Homosexuals, and Heterosexuals," *Archives of Sexual Behavior, 10* (no. 4), 357-370 (1981).

476 John T. Talamini, *Boys Will Be Girls: The Hidden World of the Heterosexual Male Transvestite* (Lanham, MD: Univ. Press of America, 1982), chapter 6.

477 Ibid, p. 66.

478 Richard F. Docter & James S. Fleming, "Measures of Transgender Behavior," *Archives of Sexual Behavior, 30* (no. 3), 255-271 (2001). For report of mean differences between groups see Table II.

479 D. J. Ziegler, "Transvestism," in R. J. Corsini (Ed.), *Encyclopedia of Psychology*, 2nd ed. (N. Y.: John Wiley & Sons, 1994), p. 551f. Ellipses mark deletion of reference citations, not content.

Q. 28 Notes

480 Janet Thompson, "Transvestism: An Empirical Study," *International Journal of Sexology, 4*, 216-219 (1951).

481 H. Taylor Buckner's master's thesis results were reported in Harry Benjamin, *The Transsexual Phenomenon* (N.Y.: The Julian Press, 1966), chapter 3, " The Transvestite in Older and Newer Aspects," n. 8. This book has been reprinted on the Symposion.com website as an IJT Electronic Book. Accessed online at http://www.symposion.com/ijt/benjamin/index.htm.

482 Virginia Prince & P. M. Bentler, "Survey of 504 Cases of Transvestism," *Psychological Reports, 31*, 903-917 (1972), p. 906, Table 1.

483 Peter M. Bentler, "A Typology of Transsexualism: Gender Identity Theory and Data," *Archives of Sexual Behavior, 5* (no. 6), 567-584 (1976), p. 574, Table IV. Bentler's subjects were 42 post-operative Male-to-Female transsexuals. Bentler also identified an 'asexual' group, of whom 50% began crossdressing before age 11, but only 8% before age 5.

484 Richard Green, "One-Hundred Ten Feminine and Masculine Boys: Behavioral Contrasts and Demographic Similarities," *Archives of Sexual Behavior, 5* (no. 5), 425-446 (1976), p. 436. Green (p. 434f.) reports that 98% of the feminine boys crossdressed compared to 19% of the masculine boys.

485 Neil Buhrich & Neil McConaghy, "The Clinical Syndromes of Femmiphilic Transvestism," *Archives of Sexual Behavior, 6* (no. 5), 397-412 (1977).

486 Jack L. Croughan, Marcel Saghir, Rose Cohen, & Eli Robins, "A Comparison of Treated and Untreated Male Crossdressers," *Archives of Sexual Behavior, 10* (no. 6), 515-528 (1981), p. 518, Table II.

487 Neil Buhrich & Trina Beaumont, "Comparison of Transvestism in Australia and America," *Archives of Sexual Behavior, 10* (no. 3), 269-279 (1981).

488 Vern Bullough, Bonnie Bullough, & Richard Smith, "A Comparative Study of Male Transvestites, Male to Female Transsexuals, and Male Homosexuals," *The Journal of Sex Research, 19* (no. 3), 238-257 (1983). In this comparison study they also find that the crossdressing of transvestite males typically begins at an earlier age than for transsexual males (of 33 MtF transsexuals, only 21% report crossdressing before age 10 and 73% report *never* crossdressing).

489 Richard Green, *The 'Sissy Boy Syndrome' and the Development of Homosexuality* (New Haven, CT: Yale Univ. Press, 1987).

490 Peter J. Fagan, Thomas N. Wise, Leonard R. Derogatis, & Chester W. Schmidt, "Distressed Transvestites," *Journal of Nervous and Mental Disease, 176* (no. 10), 626-632 (1988), p. 630.

491 Richard F. Docter, *Transvestites and Transsexuals: Toward a Theory of Cross-Gender Behavior.* (N. Y.: Plenum Press, 1988), p. 131.

492 A. M. Verschoor, "Wetenschappelijk onderzoek en theorievorming," in A. M. Verschoor & J. Poortinga (Eds.), *Een Dubbel Bestaan*, pp. 101-133 (Swetz & Zietlinger, 1990).

493 C. D. Doorn, J. Poortinga, & A. M. Verschoor, "Cross-Gender Identity in Transvestites and Male Transsexuals," *Archives of Sexual Behavior, 23* (no. 2), 185-201 (1994).

494 Richard L. Schott, "The Childhood and Family Dynamics of Transvestites," *Archives of Sexual Behavior, 24* (no. 3), 309-327 (1995), p. 315f.

495 Vernon Coleman, *Men in Dresses: A Study in Transvestism/Crossdressing.* European Medical Journal. (Chilton Designs Publishers, 1996). Accessed online at http://www.vernoncoleman.com/downloads/mid.htm. See §1, 'At What Age Do Crossdressers Start to Wear Women's Clothes?' The 1,014 subjects reported in the table reflect two sources: 414 men who answered a questionnaire and 600 other men who had written communication with Coleman during the period (July-August, 1995) he did his research.

496 Bonnie Bullough & Vern Bullough, ""Men Who Cross-Dress: A Survey," in B. Bullough, V. L. Bullough, & J. Elias (Eds.), *Gender Blending*, pp. 174-188 (Amherst, NY: Prometheus Books, 1997), p. 178.

497 Richard F. Docter & Virginia Prince, "Transvestism: A Survey of 1032 Cross-Dressers," *Archives of Sexual Behavior, 26* (no. 6), 589-605 (1997), Table II.

498 Yvonne, "Who We Are," *Yvonne's Place for Crossdressers* (1999). Accessed online at http://www.yvonnesplace.net/index2.html. This survey does not claim to be scientific; the results come from a total of more than one thousand participants, whose information was received by email.

499 Yik Koon Teh, "*Mak Nyahs* (Male Transsexuals) in Malaysia: The Influence of Culture and Religion on Their Identity," *International Journal of Transgenderism, 5* (no. 3) (2001), accessed online at http://www.symposion.com/ijt/ijtvo05no03_04.htm.

500 The work of Wing Foo Tsoi suggests that female-to-male transsexuals may start crossdressing at an earlier age than do male-to-female transsexuals. See W. F. Tsoi, "Developmental Profile of 200 Male and 100 Female Transsexuals in Singapore," *Archives of Sexual Behavior, 19* (no. 6), 595-605. Cf. W. F. Tsoi, "Male and Female Transsexuals: A Comparison," *Singapore Medical Journal, 33* (no. 2), 182-185 (1992).

501 N. Lukianowicz, "Survey of Various Aspects of Transvestism in the Light of Our Present Knowledge," *Journal of Nervous and Mental Disease, 128* (no. 1), 36-64 (1959), p. 51.

502 Ingrid M. Sell, "Third Gender: A Qualitative Study of the Experience of Individuals Who Identify as Being Neither Man Nor Woman," *The Psychotherapy Patient, 13* (nos. 1-2), 131-145 (2004), p. 139.

Q. 29 Notes

503 Gerald P. Mallon & Theresa DeCrescenzo, "Transgender Children and Youth: A Child Welfare Practice Perspective," *Child Welfare, 85* (no. 2), 215-241 (2006), p. 217.

504 Neil Buhrich & Trina Beaumont, "Comparison of Transvestism in Australia and America," *Archives of Sexual Behavior, 10* (no. 3), 269-279 (1981). They set as the criterion that such labeling had occurred at least twice between ages 6-12.

[505] Richard L. Schott, "The Childhood and Family Dynamics of Transvestites," *Archives of Sexual Behavior, 24* (no. 3), 309-327 (1995), p. 324.

[506] Mallon & DeCrescenzo, p. 217.

[507] Emily W. Kane, "'No Way My Boys Are Going to Be Like That!' Parents' Responses to Children's Gender Nonconformity," *Gender & Society, 20* (no. 2), 149-176 (2006). Quote is from p. 158.

[508] Gianna E. Israel & Donald E. Tarver, *Transgender Care: Recommended Guidelines, Practical Information, and Personal Accounts* (Phila.: Temple Univ. Press, 1997).

[509] Mallon & DeCrescenzo, p. 223.

[510] Neil Buhrich & Trina Beaumont, "Comparison of Transvestism in Australia and America," *Archives of Sexual Behavior, 10* (no. 3), 269-279 (1981), Table 1. 'Characteristics of Feminine Gender Identity.'

[511] Neil Buhrich & Neil McConaghy, "Preadult Feminine Behaviors of Male Transvestites," *Archives of Sexual Behavior, 14* (no. 5), 413-419 (1985).

[512] Shannon Wyss, "'This Was My Hell': The Violence Experienced By Gender Non-conforming Youth in US High Schools," *International Journal of Qualitative Education, 17* (no. 5), 709-730 (2004), p. 710.

[513] Jody Norton, "Transchildren, Changelings, and Faeries: Living the Dream and Surviving the Nightmare in Contemporary America," in G. E. Anzaldua & E. Keating (Eds.), *This Bridge We Call Home*, pp. 145-154 (N. Y.: Routledge, 2002), p. 149.

[514] Mallon & DeCrescenzo, pp. 223-224.

[515] Cf. John Money & Anthony J. Russo, "Homosexual vs. Transvestite or Transsexual Gender-Identity/Role: Outcome Study in Boys," *International Journal of Family Psychiatry, 2* (nos. 1-2), 139-145 (1981).

[516] Erik H. Erikson, *Childhood and Society*, 2nd ed. (N. Y.: W. W. Norton, 1963), p. 261.

[517] Ibid, p. 262. Also see Erik H. Erikson, "The Problem of Ego Identity," in E.Erikson, *Identity and the Life Cycle*, pp. 108-175 (N. Y.: W. W. Norton, 1980 reprint of 1959 ed.).

[518] Mallon & DeCrescenzo, p. 224.

Q. 30 Notes

[519] Gianna E. Israel, "Tired of Transgender?" *Gianna Israel Gender Library* (2000). Available online at http://www.firelily.com/gender/gianna/tired.html.

[520] Mary T. Hogan-Finlay, *Development of the Cross-Gender Lifestyle and Comparison of Cross-Gendered Men with Heterosexual Controls*. Ph.D. dissertation. (Carleton University, 1995).

[521] Among the various studies to confirm this change, see C. D. Doorn, J. Poortinga, & A. M. Verschoor, "Cross-Gender Identity in Transvestites and Male Transsexuals," *Archives of Sexual Behavior, 23* (no. 2), 185-201 (1994). The authors note that the growing need for crossdressing experienced in adulthood by many transvestites is accompanied by a "clearly diminishing fetishistic motivation, in favor, as can be assumed, of a gender identity motivation."

[522] Mary T. Hogan-Finlay, *Development of the cross-gender lifestyle and comparison of cross-gendered men with heterosexual controls*. PH.D. Thesis (Carleton University, 1995).

[523] Ibid.

[524] Harry Benjamin, *The Transsexual Phenomenon* (N.Y.: The Julian Press, 1966), chapter 3, " The Transvestite in Older and Newer Aspects." This book has been reprinted on the Symposion.com website as an IJT Electronic Book. Accessed online at http://www.symposion.com/ijt/benjamin/index.htm. For more on Benjamin's views, see the answer to Q. 95.

[525] Neil Buhrich & Trina Beaumont, "Comparison of Transvestism in Australia and America," *Archives of Sexual Behavior, 10* (no. 3), 269-279 (1981). Percentage compiled from data presented in Table II. 'Characteristics of Crossdressing.'

[526] Vernon Coleman, (1996). *Men in Dresses: A Study in Transvestism/ Crossdressing.* European Medical Journal. Chilton Designs Publishers, §15, 'Hours a Week Cross-dressed: Reality & Expectation.' Accessed online at http://www. vernoncoleman.com/downloads/ mid.htm.

[527] Bonnie Bullough & Vern Bullough, ""Men Who Cross-Dress: A Survey," in B. Bullough, V. L. Bullough, & J. Elias (Eds.), *Gender Blending*, pp. 174-188 (Amherst, NY: Prometheus Books, 1997), p. 184, Table 5. 'Current Cross-Dressing Patterns (Full Dress or Selected Items).'

[528] Yvonne, "Who We Are," *Yvonne's Place for Crossdressers* (1999). Accessed online at http://www.yvonnesplace.net/index2.html.

[529] Ibid.

[530] Buhrich & Beaumont (percentage compiled from data presented in Table II).

[531] Coleman, §15.

[532] Bullough & Bullough, p. 184, Table 5.

[533] Yvonne.

[534] Benjamin, see the end of chapter 3.

[535] Virginia Prince & P. M. Bentler, "Survey of 504 Cases of Transvestism," *Psychological Reports, 31*, 903-917 (1972), pp. 913-916.

[536] Coleman, §4, 'Extent of Cross Dressing.' Coleman noted 'complete' included not only feminine dress, but use of a wig and cosmetics.

[537] Richard F. Docter & Virginia Prince, "Transvestism: A Survey of 1032 Cross-Dressers," *Archives of Sexual Behavior, 26* (no. 6), 589-605 (1997), Table II and following discussion.

[538] Coleman, §8, 'Bra and Panties Beneath the Suit: The Number of Crossdressers Who Wear Women's Underwear When Dressed in Ordinary Male Clothes.'

[539] Buhrich & Beaumont, Table II (percentage calculated from table data).

[540] Ibid.

[541] Virginia Prince & P. M. Bentler, "Survey of 504 Cases of Transvestism," *Psychological Reports, 31*, 903-917 (1972), p. 914.

Q. 31 Notes

[542] A number of studies have shown the desirability of psychological androgyny.

[543] Jung thinks that every man possesses within himself a feminine archetype called the *anima* and every woman possesses within herself a male archetype called the *animus*.

[544] Gianna E. Israel, "Closeted crossdresser dilemmas," *Gianna Israel Gender Library* (1998). Accessed online at http://www.firelily.com/gender/gianna/closeted. dilemmas.html.

545 Jon K. Meyer, Norman J. Knorr, & Dietrich Blumer, "Characterization of a Self-Designated Transsexual Population," *Archives of Sexual Behavior, 1* (no. 3), 219-230 (1971), p. 227.

546 The designation of 'marginal transvestites' comes from work done by researchers Neil Buhrich and Neil McConaghy. See Neil Buhrich & Neil McConaghy, "Three Clinically Discrete Categories of Fetishistic Transvestism," *Archives of Sexual Behavior, 8* (no. 2), 151-157 (1979). Cf. Neil Buhrich & Neil McConaghy, "The Discrete Syndromes of Transvestism and Transsexualism," *Archives of Sexual Behavior, 6* (no. 6), 483-495. Also, Neil Buhrich & Neil McConaghy, "Clinical Comparison of Transvestism and Transsexualism: An Overview," *Australian and New Zealand Journal of Psychiatry, 11* (no. 2), 83-86 (1977).

547 Virginia Prince & P. M. Bentler, "Survey of 504 Cases of Transvestism," *Psychological Reports, 31*, 903-917 (1972), p. 909.

548 Yvonne, "Who We Are," *Yvonne's Place for Crossdressers* (1999). Accessed online at http://www.yvonnesplace.net/index2.html. There were 1,206 respondents on this matter.

549 Meyer, Knorr, & Blumer, p. 229.

550 Yvonne, 1999.

551 Meyer, Knorr, & Blumer, p. 227; see Table IV.

552 Prince & Bentler, p. 909. The authors also note that more than a third (34%) report that had it been financially possible, and legal, to have a sex change operation they would have done so when younger. But, say the authors, some of these men may be expressing "fantasy exploration" rather than a strong transsexual desire; they point (p. 910) to Harry Benjamin's conclusion that the notion of a sex change can be attractive to transvestites even though they reject actually pursuing such a conversion. (See Harry Benjamin, *The Transsexual Phenomenon* (N. Y.: Julian Press, 1966), p. 22.)

553 Yvonne, 1999. The respondent pool on this matter numbered 1,171.

554 Bullough, Bullough, & Smith, p. 252, Table 10. The differences between transvestites and transsexuals in this respect is pronounced. Almost half (49%) of the transsexual participants had at one time or another taken sex hormones and a full third (33%) had undergone surgery; another 15% are so inclined.

555 Vernon Coleman, *Men in Dresses: A Study in Transvestism/Crossdressing.* European Medical Journal. (Chilton Designs Publishers, 1996), §3, 'The Incidence of Transsexualism Among Crossdressers.' Accessed online at http://www.vernoncoleman.com/downloads/mid.htm.

Q. 32 Notes

556 Peggy Rudd, *Crossdressing with Dignity: The Case for Transcending Gender Lines.* (Katy, TX: PM Publishers, 1990), p. 16.

557 Jack L. Croughan, Marcel Saghir, Rose Cohen, & Eli Robins, "A Comparison of Treated and Untreated Male Crossdressers," *Archives of Sexual Behavior, 10* (no. 6), 515-528 (1981), Table VIII (and discussion following it).

558 Vernon Coleman, *Men in Dresses: A Study in Transvestism/ Crossdressing* (European Medical Journal. Chilton Designs Publishers, 1996), §5, 'The Negative Social Impact of Crossdressing on Crossdressers Themselves.' Accessed online at http://www. vernoncoleman.com/downloads/mid.htm.

559 H. Taylor Buckner, "The Transvestic Career Path," *Psychiatry, 33* (no. 3), 381-389 (1970). For more description of his thesis, see the answer to Q. 22. Cf. the notion of *autogynephilia* advanced by Ray Blanchard and others (see the answers to Q. 96, 98).

560 Some have carped that such reports tend to come from spouses involved in groups supportive of crossdressing and thus may be biased. I doubt they are any more biased, though, than those who appeal to theories they find agreeable to their values quite apart from any empirical evidence. Cf. the answer to Q. 38 for more on Docter's findings and further information.

561 David F. Greenberg, *The Construction of Homosexuality* (Chicago: Univ. of Chicago Press, 1988), p. 2.

562 Rudd, p. 16.

563 Neil Buhrich & Trina Beaumont, "Comparison of Transvestism in Australia and America," *Archives of Sexual Behavior, 10* (no. 3), 269-279 (1981). Percentage calculated from data presented in Table II. 'Characteristics of Crossdressing.'

564 Coleman, §2, 'Why Do Men Crossdress?'

565 Ibid.

566 Jason Cox & Helga Dittmar, "The Functions of Clothes and Clothing (Dis)satisfaction: A Gender Analysis Among British Students," *Journal of Consumer Policy, 18* (nos. 2-3), 237-265 (1995), p. 251.

567 Manuel X. Zamarripa, Bruce E. Wampold, & Erik Gregory, "Male Gender Role Conflict, Depression, and Anxiety: Clarification and Generalizability to Women," *Journal of Counseling Psychology, 50* (no. 3), 333-338 (2003), p. 333. This research is discussed in answering Q. 7.

Q. 33 Notes

568 Julie A. Seaman, "The Peahen's Tale, Or Dressing Our Parts At Work," *Duke Journal of Gender Law and Policy, 14*, 423-466 (2007), p. 423. Accessed online at http://www.law.duke.edu/journals/cite.php?14+Duke+J.+Gender+L.+&+Pol'y+423 #FA0.

569 Roberta Gilchrist, *Gender and Archaeology: Contesting the Past* (N. Y.: Routledge, 1999), p. 65.

570 See, for example, the practice among Chinese nobility, in Tsui-mei Huang, "Gender Differentiation in Jin State Jade Regulations," in K. M. Linduff & Y. Sun (Eds.), *Gender and Chinese Archaeology*, pp. 137-160 (Walnut Creek, CA: AltaMira, 2004), p. 159.

571 Rosemary A. Joyce, "Beauty, Sexuality, Ornamentation and Gender in Ancient Mesoamerica," in S. Nelson & M. Rosen-Ayalon (Eds.), *In Pursuit of Gender*, pp. 81-92 (Walnut Creek, CA: AltaMira Press, 2002).

572 Laura L. Runge, *Gender and Language in British Literary Criticism, 1660-1790* (N.Y.: Cambridge Univ. Press, 1997), p. 189.

573 Cf. Marjorie B. Garber, *Vested Interests: Cross-Dressing and Cultural Anxiety* (N. Y.: Routledge, 1997), p. 207. Also cf. Susan J. Bradley & Kenneth J. Zucker, *Gender Identity Disorder and Psychosexual Problems in Children and Adolescents* (N. Y.: Guilford, 1995), p. 49.

574 Richard Ekins, *Male Femaling: A Grounded Theory Approach to Cross-Dressing and Sex-Changing* (N. Y.: Routledge, 1997), p. 78.

575 Ibid, p. 431f.

576 Sofie Van Bauwel, "Representing Gender Benders: Consumerism and the Muting of Subversion," in J. Hands & E. Siapera (Eds.), *At the Interface: Continuity and Transformation in Culture and Politics*, pp. 17-38 (Amsterdam-N. Y.: Rodopi, 2004), p. 20.

577 Ekins, p. 42.

578 Richard J. Novic, *Alice in Genderland: A Crossdresser Comes of Age* (Lincoln, NE: iUniverse, 2005), p. 147.

579 Richard Ekins & Dave King, *Blending Genders: Social Aspects of Cross-Dressing and Sex-Changing* (N. Y.: Routledge, 1996), p. 46.

580 See, for example, the remark by Rudy Makoul, *Hollywood, Sight Unseeing* (Victoria, Canada: Trafford Publishing, 2004), p. 186.

Q. 34 Notes

581 Arlene Istar Lev, *Transgender Emergence: Therapeutic Guidelines for Working with Gender-Variant People and Their Families* (N. Y.: Haworth Clinical Practice Press, 2004), p. 241.

582 See Stephen Whittle, "The Trans-Cyberian Mail Way," *Social & Legal Studies, 7* (no. 3), 389-408 (1998). Also see Patricia Gagne, Richard Tewksbury, & Deanna McGaughey, "Coming Out and Crossing Over: Identity Formation and Proclamation in a Transgender Community," *Gender & Society, 11*, 478-508 (1997). Cf. James P. Sampson, Jr., "The Internet as a Potential Force for Social Change," in C. C. Lee & G. R. Walz (Eds.), *Social Action: A Mandate for Counselors*, pp. 213-225 (Alexandria, VA: American Counseling Association, 1998).

583 Alex Fernando Teixeira Primo, Vanessa Andrade Pereira, & Angélica Freitas, "Brazilian Crossdresser Club," *CyberPsychology & Behavior, 3* (no. 2), 287-296 (2000).

584 Alan L. Ellis, Liz Highleyman, Kevin Schaub, & Melissa White (Eds.), *The Harvey Milk Institute Guide to Lesbian, Gay, Bisexual, Transgender, and Queer Internet Research* (Binghamton, NY: Haworth Press, 2002). This volume is divided sensibly into chapters that can assist one in conducting internet research. An entire chapter is given to *how* to conduct internet research, followed by one identifying major LGBTQ internet research tools. Subsequent chapters offer focus on specific areas: Queer studies, bisexual studies, transgender and intersex studies, and so forth. Subjects covered include sexuality, law, and health, among others.

585 Accessed online at http://www.gender.org.uk/gendys/bokrevw.htm. The GENDYS Network is a London-based site that advertises itself on its homepage as "For all who have encountered gender identity problems personally, transsexuals, transgendered people and gender dysphoric people of either sex, and for those who provide care, both professional and lay." Accessed online at http://www.gender.org.uk/gendys/index.htm.

586 This internet domain has as its cornerstone youth suicide problems related to gay and bisexual males; see the homepage accessed online at http://www.youth-suicide.com/gay-bisexual/index.htm. However, this comprehensive source offers links to many, many materials. The GLBT Web-Based Education Index lists 22 subject areas and is accessed online at http://www.youth-suicide.com/gay-bisexual/educate.htm.

587 This material is drawn principally from the following sources: Dave King & Richard Ekins, *Pioneers of Transgendering: The Life and Work of Virginia Prince* (2000), accessed online at http://www.gender.org.uk/conf/2000/king20.htm. This material was prepared for the GENDYS Conference, 2000. Also see by the same authors, *Virginia Prince: Pioneer of Transgendering* (N. Y.: Haworth, 2006). Also see Jane Ellen Fairfax, *A*

Brief History of Tri-Ess (2006), accessed online at the Tri-Ess website, at http://www.tri-ess.org/history.html. Also see Laura Granger & Joan Huff, *Tiffany Club of New England* (2004). Accessed online at http://www.tcne.org/club_history.htm.

[588] Various sources offer one or the other name.

[589] King & Ekins; also Fairfax.

[590] Fairfax.

[591] Jane Ellen Fairfax, *3 S's of Tri-Ess* (2001; updated Jan. 5, 2006). Accessed online at http://www.tri-ess.org/3sss.html.

[592] Jane Ellen Fairfax, *A Crossdressers' Bill of Rights* (1998-2000; updated Jan. 29, 2005). Accessed online at http://www.tri-ess.org/Wives_CDs_BofR.html. The Bill of Rights has been summarized in the text; please see the original document for greater detail.

[593] Frances Fairfax, *A Wives' Bill of Rights* (1998-2000; updated Jan. 29, 2005). Accessed online at http://www.tri-ess.org/Wives_CDs_BofR.html. This Bill of Rights was first published in 1994 in *Sweetheart Connection*. The Bill of Rights has been summarized in the text; please see the original document for greater detail.

[594] *AEGIS Online* (1997, 1999, 2000). Accessed online at http://www.gender.org/aegis/. Also see Gender.org, the website for GEA, accessed online at http://www. gender.org/.

[595] *About* page for Gender Public Advocacy Coalition (n.d.). Accessed online at http://www.gpac.org/about/.

[596] For more on her role in the founding of the Tiffany Club, see Granger & Huff.

[597] *Transgender Tapestry & The International Foundation for Gender Education FAQs (frequently-asked questions)* (2006). Accessed online at http://www.ifge.org/index.php?name=FAQ&id_cat=2.

[598] This page is archived at the organization's website. Accessed online at http://www.ifge.org/intro.htm.

[599] Mission statement found on the NCTE 'About' page, accessed online at http://nctequality.org/About/about.asp.

[600] *Transgendered Cop Says He Was Unfairly Forced from Job* (2004, Mar. 1). This Associated Press news story found at the Human Rights Campain website, accessed online at http://www.hrc.org/Template.cfm?Section=Home&CONTENTID=17082&TEMPLATE=/ContentManagement/ContentDisplay.cfm.

[601] *Former IFGE Board Member Wins VT Discrimination Case* (2004). Article archived at the IFGE Transgender Tapestry website, accessed online at http://www.ifge.org/index.php?name=News&file=article&sid=13.

[602] Julie Marin, *Vision* (2005); also, *Welcome* page, both at the T-COPS website, accessed online at http://www.tcops.org/.

[603] PFLAG's Home page accessed online at http://www.pflag.org/. The Vision Statement (*Our Vision*) accessed online at http://www.pflag.org/Vision__Mission_and_Strategic_Goals.mission.0.html. Basic information cited in the text comes from the *About PFLAG* webpage, accessed online at http://www.pflag.org/FAQs_Facts.pflag_faq.0.html.

[604] FPC's Home page accessed online at http://www.familypride.org. The history material accessed online at http://www.familypride.org/history.html. The remaining

material accessed online at http://www.familypride.org/site/pp.asp?c=bhKP17PFIm E&b=313485.

[605] SSN's Home page accessed online at http://www.straightspouse.org/index .shtml. The 'What We Do' page accessed online at http://www.straightspouse.org/ whatwe.shtml.

[606] Helen Boyd, *My Husband Betty. Love, Sex, and Life with a Crossdresser* (N. Y.: Thunder's Mouth Press, 2004).

[607] Helen Boyd, *She's Not the Man I Married: My Life with a Transgender Husband* (Emeryville, CA: Seal Press, 2007).

[608] Virginia Erhardt, *Head Over Heels. Wives Who Stay with Cross-Dressers and Transsexuals* (N. Y.: Haworth Press, 2007).

[609] CrossDressersWives.com accessed online at http://crossdresserswives.com/. The *Mission Statement* accessed online at http://crossdresserswives.com/601.html.

[610] The Laura's Playground website's Home Page accessed online at http://www. lauras-playground.com/index.htm.

[611] The credentials of the moderator staff for Laura's Playground accessed online at http://www.lauras-playground.com/staff.htm.

[612] Accessed online at http://www.lauras-playground.com/support_index.htm.

[613] CDWSOS maintains a simple webpage, accessed online at http://www. angel-fire.com/tv2/cdwsos/.

Q. 35 Notes

[614] Darryl B. Hill, "'Feminine' Heterosexual Men: Subverting Heteropatriarchal Sexual Scripts?" *Journal of Men's Studies, 14* (no. 2), 145-159 (2006).

[615] Marjorie Garber, *Vested Interests: Cross-Dressing and Cultural Anxiety* (N. Y.: Routledge, 1992), p. 131.

[616] Jason Cromwell, *Transmen and FTMs. Identities, Bodies, Genders, and Sexualities* (Chicago: Univ. ofChicago Press, 1999), p. 63.

[617] Wilhelm Stekel and Emil Gutheil were the most prominent advocates of this theory; see the answer to Q. 95 for more information on their ideas.

[618] Albert C. Kinsey, Wardell B. Pomeroy, Clyde E. Martin, & Paul H. Gebhard, *Sexual Behavior in the Human Female* (Philadelphia: W. B. Saunders, 1953), p. 681. Also see Harry Benjamin, *The Transsexual Phenomenon* (N.Y.: The Julian Press, 1966), chapter 3, " The Transvestite in Older and Newer Aspects." This book has been reprinted on the Symposion.com website as an IJT Electronic Book. Accessed online at http://www. symposion.com/ijt/benjamin/index.htm. For more on Benjamin's views, see the answer to Q. 95.

[619] Gianna E. Israel, "Translove: Transgender Persons and Their Families," *Journal of GLBT Family Studies, 1* (no. 1), 53-67 (2005), p. 56.

[620] Ibid, p. 57.

[621] Virginia Prince & P. M. Bentler, "Survey of 504 Cases of Transvestism," *Psychological Reports, 31*, 903-917 (1972), p. 908. It is important to note that this survey was specifically aimed at crossdressing men who were subscribers to *Transvestia* magazine, a publication aimed at *hetero*sexual males.

[622] Vern Bullough, Bonnie Bullough, & Richard Smith, "A Comparative Study of Male Transvestites, Male to Female Transsexuals, and Male Homosexuals," *The Journal of Sex Research, 19* (no. 3), 238-257 (1983), p. 250, Table 8. This comparative study involv-

ing male transvestites, transsexuals, homosexuals and others, poses the question, "Are you more sexually attracted to females, males, both, or neither?" The percentage reported in the table is for those subjects identified as transvestites. The incidence of the response "male" (6%) by transvestites is comparable to the rate established for the general population (4-10%), and substantially less than for transsexuals (52%) or homosexuals (80%).

623 Richard F. Docter, *Transvestites and Transsexuals: Toward a Theory of Cross-Gender Behavior.* (N. Y.: Plenum Press, 1988), p. 128. The figure in the table includes those who designate themselves "exclusively" heterosexual (60%) and those who are "predominantly" so, while admitting incidental homosexual contact (28%).

624 Richard L. Schott, "The Childhood and Family Dynamics of Transvestites," *Archives of Sexual Behavior, 24* (no. 3), 309-327 (1995), p. 318, Table IV. The results in the table are for designated as transvestites; only 8% of the transsexuals make such a claim.

625 Vernon Coleman, *Men in Dresses: A Study in Transvestism/ Crossdressing.* European Medical Journal (Chilton Designs Publishers, 1996), §10, 'Homosexual Experiences Among Crossdressers.' Accessed online at http://www.vernoncoleman.com/ downloads/ mid.htm. Coleman phrases the question as "Have you ever had sex with another man?" Presumably, some portion of those who answer 'Yes' (20%) would not acknowledge that such an encounter means they are homosexual. Thus the 80% reported in the table is best regarded as a 'most conservative' figure.

626 Bonnie Bullough & Vern Bullough, ""Men Who Cross-Dress: A Survey," in B. Bullough, V. L. Bullough, & J. Elias (Eds.), *Gender Blending*, pp. 174-188 (Amherst, NY: Prometheus Books, 1997), p. 183, Table 4.

627 Richard F. Docter & Virginia Prince, "Transvestism: A Survey of 1032 Cross-Dressers," *Archives of Sexual Behavior, 26* (no. 6), 589-605 (1997), Table II.

628 Yvonne, "Who We Are," *Yvonne's Place for Crossdressers* (1999); see the table on 'Sexual Orientation' in the section on Sexuality. Accessed online at http://www. yvonnesplace.net/index2.html. The figure in the table is collective for the following responses: "heterosexual" (48.4%), "heterosexual but bi-curious" (23.9%), and "heterosexual with homosexual experiences" (7.2%).

629 Schott, p. 318, Table IV.

630 Bullough & Bullough, p. 183, Table 4.

631 Docter, p. 128.

632 Roselle Pineda, "Undressing Dresses," *Women in Action*, no. 3 (2002). Accessed online at http://www.isiswomen.org/pub/wia/wia302/undress.htm.

Q. 36 Notes

633 See Paisley Currah, Richard M. Juang, & Shannon Price Minter (Eds.), *Transgender Rights* (Minneapolis: Univ. of Minnesota Press, 2007).

634 John Money, *Lovemaps: Sexual/Erotic Health and Pathology, Paraphilia, and Gender Transposition* (Amherst, NY: Prometheus Books, 1989), pp. 3-4. Also see David F. Greenberg, *The Construction of Homosexuality* (Chicago: Univ. of Chicago Press, 1988), pp. 292ff.

Money himself advocates what he terms "the principle of personal sexual inviolacy." This principle is intended both to guarantee equal sexual rights for all individuals and simultaneously safeguard societal rights. Money (p. 4f) explains it as follows:

According to this principle, no one has the right to infringe upon someone else's personal sexual inviolacy by imposing his/her own version of what is or is not erotic and sexual, without the other person's informed consent. It is possible to give informed consent, and to enter into a consensual contract, only if the terms of the contract are known in full, and not taken for granted. They can be known in full only if the end is predicated by the beginning. In a sexual engagement, that means no unexpected ending, unilaterally imposed on one partner by the other.

[635] In 1696 Massachusetts prohibited crossdressing by either gender. See Patricia Bonomi, *The Lord Cornbury Scandal: The Politics of Reputation in British America* (Chapel Hill, NC: The Univ. of North Carolina Press, 1998), p. 141.

[636] William N. Eskridge, Jr., "No Promo Homo: The Sedimentation of Antigay Discourse and the Channeling Effect of Judicial Review," *New York University Law Review, 75*, 1327-1411 (2000), pp. 1334f.

[637] *GenderPAC. First National Survey of TransGender Violence* (GenderPAC, 1997), p. 4. Accessed online at http://hatecrime.transadvocacy.com/documents/ TransViolence%20Survey%20Results.pdf.

[638] P. M. Maher & A. C. Slocum, "Freedom in Dress: Legal Sanctions," *Clothing & Textiles Research Journal, 5* (no. 4), 14-22 (1987). In their review of cases, they found that judges 61% of the time ruled the sanction had been improperly applied.

[639] S. J. Lennon, K. K. P. Johnson, & T. L. Schulz, "Forging Linkages Between Dress and Law in the U.S., Part I: Rape and Sexual Harassment," *Clothing & Textiles Research Journal, 17* (no. 3), 144-156 (1999). Cf. S. J. Lennon, K. K. P. Johnson, & T. L. Schulz, "Forging Linkages Between Dress and Law in the U.S., Part II: Dress Codes," *Clothing & Textiles Research Journal, 17* (no. 3), 157-167 (1999). This article examines how dress code legal cases, while implicating issues of individual liberty, are not related to accuracy of inference in judging the dress of a code violater.

[640] L. Lewis & K. K. P. Johnson, "Effect of Dress, Cosmetics, Sex of Subject, and Causal Inference on Attribution of Victim Responsibility," *Clothing & Textiles Research Journal, 8* (no. 1), 22-27 (1989). Cf. L. Richards, "A Theoretical Analysis of Nonverbal Communication and Victim Selection for Sexual Assault," *Clothing & Textiles Research Journal, 9* (no. 4), 55-64 (1991).

[641] Sr. Mary Elizabeth, *Legal Aspects of Transsexualism* (San Juan Capistrano, CA: J2CP Information Services, 1988). Excerpts from this edition are available on the internet at various websites. The revised edition was published by Educational Resources Publication (1990).

[642] Such provisions can be annoyingly persistent. Detroit's 'annoying person' ordinance (*Code of 1964, §39-1-36*) was only repealed in July, 2002 (*Ord. No. 9-02, §1*).

[643] See, for example the ordinance of St. Paul, Minnesota that states, "No person shall appear in any street or public place in a state of nudity, nor in any indecent or lewd dress . . ." (*§280.03. Nudity, Indecency and Obscenity*). This, with *§280.06. Loitering After Midnight*, which prohibits consorting with "thieves, prostitutes, or other questionable characters," exemplifies the kinds of ordinance interactions that have been used against crossdressers. Both are listed under "Certain Miscellaneous Misdemeanors."

644 William N. Eskridge, Jr., "Privacy Jurisprudence and the Apartheid of the Closet, 1946-1961," *Florida State University Law Review, 24* (no. 4), 703-840 (1997), p. 723. Accessed online at http://www.law.fsu.edu/journals/lawreview/frames/244/eskrtxt. html#FNR98.

645 Ibid, p. 830 (Appendix E).

646 Ariadne Kane, "Cross-Gendered Persons," in P. B. Koch & D. L. Weis (Eds.), *Sexuality in America. Understanding Our Sexual Values and Behavior,* pp. 165-171 (N. Y.: Continuun, 1998), p. 170.

647 Barry Lank, "These Laws Made Sense at the Time," *Courier-Post* of Cherry Hill, NJ (2002. March 3). Accessed online at *Barry Lank's Teeny Tiny Brain* at http://www.barrylank.com/3_3_02.html. The example is Woodbury municipal code ordinance 139-8. Cf. the 1969 Municipal Code of Columbus, Ohio (§2343.04): "No person shall appear upon any public street or other public place in a state of nudity or in a dress not belonging to his or her sex, or in an indecent or lewd dress."

648 Arlene Zarembka, "Fashion vs. Gender. We Should Approach the Cross-Dressing with Tolerance," *St. Louis (Missouri) Post-Dispatch* (2 Jan., 2003). Accessed online at the tgcrossroads.org website at http://www.tgcrossroads.org/news/ archive.asp?aid=563.

649 See *City of Columbus v. Zanders*, case #31436, Franklin County Municipal Court (Oh. 1970). The case against the accused was dismissed on the legal grounds that the defendant suffered from a "mental disease or defect" which produced a lack of capacity "either to appreciate the wrongfulness of his conduct or to conform his conduct to the requirements of law." Excerpts from the trial transcript accessed online at the National Transgender Advocacy Coalition website at http://www.ntac.org/law/criminal_266 ne2d602.html. The ordinance, in *City of Columbus v. Rogers* was ruled unconstitutionally vague; see Sr. Mary Elizabeth, *Legal Aspects of Transsexualism.*

Also see, for further examples, *City of Chicago v. Wilson*, 389 N.E.2d 522, 533-34 (Ill. 1978); *Doe v. McConn* 489 F. Supp. 76, 79-80 (S.D. Tex. 1980). In the latter case Houston ordinance *§328-42.4* of the city code prohibited "a person from appearing in public dressed with the intent to disguise her or his sex as that of the opposite sex."

650 N. Lukianowicz, "Survey of Various Aspects of Transvestism in the Light of Our Present Knowledge," *Journal of Nervous and Mental Disease, 128* (no. 1), 36-64 (1959), p. 56.

651 New York City Penal Code §240.35(4). For a thorough discussion of this law and its history, see Clare Norens, *Anti-Mask: New York Penal Code §240.35(4)* (2004). Accessed online at http://www.nlgnyc. org/pdf/MaskMemo.pdf.

652 Phyllis Randolph Frye, "Facing Discrimination, Organizing for Freedom: The Transgender Community," in J. D'Emilio, W. B. Turner & U. Vaid (Eds.), *Creating Change: Public Policy and Civil Rights*, pp. 451-522 (N. Y.: St. Martin's Press, 2000), p. 518, n. 20. p. 458. Accessed online at http://www.transgenderlegal.com/.

653 Department of Defense (DoD) Directive 6130.3 ("Physical Standards for Appointment, Enlistment, and Induction") and DOD Instruction 6130.4 ("Criteria and Procedure Requirements for Physical Standards for Appointment, Enlistment, or Induction in the Armed Forces"). Interestingly, Directive 6130.3 §3.3, under 'Policy,' states as its rationale "to ensure that individuals under consideration for appointment, enlistment, or induction into the United States Armed Forces" meet five medical crite-

ria: freedom from contagious diseases that might endanger others (3.3.1); freedom from conditions that might require excessive time lost from duty or lead to discharge for medical unfitness (3.3.2); medically able to satisfactorily complete required training (3.3.3); medically adaptable to the military environment without limitations of location (3.3.4); and, medically capable of performing duties without aggravating an existing physical defect or medical condition (3.3.5). Since being transgendered is not contagious, does not require treatment or hospitalization, does not render one physically or mentally feeble, and is not exaggerated by work, presumably it is not 'adaptable to the military environment.' However that point seems to be with reference to medical conditions that limit a person's ability to be stationed abroad, and transgender hardly fits that either. Nevertheless, the DoD regards being transgendered a medical liability preventing enlistment. The directive was accessed online at http://www.dtic.mil/whs/directives/ corres/pdf/d61303_121500/d61303p.pdf.

[654] Department of Defense Instruction 6130.4, E1.29. The DoD references the International Classification of Disease (ICD) codes in parentheses for disqualifying conditions. Thus the (302) in the quotation refers to that ICD code. Accessed online at http://www.dtic.mil/whs/directives/corres/ pdf2/i61304p.pdf. For a review of court cases with reference to this matter, see Sr. Mary Elizabeth, *Legal Aspects of Transsexualism*.

[655] Oiler v. Winn Dixie Louisiana, Inc., Civ. No. 00-3114, Section AIA, 2002 U.S.

Dist. LEXIS 17417 (E.D. La. Sept. 16, 2002). Peter Oiler had worked for Winn-Dixie more than 20 years when fired after his employers learned he occasionally cross-dressed away from work. The lawsuit brought on his behalf by the ACLU sued under Title VII, the Civil Rights Act of 1964. Judge Lance Africk, while noting many might find Winn-Dixie's stance morally wrong, also observed that despite 31 proposed bills in Congress between 1981-2001 to amend Title VII to ban employment discrimination based on either affectional or sexual orientation, none had passed. Title VII protection, therefore, does not apply to the transgendered.

[656] Frye, p. 458. Frye references JoAnna McNamara, "Employment Discrimination and the Transsexual," *Proceedings IV*, Appendix E (Houston: ICTLEP, 1995). The cases were *Holloway v. Arthur Anderson Company* (9th Circuit, 1977; 566 F2d 659), *Sommers v. Budget Marketing, Inc.* (8th Circuit, 1982; 667 F2d 748), and *Ulane v. Eastern Airlines, Inc.* (7th Circuit, 1984; 742 F2d 1081).

[657] Doe v. United Consumer Financial Svcs., No. 1:01 CV 1112 (N.D. Ohio 2001).

[658] Price Waterhouse v. Hopkins, 490 U.S. 228. The case was heard before the Supreme Court on October 31, 1988 with a decision handed down May 1, 1989. The opinions of the justices may be accessed online at a number of websites. The majority opinion was accessed online at the Legal Information Institute of Cornell University website at http://supct.law.cornell.edu/supct/html/historics/USSC_CR_0490_ 0228_ZS.html.

[659] R. V. Shervin, "The Legal Problem in Transvestism," *American Journal of Psychotherapy, 8*, 243-244 (1954).

[660] Frye, p. 458. Cf. 2000 California Assembly Bill 1851 (A.B. 1851), which concerned court procedures to be followed when transsexuals apply for legal recognition of their new sex status; it was vetoed by the governor.

[661] *Jones v. Brinkley*, 174 N.C. 23, 27, 93 S.E. 372, 373 (1917).

[662] *State v. Mann*, 317 N.C. 164, 170, 345 S.E.2d 365, 369 (1986). Here the definition reads: "an act of inherent baseness in the private, social, or public duties which one

owes to his fellowmen or to society, or to his country, her institutions and her government." An example of the continuing application of the concept can be found in *Dew v. NCDMV* (1997), an appellate court case. Accessed online at *FindLaw* at http:// caselaw.lp.findlaw.com/scripts/getcase.pl?court=nc&vol=appeals97%5Cappeals0819% 5C&invol=dew.

[663] Office of Disciplinary Counsel vs. Klaas. Accessed online at FindLaw at http://caselaw.lp. findlaw.com/scripts/getcase.pl?court=oh&vol=001109&invol=1.

[664] *State v. Harrison*, 298 S.C. 333, 336, 380 S.E.2d 818, 819 (1989). South Carolina defines moral turpitude as "an act of baseness, evilness, or depravity in the private and social duties which man owes to his fellow man or to society in general, contrary to the customary and accepted rule of right and duty between man and man" (*State v. Major*, 301 S.C. 181, 391 S.E.2d 235 (1990)).

[665] Michael G. Okun & John Rubin, "Employment Consequences of a Criminal Conviction in North Carolina," *Popular Government, 63* (no. 2), 13-24 (1998). See section titled "License Restrictions" and notes 22-23. Accessed online at http://ncinfo.iog. unc.edu/pubs/electronicversions/pg/rubin.htm.

[666] Cf. Eskridge, p. 723. One example: at the end of March, 2005, a New York State appeals court dismissed a suit brought by the Hispanic AIDS Forum, which contended that the loss of an agreed upon lease extension was the result of discrimination based on sex and gender. The defendant had declined to honor the extension, citing concerns over complaints arising from bathroom facility use by transgendered clientele. The Court ruled that no discrimination had occurred because the individuals had been barred from using restrooms that did not conform to their biological sex since this was an expectation for all tenants.

[667] *Cruzan v. Special School District, #1, et al.* (294 F. 3d 981 (Minn. 2002)). Accessed online at http://caselaw.lp.findlaw.com/data2/circs/8th/013417p.pdf. Carla Cruzan contested the right of Debra Davis, a male-to-female (MtF) transsexual, to use the women's restroom at the public school where both were employed. Cf. *Cruzan v. Minneapolis Public School System* (165 F. Supp. 2d 964 (D. Minn. 2001)).

[668] Harry Benjamin, *The Transsexual Phenomenon* (N.Y.: The Julian Press, 1966), chapter 9, "Legal Aspects in Transvestism and Transsexualism." This book has been reprinted on the Symposion.com website as an IJT Electronic Book. Accessed online at http://www.symposion.com/ijt/benjamin/index.htm. In this chapter, Benjamin observed that in the mid-1960s arrests and convictions of crossdressers occurred "daily." For more on Benjamin's views, see the answer to Q. 93.

[669] Jon K. Meyer, Norman J. Knorr, & Dietrich Blumer, "Characterization of a Self-Designated Transsexual Population," *Archives of Sexual Behavior, 1* (no. 3), 219-230 (1971), p. 223.

[670] Jack L. Croughan, Marcel Saghir, Rose Cohen, & Eli Robins, "A Comparison of Treated and Untreated Male Crossdressers," *Archives of Sexual Behavior, 10* (no. 6), 515-528 (1981), p. 518 and Table VIII.

[671] Vernon Coleman, *Men in Dresses: A Study in Transvestism/Cross-dressing.* European Medical Journal (Chilton Designs Publishers, 1996), §12, 'Crossdressers' Experience of the Law.'

[672] See, for example, Shannon Minter, *Representing Transsexual Clients: Selected Legal Issues* (2003). Accessed online at http://www.nclrights.org/publications/pubs/tgclients.pdf.

[673] Sr. Mary Elizabeth, Legal Aspects of Transsexualism.

[674] Jon K. Meyer, Norman J. Knorr, & Dietrich Blumer, "Characterization of a Self-Designated Transsexual Population," Archives of Sexual Behavior, 1 (no. 3), 219-230 (1971), p. 223. Of the 599 transsexuals in their study, 23% of males and 15% of females reported they had been in trouble with the law, which the authors remark as "low considering the extent of cross-dressing practices and the experience of the Clinic that arrest for impersonation is a common cause of legal complications in this group."

[675] Eugene de Savitsch, Homosexuality, Transvestism and Change of Sex (London: William Heinemann Medical Books, 1958), p. 16. The Leber decision is found Appendix A of de Savitsch's book. It is available online at http://www.ntac.org/law/nonus_inreleber.html.

[676] Ibid.

[677] Ibid.

[678] Ibid.

[679] Ibid.

[680] Ibid.

[681] The International Lesbian and Gay Association's *World Legal Survey* (1999), accessed online at http://www.ilga.info/Information/Legal_survey/Summary%20information/transgender_rights.htm, lists Australia (South Australia), Austria, Brazil, Czech Republic, Egypt, Germany, Greece, Italy, Japan, Singapore, Slovakia, Switzerland, and Ukraine. To these may be added Canada, Iran, Turkey the United Kingdom (see the Gender Recognition Act of 2004, at the Department for Constitutional Affairs website accessed online at http://www.dca.gov.uk/constitution/transsex/legs.htm), and the United States. It should also be added that some nations tolerate the practice of SRS without legally sanctioning it.

[682] The text of H.R. 2662 accessed online through the Library of Congress website at http://thomas.loc.gov/cgi-bin/query/D?c109:1:./temp/~c109v6v4mI::.

[683] The text of S. 1145 accessed online through the Library of Congress website at http://thomas.loc.gov/cgi-bin/query/z?c109:S.1145:.

[684] *U. S. House of Representatives Passes Historic Hate Crimes Bill* (2007, May 3). Article posted at Human Rights Campaign website, accessed online at http://www.hrc.org/Template.cfm?Section=Home&CONTENTID=36637&TEMPLATE=/Content Management/ContentDisplay.cfm.

[685] Matthew Shepard was a 21-year-old University of Wyoming student brutally murdered near Laramie, Wyoming in 1998. He was killed because he was gay. For more information, contact the Matthew Shepard Foundation or visit Matthew's Place website, accessed online at http://www.matthewsplace.com/.

[686] *Statement of Administration Policy: H.R. 1592—Local Law Enforcement Hate Crimes Prevention Act of 2007* (2007, May 3). Accessed online at http://www.whitehouse.gov/omb/legislative/sap/110-1/hr1592sap-h.pdf.

[687] *GLAD Wins Tax Deducation for Sex Reassignment Surgery* (2004, Nov. 30). Accessed online at http://www.glad.org/News_Room/press83-11-30-04.html. Also see at the

GLAD website more on the case of Rhiannon O'Donnabhain. Accessed online at http://www.glad.org/GLAD_Cases/index.shtml#Rhia_IRS.

688 *Office of Chief Counsel, Internal Revenue Service: Memorandum (Number 200603025)* (2006, Jan. 20). Accessed online at http://www.irs.gov/pub/irs-wd/0603025.pdf. Also see Doanld H. Read, "IRS Plays Politics with Tax Code," *San Francisco Chronicle* (2006, Apr. 16). Accessed online at http://www.sfgate.com/cgi-bin/article.cgi?file=/chronicle/archive/2006/04/16/INGOLI8NRI1.DTL.

689 The Petition can be found at the GLAD website, accessed online at http://www.glad.org/GLAD_Cases/ODonnabhainTaxCourtPetition.pdf.

690 Jennifer J. Smith, "New HRC Survey Changes Trans Politics, Activists Say," *Washington Blade* (2002, October 11). Accessed online at http://www.tgcrossroads.org/news/archive.asp?aid=399.

691 A summary of the legal situation, pertinent to the wider transgender community (i.e., including gays and lesbians) is available through Lambda Legal's website (lambdalegal.org). Lambda Legal, a national organization "committed to achieving full recognition of the civil rights of lesbians, gay men, bisexuals, the transgendered, and people with HIV or AIDS through impact litigation, education, and public policy work," keeps track of states, counties and cities which prohibit discrimination based on sexual orientation. Accessed online at http://www.lambdalegal.org/cgibin/iowa/documents/record?record=217.

692 The wording quoted is taken from the Minnesota code, ch. 363.03, "Definitions," subdivision 44, "Sexual Orientation" (1992), accessed online at http://www.revisor.leg.state.mn.us/stats/363A/03.html. The chapter concerns the Department of Human Rights. Also cf. 611A.79, on civil damages for bias offenses.

693 Vermont Statute Title 13, 'Crimes and Criminal Procedure': Part 1. Crimes: Chapter 31. Discrimination. §1455. Hate Crimes. Cf. §1458. Definitions. (1999).

694 Lauren Ober, "Transgender Bill Gets Governor's Signature," *Burlington Free Press* (2007, May 25). Accessed online at http://www.burlingtonfreepress.com/apps/pbcs.dll/article?AID=/20070525/NEWS02/705250308/1007/RSS02.

695 Missouri State Statutes 557.035.1. (1999). Accessed online at http://www.moga.state.mo.us/statutes/c500-599/5570035.htm.

696 Hawaii Statutes HRS Chapter 0846. Hawaii Criminal Justice Data Center; Civil Identification: Part IV. Hate Crime Reporting: §846-51. Definitions. (2003). The text reads: "'Gender identity or expression' includes a person's actual or perceived gender, as well as a person's gender identity, gender-related self-image, gender-related appearance, or gender-related expression; regardless of whether that gender identity, gender-related self image, gender-related appearance, or gender-related expression is different from that traditionally associated with the person's sex at birth." Accessed online at http://www.capitol.hawaii.gov/hrscurrent/vol14_ch0701-0853/hrs0846/hrs_08460051.htm.

697 New Mexico State Statute Article 18B. Hate Crimes: §31-18B-2. Definitions (2003). The text reads: "'gender identity' means a person's self-perception, or perception of that person by another, of the person's identity as a male or female based upon the person's appearance, behavior or physical characteristics that are in accord or opposed to the person's physical anatomy, chromosomal sex or sex at birth." Accessed online at http://legis.state.nm.us/Sessions/03%20Regular/bills/senate/SB0249JUS.pdf.

[698] Maine's LD 1196 prohibits discrimination based on sexual orientation, which is defined to include "a person's actual or perceived heterosexuality, bisexuality, homosexuality, or gender identity or expression" (5 Me. Rev. St. §4553 (9-C)).

[699] HB 2661, which expands the jurisdiction of the state Human Rights Commission, was accessed online at http://apps.leg.wa.gov/billinfo/summary.aspx?year =2005&bill=2661. Note §4.(15), which amends RCW 49.60.040 and 1997 c 271 s 3 to read, "'Sexual orientation' means heterosexuality, homosexuality, bisexuality, and gender expression or identity. As used in this definition, 'gender expression or identity' means having or being perceived as having a gender identity, self-image, appearance, appearance, behavior, or expression, whether or not that gender identity, self-image, appearance, behavior, or expression is different from that traditionally associated with the sex assigned to that person at birth." Also see Rachel La Corte, "Wash. Legislature Passes Gay Rights Bill" (Olympia: Associated Press, Jan. 28, 2006); article published online. Accessed at the *Washington Post* website at http://www.washingtonpost .com/wp-dyn/content/article/2006/01/27/AR2006012701190.html

[700] California A.B. 1999 (1998). Accessed online at http://info.sen.ca.gov/pub/97-98/bill/asm/ab_ 1951-2000/ab_1999_bill_19980928_chaptered.html. See Penal Code §422.76. Accessed online at http://www.leginfo.ca.gov/cgibin/displaycode?section= pen&group=00001-01000&file=422.6-422.95.

[701] A.B. 1851. Accessed online at http://www.leginfo.ca.gov/pub/99-00/bill/ asm/ab_1851-1900/ab_1851_bill_20000831_enrolled.html.

[702] *GPAC Applauds KY Non-Discrimination Order*, accessed online at http://www. gpac.org/archive/news/notitle.html?cmd=view&msgnum=0485 GPAC stands for Gender Public Advocacy Coalition.

[703] *GPAC Applauds PA Non-Discrimination Order, First Executive Order to Include Gender Expression*, accessed online at http://www.gpac.org/archive/news/index .html? cmd=view&archive=news&msgnum=0493.

[704] California A.B. 196. Accessed online at http://www.leginfo.ca.gov/pub/bill/ asm/ab_0151-0200/ab_196_bill_20030802_chaptered.html. Cf. the press release from the office of the bill's sponsor, Assemblyman Mark Leno, accessed online at http:// democrats.assembly.ca.gov/members/a13/press/ a132003032.htm.

[705] ORS 659A.118(2). ORS is the abbreviation for Oregon Revised Statutes. Chapter 659A is titled "Unlawful Discrimination in Employment, Public Accom-modations and Real Property Transactions; Administrative and Civil Enforcement." Accessed online at http://landru.leg.state.or.us/ors/659a.html. Cf. the Oregon Civil Rights of Disabled Persons Act.

[706] OAR 839-006-0206(2). OAR is the abbreviation for Oregon Administrative Rules. OAR 839-006-0206 is titled "Examples of Reasonable Accommodation." Accessed online at http://arcweb.sos.state.or.us/rules/OARS_800/OAR_839/839_006 .html.

[707] For a more complete and relatively current list, see the chart maintained by the Lambda website entitled *Summary or States, Cities, and Counties Which Prohibit Discrimination Based on Sexual Orientation* (1997-2005), accessed online at http://www.lambdalegal.org/ cgi-bin/iowa/news/resources.html?record=217.

[708] The new ordinance was met by opposition organized under the banner 'Equal Rights Not Special Rights.' A referendum to amend the ordinance, 'Issue 3,' was placed

on the 1993 ballot and passed handily. Issue 3 changes the City Charter to prohibit any law granting preferential treatment based on sexual orientation. In response, a group including the Equality Foundation sued the city, arguing the amendment violated their rights. A U.S. District judge struck down the amendment as unconstitutional. By a narrow margin the City Council in 1995 voted to remove the phrase 'sexual orientation.' But the legal wrangling continued. The U.S. 6th Circuit Court of Appeals overturned the District Court decision. The U.S. Supreme Court, in 1998, declined to review the matter, letting the Appeals Court decision stand.

For a more in-depth review of the history of the ordinance, see Julie Irwin, "Law Denying Gay Protection Stands," *Cincinnati Enquirer* (1998, Oct. 14). Accessed online at http://www.enquirer.com/ editions/1998/10/14/loc_gayrights14.html.

[709] IFGE website accessed online at http://www.ifge.org/. See story, "Austin Becomes the 3rd City in Texas to Extend Civil Rights Based on Gender Identity" (2004, July 10), accessed online at http://www. ifge.org/modules.php?op=modload&name=News&file=article&sid=25&mode=thread&order=0&thold=0.

[710] *New Orleans Municipal Code §86-1.5. Definitions.* Accessed online at *Municode Online Codes* (Municode.com) at http://livepublish.municode.com.

[711] Ibid. This exclusion is typical in the U.S. and prevents claims of discrimination against crossdressers under provisions of Federal Law protecting the disabled.

[712] *New Orleans Municipal Code §86-19(8). Exclusions.* Accessed online at *Municode Online Codes* (Municode.com) at http://livepublish.municode.com.

[713] *Atlanta Municipal Code §94-112. Unlawful Employment Practices.* Accessed online at *Municode Online Codes* (Municode.com) at http://livepublish.municode.com. According to *94-10. Definitions,* 'gender identity' means "self-perception as male or female, and shall include a person's identity, expression, or physical characteristics, whether or not traditionally associated with one's biological sex or one's sex at birth, including transsexual, transvestite, and transgendered, and including a person's attitudes, preferences, beliefs, and practices pertaining thereto, including but not limited to assumption of male or female identity by appearance or medical treatment."

[714] Boston Municipal Code 10-3.1 Policy of the City of Boston. Accessed online at American Legal Publishing Corporation at http://www.amlegal.com/. Cf. 24-215. Definitions with reference to "Boston Jobs and Living Wage Ordinance." At 12-9.1. Policy, in the section on "Human Rights" in the chapter on "Public Health and Welfare," the code states: "It is clear that behavior which denies equal treatment to any of our citizens as a result of their religious creed, race, color, sex, gender identity or expression, age, disability, national origin, ex-offender status, prior psychiatric treatment, sexual orientation, military status, marital status or parental status, or which is sexually or racially harassing undermines civil order and deprives persons of the benefits of a free and open society."

[715] Chicago Municipal Code 5-8-030. Unfair Housing Practices. Accessed online at Municode Online Codes (Municode.com) at http://livepublish.municode.com. At 2-160-020. Definitions, 'gender identity' is defined as "the actual or perceived appearance, expression, identity or behavior, of a person as being male or female, whether or not that appearance, expression, identity or behavior is different from that traditionally associated with the person's designated sex at birth."

716 Iowa City City Code 2-3-1. Employment; Exceptions. This section is under Title II, "Human Rights," chapter 3, "Discriminatory Practices." Accessed online at http://66. 113.195.234/IA/Iowa%20City/index.htm. At 2-1-1. Definitions, 'gender identity' is defined as "a person's various individual attributes, actual or perceived, in behavior, practice or appearance, as they are understood to be masculine and/or feminine."

717 Los Angeles Municipal Code 49.72. Employment. Accessed online at American Legal Publishing Corporation at http://www.amlegal.com/. At 49.71.4. Definitions, the following is offered: "As used in this ordinance, the term 'sexual orientation' shall mean an individual having or manifesting an emotional or physical attachment to another consenting adult person or persons, or having or manifesting a preference for such attachment, or having or projecting a self-image not associated with one's biological maleness or one's biological femaleness." Cf. Los Angeles Enacts Transgender Protections—21 Years Ago (NTAC Press Release, December 23, 2000), at the National Transgender Advocacy Coalition website accessed online at http://www.ntac.org/pr/001223la.html, where it notes LA's ordinance was adopted in 1979 and the wording taken verbatim from a Minneapolis city ordinance enacted in 1975.

718 Minneapolis Municipal Code 15.150. Discrimination or Harassment. Accessed online at Municode Online Codes (Municode.com) at http://livepublish.municode.com. At 139.20. Definitions, the term 'affectional preference' is defined as "Having or manifesting an emotional or physical attachment to another consenting person or persons, or having or manifesting a preference for such attachment, or having or projecting a self-image not associated with one's biological maleness or one's biological femaleness."

719 Santa Cruz Municipal Code 9.83.010. Purpose and Intent. Accessed online at http://nt2.scbbs.com/cgi-bin/om_isapi.dll?clientID=602767&infobase=procode1& record={1002E89} &softpage=Document. At 9.83.020. Definitions, 'gender' is defined as "'Gender' shall have the same meaning as 'sex' as that term is used herein and shall be broadly interpreted to include persons who are known or assumed to be transgendered."

720 Seattle Municipal Code 3.110.260. Accessed online at http://clerk.ci.seattle. wa.us/. Cf. Seattle Office of Civil Rights Rules, chapter 40, which includes in the definition of 'sexual orientation' "actual or perceived male or female heterosexuality, bisexuality, homosexuality, transsexuality or transvestism and includes a person's attitudes, preferences, beliefs and practices pertaining thereto" (SHRR40-015a(xvi)) accessed online at http://www.cityofseattle.net/civilrights/documents/chap40.pdf. Cf. SMC 12A.06.115 .D Malicious Harassment (amended Aug. 30, 1999), accessed online at http:// clerk.ci.seattle.wa.us/~scripts/nphbrs.exe?d=CBOR&s1=119628.ordn.&Sect6=HIT OFF&l=20&p=1&u=/~public/cbor2.htm&r=1&f=G, where it is specified that, "'Gender identity' means a person's identity, expression, or physical characteristics, whether or not traditionally associated with one's biological sex or one's sex at birth, including transsexual, transvestite, and transgendered, and including a person's attitudes, preferences, beliefs, and practices pertaining thereto."

721 The issue of whether they should enjoy such rights remains a matter of debate. In a sense, this entire project is about how that matter is best answered on rational, empirical, moral, and religious grounds.

722 *Human Rights News. Sexual Orientation and Gender Identity: Briefing to the 60ᵗʰ Session of the UN Commission on Human Rights* (2004). Accessed online at the Human Rights Watch website at http://hrw.org/english/docs/2004/02/02/global7249.htm. The written document submitted to the Human Rights Commission accessed online at http://www.unhchr.ch/Huridocda/Huridoca.nsf/(Symbol)/E.CN.4.2004.NGO.232. En?Opendocument.

723 *Notes for an Address by the Honourable Pierre Pettigrew, Minister of Foreign Affairs to the 61ˢᵗ Session of the Commission on Human Rights.* Accessed online at the website for the Canadian Permanent Mission—Geneva (site maintained by the Department of Foreign Affairs and International Trade), at http://www.dfait-maeci.gc.ca/canada_un/geneva/Minister_speech_Mar14_2005-en.asp. The Commission met from March 14-April 22, 2005.

724 See *Letter to Nepal's Minister of Justice and Minister of Home Affairs* (2004). Found at the Human Rights Watch website, accessed online at http://hrw.org/english/docs/2006/01/12/nepal12420.htm.

725 *Christine Goodwin v UK Government*, application No. 28957/95 (1995) ECHR, *I v UK* Government, application No. 25608/94 (1994) ECHR. See *Case of Christine Goodwin v. United Kingdom* accessed online at http://www.homo.se/upload/homo/pdf_homo/rattsfall/CASE_OF_CHRISTINE_GOODWIN_v._THE_UNITED_KINGDOM.doc.

726 Dina Dobrkovic (Ed.), *Human Rights in Serbia 2006. Legal Provisions and Practice Compared to International Human Rights Standards* [Series Reports 10] (Belgrade: Belgrade Centre for Human Rights, 2007), p. 151. See §4.15.2 Marriage. Accessed online at http://www.bgcentar.org.yu/documents/Human%20Rights%20in%20Serbia%202006.pdf.

727 Keeping track of international law is a daunting task. The information presented in the table is thus necessarily general and should be checked with sources from each country. Material in the table developed from various sources, especially The International Lesbian and Gay Association's *World Legal Survey* (1999), accessed online at http://www.ilga.info/Information/Legal_survey/summary_information_by_subject .htm#*Anti and also *The Fact Sheet: Worldwide Antidiscrimination Laws and Policies Based on Sexual Orientation* (1999), on The Body website, accessed online at http://www. thebody.com/siecus/ report/discrimination.html.

728 The prototype for the IBGR, written by JoAnn Roberts, Ph.D., was accessed online at http://www. transgender.org/stlgf/gender.html.

729 Phyllis Randolph Frye, *International Bill of Gender Rights* (2001), accessed online at http://www.transgender legal.com/ibgr.htm. Frye is an attorney and was one of the major contributors to the committee work on the IBGR.

730 Ibid. The text of the June 17, 1995 version of the IBGR has been widely distributed and was accessed online at sexuality.org at http://www.sexuality.org/l/ transgen/ibgr.html, and at http://www. pfc.org.uk/gendrpol/gdrights.htm.

731 Phyllis Randolph Frye, *History of the International Conference on Transgender Law and Employment Policy, Inc.* (2001), accessed online at http://transgenderlegal.com/.

Q. 37 Notes

[732] H. Taylor Buckner, "The Transvestic Career Path," *Psychiatry, 33* (no. 3), 381-389 (1970), p. 387. Accessed online at http://www.tbuckner.com/TRANSVES.HTM. For more on Buckner's ideas, see the answer to Q. 22.

[733] See Virginia Prince & P. M. Bentler, "Survey of 504 Cases of Transvestism," *Psychological Reports, 31*, 903-917 (1972), p. 906, 914.

[734] Vernon Coleman, *Men in Dresses: A Study in Transvestism/ Crossdressing* European Medical Journal (Chilton Designs Publishers, 1996), §6, 'Interpersonal Recreational External Socialization in Controlled and Uncontrolled Situations (Going Out and Having Fun).' Accessed online at http://www. vernoncoleman.com/ downloads/mid.htm.

[735] Richard F. Docter & Virginia Prince, "Transvestism: A Survey of 1032 Cross-Dressers," *Archives of Sexual Behavior, 26* (no. 6), 589-605 (1997), Table II. The authors reflect that the data compared to the 1972 report shows a substantially greater willingness of respondents to appear in public while crossdressed than a generation earlier.

[736] Yvonne, "Who We Are," *Yvonne's Place for Crossdressers* (1999). Accessed online at http://www.yvonnesplace.net/index2.html. This survey was available online in 1999 and solicited voluntary responses, which were submitted by email. Altogether, 1,316 people responded, though not every person responded to every survey item. The study acknowledges its limitations.

[737] D. G. Brown, "Transvestism and sex-role inversion," in A. Ellis & A. Abarbanel (Eds.), *The Encyclopedia of Sexual Behavior, vol. 2.* (N. Y.: Hawthorne Books, 1961).

[738] Coleman, §11, 'The Extent and Significance of Fear of Exposure.'

[739] Peggy Rudd, *My Husband Wears My Clothes.* (Katy, TX: PM Publishers, 1990), p. 3.

[740] Virginia Prince & P. M. Bentler, "Survey of 504 Cases of Transvestism," *Psychological Reports, 31*, 903-917 (1972), p. 915f.

[741] Mary Boes & Katherine van Wormer, "Social Work with Lesbian, Gay, Bisexual, and Transgendered Clients," in A. R. Roberts & G. J. Greene (Eds.), *Social Worker's Desk Reference*, pp. 619-623 (N. Y.: Oxford Univ. Press, 2002), p. 619.

[742] Phyllis Randolph Frye, "Facing Discrimination, Organizing for Freedom: The Transgender Community," in J. D'Emilio, W. B. Turner & U. Vaid (Eds.), *Creating Change: Public Policy and Civil Rights*, pp. 451-522 (N. Y.: St. Martin's Press, 2000), p. 453. Accessed online at http://www.transgenderlegal.com/.

[743] Gregory M. Herek, "On Heterosexual Masculinity: Some Psychical Consequences of the Social Construction of Gender and Sexuality," *American Behavioral Scientist, 29* (no. 5), 563-577 (1986). Cf. G. G. Bolich, *Conversin on Gender. A Primer for Entering Dialog* (Raleigh, NC: Psyche's Press, 2007), pp. 209-211.

[744] Jason Cox & Helga Dittmar, "The Functions of Clothes and Clothing (Dis)satisfaction: A Gender Analysis Among British Students," *Journal of Consumer Policy, 18* (nos. 2-3), 237-265 (1995), p. 251.

[745] Stephen J. Gould & Barbara B. Stern, "Gender Schema and Fashion Consciousness," *Psychology & Marketing, 6* (no. 2), 129-145 (1989), p. 142.

[746] John L. Moulton, III, "Homosexuality, Heterosexuality, and Cross-Dressing: Perceptions of Gender-discordant Behavior," *Sex Roles, 37* (nos. 5-6), 441-450 (1997).

[747] Tina Brandon was the subject of the 1999 film, "Boys Don't Cry." Brandon, a genetic female, assumed the role of a male, using the name Brandon Teena. Things

went horribly wrong for Brandon in 1993 when, after being discovered as an anatomical female, she was brutally murdered by two young men who had befriended Brandon as a male.

Just as disturbing, in an entirely different setting and context, is what happened to Tyra Hunter, a 24-year-old male-to-female (MtF) transsexual in August, 1995. A passenger in an automobile accident, Hunter bled to death after Fire Department EMTs at the scene stopped treatment following the discovery of a mismatch between genitalia and gender presentation. Instead, they made crude jokes until pressure by witnesses brought others to help—but too late.

[748] Viviane K. Namaster, *Invisible Lives. The Erasure of Transsexual and Transgendered People* (Chicago: Univ. of Chicago Press, 2000), p. 145. TS stands for "transsexual" and TG for "transgendered."

[749] *Transphobia and CT Hate Crime Legislation* (The Connecticut TransAdvocacy Coalition, 2004). Accessed online at the TransAdvocacy.com website at http://hatecrime.transadvocacy.com/index.htm.

[750] Moulton, p. 442.

[751] Hate crimes are motivated by intolerance toward members of one or another group simply because they belong to that group, which the perpetrator objects to. There are other defining characteristics. Hate crimes are meant to send a message; by victimizing one member of the group the entire group is targeted. The fact that one has been targeted by virtue of whom he or she is, plus the awareness that the victimization intends to have a chilling effect on others, may be why such crimes tend to carry more psychological impact. In effect, the perpetrator has managed at one and the same time to say, 'I picked you because of who you are, but who you are doesn't matter to me because I hate the entire group you belong to.' The hate crime is thus highly personal even as it depersonalizes the victim.

[752] For more information on GenderPAC, see their website, accessed online at http://www.gpac.org/. GenderPAC's address is 274 W. 11th St, New York, NY 10014.

[753] *GenderPAC. First National Survey of TransGender Violence* (GenderPAC, 1997). Accessed online at http://hatecrime.transadvocacy.com/documents/TransViolence%20Survey%20Results.pdf. Percentages reported have been rounded. See 'Data Summary' on p. 1. The report also documents variations due to factors such as age and economic conditions, and details aspects such as locations of incidents and relationship of the victim to the perpetrator.

[754] Ibid, pp. 18 (Table 10), 19 (Table 11), 20 (Table 12), 21f. (Table 13); cf. 'Data Summary,' p. 1.

[755] Ibid, p. 5.

[756] Yvonne, "Who We Are," *Yvonne's Place for Crossdressers* (1999). Accessed online at http://www.yvonnesplace.net/index2.html.

[757] Brian Tully, *Accounting for Transsexuality and Transhomosexuality: The Gender Identity Careers of Over 200 Men and Women Who Have Petitioned for Surgical Reassignment* (London: Whiting and Birch, 1992), p. 266. Tully's work discloses the results of a large scale, systematic study of 204 transsexuals that was conducted by the Gender Identity Clinic at Charing Cross Hospital in London.

[758] Kelly Kleiman, "Drag=Blackface," *Chicago-Kent Law Review*, 75, 669-686 (2000), p. 683. Accessed online at http://lawreview.kentlaw.edu/articles/75-3/AFTER MACROKleiman.pdf.

[759] Gianna E. Israel, "Closeted Forever?" *Gianna Israel Gender Library* (2000). Accessed online at http://www.firelily.com/gender/gianna/closeted.forever.html.

[760] Tully, p. 266.

[761] "Adding Sexual Orientation and Gender Identity to Discrimination and Harassment Policies in Schools," *SIECUS Report*, 28 (no. 3), 17-18 (2000, Feb.-Mar.), p. 17. Also see Shannon Wyss, "'This Was My Hell': The Violence Experienced By Gender Non-conforming Youth in US High Schools," *International Journal of Qualitative Education, 17* (no. 5), 709-730 (2004).

[762] Ibid, p. 18.

[763] Joseph G. Kosciw, *The GLSEN 2001 National School Climate Survey: The School-Related Experiences of Our Nation's Lesbian, Gay, Bisexual and Transgender Youth* (N. Y.: Gay, Lesbian, and Straight Education Network, 2002), p. 11.

[764] Ibid, p. 17.

[765] Ibid, pp. 18-20.

[766] Ibid, p. 17.

[767] Ibid, p. 22.

[768] Linda McCarthy, "What About the 'T'? Is Multicultural Education Ready to Address Transgender Issues?" *Multicultural Education, 5* (no. 4), 46-48 (2003).

[769] Ibid, p. 46.

[770] Kosciw, p. 32.

[771] These figures are as reported in two accounts: Jennifer J. Smith, "New HRC Survey Changes Trans Politics, Activists Say," *Washingtom Blade* (2002, October 11). Accessed online at http://www.tgcrossroads.org/ news/archive.asp?aid=399, and Mubarak Dahir, "HRC: Transgender Breakthrough," *The Advocate* (2002, Oct. 15). Accessed online at http://www.tgcrossroads.org/news/archive.asp?aid=384.

[772] Mubarak Dahir, "HRC: Transgender Breakthrough," *The Advocate* (2002, Oct. 15). Accessed online at http://www.tgcrossroads.org/news/archive.asp?aid=384.

[773] Kosciw, p. 33f. These changes were noted in comparing GLSEN's 1999 and 2001 surveys.

[774] Dahir. The description reads:
> A transgender person is someone who is born as one gender but feels they are the opposite gender. This person may do certain things so that their outward appearance fits who they feel they are on the inside. They might dress as a person of the opposite gender, get medical treatment such as hormone therapy, or have surgery to change their appearance so they look like the gender that they feel they are. This could be a man changing to a woman or a woman changing to a man.

[775] Ibid. Dahir reports the numbers as follows with regard to the query whether the respondent felt 'favorable,' 'neutral,' or 'unfavorable' toward transgendered people:

	Unfavorable	Neutral
Before hearing description	24%	32%
After hearing description	31%	26%

And with reference to believing transgenderism is "morally wrong" and "a choice":

	Morally wrong	Choice
Before hearing description	26%	42%
After hearing description	33%	47%

776 Elizabeth Reis, "Teaching Transgender History, Identity, and Politics," *Radical History Review, 88*, 166-177 (2004), p. 166.

777 Ibid, p. 168.

778 Larry M. Lance, "Acceptance of Diversity in Human Sexuality: Will the Strategy Reducing Homophobia Also Reduce Discomfort of Cross-Dressing?" *College Student Journal, 36* (no. 4), 598-602 (2002). Accessed online at http://articles. findarticles.com/p/articles/mi_m0FCR/is_4_36/ai_96619966. It should be noted that the study applied 'contact theory,' which hypothesizes that intergroup interaction will decrease prejudices and fears. However, results from various studies indicate that positive results follow from positive interactions; negative interactions may actually reinforce stereotypes and prejudices.

779 Cindi M. Penor Ceglian & Nancy N. Lyons, "Gender Type and Comfort with Cross-Dressers," *Sex Roles, 50* (nos. 7/8), 539-546 (2004).

780 *SIECUS Report*, p. 18.

Q. 38 Notes

781 While I draw on a large number of diverse resources in this work—and for answering this question—I prefer relying on matter that tries not to have an obvious axe to grind (although even scientific research can find it hard to avoid such axes). Still, the paucity of really solid scientific research often means needing to draw on what seems to me to be representative samples of the anecdotal material. That is certainly the case in answering this question. Moreover, the surveys themselves have problems: most obtain information from the crossdresser rather than the partner, and at least one (the 1999 online survey) has some methodological problems.

782 See the answer to Q. 26 for specifics. Interestingly, sexologist Roger Peo suggests that many crossdressing men use a relationship with a woman to help them eliminate the desire to crossdress, but that the sight of the woman dressing and undressing may actually reinforce the desire. See Roger E. Peo, "Transvestism," *Journal of Social Work & Human Sexuality, 7* (no. 1), 57-75 (1988).

783 J. L. McCary, J. L., *Human sexuality*, 3rd ed. (N. Y.: Van Nosstrand, 1978), p. 218.

784 Cultural stereotypes tend to be accompanied by preprogrammed response patterns to guide our behavior in conformity with the stereotyped perception. Since crossdressing is stereotyped negatively the accompanying automatic response pattern is negative. To respond in any other fashion is to challenge the stereotype. For more on stereotypes and responses, see the answer to Q. 8 in volume 1.

785 Richard F. Docter, *Transvestites and Transsexuals: Toward a Theory of Cross-Gender Behavior*. (N. Y.: Plenum Press, 1988), p. 169.

786 John B. Bancroft, *Human Sexuality and Its Problems*, 2nd ed. (N. Y.: Elsevier Health Sciences, 1989), p. 345. Bancroft concludes we should infer from this a need to be cautious in judging a marriage fails because of crossdressing, which may be a symptom more than a principal cause of relational breakdown.

787 While all questions between an intimate couple should be permitted, some will prove more useful than others, especially at the start. Thinking beforehand about what to ask will help. Perhaps a sensible course is to begin with general questions about when the crossdressing started, how it proceeded, and what it means to the crossdresser. Other 'safe' questions might be: how do they obtain clothes? How do they decide what to wear? How do they feel different when crossdressed? After a time the harder questions may be easier to discuss, such as: What do you see the future holding? Do you want to change your body? Are you sexually attracted to members of the same sex? The point is, dialog should be reciprocal and ongoing. There may be internal pressure to have all one's questions asked and answered in a sitting, but such a course is unlikely to prove as satisfying or productive as being patient. Give time to digest what is learned.

788 Harry Benjamin, *The Transsexual Phenomenon* (N. Y.: Julian Press, 1966), p. 44.

789 George R. Brown, "Women in Relationships with Cross-Dressing Men: A Descriptive Study from a Nonclinical Setting," *Archives of Sexual Behavior, 23* (no. 5), 515-530 (1994), p. 527.

790 Virginia Prince & P. M. Bentler, "Survey of 504 Cases of Transvestism," *Psychological Reports, 31*, 903-917 (1972), p. 913. N.B. the actual percentage on the page is 27%, not 72%; that this is an unintended reversal of numbers becomes clear when reading the later report of Docter and Prince.

791 Betty Ann Lind, "A Survey of Wives," in Jed Bland (Ed.), *He, She, We, They. Partners of Cross Dressers*. Published by the Derby TV/TS Group, c/o Derby CVS Self Help Team, 4, Charnwood Street, Derby. Accessed online at http://www.gender. org.uk/ derby/wives.htm.

792 Thomas N. Wise, Carol Dupkin, & Jon K. Meyer, "Partners of Distressed Transvestites," *American Journal of Psychiatry, 138* (no. 9), 1221-1224 (1980), p. 1222. Some 44% discovered the crossdressing 2-5 years after marriage.

793 Docter, p. 171.

794 Vernon Coleman, Men in Dresses: A Study in Transvestism/
Crossdressing. European Medical Journal (Chilton Designs Publishers, 1996), §14, 'Partners' Attitudes Towards Crossdressing Males.' Accessed online at http://www. vernoncoleman. com/downloads/mid.htm.

795 Richard F. Docter & Virginia Prince, "Transvestism: A Survey of 1032 Cross-Dressers," Archives of Sexual Behavior, 26 (no. 6), 589-605 (1997), Table II.

796 Yvonne, "Who We Are," *Yvonne's Place for Crossdressers* (1999). Accessed online at http://www.yvonnesplace.net/index2.html. There were 836 respondents on this matter.

797 "Survey Results," *Connectivity*, 7 (no. 1), accessed online at http"//www.forge-forward.org/newsletters/v07i01/surveyresults.htm. Forge (For Ourselves: Reworking Gender Expression) is a national education, advocacy, and support organization for female-to-male transsexual and female transgenderists, among others. See the home page on their website, accessed online at http://www.forge-forward.org/index.php. The survey uses a convenience sample and must be understood in light of the population responding.

[798] Ibid.

[799] Ibid, 'A Survey of Wives.'

[800] A CD Wife, *How I Learned My Husband Was a Crossdresser* (2004). This is Michelle Renee's wife's story. Accessed online at http://www.geocities.com/ms_ michelle_renee/wfsstory.html; also at Jenelle Rose's website; see http://www. jenellerose.com/htmlpostings/ cdwivesperstive.html.

[801] Virginia Prince, *The Crossdresser and His Wife* (Los Angeles: Chevalier Books, 1967); also issued under the title, *The Transvestite and His Wife*.

[802] Helen Boyd, *My Husband Betty. Love, Sex, and Life with a Crossdresser* (N. Y.: Thunder's Mouth Press, 2004). See chapter 3, "Crossdressers' Wives, Girlfriends, and Partners."

[803] Partners at Fantasia Fair 1986, "He, She, We, They: Partners of Crossdressers," in Jed Bland (Ed.), *He, She, We, They. Partners of Cross Dressers*. Published by the Derby TV/TS Group, c/o Derby CVS Self Help Team, 4, Charnwood Street, Derby DE1 2GT, England. Though now out of print, the booklet has been archived online. Accessed online at http://www.gender.org.uk/derby/wives.htm.

[804] Ibid.

[805] Kathleen V. Cairns, "Counselling the Partners of Heterosexual Male Cross-Dressers," *The Canadian Journal of Human Sexuality, 6* (o. 4), 297-306 (1997).

[806] Thomas N. Wise, "Coping with a Transvestic Mate: Clinical Implications," *Journal of Sex and Marital Therapy, 11* (no. 4), 293-300 (1985).

[807] Cairns, especially, p. 303f.

[808] Yvonne, 1999.

[809] Gianna E. Israel, "Secret Lives." *Gianna Israel Gender Library* (1996). Accessed online at http://www.firelily.com/gender/gianna/lives.html.

[810] Annie Woodhouse, *Fantastic Women. Sex, Gender and Transvestism.* (New Brunswick, NJ: Rutgers Univ. Press, 1989). Cf. Annie Woodhouse, "Forgotten Women: Transvestism and Marriage," *Women's Studies International Forum, 8,* 583-592. The sentiment expressed by Woodhouse is echoed by the authors—all partners of crossdressers—of the booklet *He, She, We, They*, referenced above.

[811] Vern L. Bullough & Thomas S. Weinberg, "Alienation, Self-Image and the Importance of Support Groups for Wives of Transvestites. *Journal of Sex Research, 24,* 262-268 (1988). See the remarks at the end of the answer to Q. 34.

[812] Brown, pp. 515-530. When placed together with the data that most crossdressing men tell their partners before marriage, the resultant picture suggests that the revelation is done cautiously; not immediately, but usually before a binding commitment.

[813] Ibid. See especially pp. 515-519.

[814] Ibid, p. 520. Similarly, a research study found that male transvestites had the lowest rate of alcoholism of any group of men diagnosed with a paraphilia. See S. H. Allnut, John Macdonald Wilson Bradford, D. M. Greenberg, & S. Curry, "Co-Morbidity of Alcoholism and the Paraphilias," *Journal of Forensic Sciences, 41* (2), 234-239 (1996). The study encompassed 728 men diagnosed with a paraphilia.

[815] Docter, p. 192, characterizes the wives of his study as "unremarkable" (i.e., not different from other normal folk) in terms of personal adjustment.

[816] Deborah H. Feinbloom, *Transvestites and Transsexuals: Mixed Views* (N. Y.: Delacorte Press, 1976).

[817] Brown, p. 525.

[818] Docter, p. 167.

[819] Brown, p. 526. Peo (pp. 57-75) maintains that the woman's ability to stay in the relationship depends both on high self esteem and her acceptance of the crossdressing behavior.

[820] Woodhouse, p. 127. How many spouses share this dilemma is unknown, but Woodhouse is surely right in urging that researchers be careful to interview crossdressers' partners apart so that they can be more candid.

[821] Bullough & Weinberg, pp. 262-268. Cf. Bonnie Bullough & Vern L. Bullough, "Locus of Control for Wives of Transvestites," in C. M. Davis, W. L. Yarber, R. Bauserman, G. Schreer, & S. L. Davis (Eds.), *Handbook of Sexuality Related Measures*, p. 583 (Thousand Oaks, CA: Sage, 1998).

[822] Gianna E. Israel, "Impact on children." *Gianna Israel Gender Library* (1997). Available online at http://www.firelily.com/gender/gianna/impact.children.html.

[823] Brown, p. 521. Cf. Benjamin's experience with more than a dozen wives, which left him with the impression that while most put up a brave front, they were not happy with the crossdressing; see Harry Benjamin, *The Transsexual Phenomenon* (N.Y.: The Julian Press, 1966), chapter 3, " The Transvestite in Older and Newer Aspects." This book has been reprinted on the Symposion.com website as an IJT Electronic Book. Accessed online at http://www.symposion.com/ijt/benjamin/index.htm.

[824] Prince & Bentler, p. 913. What acceptance means in terms of behavior is explored later in the answer.

[825] John T. Talamini, *Boys Will Be Girls: The Hidden World of the Heterosexual Male Transvestite* (Lanham, MD: Univ. Press of America, 1982), chapter 3. Like other research reported in this answer, Talamini found that many partners did not know of their spouse's crossdressing before marriage; the men were afraid the knowledge would drive their beloved away. While Talamini is not specific about what 'acceptance' means, it apparently refers to a level of support for crossdressing conducted outside the spouse's presence.

[826] Docter, p. 172. He used a 9 point scale; 4 response types fit the positive attitudes, 4 fit the negative attitudes, and 1 was neutral. Relatively even distributions were reported among the positive responses. The negative responses were disproportionately clustered (69%) at point 7 on the scale, which reads, "I dislike it somewhat. It causes me unhappiness."

[827] Brown, p. 522. It should be noted that Brown felt he could only classify 83% of the wives. He clarifies each status as follows: "Low acceptors" (19%) both have seriously considered ending the relationship and view their own overall level of acceptance as low. "Moderate acceptors" (25%) both have never considered separation or divorce and desire to be more tolerant or accepting. "High acceptors" (39%) both have never considered terminating the relationship and see themselves as already accepting.

[828] Coleman, §14, 'Partners' Attitudes Towards Crossdressing Males.'

[829] Docter & Prince, Table II.

[830] Yvonne, 1999. Of the partners rated as "supportive," 'significant others' (69%) were more often supportive than marriage partners (59%). Significantly, a partner's supportiveness seems directly related to the likelihood of others being supportive. The sur-

vey found that where the partner was supportive, others who know are much likelier to be supportive.

831 Brown, p. 522.

832 Ibid, p. 521f.

833 Ibid., p. 523.

834 Many of these women write under a pseudonym in order to protect themselves and their partners.

835 Peggy Rudd, *My Husband Wears My Clothes.* (Katy, TX: PM Publishers, 1990). Also see, Peggy Rudd, *Crossdressers: and Those Who Share Their Lives* (Katy, TX: PM Publishers, 1995), p. x.

836 Rachel Miller, *The Bliss of Becoming One! Integrating Feminine" Feelings Into the Male Psyche Mainstreaming the Gender Community* (Highland City, FL: Rainbow Books, 1996), p. 12. It must be noted that not all accounts are so rosy; some writers contend that transvestite males have problems with intimacy (see the answer to Q. 27).

837 Lind, "A Survey of Wives," in Bland (1993). Of the 43 women interviewed, 13 knew about the crossdressing before marriage; 10 of them thought marriage would end the behavior. Anecdotal evidence from male crossdressers suggests some of them also believe marriage will effect a 'cure.'

838 Brown, p. 521.

839 I am reminded of a study I read some years ago in which two groups were followed who had experienced major changes. One group was comprised of people who had become paraplegics; the other was made up of folk who had won a million dollars or more in the lottery. As one might expect, immediately after these events there was a great difference between the groups in happiness. But a year later—after habituation—no significant differences pertained. We can adjust and move on even when faced with radical changes.

840 Brown, p. 524.

841 Janet L. Davies & Ellen H. Janosik, *Mental Health and Psychiatric Nursing. A Caring Approach* (Boston: Jones and Bartlett, 1991), p. 385.

842 Prince & Bentler, p. 908. One caveat should be noted, though. This same survey finds that 28% have experienced at least one same-sex sexual encounter. While this may seem high, it is lower than the 37% for the general population that Albert Kinsey finds in his 1948 study of male sexuality. A 2001 study involving 455 male transvestites finds only 6% report it is usual for them to have a same sex partner; see Richard Docter and J. S. Fleming, "Measures of Transgender Behavior," *Archives of Sexual Behavior, 30* (no. 3), 255-271 (2001). Measuring this behavior has always proved elusive and figures presented in various studies range considerably.

843 Docter & Prince, Table II.

844 Vern Bullough, Bonnie Bullough, & Richard Smith, "A Comparative Study of Male Transvestites, Male to Female Transsexuals, and Male Homosexuals," *The Journal of Sex Research, 19* (no. 3), 238-257 (1983), p. 250, Table 8.

845 Boyd, *My Husband Betty.* See chapter 5, "Slippery Slope."

846 Bullough, Bullough, & Smith, p. 252, Table 10. The differences between transvestites and transsexuals in this respect is pronounced. Almost half (49%) of transsexuals in the study have at one time or another taken sex hormones and a full third (33%) have undergone surgery; another 15% are so inclined.

[847] Coleman, §3, 'The Incidence of Transsexualism Among Crossdressers.'

[848] P. J. Huxley, J. C. Kenna, & S. B. Brandon, "Partnership in Transsexualism: II. The Nature of the Partnership," *Archives of Sexual Behavior, 10* (no. 2), 143-160 (1981). This research looks at transsexuals in various relationship patterns, including 6 male-to-female transsexuals still living with their marriage partners.

[849] Betty W. Steiner & Stephen M. Bernstein, "Female-to-Male Transsexuals and Their Partners," *Canadian Journal of Psychiatry, 26* (no. 3), 178-182 (1981).

[850] Peggy J. Rudd, *Crossdressers: And Those Who Share Their Lives* (Salt Lake City, UT: Publishers Press, 2000), p. 56.

[851] Docter, p. 173, Table 41.

[852] Feinbloom, *Transvestites and Transsexuals: Mixed Views.* Feinbloom founded Boston's Gender Identity Service.

[853] Sally Hunt & Terri L. Main, "Sexual Orientation Confusion Among Spouses of Transvestites and Transsexuals Following Disclosure of Spouse's Gender Dysphoria," *Journal of Psychology & Human Sexuality, 9* (no. 2), 39-51 (1997). Accessed online from the Research Archives of Trans-Gender Expressions (International Transgender Peer Support) at http://www.tg2tg.org/sosupport/research/soffa-study1.htm.

[854] Brown, p. 520f.

[855] Davies & Janosik, p. 385.

[856] Woodhouse, p. 132.

[857] Partners at Fantasia Fair 1986, in Bland (1993).

[858] Bullough & Weinberg, p. 266.

[859] Docter, pp. 182-184.

[860] Brown, p. 526. Prince (p. 48) goes so far as to say, "If a wife really comes to understand the feminine personality within her husband she will have a fuller relationship with her spouse than could otherwise be the case because she can enjoy and live with both at the same time." However, Woodhouse (p. 128) points out that this phenomenon of personality changes can also be a problem: "In this sense a wife may feel that she is living with two people and feel confused about her relationship with her husband." The more pronounced the personality changes the more likely this dilemma may be.

[861] Havelock Ellis, "Eonism and Other Supplementary Studies," vol. 2, pp. 1-110 in H. Ellis, *Studies in the Psychology of Sex*, 2 vols. (N. Y.: Random House reprint of 1941-1942; original work published 1905-1928), vol. 2, p. 108. For more on Ellis' thoughts, see the answer to Q. 95.

[862] Prince & Bentler, p. 913.

[863] Yvonne, 1999. These percentages are skewed a bit toward the low end by the nature of the question—"Which best describes your wife's/SO's feelings about your crossdressing?"—and eight possible responses, most of which are nonexclusive. Thus, for example, a partner who might be accepting of crossdressing at home but not in public could be placed in any of several categories (e.g., "her feelings vacillate between acceptance and rejection," "she accepts but doesn't want family/friends to find out," "she accepts but doesn't want me to leave the house crossdressed," or "she accepts but won't go out in public with me"), depending on what her spouse thought *best* described her.

[864] Coleman, §14, "Partners' Attitudes Towards Crossdressing Partners.'

[865] Docter, p. 173, Table 41.

[866] Boyd, p. 69f.

867 Arlene Istar Lev, *Transgender Emergence: Therapeutic Guidelines for Working with Gender Variant People and Their Families* (N. Y.: Haworth Clinical Practice Press, 2004), p. 302.

868 Thomas N. Wise, Peter J. Fagan, Chester W. Schmidt, Yula Ponticas, & Paul T. Costa, "Personality and Sexual Functioning of Transvestitic Fetishists and Other Paraphilics," *Journal of Nervous and Mental Disease, 179* (no. 11), 694-698 (1991), p. 697.

869 Wise, Dupkin, & Meyer, pp. 1223-1224. Cf. Roy C. Calogeras, "The Transvestite and His Wife," *Psychoanalytic Review, 74* (no. 4), 517-535 (1987). Calogeras offers his summation of psychoanalysis of a crossdressing man, in which he found complementary pathology in both the man and his wife contributing to their marital difficulties.

870 Yvonne, 1999.

871 Docter, pp. 178-179.

872 Ibid, pp. 179-180.

873 Ibid, pp. 184-189. Please note that the characterizations of movement and power are my own formulations though they are based on how Docter describes each pattern.

874 'A CD Wife.' Accessed online at http://www.geocities.com/ms_michelle_renee/wfsstory.html; also at Jenelle Rose's website; see http://www.jenellerose.com/htmlpostings/cdwivesperstive.html.

Q. 39 Notes

875 Gerald P. Mallon & Theresa DeCrescenzo, "Transgender Children and Youth: A Child Welfare Practice Perspective," *Child Welfare, 85* (no. 2), 215-241 (2006), p. 217.

876 Gianna E. Israel, "Contentious Family Issues." *Gianna Israel Gender Library* (2003). Accessed online at http://www.firelily.com/gender/gianna/contentious.html.

877 Ibid.

878 Gianna E. Israel, "Translove: Transgender Persons and Their Families," *Journal of GLBT Family Studies, 1* (no. 1), 53-67 (2005), p. 54.

879 Ibid, p. 55.

880 Richard Docter observes that most crossdressers keep the behavior secret from their children and that it is a rare couple who disclose its existence to young children. See Richard Docter, *Transvestites and Transsexuals: Toward a Theory of Cross-Gender Behavior* (N. Y.: Plenum Press, 1988), p. 175.

881 Yvonne, "Who We Are," *Yvonne's Place for Crossdressers* (1999). Accessed online at http://www.yvonnesplace.net/index2.html. This survey makes no pretence at being scientific, and has some admitted methodological flaws, so results should be held loosely. Though urging caution because of the limited data, the online survey of 1999 found that support peaked before puberty (ages 6-11), and again in young adulthood (ages 24-29), presumably after the children were out of the home.

882 George R. Brown, "Women in Relationships with Cross-Dressing Men: A Descriptive Study from a Nonclinical Setting," *Archives of Sexual Behavior, 23* (no. 5), p. 519.

883 John T. Talamini, *Boys Will Be Girls: The Hidden World of the Heterosexual Male Transvestite* (Lanham, MD: Univ. Press of America, 1982).

884 Ibid.

885 Israel, "Translove: Transgender Persons and Their Families," p. 65.

886 Brown, p. 521.

887 Ibid, p. 525.

[888] Harry Benjamin, *The Transsexual Phenomenon* (N.Y.: The Julian Press, 1966), chapter 3, " The Transvestite in Older and Newer Aspects." This book has been reprinted on the Symposion.com website as an IJT Electronic Book. Accessed online at http://www.symposion.com/ijt/benjamin/index.htm. For more on Benjamin's views, see the answer to Q. 95.

[889] Docter, p. 175.

[890] Israel, "Translove: Transgender Persons and Their Families," p. 65.

[891] Yvone, 1999.

[892] Cf. Israel, "Translove: Transgender Persons and Their Families," p. 62.

Q. 40 Notes

[893] With respect to eugenics and abortion, cf. the remarks made in J. Michael Bailey, *The Man Who Would Be Queen: The Science of Gender-Bending and Transsexualism* (Washington, D.C.: National Academies Pres, 2003), pp. 114-115. Bailey (p. 114) remarks, for example, "The issue is not whether abortion is acceptable. Instead, the real question is whether parental selection in favor of heterosexuality is acceptable. To focus on this question, we have to assume that whatever means parents will use to do this are, in themselves, morally acceptable." Bailey's book—and public remarks in lectures—raised a firestorm both in the academic community and transgender community. For a review from a leading scholar and therapist, see Walter O. Bockting, "Biological Reductionism Meets Gender Diversity in Human Sexuality [Book Reviews]," *The Journal of Sex Research,* 42 (no. 3), 267-270 (2005). The specter of eugenics applied to transgender is appalling to most folk. For example, transgender person Stephen Whittle says, "I do not care whether I was 'born this way' or 'became this way.' The question of the 'gay gene' or the 'tranny brain' is a potentially frightening route to another eugenics programme to destroy the brilliance of difference in the world, and the sooner we reject these projects the better." Stephen Whittle, "Where Did We Go Wrong? Feminism and Trans Theory—Two Teams On the Same Side" (2000). Speech given at the True Spirit Conference, Alexandria, Virginia, February, 2000, quoted in Arlene Istar Lev, *Transgender Emergence: Working with Gender-Variant People and Their Families* (N. Y.: Haworth Clinical Practice Press, 2004), p. 131.

[894] Ivan Illich, *Gender* (N. Y.: Pantheon Books, 1982), p. 145f.

[895] Ibid, p. 146.

[896] Victor Turner, "Frame, Flow and Reflection: Ritual and Drama as Public Liminality," *Japanese Journal of Religious Studies, 6* (no. 4), 465-499 (1979), p. 474.

Crossdressing in Context.
Dress, Gender, Transgender, and Crossdressing.

Table of Contents for 5 Volume Set

Q. 16   What do people find entertaining about crossdressing?

Q. 17   Why do some homosexuals crossdress?

Q. 18   What is 'transvestism'?

Q. 19   What is 'transsexualism'?

Q. 20   What does 'transgender' mean?

Question Set 3: What causes crossdressing?

Q. 21   Is crossdressing 'natural'?

Q. 22   Is crossdressing learned behavior?

Q. 23   Is crossdressing developmental (i.e., "just a 24phase")?

Q. 24   Is crossdressing caused by sexual abuse?

Q. 25   Is crossdressing a choice?

Question Set 4: What is it like to be a transgendered crossdresser?

Q. 26   How do crossdressers describe themselves?

Q. 27   What is the profile of a 'typical' crossdresser?

Q. 28   When does crossdressing usually start?

Q. 29   What is childhood and adolescence like?

Q. 30   What is adulthood like for a crossdresser?

Q. 31   Does crossdressing lead to a sex change operation?

Q. 32   Is crossdressing harmful?

Q. 33   What is involved in crossdressing?

Q. 34   Where do crossdressers find support?

Q. 35   Are all crossdressers homosexual?

Question Set 5: How are transgender realities regarded by others?

Q. 36   What is the legal status of crossdressers?

Q. 37   How are crossdressers treated in public?

Q. 38   How do partners handle the crossdressing of their significant others?

Q. 39   How does crossdressing affect families?

Q. 40   Why does society tolerate crossdressing?

Volume 3: Transgender History & Geography

Question Set 6: What is the history of crossdressing?

    Q. 41   What did the ancient world think?

    Q. 42   Who are some famous crossdressers of mythology?

    Q. 43   Who are some famous ancient crossdressers?

    Q. 44   What is the history of crossdressing and the theater?

    Q. 45   What was the history of gender, transgender and crossdressing in the Middle Ages?

    Q. 46   What is the history since the Middle Ages?

    Q. 47   What is the history in the United States?

    Q. 48   Who are some famous crossdressing women?

    Q. 49   Who are some famous crossdressing men?

    Q. 50   What will the present likely be noted for?

Question Set 7: Where in the world is crossdressing found?

    Q. 51   Is crossdressing only found in the Western world?

    Q. 52   Where is it found in the East?

    Q. 53   Where is it found in the Middle East?

    Q. 54   Where is it found in Africa?

    Q. 55   Where is it found in Latin America?

    Q. 56   Where is it found in Europe?

    Q. 57   Where is it found in the Pacific Ocean nations?

    Q. 58   Where is it found in North America?

    Q. 59   Where is it found in Native American groups?

    Q. 60   If it is so common, what role does it play in culture?

Volume 4: Transgender & Religion

Question Set 8: What does the Bible say about crossdressing?

    Q. 61   Where does the Bible address crossdressing?

    Q. 62   What are the key issues for understanding what the Bible says?

    Q. 63   What do Jewish commentators say?

Q. 64   What do Christian commentators say?

Q. 65   What constitutes a 'reasonable' position to take?

Question Set 9: What does Christianity say about crossdressing?

Q. 66   What does the New Testament say?

Q. 67   What did the Church Fathers say?

Q. 68   Are there crossdressing saints?

Q. 69   Are there notable crossdressing Christian women?

Q. 70   Are there notable crossdressing Christian men?

Q. 71   Are there Christian festivals where crossdressing is accepted?

Q. 72   Has the Church said anything "officially" about crossdressing?

Q. 73   What do Christians today who oppose transgender realities say?

Q. 74   What do transgender Christians and their supporters today say?

Q. 75   Are there resources for transgender Christians?

Question Set 10: What do other religions say about crossdressing?

Q. 76   How did crossdressing figure in ancient and pre-modern religions?

Q. 77   What stance does Judaism take on crossdressing?

Q. 78   What role has crossdressing played in Islam?

Q. 79   How does Hinduism regard crossdressing?

Q. 80   Is Buddhism tolerant of crossdressing?

Q. 81   Is crossdressing found in Japanese religions?

Q. 82   Can transgender elements be found in other Eastern religions?

Q. 83   What roles do crossdressing and transgender play in African religions?

Q. 84   Are transgender realities found in Native American religiosity?

Q. 85   What role does crossdressing play in religion?

Volume 5: Transgender & Mental Health

Author Index

M

Main, Terri, 299
Makinen, Merja, 47, 65-66
Mallon, Gerald, 290, 292, 294, 296, 305
Mason, Bob, 108
McCarthy, Linda, 276
McCary, J. L., 18, 19, 282
McClintock, Martha, 120f
McConaghy, Neil, 73, 160, 181, 186, 194
Meyer, Jon, 164, 289

Michel, Aude, 79-81
Miller, Rachel, 296
Money, John, 118, 119, 135, 244, 362 n. 630
More, K., 95
Mormont, Christian, 79-81
Moulton, John III, 271
Munroe, Robert & Monroe, Ruth, 127
Mustanski, Brian, 114

N

Namaster, Viviane, 272
Newman, Esther, 64

Norton, Jody, 194
Novic, Richard, 223

O

Okun, Michael, 251
Ovesey, Lionel, 63

Owomoyela, Oyekan, 42

P

Paul, Andreas, 109
Pauly, Ira, 47-48, 131f.
Person, Ethel, 63
Philbert, M., 117f.
Pillard, Richard, 119
Pineda, Roselle, 64

Portinga, J., 186
Prince, Virginia, 80, 94, 98, 159, 160-161 163-165, 167, 168-172, 176-177, 186-187, 202, 205-206, 219, 268-269 289-290, 295, 301

Q, R

Reinisch, June, 118
Reis, Elizabeth, 278
Robins, Eli, 186
Roscoe, Will, 99

Roughgarden, Joan, 106-107
Rubin, John, 251
Rudd, Peggy, 42, 211, 217, 269, 295, 298

S

Saddock, Benjaim & Saddock, Virginia, 149
Saghir, Marcel, 186
Schacht, Steven, 64
Schmidt, Chester, 186
Schnittker, Jason, 128
Schott, Richard, 18, 159-160, 162, 186, 191, 193, 239
Seaman, Julie, 221
Sears, Lonnie, 111
Sell, Ingrid, 99, 164-165, 187
Sharpe, Andrew, 84-85

Sherman, Richard, 176
Shervin, R. V., 249
Shine, Rick, 108
Sifuentes-Jauregui, Ben, 62
Sister Mary Elizabeth, 246, 253
Smith, Richard, 112, 161, 186, 239
Stayton, William, 36
Stern, Barbara, 271
Stoller, Robert, 47, 130
Stone, Gregory, 132
Swarr, Amanda, 64

T

Talamini, John, 182, 194, 307
Teh, Yik Koon, 187
Tewksbury, Richard, 96
Thom, B., 95

Thompson, Janet, 141, 150, 185
Thompson, Mark, 64
Turner, Victor, 315
Tsoi, W. F., 84

Subject Index

www.ingramcontent.com/pod-product-compliance
Lightning Source LLC
Chambersburg PA
CBHW020601270326
41927CB00005B/122